THE PE

FOUNDER EDIT

Edit

CICERO'S LETTERS TO HIS FRIENDS · 2

CICERO, MARCUS TULLIUS (106–43 B.C.), Roman orator and statesman, was born at Arpinum of a wealthy local family. He was taken to Rome for his education with the idea of a public career and by the year 70 he had established himself as the leading barrister in Rome. In the meantime his political career was well under way and he was elected praetor for 66. His ambitious nature enabled him to obtain those honours which would normally only have been conferred upon members of the Roman aristocracy, and he was duly elected consul for 63. One of the most permanent features of his political life was his attachment to Pompey. As a politician his notable quality was his consistent refusal to compromise; as a statesman his ideals were more honourable and unselfish than those of his contemporaries. Cicero was the greatest of the Roman orators, possessing a wide range of technique and an exceptional command of the Latin tongue. He followed the common practise of publishing his speeches, but he also produced a large number of works on the theory and practice of rhetoric, on religion, and on moral and political philosophy. He played a leading part in the development of the Latin hexameter. Perhaps the most interesting of all his works is the collection of 900 letters published posthumously. These not only contain a first-hand account of social and political life in the upper classes at Rome, but also reflect the changing personal feelings of an emotional and sensitive man.

D. R. SHACKLETON BAILEY was born in 1917 and educated at Lancaster Royal Grammar School and at Gonville and Caius College, Cambridge, where he was a Fellow from 1944 to 1955, and again, as Deputy and Senior Bursar, from 1964 to 1968. From 1948 to 1968 he was University Lecturer in Tibetan and from 1955 to 1964 Fellow and Director of Studies in Classics at Jesus College, Cambridge. From 1968 to 1974 he was Professor of Latin at the University of Michigan and has been Professor of Greek and Latin at Harvard University since 1975. He is a Doctor of Letters (Cambridge, 1957), a Fellow of the British Academy (1958), and a member of the American Philosophical Society (1977). Among his classical publications are *Propertiana* (1956), *Towards a Text of Cicero ad Atticum* (1960), *Ciceronis Epistulae II.ii* (1961), *Cicero's Letters to Atticus* (1965–70), *Cicero* (1971), *Two Studies in Roman Nomenclature* (1976), *Cicero, Epistulae ad Familiares* (1977).

CICERO

CICERO'S LETTERS TO HIS FRIENDS

VOLUME TWO

Translated with Introductions by
D. R. Shackleton Bailey

PENGUIN BOOKS

Penguin Books Ltd, Harmondsworth, Middlesex, England
Penguin Books, 625 Madison Avenue, New York, New York 10022, U.S.A.
Penguin Books Australia Ltd, Ringwood, Victoria, Australia
Penguin Books Canada Ltd, 2801 John Street, Markham, Ontario, Canada L3R 1B4
Penguin Books (N.Z.) Ltd, 182–190 Wairau Road, Auckland 10, New Zealand

—

This translation first published 1978

—

—

Printed in the United States of America by
Offset Paperback Mfrs., Inc., Dallas, Pennsylvania
Set in Monotype Bembo

48,574

876.01
Ca85c
vol2

3.95

B+L

4
2.8.9

CONTENTS

INTRODUCTION

THE collection of Cicero's 'Letters to Friends' (*Epistulae ad Familiares*) did not originally appear as such. Our manuscripts have it in sixteen 'Books'. Some of these consist entirely or mainly of letters to or from a single correspondent: Lentulus Spinther in 'Book' I, Appius Claudius Pulcher in 'Book' III, Caelius in 'Book' VIII, Terentia in 'Book' XIV, Tiro in 'Book' XVI. 'Book' XIII consists of letters of recommendation, 'Books' X–XII of correspondence relating to the struggle with Antony in 44–43. The other 'Books' show more or less of internal cohesion. The evidence suggests that they were arranged and published separately or in groups during the Augustan period by a single editor, who was in all probability Cicero's faithful secretary, Tiro; he is also likely to have produced the now lost collections of letters to individual correspondents other than Atticus known to have existed in antiquity, Caesar, Pompey, Octavian and others, as well as those surviving to Quintus Cicero and Marcus Brutus. At what time the collection of sixteen 'Books' came into being is unknown. The title 'Letters to Friends' seems to be no older than the Renaissance.

The 'friends' are a motley group. Some of them, as Trebatius Testa, Caelius, and Papirius Paetus, really were familiars, to whom Cicero could write as informally, though not as intimately, as to Atticus or to his brother. With powerful aristocrats like Cato, Lentulus Spinther, and Appius Pulcher he was on no such easy footing, and his letters to them are in as elaborate a style as his published works. The high sentiments, stately flatteries, and courteously veiled rebukes might have transposed naturally into eighteenth-century English, but put a modern translator at a disadvantage. In contrast with both types are a series of official or semi-official documents, including two dispatches from Cilicia, both models of elegant, straightforward language.

The letters are arranged and numbered as in my edition of the Latin texts (Cambridge, 1977), partly chronologically, partly by grouping according to correspondent or genre, and are translated from its text.

BIBLIOGRAPHICAL NOTE

THIS translation follows my recently published text and commentary, nos. 16–17 in the Cambridge Classical Texts and Commentaries series (Cambridge University Press, 1977). My *Cicero* (Gerald Duckworth, 1971) may be of use as a biographical and historical companion to the Correspondence. As a general history of the period T. Rice Holmes, *The Roman Republic* (3 vols., Oxford University Press, 1923), can still be recommended. Mommsen's *History of Rome*, however outmoded its ideological bias, keeps its fascination as a work of genius. Among contributions by living scholars R. Syme's *Roman Revolution* (Oxford University Press, 1939) is an established classic (largely, however, concerned with the period after Cicero's death). Anything by E. Badian and P. A. Brunt is worth reading. For penetrating analysis of the problems and determinants underlying late-republican politics I know nothing to equal the work of Christian Meier, especially *Res Publica Amissa* (Wiesbaden, Steiner, 1966) and *Caesars Bürgerkrieg* (1964; republished in *Entstehung des Begriffs Demokratie*, Frankfurt am Main, Suhrkamp Verlag, 1970); unfortunately it has not been translated.

Gaston Boissier's *Cicéron et ses amis* (1865; Engl. tr. 1897) can never be superseded as a delightful and sympathetic account of the man and his milieu. The straightforward biographies tend to be soporific. The only modern commentary on the whole Correspondence, that of Tyrrell and Purser (7 vols., 1904–33), is a mine of honest misinformation. On the other hand, J. Carcopino's *Les Secrets de la correspondance de Cicéron* (2 vols., 1947; Engl. tr. 1951), a farrago of garbled facts and false inferences, is more worthy of an unscrupulous prosecuting attorney than of a serious scholar.

NOTE

This translation (in two volumes) of *Cicero's Letters to his Friends* is a companion to *Cicero's Letters to Atticus* (Penguin Classics).

CICERO'S LETTERS TO HIS FRIENDS
(continued)

SERVIUS SULPICIUS RUFUS TO CICERO

Athens, mid March 45

From Servius to Cicero greetings.

When the report reached me of the death of your daughter Tullia, I was indeed duly and deeply and grievously sorry, and I felt that the blow had struck us both. Had I been in Rome, I should have been with you and shown you my grief in person. And yet that is a melancholy and bitter sort of comfort. Those who should offer it, relations and friends, are themselves no less afflicted. They cannot make the attempt without many tears, and rather seem themselves to stand in need of comfort *from* others than to be capable of doing their friendly office *for* others. None the less, I have resolved to set briefly before you the reflections that come to my mind in this hour, not that I suppose you are unaware of them, but perhaps your grief makes them harder for you to perceive.

What reason is there why your domestic sorrow should affect you so sorely? Think how fortune has dealt with us up to now. All that man should hold no less dear than children – country, dignity, standing, distinctions – has been snatched away from us. Could this one further mishap add appreciably to your grief? How should not any heart practised in such experience have grown less sensitive and count all else as of relatively little consequence?

But I suppose you grieve for *her*. How often must you have thought, and how often has it occurred to me, that in this day and age they are not most to be pitied who have been granted a painless exchange of life for death! What was there after all to make life so sweet a prospect for her at this time? What did she have or hope? What comfort for her spirit? The thought perhaps of spending her life wedded to some young man of distinction? Do you suppose it was possible for you to choose from this modern generation a son-in-law suitable to your standing, to whose protection you could feel safe in confiding your child? Or the thought of bearing children herself, whose bloom would cheer her eyes, sons who could maintain their patrimony, would seek public office in due course, and act in public affairs and in their friends' concerns like free men? Was not all this taken away before it was granted? The loss of children is a calamity, sure enough – except that it is a worse calamity to bear our present lot and endure.

I want to tell you of something which has brought *me* no slight comfort,[737] in the hope that perhaps it may have some power to lighten your sorrow too. As I was on my way back from Asia,[738] sailing from Aegina towards Megara, I began to gaze at the landscape around me. There behind me was Aegina, in front of me Megara, to the right Piraeus, to the left Corinth; once flourishing towns, now lying low in ruins before one's eyes. I began to think to myself: 'Ah! How can we manikins wax indignant if one of us dies or is killed, ephemeral creatures as we are, when the corpses of so many towns lie abandoned in a single spot? Check yourself, Servius, and remember that you were born a mortal man.' That thought, I do assure you, strengthened me not a little.[739] If I may suggest it, picture the same spectacle to yourself. Not long ago so many great men died at one time, the Roman Empire was so gravely impaired, all its provinces shaken to pieces; can you be so greatly moved by the loss of one poor little woman's frail spirit? If her end had not come now, she must none the less have died in a few years' time,

737. If Sulpicius had suffered a bereavement we do not know what it was.

738. i.e. from Samos. Sulpicius will have been returning to Rome in the autumn of 47.

739. Byron refers to this passage in *Childe Harold* (Canto V, stanza 4), as does Sterne, *Tristram Shandy*, V, 3, who probably got it from Burton.

for she was mortal. You too must take your mind and thoughts away from such things, and dwell instead on recollections worthy of the character you hold. Tell yourself that she lived as long as it was well for her to live, and that she and freedom existed together. She saw you, her father, Praetor, Consul, and Augur. She was married to young men of distinction. Almost all that life can give, she enjoyed; and she left life when freedom died. How can you or she quarrel with fortune on that account?

And then, do not forget that you are Cicero, a man accustomed to give rules and advice to others. Do not be like a bad physician, who professes medical knowledge to his patients but does not know how to treat himself. Rather lay to your heart and place before your mind the precepts you are wont to offer others. There is no grief that is not lessened or softened by the passage of time. For *you* to wait for this time to pass, instead of anticipating the result by your own good sense, does you discredit. And if consciousness remains to those below, loving you as she did, dutifully fond as she was of all her family, *she* assuredly does not wish you to act so. Listen then for her dead sake, for the sake of others, your well-wishers and friends who are sad for your grief, and for your country's sake, so that if need arise she may have the benefit of your service and counsel. And then, since in the pass to which we have come we must not disregard even *this* aspect, do not let anyone suppose that it is not so much a daughter you are mourning as the public predicament and the victory of others.

I am ashamed to write at greater length to you on this matter, lest I seem to doubt your good sense, and so I shall end my letter with one final observation. We have seen more than once how nobly you sustain prosperity, and how great the glory you gain thereby. Let us recognize at last that you are no less able to bear adversity, and that you count it no heavier load than you should, lest of all fine qualities you may seem to lack this only.[740]

740. Livy wrote of Cicero that he bore none of his misfortunes like a man except death.

As for me, I shall inform you of what is going on here and of the state of the province when I hear that your mood is calmer. Goodbye.

249 (IV. 6)

CICERO TO SERVIUS SULPICIUS RUFUS

Atticus' villa near Nomentum, mid April 45

From M. Cicero to Ser. Sulpicius greetings.

Yes, my friend, I wish you had been with me, as you say, in my most grievous affliction. How much your presence would have helped me by consolation and by sorrow well-nigh equal to my own I readily recognize from the measure of easement I felt when I read your letter. You have written the words that could alleviate mourning and your own no small distress has given you the means of comforting mine. But your son Servius has shown by every friendly attention that could be rendered at such a time how much he thinks of me and how welcome he believes such a disposition on his part will be to you. I have often felt more pleasure in his attentions than I feel now (as you may imagine), but never more grateful.

Not only am I comforted by your words and (I might almost say) your fellowship in sorrow, but by your counsel as well. I feel it discreditable in me not to bear my bereavement as so wise a man as you considers it should be borne. But sometimes I am overwhelmed, and scarcely offer any resistance to grief, because I have no such solaces as others in similar plight, whose examples I set before my mind, did not lack. Q. Maximus[741] lost a son of consular rank, high reputation, and splendid record.

741. Q. Fabius Maximus 'Cunctator'.

L. Paulus[742] lost two in a single week. Then there was Galus in your own family[743] and M. Cato,[744] who lost a son of the highest intellectual and moral qualities. But they lived in periods when the honourable standing they enjoyed in public life assuaged their mourning. *I* had already lost those distinctions which you yourself mention and which I had gained by dint of great exertions. The one comfort still left to me was that which has now been snatched away. Neither my friends' concerns nor the administration of the state detained my thoughts. I had no wish to appear in the courts, I could not endure the sight of the Senate-House. I considered, as was the fact, that I had lost all the fruits of my work and success. However, I reflected that I shared this situation with yourself and certain others; I conquered my feelings and forced myself to bear it all patiently. But while I did so, I had a haven of refuge and repose, one in whose conversation and sweet ways I put aside all cares and sorrows.

Now this grievous blow has again inflamed the wounds I thought healed. When in the past I withdrew in sadness from public affairs, my home received and soothed me; but I cannot now take refuge from domestic grief in public life, to find relief in what it offers. And so I stay away from home and Forum alike, for neither public nor private life can any longer comfort the distress which each occasions me.

All the more then do I look forward to your return and desire to see you as soon as possible. No abstract reflection can bring me greater comfort than our fellowship in daily life and talk. However, from what I hear, I hope your arrival is imminent. One reason among many why I am anxious to see you as soon as may be is that I should like us to ponder together how we

742. L. Aemilius Paulus, victor of Pydna.

743. i.e. *gens*. C. Sulpicius Galus was Consul in 166.

744. The Censor. Cicero had collected many such examples in his lost 'Consolation', addressed to himself.

should best pass through this present time, all of which must be accommodated to the wishes of a single individual. He is a man of sense and generosity, and I think I have cause to believe him no enemy of mine and a very good friend of yours. Even so, what line we are to take needs careful consideration. I am not thinking of any positive action, but of retirement by his leave and favour.

Goodbye.

250 (IX. 11)

CICERO TO DOLABELLA

Atticus' villa near Nomentum, April (late) 45

From Cicero to Dolabella greetings.

I would rather my failure to write had been due to my own death than to the grievous calamity which has come upon me. I should surely bear it less hard if I had you beside me. Your wise words and signal affection for me would be a great solace. However, I shall soon be seeing you, so we think here. You will find me in a state which offers plenty of scope for your assistance. Not that I am so far broken down as to forget my human lot or to think it right to sink under fortune's blows. But the gaiety and charm which people saw in me, and you in particular used to find agreeable, is all swept away. My fortitude and resolution, however, if I ever possessed those qualities, you will recognize as no whit diminished.

You tell me that you have to fight my battles.[745] I am less concerned that you should rebut my detractors than anxious that your affection for me should be recognized, as it surely is.

745. Against his nephew, the younger Q. Cicero, now also with Caesar's forces in Spain. Reports of his evil tongue had arrived from other quarters (cf. *Letters to Atticus* 346 (XIII.37).2).

Let me earnestly request you to act accordingly, and to forgive the brevity of this letter. I expect we shall shortly be together, and I have not yet sufficiently regained my strength for writing.

251 (V. 14)

LUCCEIUS TO CICERO

Rome, 9 May 45

From L. Lucceius, son of Quintus, to M. Tullius, son of Marcus, greetings.

I hope you are well, as I am – that is, I am in my usual state of health, but just a little worse even than usual.

I have often asked after your whereabouts in the hope of seeing you. I was surprised that you have not been in Rome[746] since you left, and it still surprises me. What chiefly draws you away I am not sure. If you enjoy solitude while writing or engaged in one of your usual occupations, I am glad and make no criticism of your plan. Nothing can be more agreeable even in calm, prosperous times, let alone in these dark days of mourning, especially as yours is a weary mind, needing rest now from the heavy pressure of affairs, and a well-instructed one, ever creating something to delight others and shed lustre on yourself.

If, on the other hand, as before you left, you have abandoned yourself to tears and sorrow, I grieve in your grievous pain; but, if you allow me to speak my mind plainly, I cannot help taking you to task. For consider: Will you, whose intelligence pierces the darkest abstrusities, alone be blind to the obvious? Will you not understand that you gain nothing by constant complaining, that you double the cares which your good sense enjoins you to make lighter?

746. i.e. even for a short visit.

If advice can be of no avail, then I ask as a personal favour and beg of you, if you have any regard for me, to loose yourself from the bonds of your distresses and come back to live with us and to your normal way of life, both that which you share with the rest of us and that which is personal and peculiar to yourself. I am anxious not to importune you, if you find my concern irksome; and I am anxious to turn you from perseverance in this course. These two conflicting desires confuse me. As to the latter, I hope you will comply with my request, if you can; or else, as to the former, I hope you will take no offence.

Goodbye.

252 (v. 15)

CICERO TO LUCCEIUS

Astura, mid May 45

From M. Cicero to L. Lucceius, son of Quintus, greetings.

All your affection stands revealed from every angle in the letter I have lately received from you, an affection not unknown to me indeed, but none the less welcome and wished for; I should say 'pleasant', had I not lost that word forever. The reason is not only the one which you suspect, and for which, in terms of the most loving gentleness, you take me in effect severely to task; it is also that the remedies appropriate to my grievous wound no longer exist. For consider: Am I to have recourse to my friends? How many do I have? You know, for most of them were yours too. Some have perished, others have somehow grown less feeling. With you, it is true, I could live, and should greatly so desire. Old acquaintance, affection, habit, community of pursuits – what tie, pray, is wanting to our attachment? Can we then be together? Upon my word, I do not know what hinders us. Yet the fact is that hitherto we have not been so, neighbours though we were at Tusculum and Puteoli – of Rome I say nothing, for where the Forum is common ground there is no need to live next door.

But by some malign chance our lot has fallen in times when, at what should be the crown of our careers, life itself seems a dishonour. Bereft of embellishment and solace indoors and out, what refuge could I find? Books, to be sure. I go to them constantly; what else am I to do? And yet they too seem somehow to bar my way to haven and refuge, and almost to reproach me for lingering in a life that has nothing to offer save the protraction of sad days.

In these circumstances are you surprised that I stay away from Rome, where my home can afford me no pleasure, while I am mortally weary of times and men, of Forum and Senate-House? So I go to my books, on which I spend all my time, not looking for a lasting cure but only for brief forgetfulness of pain. But if you and I had done what continual alarms prevented us even thinking of, and had been always together, your health would be no burden to me nor my mourning to you. Let us, as far as may be, bring that to pass. Both of us will surely find our account in it. I shall see you soon then.

253 (IV. 12)

SERVIUS SULPICIUS RUFUS TO CICERO

Athens, 31 May 45

From Servius to Cicero cordial greetings.

I know that my news will not be of the most agreeable[747] to

747. An odd meiosis; but Sulpicius' writing is not of the most sensitive.

you and other friends. But chance and nature are our masters. Stand the matter how it may, I feel it my duty to inform you.

On 23 May I took ship from Epidaurus to Piraeus, where I met my colleague M. Marcellus, and spent the day there to be with him. I took leave of him the following day, intending to travel from Athens to Boeotia and conclude what remained of my assizes. He proposed, as he told me, to sail round Cape Malea towards Italy. Two days later I was about to set out from Athens, when about three o'clock in the morning a friend of his, P. Postumius, arrived to tell me that my colleague[748] M. Marcellus had been attacked with a dagger by P. Magius Cilo, a friend of his, after dinner, and had received two wounds, one in the stomach and one in the head behind the ear. He hoped, however, that there was a chance for his life. Magius had later committed suicide, and he himself had been sent to me by Marcellus to tell me what had occurred and ask me to send him doctors. Accordingly, I collected some doctors and set out straight away for Piraeus as day broke. I was not far away, when a boy of Acidinus' met me on the road with a note which stated that Marcellus had breathed his last shortly before dawn. So a very eminent man has been tragically murdered by a villain. He was spared by the respect of his enemies only to meet his death at the hand of a friend.

None the less I proceeded to his tent. I found two freedmen and a handful of slaves. They said the rest had fled in a panic, because their master had been killed in front of his tent. I had to bring him back to the city in the litter in which I myself had travelled, using my own bearers; and there I saw to his funeral, on as handsome a scale as the resources of Athens could provide. I could not induce the townspeople to grant him burial within the city precincts; they pleaded a religious bar, and it is a fact that they had never given such permission in the past. The next best thing they did allow, to bury him in a public hall, whichever I wished. So I chose a spot in the most celebrated hall in the

748. As Consul in 51.

world, the Academy. There we cremated him, and I later saw to it that the people of Athens should arrange for the erection of a monument to him in marble on the spot. So I have done all that in me lay for my colleague and kinsman, in life and in death.

Goodbye.

Dispatched 31 May, Athens.

254 (IX. 8)[749]

CICERO TO VARRO

Tusculum, 11 or 12 July 45

From Cicero to Varro.

To dun a man for a present, though promised, is in poor taste – even the crowd does not demand a show[750] unless stirred up to it. None the less my impatience for the fulfilment of your promise[751] impels me – not to dun, but to remind you. And I am sending you four monitors[752] not of the most bashful. I am sure you know how assertive this younger Academy[753] can be; well, the quartet I am sending you has been summoned from its

749. This letter, of which Cicero wrote to Atticus (333 (XIII.25).2) that he would never take so much trouble over anything again, accompanied the presentation of the four Books of his dialogue *Academic Questions*. Varro had a major role in the final version.

750. *munus* has the double meaning of 'present' and 'show'; cf. Letter 47 (II.3).

751. Several years previously Varro had promised to dedicate his work *On the Latin Language* to Cicero; cf. *Letters to Atticus* 320 (XIII.12). 2.

752. The four Books of the *Academic Questions*.

753. The sceptical school of Arcesilas and Carneades. Elsewhere Cicero calls it the 'New Academy'.

headquarters. I am afraid they *may* dun you, but I have charged them to *request*. To be sure, I have been waiting quite a while and holding back, so as not to address a piece to you before I received one and thus repay you as nearly as possible in your own coin. But since you are proceeding rather slowly (and that is to say, as I interpret, carefully), I could not refrain from advertising the bond of common pursuits and affection between us by such a form of composition as lay within my powers. Accordingly, I have staged a conversation between us at Cumae, Pomponius also being present. I have assigned the exposition of Antiochus' tenets (being under the impression that you approve of them) to your role, that of Philo's to my own. I dare say you will be surprised when you read to find that you and I have discussed a subject which in fact we never *háve* discussed; but you know the conventions of Dialogue. In future, my dear Varro, we shall have talks in plenty, if so minded, between ourselves and to please ourselves. Late in the day perhaps. But let the public destiny answer for what is past; the present is our own responsibility. If only we could pursue these studies together in peaceful times and a settled, if not satisfactory, state of the community! And yet, if that were so, there would be other claims upon us, calling us to honourable responsibilities and tasks. As matters stand, why should we desire life without our studies? For my part, I have little enough desire for it even with them; take them away, and I should lack even that little. But all this we will talk over together and often.

All good luck to your change of residence and your new purchase. I think you are doing wisely. Take care of your health.

255 (V. 9)

VATINIUS TO CICERO

Narona, 11 July 45

From Vatinius, Imperator, to his friend Cicero greetings.

I trust you are well, as I am and my army.

Do you keep up your practice of standing by old clients? If so, here comes one of them by the name of P. Vatinius, who wants an advocate to take his case! Surely you won't turn your back now I stand well in the world after taking me on when it was touch and go. As for me, whom should I choose and turn to but my old defender, who taught me how to win? When I think what a combination of powerful persons you disregarded to save my life, I can hardly doubt your readiness to smash and squash a set of petty backbiters with their spiteful tittle-tattle, when it's a question of an honour.[754]

Well then, if you love me as you usually do, let me put myself wholly in your hands. Look upon this load, such as it is, as yours to shoulder, a task you ought to perform for the sake of my standing. You know that somehow or other my career is apt to find tongues to carp at it – truly no fault of mine, but what difference does that make if the thing happens just the same, fated as it were? If anyone *does* show a disposition to stand in my light, may I ask you to defend me in my absence with no less than your usual generosity? I am appending the text of my dispatch to the Senate on my military operations for your perusal.

They tell me that a runaway slave[755] of yours, a reader, is with the Vardaei. You gave me no commission about him, but I have

754. A Supplication for Vatinius' military successes in Illyricum.
755. Cf. Letter 212 (XIII.77).

none the less issued instructions in advance that he be searched for by land and sea, and no doubt I shall find him for you, unless he has made off into Dalmatia – though even there I shall winkle him out sooner or later. Don't forget me.

Goodbye.

11 July, from camp at Narona.

256 (V. 10a. 3)

VATINIUS TO CICERO

Narona, early November 45

Caesar is treating me badly so far. He is still not putting the motion about my Supplications and my Dalmatian successes. One might think I had not done fully enough in Dalmatia to entitle me to a Triumph![756] Or am I supposed to wait until I have finished the whole war? Dalmatia has twenty towns of ancient foundation, more than sixty adopted later into the confederacy. If no Supplications are decreed me until I take them all, then I am on a very different footing from other generals.

257 (V. 11)

CICERO TO VATINIUS

Rome, early December (?) 45

From M. Cicero to Vatinius, Imperator, greetings.

It is no surprise to me to find you appreciative of my good offices, for I know you of old as the most grateful of mankind,

756. Vatinius was finally granted a Triumph by the Triumvirs in 42.

and I have never been behindhand in proclaiming it. You not only felt but *showed* your gratitude to me in deed, and in more than ample measure. Accordingly, in all your future concerns you shall find my devotion no less and my sentiments towards you unchanged.

As soon as I had read your letter, in which you commend to me your excellent lady Pompeia, I had a word with our friend Sura and asked him to tell her from me to let me know of any service she might require, and to promise that I should give my most sedulous endeavours to perform her wishes. And so I shall, and, if need appears, I shall see her in person. But will you please write and tell her that she must not consider anything too big or too small? I shall find nothing too difficult and nothing beneath my attention. No part I take in your affairs will appear to me either troublesome or unbecoming.

Do please settle this affair of Dionysius. I shall honour any undertaking you make him. If he behaves like the scoundrel he is, you shall lead him captive at your Triumph. Deuce take these Dalmatians, who are giving you so much trouble! But, as you say, they will soon be in the bag and will shed lustre on your successes, for they have always been accounted a warrior race.

258 (v. 10b)

VATINIUS TO CICERO

Narona, 5 December 45

After the Supplications in my honour were decreed, I set out for Dalmatia. I took six towns by storm. The single town of ✳, the biggest of the lot, was captured by me four times over, for I took four towers and four walls and their whole citadel, from which snow, frost, and rain dislodged me. Thus, my dear Cicero, I had to leave the town I had taken and the war I had won; it was too bad. Please plead my cause with Caesar, if need arises, and regard me as yours to defend on all fronts, believing that you have no more devoted friend than me.

Goodbye.

Dispatched Nones of December, from Narona.

259 (v. 10a. 1–2)

VATINIUS TO CICERO

Narona, late December 45 or January 44

From Vatinius to his friend Cicero greetings.

I trust you are well, as I am and my army.

So far I cannot fish anything out about your man Dionysius, especially as the Dalmatian cold, which drove me out from there, has frozen me up here too. But I shall not give up till sooner or later I winkle him out. But you are a hard taskmaster! You write me what reads like a very earnest intercession on behalf of Catilius. Get along with you, and our friend Sex. Servilius too! Upon my word, I think a lot of him, as you do. But is this the kind of client and case you people take on – a monster of savagery, who has murdered and kidnapped and ruined all those freeborn men and matrons and Roman citizens, and laid whole districts waste? This ape, this worthless ruffian, bore arms against me, and I took him prisoner of war. But really, my dear Cicero, what can I do? Upon my word, I am anxious to obey your every command. My own right to inflict condign punishment upon him as my captive, which I was going to exercise, I forgo in deference to your request. But what am I to say to those who demand redress by process of law for the plunder of their property, the seizure of their ships, the slaughter of brothers, children, and parents? Upon my word, I could not face it out, not if I had the impudence of Appius, whose shoes I wear.[757] Well then, I shall spare no pains to meet your wishes, as I know them. He is defended by Q. Volusius, a pupil of yours[758] – perhaps that circumstance may rout the other side. There lies the best hope. You will defend me in Rome, if need arises.

260 (VII. 24)

CICERO TO M. FABIUS GALLUS

Tusculum, 22 August 45

From M. Cicero to M. Fabius Gallus greetings.

Everywhere I turn I come across traces of your affection, as most recently in the affair of Tigellius.[759] I could see from your letter that you have been very much concerned. So I thank you for the kind intention. But on the matter itself, one or two observations. Cipius I think it was who said on a certain occasion 'I am not asleep to everybody.'[760] Just so, my dear Gallus, *I* am not a slave to everybody. Though I don't know why I talk of slavery. In the old days, when I was supposed to be an autocrat, I was never so courted as I now am by Caesar's closest intimates, all except your friend. I consider myself so much the

757. Literally 'into whose place I was elected'. Vatinius had succeeded to the vacancy in the College of Augurs left by Ap. Pulcher's death in 48.

758. He may have taken lessons in declamation from Cicero, like Hirtius and Dolabella.

759. On this see *Letters to Atticus* 347 (XIII.49).

760. The story (or an allusion to it) could be found in Lucilius. Cipius pretended to be asleep at dinner so that he could ignore his wife's misbehaviour. But when a slave tried to make off with some wine, he started up with the words quoted.

luckier, not to have to put up with the fellow – more pesti-
lential than his native climate![761] I regard him as knocked down
to the highest bidder all those years ago in Licinius Calvus'
Hipponactean advertisement![762]

However, let me tell you about his grievance. I had taken on
Phamea's case, for his own sake – he was quite a friend of mine.
He came and told me that the judge had fixed a day for the
hearing, being the very day that the jury had to consider their
verdict in P. Sestius' case.[763] I replied that I could not possibly
manage it; if he picked any other day he liked, I should not fail
him. However, conscious of having a nephew, a pretty per-
former on the flute and a tolerable hand with the oil-can,[764] he
took his leave, in something of a huff, I thought. So there you
are: 'Sardinians for sale, each worse than t'other.'[765] You now
know my side, and can see how unreasonable this beggar on
horseback is being.

Send me your 'Cato'[766] – I am anxious to read it. It's a disgrace to us both that I have not read it already.

761. Sardinia was notoriously unhealthy.
762. Calvus had composed a lampoon upon Tigellius after the manner
and in the metre of the sixth-century Hipponax of Ephesus. The first
line is preserved: 'Sardinian Tigellius for sale – stinking goods!'
763. Sestius was accused of electoral corruption in 52.
764. Presumably in training athletes. But Manutius' conjecture
cantorem ('singer') for *unctorem* ('anointer') is attractive.
765. A proverb quoted elsewhere and variously interpreted.
766. After Cato's death in April 46 there was a brisk output of pamphlets for and against his character and record. Cicero's had appeared
about a year previously.

261 (VII. 25)

CICERO TO M. FABIUS GALLUS

Tusculum, 23 or 24 August 45

From Cicero to M. Fabius Gallus greetings.

Don't distress yourself about the letter which you are so sorry you tore up. I have it safe at home.[767] You can ask for it any time you like. As for your word of warning, I'm very grateful, and hope you will always so favour me. Apparently you are afraid that, if we make mock of your friend, we may come to laugh – *sard*onically![768]

Attention now! No more writing![769] Here comes the beak, sooner than expected! It's the cat for Catonians, I fear.

My dear Gallus, that part of your letter from 'all goes downhill' onwards – depend upon it, it's the best thing ever. This for your private ear, keep it to yourself – not a word to your freedman Apella even. Nobody but us two talks in this style – good or bad, that's another question; but whatever it is, it's *ours*. So press on and don't budge a nail's breadth, as they say, from your pen. The pen makes the author! For my own part, I work o'nights nowadays as well as in the day-time.

767. i.e. a copy. The letter was probably Letter 260 (VII.24).

768. The Greek phrase *sardonion gelan*='to laugh scornfully' or 'bitterly' ('the wrong side of one's mouth') was variously explained in antiquity. Cicero of course alludes to the Sardinian origin of Tigellius.

769. Literally 'hands off the tablet'. When the schoolmaster comes in the boys must stop writing their exercise. The schoolmaster here is Caesar.

262 (VI. 19)

CICERO TO LEPTA

Astura, August (end) 45

From Cicero to Lepta.

Glad to hear that Macula has behaved as he should.[770] I always thought his Falernian place suitable for a lodge, provided there is enough shelter for my entourage. In other respects I don't dislike the place. But I shall not on that account give up your Petrine establishment – the house and amenities generally are for residence, not just a lodge.

I have spoken to Oppius about a Curatorship of the royal shows[771] (Balbus I have not seen since you left; the gout in his feet is so bad that he doesn't want visitors). To be sure, I think you would be wiser to forget the whole thing. You will stand no chance of gaining the object for which you put yourself to such drudgery. He[772] has so many intimates that there is more likelihood of one dropping out than of any opening for a newcomer, especially one who has nothing to contribute except his services; and as for them, he will think he has conferred a favour (if he so much as knows of it) rather than received one. However, we'll try to find something that looks well; otherwise I think that, far from seeking such employment, you should steer clear of it.

770. Probably a relative of Lepta who had died leaving him money; cf. the beginning of *Letters to Atticus* 65 (III.20). Lepta seems to have suggested that Cicero might like to acquire part of the estate, a small property in the Falernian district eastward of Sinuessa, as a lodge for use on his journeys up and down the Appian Way; cf. Letter 339 (XII.20).

771. Cf. *Letters to Atticus* 338 (XIII.46).1. 'Royal', of course, is a hostile reference to Caesar, called *rex* in *Letters to Atticus* 346 (XIII.37)2.

772. Caesar.

I think I shall stay at Astura until I learn his route and time of arrival.

Goodbye.

263 (IX. 12)

CICERO TO DOLABELLA

A villa, December 45 (?)

From Cicero to Dolabella.

I congratulate our Baiae if, as you say, it has suddenly become a healthy spot.[773] But perhaps it is out of fondness and flattery towards yourself; perhaps the place has forgotten its nature so long as you are there. If that is the explanation, I am not in the least surprised that even air and soil put aside their natural properties for your benefit.

Contrary to what I thought, I find I have with me the little speech in defence of Deiotarus[774] which you were asking for, and so I am sending it to you. Please bear in mind, when you read it, that the case was a meagre, paltry affair, hardly worth writing up. But I wanted to send my old friend and host a little present – on the light, coarse-spun side, as his own presents are apt to be.

I wish you good sense and courage, so that your moderation and steadiness will bring shame on the misconduct of others.

773. The apparent implication that this most famous of Roman pleasure-resorts was unhealthy is surprising.

774. Accused of an attempt on Caesar's life. Cicero's defence survives.

264 (VII. 29)

MANIUS CURIUS TO CICERO

Patrae, 29 October 45

From his friend Curius to M. Cicero greetings.

I trust you are well.

I say '*his* friend', for I am yours in usufruct, though I belong to our good Atticus by right of ownership. You have the enjoyment, and he the title. If he puts the goods up for sale as a job lot, he won't get much by it. But *I* advertise that everything I am and have, my entire place in society, comes from you. That's worth something! So, Cicero mine, carry on your good work. Keep me in good shape, and give me a first-class recommendation to Sulpicius' successor,[775] thus making it easier for me to obey your precepts, and see you gladly come spring, and pull up stakes here, and take my all safely home.

Only, exalted friend, please don't show Atticus this letter. Leave him in his delusion. Let him go on thinking me a man of honour, not one to cover two walls from the same pot of whitewash.

And so, patron mine, a very good day to you. Give my regards to my good friend Tiro.

Dispatched 29 October.

775. As governor of Achaia. His name was Acilius.

265 (VII. 30)

CICERO TO MANIUS CURIUS

Rome, January 44

From Cicero to Curius greetings.

Not so. I no longer urge you or ask you to come home. On the contrary, I am anxious to take wing myself and go to some place 'where nevermore of Pelops' line I'll hear the name or deeds'.[776] You cannot imagine the sense of personal dishonour I feel at living in the Rome of today. Farsighted indeed you turn out to have been when you fled this country. Although the happenings here are painful enough in the report, yet it is more tolerable to hear of them than to see them. At least you were not in the Campus when the elections to the Quaestorship began at nine o'clock in the morning. A chair of state had been placed for Q. Maximus, whom these people used to call Consul. His death was announced, and the chair removed. Whereupon *he*,[777] having taken auspices for an assembly of the Tribes, held an assembly of the Centuries,[778] and at one o'clock of the afternoon declared a Consul elected, to remain in office until the Kalends of January, the next morning that was to be. So in the Consulship of Caninius[779] you may take it that nobody had breakfast! However, at any rate no crime was committed during the same period – the Consul's vigilance was extraordinary. Throughout his entire term of office he never closed an eye! You find such things laughable, for you are not on the

776. See n. 627.

777. Caesar.

778. For the election of a Consul. Quaestors were elected by the Assembly of Tribes.

779. C. Caninius Rebilus.

spot; if you were here to witness, you would have to weep. What if I were to tell you the rest? Incidents of the same character are innumerable. I could not bear them, if I had not brought my boat into the harbour of philosophy, and if I did not have our dear Atticus to share my pursuits. You say you belong to him by legal ownership, but to me by use and enjoyment. I am quite satisfied with that position. What a man uses and enjoys *is* what belongs to him. But of this more anon.

Acilius, who has been sent to Greece with an army, is under a great obligation to me, having been twice defended by me in better days on a capital charge. He is not without a sense of gratitude, and pays me many attentions. I have written to him on your behalf with all care and am enclosing my letter herewith. I should be glad if you would write and tell me how he receives it, and what promises he makes you.

266 (XIII. 50)

CICERO TO ACILIUS

Rome, January (beginning) 44

From Cicero to Acilius greetings.

In view of your habitual courtesy towards me, of which I had full experience throughout the time of my residence in Brundisium, I have made bold to write to you without ceremony and almost as of right on any matter which deeply concerns me.

Manius Curius, who is in business at Patrae, is on the closest and most familiar terms with me. I am indebted to him for many services, as he is to me. And, what is most important, there is a cordial and reciprocal affection between us. That being so, if you pin any hopes upon my friendship, if you wish to

make me even more grateful for the services you so readily
rendered me in Brundisium (though most grateful I am), and if
you see that all those near to you hold me in affection, then of
your favour grant me this request: Keep Manius Curius in good
fettle, as the phrase goes, safe and sound and free of all embar-
rassment, loss, and trouble. I give you my personal guarantee
(and all your people will undertake as much on my behalf) that
my friendship and your good offices to me will yield you no
small returns and no slight pleasure.

Goodbye.

267 (VII. 31)

CICERO TO MANIUS CURIUS

Rome, February 44

From Cicero to Curius greetings.

I readily perceive from your letter that you have a great
regard for me, and that you are aware of my affection for yourself. It has always been my endeavour that this should be so.
Having both achieved this result, we now have only to vie with
one another in acts of friendship, a contest in which the victory
of either will leave me equally content.

Just as well that you had no need to give my letter to Acilius.
I understand from yours that you did not much require Sulpicius' help,[780] because your affairs have contracted to a point at
which, as you say, 'there is neither head nor foot to them'[781] –
for my part I wish they had *feet*, to bring you home at long last.
You see how the sources of ancient wit have dried up. Our
friend Pomponius can truly say 'Save that we few keep the

780. Cf. Letter 283 (XIII.17).
781. i.e. 'they are worth nothing'.

ancient Attic glory living still.'[782] He is your successor, and I am his. Pray then come back, so that the seed of wit at least does not perish along with the commonwealth.

268 (XIII. 43)

CICERO TO Q. GALLIUS[783]

Rome, winter of 47–46

From M. Cicero to Q. Gallius.

I hope your affection for me, which to be sure has long been apparent, will be shown in many contexts, but here you have a matter in which you can easily demonstrate your good-will towards me. A friend of mine, L. Oppius, son of Marcus, is in business at Philomelium. I recommend him to you very specially, all the more so because, besides the regard I have for himself, he is managing the affairs of L. Egnatius Rufus. Now Egnatius is of all Roman Knights on the most familiar terms with me; daily intercourse and many important services rendered have created a close attachment.

So I am asking you to look kindly on Oppius, who is on the spot, and to protect Egnatius' interests in his absence just as though his affairs were mine. I should be grateful if, to aid your memory, you would write a few lines to be delivered to you in the province – but write in such terms that, when you read them, you can readily recall the urgency of this recommendation of mine. This I beg of you as a special favour.

782. Source unknown.

783. The manuscripts vary and the name of the addressee (also in Letter 270 (XIII.44)) may have been Q. (?) Quintius Gallus – an unknown. In any case he was about to join Q. Marcius Philippus, governor of Cilicia, as Quaestor or Legate.

269 (XIII. 74)

CICERO TO Q. PHILIPPUS

Rome, early 46

From M. Cicero to Q. Philippus, Proconsul, greetings.

Although, in view of your attentiveness to me and the friend-ship between us, I do not doubt that you are bearing my recommendation in mind, I would none the less recommend to you yet again my friend L. Oppius, who is on the spot, and the affairs of my very good friend L. Egnatius, who is not. My connection with the latter is so close and familiar that I should not be more concerned if my own money were at stake. So you will greatly oblige me if you make clear to him that your affection for me is as great as I myself believe it to be. You can do nothing to oblige me more, and I beg it of you earnestly.

270 (XIII. 44)

CICERO TO Q. GALLIUS

Rome, early 46

From Cicero to Gallius greetings.

Letters from yourself and from my good friend L. Oppius have informed me that you have been mindful of my recom-mendation, which in view of your notable good-will towards me and the attachment between us did not at all surprise me. However, I should like once again to recommend L. Oppius, who is on the spot, and the affairs of my very close friend L. Egnatius, who is not. My connection with the latter is so close and intimate that I should not be more concerned if my own money were at stake. So you will very much oblige me if you make it clear to him that your affection for me is as great as I myself believe it to be. You can do nothing to oblige me more, and I beg it of you earnestly.

271 (XIII. 45)

CICERO TO APPULEIUS

Rome, 46

From Cicero to Appuleius, Proquaestor.[784]

Of all Roman Knights L. Egnatius stands on the most familiar footing with me, and I recommend to you his slave Anchialus and his business affairs in Asia as warmly as if I were writing of my personal interests. I should like you to be aware that apart from a great deal of day-to-day contact we are indebted to one another for important services mutually rendered. So let me earnestly request you to let him understand that I have written to you in appropriately pressing terms – for as to your friendly disposition towards me he is in no doubt. May I particularly beg this favour of you?

Goodbye.

784. Evidently in the province of Asia. He cannot be securely identified with any of the contemporary Ap(p)uleii.

272 (XIII. 46)

CICERO TO APPULEIUS

Rome, 47–46

From Cicero to Appuleius greetings.

L. Nostius Zoilus is my co-heir and the estate is that of his former master. I mention these two particulars so you may know that I have cause to be his friend and may judge him a man of good character to be favoured by his ex-master with such a mark of esteem. So I recommend him to you as though he were one of my own domestic circle. It will be very agreeable to me if you will let him understand that this recommendation has done him great service with you.

273 (XIII. 73)

CICERO TO Q. PHILIPPUS

Tusculum (?), summer of 46

From M. Cicero to Q. Philippus, Proconsul, greetings.

I congratulate you on your safe return from your province to the bosom of your family with your reputation and the public interest unimpaired. If I had been in Rome, I should have seen you, and thanked you in person for taking care of my very good friend L. Egnatius in his absence and of L. Oppius on the spot.

My relations with Antipater of Derbe[785] are not only of hospitality, but of the most familiar acquaintance. I heard that

785. 'A local dynast in south Lycaonia, holding Derbe and Laranda, both places of some consequence' (R. Syme).

you have been very angry with him and was sorry for it. On the merits of the case I can make no judgement, apart from my persuasion that, being the man you are, you have done nothing without due consideration. But in virtue of our old friendship, I would urgently request you to spare his sons, who are in your hands, if only as a favour to me, unless you think your reputation would thereby be in any way compromised. If *I* thought that, I should not dream of asking you – your credit would be of much more consequence in my eyes than the connection I have mentioned. But I am persuaded (I may be wrong) that such action will bring you commendation rather than criticism. If it is not troubling you too much, I should be glad to learn from you what can be done, and what you can do for my sake – of your will I have no doubt.

274 (XIII. 47)

CICERO TO P. SILIUS

Date uncertain

From Cicero to Silius greetings.

Why should I recommend to you a person for whom you yourself have a regard? However, to let you know that I have not only a regard but an affection for him, I am writing you these lines. Of all your good offices, which are many and great, it will be to me the most agreeable if you will deal with Egnatius so as to make him feel that I am fond of him and that you are fond of me. I beg this of you as a special favour.

You may take it that those plans[786] of mine have fallen through. Well, let me apply the proverbial comfort – it may all be for the best. But of this when we meet. Be sure to keep your affection for me, and be satisfied of mine for you.

786. Reference uncertain.

275 (XIII. 78)

CICERO TO A. ALLIENUS

47–46? (perhaps c. 62)

From M. Cicero to Allienus[787] greetings.

Demetrius of Sicyon is not only a former host of mine, but a familiar friend, which not many (especially Greeks) can say. He is a most honest, worthy, and sedulously hospitable person, and pays me particular respect and attention and regard. You will find that he is the leading man, not only in his own town, but almost in Achaia as a whole. I would only open the door and pave his way into your acquaintance. Once you get to know him, your own disposition will do the rest: you will judge him worthy of your friendship and hospitality. So may I request you after reading this letter to take him under your wing, and promise to do all you can for him for my sake? As for what may follow, if, as I am confident will be the case, you find him deserving of your friendship and hospitality, I would ask you to make much of him and include him in your circle. I shall be greatly obliged.

Goodbye.

787. The following letter (276 (XII.79)) is addressed to Allienus as Proconsul, which he was, in Sicily, in 48–46. But the recommendation of a citizen of Sicyon suggests that this letter belongs to an earlier period in his career when he may have been serving in Greece. He was probably Quaestor *c.* 62.

276 (XIII. 79)

CICERO TO A. ALLIENUS

Rome, 47–46

From M. Cicero to Allienus, Proconsul, greetings.

I think you know how high a regard I had for C. Avianius
Flaccus, and I heard from his own lips (he was an excellent man,
most appreciative of a kindness) how handsomely you treated
him. His sons are thoroughly worthy of their father, and very
dear friends of mine. May I recommend them to you as warmly
as I possibly can? C. Avianius is in Sicily, Marcus is here with us.
I beg you to enhance the standing of the former, who is on the
spot, and to protect the interests of both. You can do nothing in
your present province to oblige me more, and I do most
particularly request it of you.

277 (XIII. 10)

CICERO TO M. BRUTUS

Rome, early (?) 46

From Cicero to Brutus greetings.

When your Quaestor, M. Varro,[788] was setting off to join
you I did not think he needed any recommendation. Traditional
usage, I thought, was in itself sufficient to recommend him to
you – which, as you are aware, has decreed that the relationship
of Quaestor to superior should stand next to that of children to

788. M. Terentius Varro Gibba. Brutus was governor of Cisalpine
Gaul.

parents. But Varro himself is persuaded that a carefully drafted letter of mine concerning him will carry great weight with you, and urges me to write as fully as possible. So I have thought it better to comply with my friend's wish, since he attaches so much importance to it.

To show you then that in so doing I am fulfilling an obligation, let me mention that when M. Terentius first entered public life he sought my friendship. Then, when he had established himself in the world, two additional circumstances served to increase my good-will towards him. One was that he was engaged in my own chosen avocation,[789] in which even today I take most pleasure, showing natural ability, as you know, and considerable application; the other, that at an early age he involved himself in the companies managing public contracts – to my regret, for he lost a great deal of money. However, the common interest of a class which stands very high in my regard made our friendship the firmer. Then, after a record of highly conscientious and creditable activity on both benches,[790] he applied himself to a political career (that was before this recent constitutional upheaval), and regarded the office as the most honourable reward of his hard work. I may add that latterly he travelled from Brundisium with a letter and oral message from myself to Caesar. I was impressed by his friendly spirit in undertaking this mission and the conscientiousness with which he discharged and reported it.

I had intended to deal specifically with his good character and personality after explaining the reason why I have so high a regard for him, but it seems to me that in doing the latter I have sufficiently covered the former. However, I do specifically promise and personally guarantee that he will make you a pleasant and useful associate. You will find him a man of modesty and good sense, a stranger to any form of self-seeking, active and painstaking furthermore in the highest degree.

789. Forensic oratory.
790. As prosecutor and defender.

I ought not to promise what you will have to judge for yourself when you come to know him well. Still, in all new associations something depends on the nature of the first approach, the sort of recommendation which opens as it were the door of friendship. That was my purpose in this letter. It should have been achieved, to be sure, by the official bond automatically; all the same, that bond will be none the frailer for this extra link. So if you think as much of me as Varro believes and I myself am conscious that you do, I trust you will make it your business to show me as soon as possible that this recommendation of mine has proved as advantageous to him as he expects (and I do not doubt) it will.

278 (XIII. 11)

CICERO TO M. BRUTUS

Rome, 46

From Cicero to Brutus greetings.

I have always noticed the particular care you take to inform yourself of all that concerns me, so I do not doubt that you not only know which township I hail from but also know how attentively I look after the interests of my fellow-townsmen of Arpinum. All their corporate income, including the means out of which they keep up religious worship and maintain their temples and public places in repair, consists in rents from property in Gaul.[791] We have dispatched the following gentlemen, Roman Knights, as our representatives to inspect the properties, collect sums due from the tenants, and take general cognizance and charge: Q. Fufidius, son of Quintus; M. Faucius, son of Marcus; Q. Mamercius, son of Quintus.

791. Cisalpine.

May I particularly request of you in virtue of our friendship to give your attention to the matter, and to do your best to see that the business of the municipality goes through as smoothly and rapidly as possible with your assistance. As for the persons named, let me ask you to extend them, as you naturally would, all possible courtesy and consideration. You will attach some worthy gentlemen to your connection and your favour will bind a township which never forgets an obligation. As for myself, I shall be even more beholden than I should otherwise have been, because, while it is my habit to look after my fellow-townsmen, I have a particular concern and responsibility towards them this year. It was my wish that my son, my nephew, and a very close friend of mine, M. Caesius, should be appointed Aediles this year to set the affairs of the municipality in order – in our town it is the custom to elect magistrates with that title and no other. You will have done honour to them, and above all to me, if the corporate property of the municipality is well managed thanks to your good-will and attention. May I again ask you this favour most earnestly?

279 (XIII. 12)

CICERO TO BRUTUS

Rome, same date as preceding

From Cicero to Brutus greetings.

In a separate letter I have recommended the representatives of the people of Arpinum jointly to your favour as warmly as I was able. In this letter I am recommending Q. Fufidius, with whom I have all manner of friendly ties, individually and with special warmth; not in any way to detract from the force of my other recommendation, but to add this one. He is the stepson of my particular friend and connection M. Caesius, and served with me as Military Tribune in Cilicia. His conduct in that capacity was such as to make me feel that I had not conferred a favour but received one. Furthermore, a point to which you attach special importance, he is not without a leaning towards our favourite pursuits. So I hope you will give him the most generous of welcomes, and do your best to ensure that his activity in a mission which he undertook contrary to his own convenience in deference to my wishes may shine as conspicuously as possible. He is desirous (the natural instinct of a man of mould) to gain all the commendation he can from me, his instigator, and from the municipality. In that he will succeed, if through this recommendation of mine he enlists your goodwill.

280 (XIII. 13)

CICERO TO M. BRUTUS

Rome, 46

From Cicero to Brutus greetings.

L. Castronius Paetus is without question the leading man in Luca, a gentleman of distinction and consequence, always ready to serve a friend – a thoroughly honourable man, whose virtues (if it be anything to the purpose) are set off by worldly fortune. He is also an intimate of mine; in fact there is no member of our order[792] whom he cultivates more assiduously. So I recommend him as my friend and worthy to be yours. Any service you render him will, I feel sure, tend to your own gratification, as it will certainly oblige me.

Goodbye.

792. The senatorial.

281 (XIII. 14)

CICERO TO M. BRUTUS

Rome, 46

From Cicero to Brutus greetings.

L. Titius[793] Strabo, one of our most respected and distinguished Roman Knights, is on intimate terms with me, and we can claim from one another all that belongs to the closest of connections. He is owed money in your province by P. Cornelius. Vulcatius, as City Praetor, has remitted the matter for adjudication in Gaul.

May I request you particularly (more so than if the case were mine, in so far as one is more respectably concerned about a friend's money than about one's own) to see that the affair is settled? Take it up personally and put it through. Try to arrange, so far as seems to you right and fair, that Strabo's freedman, who has been dispatched for the purpose, settles the business on the most favourable terms and collects the cash. I shall be deeply beholden, and you yourself will find L. Titius well worthy of your friendship. Let me once more earnestly beg of you to attend to this, as you habitually do to any wish of mine within your knowledge.

793. Perhaps 'Tidius'; he may have been the father of the person mentioned in Letter 376 (XII.6).

282 (XIII. 29)

CICERO TO L. PLANCUS

Rome, 46 (early)

From M. Cicero to L. Plancus greetings.

I am sure you know that among the connections you inherited from your father I stand pre-eminently close to you, not only on such grounds as present the façade of an intimate association, but on those of familiar intercourse – for, as you are aware, I had such a relationship, most valid and most delightful, with your father. Such were the origins of my affection for yourself. It strengthened my association with your father, the more so because I observed that, from the time when you were old enough to discriminate in your regard for this person or that, I was the object of your special notice and fond attention. Add to this the strong attachment of common pursuits, important in itself, and of such pursuits and accomplishments as automatically link those who share the love of them in the bonds of familiar friendship.

I expect you are wondering where this long-drawn exordium may be tending. Well, let me begin by assuring you that I have not mentioned these points without good and ample reason.

I am on the closest terms with C. Ateius Capito. You know the vicissitudes of my career. In all the various advancements and tribulations which have come my way C. Capito has been mine to command. His spirit and his time, his public and personal influence, even his private fortune, have been at my service in good times and bad.

Capito had a relative, T. Antistius. As Quaestor he was appointed by lot to Macedonia, and was in charge of that province, no one having come to replace him, when Pompey and his army arrived. There was nothing Antistius could do. Given the opportunity, he would have preferred above all things to rejoin Capito, whom he loved as a father, especially as he knew how deeply attached Capito was and has always been to Caesar. But taken as he was by surprise, he touched only such employment as he could not refuse. When money was minted at Apollonia, I cannot assert that he was not in charge, and I cannot deny that he was present, though for no more than two or perhaps three months. After that he kept away from the army and shunned all activity. I hope you will take my word for this as an eye-witness. He saw my despondency in that war, and shared all his thoughts with me. So he hid himself in a corner of Macedonia as far away as possible from the army, so as not to be present at any activity, let alone in command. After the battle he went to Bithynia, to a person with whom he had connections, A. Plautius. There Caesar saw him, and without a word of harshness or reproof told him to return to Rome. Directly afterwards he fell ill, and never recovered. He arrived in Corcyra a sick man, and there died. Under his will, made in Rome in the Consulship of Paulus and Marcellus, he left Capito five-sixths of his estate. The remaining sixth is left to persons whose portion may be confiscated to the state without exciting any complaint. It amounts to HS3,000,000. But this is Caesar's business.

Now, my dear Plancus, I appeal to you in the name of my friendship with your father and our mutual affection, of our studies and the whole tenor of our lives in which we are so much alike: I beg you with all possible earnestness and urgency to take this matter up and regard it as mine. Press with all your strength. Bring it about that by dint of my recommendation, your active support, and Caesar's good favour C. Capito enjoys his relative's estate. If you grant me this, I shall feel that you have spontaneously laid in my lap all the advantages which, in your present plenitude of influence and power, I could have had of you for the asking.

There is a point which I hope will help you, one of which Caesar himself is in the best possible position to judge. Capito has always cultivated and regarded Caesar. But Caesar himself is witness to that. I know what an excellent memory he has, so I do not attempt to brief you. When you speak to Caesar, assume on Capito's behalf just so much as you find *his* recollection acknowledges. For my part, let me put before you what I have been able to test in personal experience – how much weight it should carry you must judge. You are not unaware what party and cause I championed in public life, and on what persons and classes I relied for support and protection. Please believe me when I say that in this very war any action of mine not in accordance with Caesar's wishes (and I know Caesar realizes that such action was very much contrary to my own inclination) was taken by the advice, instigation, and influence of others; whereas the fact that I was the most moderate and temperate member of that party was due above all to the influence of Capito. Had my other friends been similarly minded, I might have done something for the state and should certainly have greatly benefited myself.

If you put this matter through, my dear Plancus, you will confirm my hopes of your kindly disposition towards me, and in Capito himself you will add to your connection a most appreciative, serviceable, and excellent person by conferring upon him so eminent a favour.

283 (XIII. 17)

CICERO TO SERVIUS SULPICIUS RUFUS

Rome, 46

From Cicero to Servius Sulpicius greetings.

There are many good reasons for the regard I have for Manius Curius, who is in business in Patrae. My friendship with him is of very long standing, begun when he first entered public life; and at Patrae his whole house was open to me in this recent terrible war, as well as on several earlier occasions. Had I needed, I should have used it like my own. But my principal link with Curius has, if I may so put it, a more sacred character; for he is a great intimate of our friend Atticus, whom he cultivates and regards more than anybody in the world.

If you happen to have made Curius' acquaintance already, I imagine that this letter comes too late; for he is so agreeable and attentive that I expect he will have recommended himself to you by now. If that is so, I would none the less earnestly request of you that any measure of good-will you have bestowed upon him prior to this letter of mine may be supplemented as largely as possible by my recommendation. If, on the other hand, his modesty has deterred him from putting himself in your way, or if you do not yet know him sufficiently, or if for some particular reason he requires a recommendation out of the common, then there is no man whom I could recommend to you more cordially or on better grounds. I will do what those who recommend a friend in conscience and simplicity ought to do – I will give you, or rather I do give you, my pledge and personal guarantee that Manius Curius' personality, character, and manners are such as will make you deem him, once you get to know him, worthy both of your friendship and of so studied a recommendation. Certainly I shall be deeply grateful if I find that my letter has carried as much weight with you as at the moment of writing I am confident it will.

284 (XIII. 18)

CICERO TO SERVIUS SULPICIUS RUFUS

Rome, 46

From Cicero to Servius greetings.

I won't acknowledge that your kind and charming letter gave more pleasure to our friend Atticus, whose delight I witnessed, than to myself. Our gratification was about equal, but I was the more amazed. Had you *answered* Atticus handsomely, after a request or at any rate a hint (not that we had any doubt but that you would), I should have been beholden; but you have actually written to him of your own accord, and shown him by letter such a wealth of good-will when he was not expecting it! I ought not to make a request of you in order to make you the more zealous on *my* account, for your promises go to the limit of liberality. I ought not even to thank you for what you have done for Atticus' sake and of your own volition. But this I will say, that I am deeply grateful for it. Such an expression of your esteem for my dearest friend cannot but give me the liveliest satisfaction; and, that being so, I must needs be grateful.

And yet we are so close that I may allow myself a slip when I am writing to you. So I shall proceed to do both the things I have said I must not do. I hope you *will* enhance what you have told Atticus you are ready to do for his sake by any additional favours your affection for me can prompt. And whereas I did not venture a moment ago to thank you, thank you now I do. I want you to feel that when you oblige Atticus by your good offices in connection with his affairs in Epirus or elsewhere you will by the same token be obliging me.

285 (XIII. 19)

CICERO TO SERVIUS SULPICIUS RUFUS

Rome, 46

From Cicero to Servius greetings.

With Lyso of Patrae I have an old tie of hospitality, a connection which I believe should be religiously observed. But that applies to a good many individuals, whereas the intimacy existing between myself and Lyso has no parallel among my other relationships of this sort. It has been so greatly furthered by his many services and by daily intercourse that our familiarity could not be closer. He has been in Rome for almost a year, constantly in my company. We were very hopeful that as a result of my letter of recommendation you would use your best endeavours to protect his interests while he is away; and so you have. All the same, remembering that all power resides in a single pair of hands and that Lyso had been on our side, serving in our ranks, we dreaded what each day might bring. However, his own distinction and the efforts of myself and his other erstwhile guests have carried the day. Caesar has acceded to our petitions in full, as you will gather from the letter which he has dispatched to you.

And now, far from at all abating my previous recommendation as though all our objectives were already achieved, I want to urge you all the more pressingly to take Lyso into your patronage and connection. When his fortunes hung in the balance, I was chary of saying too much to you in case of some mischance which even you would be powerless to remedy. But now that his status is secure, I most earnestly and particularly ask you for all possible assistance. Not to make a catalogue, I commend his whole household to your favour, including his young son, whom my client C. Maenius Gemellus adopted under the laws of Patrae, when he himself had become a citizen of that place during his unhappy exile. I trust that in this same matter of Maenius' inheritance you will defend his cause and rights.

The capital point is that you should admit Lyso, whom I know to be an excellent and appreciative fellow, into your connection. If you do, I have no doubt that you will form a regard for him, and in due course recommend him to others with sentiments and judgement corresponding to my own. This I ardently desire. And I also have some apprehension that, if in any particular you appear to have done less for him than you conceivably might, he will suspect that the perfunctory style of my letters has been to blame rather than your unmindfulness of myself. For how much you think of me he has been able to perceive from your own letters as well as my day-to-day conversation.

286 (XIII. 20)

CICERO TO SERVIUS SULPICIUS RUFUS

Rome, 46

From Cicero to Servius greetings.

Asclapo, a physician of Patrae, is on familiar terms with me. I liked his company, and had favourable experience of his professional skill when members of my household[794] were taken sick. He gave me satisfaction in this connection as a knowledgeable doctor, and also a conscientious and kindly one. Accordingly I am recommending him to you, and would request you

794. Tiro in 50–49, possibly others.

to let him understand that I have written about him with some particularity, and that my recommendation has been to his no small advantage. I shall be truly obliged.

287 (XIII. 21)

CICERO TO SERVIUS SULPICIUS RUFUS

Rome, 46

From Cicero to Servius greetings.

M. Aemilius Avianianus has cultivated my acquaintance from his early youth and always held me in regard. He is an honourable man and a very amiable one, most conscientious in serving his friends by every means in his power. If I thought he was now in Sicyon and had not heard that he is still staying where I left him, at Cibyra, there would be no need for me to write to you about him at any length. For I am sure that his own personality and manners without anybody's recommendation would have made you as fond of him as I and his other friends. But as I believe him to be away, let me warmly recommend to you his household in Sicyon and his interests – more especially his freedman C. Avianius Hammonius, whom I also recommend to you in his own right. I like him for his exceptional conscientiousness and fidelity towards his former master; moreover, he has rendered me personally important services, making himself available to me in the most difficult period of my life with as much loyalty and good-will as if I had given him his freedom. So let me ask you to support the said Hammonius in his former master's affairs, as the agent of the person whom I am recommending to you, and also to hold him in regard for his own sake and admit him to your circle. You will find him a modest, serviceable person, worthy of your regard.

Goodbye.

288 (XIII. 22)

CICERO TO SERVIUS SULPICIUS RUFUS

Rome, 46

From Cicero to Servius greetings.

I have a warm regard for T. Manlius, who carries on business at Thespiae. He has always made a point of cultivating my acquaintance and showing me courtesy, nor is he a stranger to our studies. Furthermore, Varro Murena takes the liveliest interest in his welfare. Although fully confident in the effect of his own letter of recommendation to you on Manlius' behalf, Varro was of the opinion that a letter of mine would contribute something additional. As for me, my friendship with Manlius and Varro's urgency have induced me to write to you as pressingly as I can.

So then, I shall be deeply obliged if you will give as much attention to this recommendation of mine as you have ever given to such a document; that is to say, if you will assist and further T. Manlius as much as possible in any way consistent with your honour and dignity. And I assure you that you will reap from his own most appreciative and amiable character the reward you are accustomed to expect from the services of honourable men.

289 (XIII. 23)

CICERO TO SERVIUS SULPICIUS RUFUS

Rome, 46

From Cicero to Servius greetings.

L. Cossinius, a friend of mine and a member of my Tribe, is

on very friendly terms with me. We have an old-established acquaintance, and our friend Atticus has made me see even more of Cossinius than I otherwise should. His whole family circle has a regard for me, in particular his freedman L. Cossinius Anchialus, a person very highly thought of by his master and his former master's connections, of whom I am one. I recommend him to you as warmly as I could if he was my own freedman and he stood in the same relation to me as to his former master. You will very much oblige me if you will admit him to your friendship and give him your assistance in any matter wherein he may require it, so far as you can do so without inconveniencing yourself. I shall be greatly obliged, and you will be glad of it later on, for you will find him a very worthy, amiable, and attentive person.

290 (XIII. 24)

CICERO TO SERVIUS SULPICIUS RUFUS

Rome, 46

From Cicero to Servius greetings.

In the consciousness of duty performed, I was already happy to remember the pains with which I had recommended to you my host and friend Lyso; but after learning in a letter from him that he had fallen under some unmerited suspicion on your part, I was glad indeed to have taken such trouble in recommending him. He tells me that my recommendation has been of the greatest help to him, because you had been informed that he was in the habit of speaking disrespectfully about you in Rome. To be sure, he writes that with your usual kindness and good nature you accepted his exculpation. None the less I should, and do, thank you most warmly for paying so much attention to my letter as to put aside after reading it all offence arising from the suspicion of Lyso which you had previously entertained. I also hope that you will believe me when I assure you that *nobody* (and in writing this I am not defending Lyso any more than the community at large) has ever spoken of you in other than the most complimentary terms. As for Lyso, who has been with me almost daily, my constant companion, he used to belaud your every act and word, not only because he thought I enjoyed listening to such talk but because he enjoyed the talking even more.

Your treatment of him is such that he no longer requires any recommendation from me and thinks that *one* letter of mine has accomplished all he needed. None the less I would particularly ask you to continue to favour him with your good offices and liberality. I should tell you what kind of a man he is, as I did in my previous letter, if I did not suppose that you know him well enough by now from personal acquaintance.

291 (XIII. 25)

CICERO TO SERVIUS SULPICIUS RUFUS

Rome, 46

Cicero to Servius greetings.

Hagesaretus of Larissa received substantial favours at my hands when I was Consul and held them in grateful memory, paying me the most sedulous attention thereafter. I recommend him to you warmly as my host and friend, an honourable man who knows the meaning of gratitude, a leading member of his community, thoroughly worthy of your friendship. You will deeply oblige me if you make him sensible that my present recommendation has carried great weight with you.

292 (XIII. 26)

CICERO TO SERVIUS SULPICIUS RUFUS

Rome, 46

From Cicero to Servius greetings.

I am bound to L. Mescinius by the fact that he was my Quaestor; but he has made that claim, to which I have always attached the importance prescribed by our traditions, all the more valid by his own merits of character and manners. I have no more familiar or pleasant companion.

I think he is confident that you will be glad to do for his own sake all you properly can, but he hoped that a letter from me would carry much additional weight with you. That was his own impression, and in his familiar intercourse with me he had often heard me refer to the close and delightful connection between us.

Accordingly let me request you, with all the warmth which you will naturally understand to be appropriate in the case of so strong and familiar a connection, to smooth and straighten his affairs in Achaia, which arise from the fact that he is heir to the estate of his brother M. Mindius,[795] who was in business at Elis. This you can do by your influence and advice as well as by your official power and prerogative. We have instructed all our agents in these affairs to submit any disputed points to you as umpire and (so far as may be consistent with your convenience) as final arbiter. May I beg you most earnestly to take this responsibility upon yourself as a compliment to me?

One further point: should any parties show an unaccommodating disposition and prove unwilling to reach a settlement out of court, you will oblige us very greatly (provided you see nothing inconsistent therein with your own high standing) by

795. See n. 450.

referring them to Rome in view of the fact that a Senator is involved. In order that you may take this course with the less hesitation, we have obtained a letter from Consul M. Lepidus addressed to yourself – not directing you on any point (that we should consider less than respectful towards you), but a sort of letter of recommendation as it were.

I could say how wisely you will be placing such a favour with Mescinius. But I am sure you know that, and besides it is for myself that I am asking. For I hope you will take it that I am as much concerned for his interest as he is himself. But while I am anxious for him to come into his own with as little trouble as possible, I am also concerned to have him think that he owes this in no trifling degree to my present recommendation.

293 (XIII. 27)

CICERO TO SERVIUS SULPICIUS RUFUS

Rome, 46

From Cicero to Servius greetings.

I might legitimately send you many letters of this kind in identical terms, thanking you for paying such careful attention to my recommendations, as I have done in other cases and shall clearly often be doing. None the less I shall not spare my pains. Like you jurists in your formulae I shall treat in my letters 'of the same matter in another way'.

C. Avianius Hammonius has written to me in transports of gratitude on his own behalf and that of his former master, Aemilius Avianianus. He writes that he himself on the spot and the interests of his absent ex-master could not have been dealt with more handsomely or with more flattering consideration. That makes me happy for their sakes. Close friendship and connection led me to recommend them to you, for of all my most intimate and familiar friends M. Aemilius is the nearest,[796] bound to me by substantial favours on my part, and the most grateful, I might almost say, of all those who may be thought to owe me anything. But it makes me far happier to find you so cordially disposed towards me that you do more for my friends than perhaps I should do myself, if I were on the spot. For I imagine that in serving them I should feel more hesitation as to how far I should go than you feel in serving me.

But of course you realize that I am grateful. What I ask you to believe is that they too are men of gratitude, which I hereby solemnly assure you is so. I hope you will try as far as you conveniently can to see that they settle whatever business they have on hand while you are governor of Achaia.

I have the closest and most agreeable association with your son Servius, and take great pleasure in observing his fine and upright character as well as his abilities and exceptional appetite for learning.

294 (XIII. 28)

CICERO TO SERVIUS SULPICIUS RUFUS

Rome, 46

From Cicero to Servius greetings.

I am generally ready enough to ask your assistance when any of my friends stands in need, but it is with far greater readiness that I write to thank you when you have acted on my recommendation, as you always do. The gratitude expressed to me by everyone I recommend to you, even without special emphasis, passes belief. All this makes me beholden, but most of all in the case of Mescinius. He tells me that as soon as you read my letter

796. Nothing is heard of this Aemilius except in letters of recommendation.

you immediately promised his agents all they asked, and that you actually did far more and better than your word. I hope you realize (I feel I cannot say it too often) that I am most deeply beholden on this score.

It makes me all the happier because I am clear that Mescinius himself will prove a source of great satisfaction to you. He is a man of fine, upright character, in the highest degree obliging and attentive, and he shares those literary interests which used to be our diversion and are now our very life. As for the future, I hope you will increase your benefactions to him by all means befitting yourself. But I have two specific requests. Firstly, if security has to be given in respect of final settlement of any claim, please see that security is given on my guarantee. Secondly, the estate consists, as near as makes no matter, of those items which Mindius' widow, Oppia, has made away with; please assist and find some means whereby the woman may be brought to Rome. It is our opinion that, if she thinks this is going to happen, we shall settle the business. Let me beg you most particularly to gain us this point.

In confirmation of what I have written above, let me personally guarantee that your past and future good offices to Mescinius will be well placed, and that you will find for yourself that you have obliged a most grateful and agreeable individual. I want this to add something to what you have done on *my* account.

295 (XIII. 28a)

CICERO TO SERVIUS SULPICIUS RUFUS

Rome, 46

From Cicero to Servius greetings.

The Lacedaemonians are confident, I imagine, that their own

prestige and that of their forefathers is all the recommendation they need to your sense of duty and justice, nor was I in any doubt, knowing you so well, that you are fully conversant with the rights and deserts of peoples. Accordingly, when Philippus of Lacedaemon asked me to recommend his community to you, I replied, though conscious of my great obligations to them, that the Lacedaemonians require no recommendation where you are concerned.

So please take it that I regard all the communities of Achaia as fortunate, considering the disorders of the present time, in having you as their governor; and, further, that I judge you to be of your own accord a good friend, now and in the future, to the people of Lacedaemon, better versed as you are in the whole history of Greece as well as Rome than any man alive. Let me then request only this: when you do for the Lacedaemonians what your conscience, your dignity, and your sense of justice will demand, indicate to them, if you please, that you are not sorry to understand that I too shall take it kindly. I have an obligation to let them feel that their interests concern me. Allow me to ask this as a particular favour.

296 (XIII. 67)

CICERO TO SERVILIUS ISAURICUS

Rome, 46–44

From M. Cicero to P. Servilius, Proconsul, greetings.

In all my province of Cilicia (to which, as you know, three districts of Asia were assigned) there was nobody with whom I was on a more friendly footing than with Andro, son of Artemo, of Laodicea. He was my host in that town and one that eminently suited my way of life and daily habit. Since leaving the province, I have come to value him far more even than at the time, having experienced in many contexts his grateful disposition and mindfulness of me. I was therefore very glad to see him in Rome. You, who have done good turns to so many people in your province, are well aware that the proportion of the grateful is less than overwhelming.

I have written the above to let you realize that my concern is not idle, and so that you yourself may account him worthy of your hospitality. You will oblige me very much indeed if you make it plain to him how much you think of me; that is to say, if you take him under your wing, and help him in every way you can with propriety and without inconvenience to yourself. That will oblige me indeed, and I would earnestly beg you so to do.

297 (XIII. 69)

CICERO TO SERVILIUS ISAURICUS

Rome, 46–44

From Cicero to his Colleague P. Servilius best greetings.

C. Curtius Mithres is, as you know, the freedman of my very good friend Postumus, but he pays as much respect and attention to me as to his own ex-master. At Ephesus, whenever I was there, I stayed in his house as though it was my home, and many incidents arose to give me proof of his good-will and loyalty to me. If I or someone close to me want anything done in Asia I am in the habit of writing to Mithres and of using his faithful service, and even his house and purse, as though they were my own.

I have told you this at some length to let you understand that I am not writing conventionally or from a self-regarding motive, but on behalf of a really intimate personal connection.

Accordingly may I request you, as a compliment to me, to accommodate Mithres in the dispute he has on hand with a certain citizen of Colophon concerning a country property, and in all other matters, so far as your conscience will permit and so far as you conveniently can – though from my knowledge of him he has too much sense of propriety to be burdensome to you in any respect. If my recommendation and his own worth win him your good opinion, he will feel that he has gained every purpose. So I do particularly ask you to take him under your wing and include him in your circle.

I shall give my most careful and devoted attention to anything that I think you would like or that appears to concern you.

298 (XIII. 70)

CICERO TO SERVILIUS ISAURICUS

Rome, 46–44

From M. Cicero to his Colleague P. Servilius best greetings.

Your good-will towards me is no secret, and so it happens that many persons want to be recommended to you by me. Sometimes I comply without much discrimination, but mostly for my friends, as in the present instance; for with T. Ampius Balbus I have the closest friendship and connection. His freedman, T. Ampius Menander, is a worthy, modest person, of whom both his ex-master and I have an excellent opinion. I specially recommend him to you. You will particularly oblige me if you will accommodate him as and when you can without trouble to yourself; and I beg you so to do as a special favour.

299 (XIII. 71)

CICERO TO SERVILIUS ISAURICUS

Rome, 46–44

From M. Cicero to his Colleague P. Servilius best greetings.

I cannot help recommending a good many people to you, since our friendship and the good-will you have for me is common knowledge. Still, though I am bound to wish well to all those I recommend, they do not all have the same claim on me.

T. Agusius was my companion in my time of tribulation. He shared all my journeys by land and water, all my fatigues and dangers. He would not have left my side now, if I had not given him leave. Accordingly I recommend him to you as a member of my domestic circle with whom I have the most intimate connection. You will oblige me very much indeed if you treat him so as to let him understand that this recommendation has been to his no small help and advantage.

300 (XIII. 72)

CICERO TO SERVILIUS ISAURICUS

Rome, 46–44

From M. Cicero to his Colleague P. Servilius greetings.

I recommended the financial interests of my friend Caerellia – her investments and property in Asia – to you, when we were together at your place in the suburbs, as warmly as I was able; and you, conformably to your habit and the constant flow of your signal services to me, undertook most handsomely to do all I asked. I expect you remember – I know you rarely forget. However, Caerellia's agents write that, because of the size of your province and the quantity of business, you should be frequently reminded.

May I request you therefore to bear in mind the ample undertaking you gave me to do all that your conscience would permit? I believe (but it is for you to consider and judge) that you have a great opportunity to accommodate Caerellia, arising out of the Senate's decree in respect of C. Vennonius' heirs. You will interpret that decree in the light of your own wisdom – I know you have always held the authority of the House in high regard. For the rest, please take it that any kindness you may do Caerellia will greatly oblige me.

301 (XIII. 30)

CICERO TO ACILIUS

Rome, 46–45

From Cicero to Acilius, Proconsul,[797] greetings.

L. Manlius Sosis was formerly a citizen of Catina, but became a Roman citizen along with the rest of the Neapolitan community and a town-councillor at Naples, having been enrolled as a citizen of that municipality before the franchise was granted to the allies and the Latins. His brother recently died at Catina. We do not expect any dispute to arise as to his title to the estate, and he is in possession of it at the present time. However, since he also has some old affairs of business in his part of Sicily, I beg to recommend to your notice this matter of his brother's estate and all other concerns of his, above all the man himself. He is

797. In Sicily.

an excellent person, a familiar friend of mine, conversant with the literary and scholarly pursuits in which I chiefly delight.

Let me then ask you (whether or not he goes to Sicily) to be aware that he is one of my closest and most intimate friends, and to let him understand by the way you treat him that my recommendation has been of substantial assistance to him.

302 (XIII. 31)

CICERO TO ACILIUS

Rome, 46–45

From Cicero to Acilius, Proconsul, greetings.

I am on very familiar terms with C. Flavius, a respected and distinguished Roman Knight. He was a great friend of my son-in-law, C. Piso, and both he and his brother L. Flavius are sedulous in their attentions to me. I hope therefore that as a compliment to me you will treat C. Flavius in the most handsome and flattering fashion in all respects consistent with your honour and dignity. Nothing could oblige me more. But furthermore I assure you (and I do so, not from any interested motive, but out of friendship and attachment, also because it is the truth) that C. Flavius' sense of obligation and attentive courtesy, together with the eminence and influence he enjoys among men of his own rank, will be a source of much gratification to yourself.

Goodbye.

303 (XIII. 32)

CICERO TO ACILIUS

Rome, 46–45

From Cicero to Acilius, Proconsul, greetings.

In the rich and famous community of Halaesa I have the closest ties of hospitality and friendship with two persons, M. Clodius Archagathus and C. Clodius Philo. But I feel some uneasiness in recommending so many people to you in special terms in case I may appear to be placing all my recommendations on a level from a self-regarding motive – not but that your response is more than gratifying both to myself and to all connected with me.

Anyhow, please take it that the family to which I refer, and these members of it especially, are bound to me by length of acquaintance, good offices, and good-will. Therefore I particularly ask you to accommodate them in all respects, so far as your conscience and dignity will allow. I shall be very sincerely beholden if you do.

304 (XIII. 33)

CICERO TO ACILIUS

Rome, 46

From Cicero to Acilius, Proconsul, greetings.

I am on a very familiar footing with Cn. Otacilius Naso, as familiar in fact as with any gentleman of his rank. His attractive manners and worth of character make my daily contacts with him very agreeable. You will not need to wait and see what words I use to recommend one with whom I am on such terms. He has affairs of business in your province, to which his freedmen Hilarus, Antigonus, and Demostratus are attending. I recommend to you these persons and all Naso's affairs exactly as though they were my own. You will oblige me deeply if I find that this recommendation has carried much weight with you.

Goodbye.

305 (XIII. 34)

CICERO TO ACILIUS

Rome, 46–45

From Cicero to Acilius, Proconsul, greetings.

My relations of hospitality with Lyso,[798] son of Lyso, of Lilybaeum, go back to his grandfather. He is most attentive to me, and I find him worthy of his grandfather and father – it is a very distinguished family. Therefore I particularly recommend his property and domestic circle to your notice, and earnestly request you to make him realize that my recommendation has tended to his great honour and advantage in your eyes.

306 (XIII. 35)

CICERO TO ACILIUS

Rome, 46–45

From Cicero to Acilius, Proconsul, greetings.

C. Avianius Philoxenus is an old host of mine and, apart

798. Nothing to do with Lyso of Patrae.

from relations of hospitality, my very good friend. Caesar through my good offices entered him as a citizen of Novum Comum.[799] He took the name of Avianius because of his especially close relations with Avianius Flaccus, a very good friend of mine, as I think you know. I have put all these facts together to let you understand that this recommendation of mine is outside the ordinary.

May I therefore request you to accommodate him in all respects, so far as you can do so without trouble to yourself, and to admit him to your circle? Let him understand that this letter of mine has been very useful to him. I shall be greatly beholden.

307 (XIII. 36)

CICERO TO ACILIUS

Rome, 46–45

From Cicero to Acilius, Proconsul, greetings.

I have old ties of hospitality with Demetrius Megas, and no native of Sicily is on such familiar terms with me. At my request Dolabella obtained the franchise for him from Caesar – I was party to the matter. So now his name is P. Cornelius. And when Caesar, on account of certain mercenary fellows who were selling his favours, gave orders for the removal of the plaque on which the names of grantees of citizenship had been engraved, he told the same Dolabella in my presence that he need not worry about Megas. In his case the favour held good.

I wanted you to know this, so that you should regard him as a Roman citizen, and in all other respects I recommend him as

799. Caesar had enrolled five hundred distinguished Greeks in his colony of Novum Comum under a law passed during his Consulship, though they did not settle there. Their Roman citizenship was now, of course, established.

warmly as I have ever recommended anyone. I shall be very much beholden to you if you deal with him so as to let him understand that my recommendation has been a great asset to him.

308 (XIII. 37)

CICERO TO ACILIUS

Rome, 46–45

From Cicero to Acilius, Proconsul, greetings.

Let me particularly recommend to you my host and friend Hippias, son of Philoxenus, of Calacte. As the matter has been represented to me, his property is being held by the state under a different name in violation of the laws of Calacte. If that is true, the nature of the case entitles him to your assistance as a just magistrate even without any recommendation of mine. But whatever the position, allow me to request you, as a compliment to me, to extricate him from his difficulty, and to accommodate him in this and other matters as far as your conscience and dignity will allow. I shall be truly beholden.

309 (XIII. 38)

CICERO TO ACILIUS

Rome, 46–45

From Cicero to Acilius, Proconsul, greetings.

L. Bruttius, a young Roman Knight of quality in every sense of the word, is one of my most familiar friends and most

sedulous in his attentions to me. I was a great friend of his
father's from the time when I was Quaestor in Sicily. Bruttius
himself is now with me in Rome, but I beg to recommend to
you his domestic circle, property, and agents with all possible
warmth. I shall be very much beholden if you will let Bruttius
understand that my recommendation has been of great assistance to him, as I undertook that it would be.

310 (XIII. 39)

CICERO TO ACILIUS

Rome, 46–45

From Cicero to Acilius, Proconsul, greetings.

There is an old connection between myself and the Titurnius
family. Its only surviving representative is M. Titurnius Rufus,
whom I am in duty bound to protect and assist to the best of my
ability. It rests with you therefore to let him feel that he has in
me a sufficiently powerful patron. Accordingly I recommend
him to you warmly and request you to let him understand that
this recommendation has been greatly to his advantage. I shall
be truly beholden.

311 (IX. 13)

CICERO TO DOLABELLA

Rome, 46 (end) or 45 (beginning)

From Cicero to Dolabella greetings.

C. Subernius of Cales is a friend of mine and very closely
attached to my intimate friend Lepta. In order to escape the war
he went to Spain with M. Varro before its outbreak, and was

living in a province where, after Afranius' defeat, none of us supposed there would be any fighting; but, as luck would have it, he found himself in the very trouble which he had tried so hard to avoid. The war which suddenly flared up caught him unawares; started by Scapula, it later gained such momentum under Pompey[800] that he could not possibly extricate himself from this wretched environment. The case of M. Planius Heres, also of Cales and a close friend of Lepta's, is almost identical.

I recommend both these persons to you, and I could not do so with a greater measure of sincere concern and anxiety. I am interested for their own sake; friendship and humanity alike move me strongly on their behalf. But when Lepta is so profoundly concerned (his whole fortune seems to be at stake), my concern must approach, or even equal, his. Therefore I should like you to persuade yourself that, often as I have experienced the warmth of your affection for me, I shall judge of it particularly in this affair. Accordingly I request you, or beg you if you will allow me, to save these unhappy persons, whose calamities are due to fortune, which there is no avoiding, rather than to any fault of their own, and to make it your wish that through you, I may confer this favour not only upon the principals, friends of mine as they are, but upon the town of Cales, with which I have a close connection, and upon Lepta, who matters to me most of all.

What I am about to say is probably not very relevant to the matter at issue, but still it can do no harm to mention it. One of the two has very little money, the other hardly up to Knight's qualification. Since, then, Caesar has generously granted them their lives and there is nothing much else which can be taken from them, get them permission (if you love me as much as I am sure you do) to return to Italy. There is nothing in that which need take up much time, except the journey; and this they are ready to undertake in order to live with their families

800. Cn. Pompeius the Younger.

and die at home. Once again I earnestly ask you to try your utmost, or rather to *do* it, for I am satisfied that you have the power.

312 (XIII. 52)

CICERO TO REX[801]

46–45(?)

From Cicero to Rex greetings.

A. Licinius Aristoteles of Malta has a very old-established tie of hospitality with me, and is furthermore attached to me by much familiar personal contact. That being so, I don't doubt that he is sufficiently recommended to your favour. Indeed I am told on all hands that a recommendation from me counts for a great deal with you. I obtained his pardon from Caesar – he had been much with me, and actually stayed in the cause longer than I did, which I imagine will make you think all the better of him. So make him understand, my dear Rex, that this letter has tended greatly to his advantage.

313 (XIII. 49)

CICERO TO CURIUS[802]

Date uncertain

From Cicero to Curius, Proconsul.

Many ties of long standing go to form my connection with Q. Pompeius, son of Sextus. He has been in the habit of protect-

801. Presumably in an official position in Sicily.
802. Nothing is known of Curius or his province or the person recommended.

CICERO'S LETTERS TO HIS FRIENDS

ing his financial interests, personal influence, and prestige by means of my recommendations; and now that you are in charge of the province, a letter from me should surely gain him enough to let him feel that he has never been better recommended to any governor. Therefore I particularly request you, bound as you are in virtue of our connection to pay as much regard to my friends as to your own, to take Pompeius under your especial patronage, so that he himself realizes that nothing could have been more to his advantage and distinction than my recommendation.

Goodbye.

314 (XIII. 2)

CICERO TO MEMMIUS[803]

Date uncertain

From Cicero to Memmius greetings.

C. Avianius Evander, who is residing in your family chapel, is a person with whom I have a good deal to do and I am on very friendly terms with his former master, M. Aemilius. May I therefore particularly request you to accommodate him in the matter of his residence as far as you can without inconveniencing yourself? It is rather sudden for him to move back on the Kalends of July, because he has a number of commissions on hand for various patrons. Modesty forbids me to ask you at much length, but I am sure that if the matter is of no consequence to you, or not much, you will feel as I should feel if you made any request of me. I shall certainly be most grateful.

803. Possibly son of the recipient of Letter 63 (XIII.1).

315 (XIII. 3)

CICERO TO C. MEMMIUS

Date uncertain

From Cicero to Memmius greetings.

A. Fufius is one of my inner circle, most attentive and devoted to me. He is a learned, highly cultivated person, thoroughly worthy to be your friend. I hope you will treat him in accordance with the promise you made me orally. I shall take it *most* kindly. Furthermore you will permanently attach to yourself a very serviceable and punctilious gentleman.

316 (XIII. 16)

CICERO TO CAESAR

Rome(?), winter of 46–45

From Cicero to Caesar greetings.

Young P. Crassus was my favourite among the whole range of our aristocracy. From his earliest youth I had good hopes of him, but he rose really high in my estimation when I saw how well you thought of him. Even during his lifetime I had a great regard and liking for his freedman Apollonius. He was warmly attached to Crassus, and admirably fitted to join him in his liberal interests, so naturally Crassus was very fond of him. After Crassus' death I thought him all the worthier of admission to my patronage and friendship because he felt it proper to pay respect and attention to those whom Crassus had loved and who had loved him in return. Accordingly he joined me in

Cilicia, where his loyalty and good sense proved very useful to me in many connections. And I believe that in the Alexandrian War such service as his zeal and fidelity could render you was not lacking.

Hoping that you are of the same opinion, he is leaving to join you in Spain, mainly on his own initiative, but not without encouragement from me. I did not promise him a recommendation, not that I did not think it would carry weight with you, but because a man who had seen military service at your side and whom Crassus' memory made one of your circle did not seem to me to need one. And if he did wish to make use of recommendations, I knew he could obtain them elsewhere. But I am glad to give him a testimonial of what I think of him, since he makes a point of it and my experience has shown me that you pay attention to such.

I know him to be a scholar, devoted to liberal studies from boyhood. For he was much in my house from an early age with Diodotus the Stoic, a most erudite person in my opinion. Now his imagination has been captured by your career, and he wants to write an account of it in Greek. I think he can do it. He has a strong natural talent cultivated by practice, and has for a long time been engaged in this type of literary work. To do justice to your immortal fame is his passionate ambition.

Well, there you have my considered testimony, but your own keen discernment will provide you with a much easier means of assessing the matter. And after all, I do recommend him to you, having said I should do no such thing. Any kindness you do him will particularly oblige me.

317 (XIII. 15)

CICERO TO CAESAR

c. May(?) 45

From Cicero to Caesar, Imperator, greetings.

Allow me to recommend Precilius to you with peculiar warmth, the son of a very worthy gentleman who is connected with you and intimate with me. I have an extraordinary regard for the young man himself because of his modesty, amiability, and notably affectionate disposition towards me; and experience has taught me to appreciate his father's unfaltering goodwill. For, mark you, he is the one man above all others who used to jeer and gird at me because I would not join you despite your most flattering invitations. But 'the heart within my breast he ne'er did sway'. For I used to hear our men of light and leading clamouring

'Be bold, and earn the praise of men unborn.'[804]
He spake; but grief's dark mist the other cloaked.[805]

But he comforts me too. Burned child as I am, they are still trying to kindle the fire of ambition in my heart:

No sluggard's fate, ingloriously to die,
But daring that which men to be shall learn.[806]

That is the way they talk. But, as you see, I am not so responsive nowadays. So I turn from Homer's magniloquence to the sound precepts of Euripides:

Who for himself's not wise, his wisdom scorn,[807]

804. *Odyssey*, I.302 (Athene to Telemachus).
805. *Odyssey*, XXIV.315 (of Laertes).
806. *Iliad*, XXII.304 f. (Hector is speaking).
807. Cf. Letter 27 (VII.6).

a verse which old Precilius extols in fine style, and says that a
man may look 'both to front and rear',[808] and yet at the same
time 'e'er be the first, o'ertopping all the rest'.[809]

But to go back to my starting point: I shall be truly grateful
if you will take the young fellow under your wing with the
kindness which is so conspicuous a trait of yours, and add my
recommendation to crown the good-will which I suppose you
to bear the Precilii for their own sakes. I have written you an
unconventional sort of letter to let you understand that this is
no ordinary recommendation.

318 (XIII. 4)

CICERO TO VALERIUS ORCA[810]

Between November 46 and July 45(?)

M. Cicero to Q. Valerius Orca, son of Quintus, Legate *pro
praetore*, greetings.

I have a very close connection with the people of Volaterrae.
Having received an important favour at my hands, they repaid
me most amply, never stinting their support either in my advancements or in my tribulations. But even if there was
nothing between me and them, I should advise and urge you
out of my warm affection for you and my consciousness of
your high regard for me to consider their financial welfare –
especially as they have an almost peculiarly strong claim to maintain their rights. By the grace of the Immortal Gods they es-

808. *Iliad*, I.343=*Odyssey*, XXIV.452.

809. *Iliad*, VI.208=XI.784. This had been Cicero's watchword in his
early days; cf. *Letters to his Brother Quintus* 25 (III.5)4.

810. Cf. Letter 57 (XIII.6). Orca was now apparently in charge of the
assignment of land in Etruria to Caesar's veterans.

caped the harsh measures of the Sullan period;[811] and they were defended by me during my Consulship with the enthusiastic support of the People of Rome.

When the Tribunes of the Plebs brought forward a highly iniquitous bill concerning their lands, I had no difficulty in persuading the Senate and People of Rome to decree the preservation of Roman citizens to whom fortune had been merciful. During his first Consulship C. Caesar approved my action in his agrarian bill, and gave the town and district of Volaterrae permanent security from any such threat. So I cannot doubt, when I see him acquiring new connections, that he wishes his old benefactions to stand. Accordingly your good sense will instruct you either to take your cue from the leader in whose wake and under whose command you have gained such high preferment, or at least to leave the whole case open for him to determine. Moreover, you ought surely to feel no doubt about the desirability of placing so important, well-established, and respectable a community as Volaterrae under a lasting obligation to yourself by conferring a signal favour.

What I have written so far is in the nature of exhortation and counsel. What follows is petitionary. I would not have you think that I am merely advising you in your own interests, and not also asking you for a favour which I personally need. Well then, I shall be greatly beholden if you decide to preserve the people of Volaterrae in complete safety and integrity. To your honour, justice, and benevolence I commend their dwellings, abodes, property, and fortunes, which the Immortal Gods and the leading men in our commonwealth have maintained intact with the wholehearted approbation of the Senate and People of Rome.

If the conditions of today permitted me to defend the people

811. Sulla had passed a law depriving the Volaterrans of Roman citizenship and confiscating their land in punishment for their long resistance to his army. But the law seems to have remained inoperative as to the first and only partially operative as to the second.

of Volaterrae as it has been my habit to support those with whom I have connections, conformably to the resources which used to be at my command, I should not fail to engage in every service, every contest indeed, in which I might possibly be of use to them. But I am confident that with yourself my voice is at the present time no less powerful than it always was with all honest men. Therefore let me request you, in the name of the close connection and reciprocally equal good-will that exists between us, to deserve well of the people of Volaterrae. Let them think that a divine providence has placed this business in charge of the man with whom of all others I, their constant champion, might exercise most influence.

319 (XIII. 5)

CICERO TO VALERIUS ORCA

46–44

From Cicero to Q. Valerius Orca, Legate *pro praetore*, greetings.

That my friendship with you should be as widely known as possible is not disagreeable to me. At the same time I have not on that account (as you are in the best possible position to judge) stood in the way of your carrying out the task you have undertaken loyally and conscientiously in accordance with the will of Caesar, who has entrusted you with so important and difficult a commission. Although I receive many requests from many people in their confidence of your friendly disposition towards me, I take good care not to embarrass you in the execution of your duty by solicitations of mine.

I have been on intimate terms with C. Curtius[812] since early youth. His iniquitous deprivation in Sulla's time was a grief to

812. Known only from this letter.

me; and when it appeared that persons who had suffered a similar injustice were allowed to return to their country, though with the loss of their entire fortunes, a concession which was universally welcomed, I lent my assistance in his rehabilitation. He owns a property in the district of Volaterrae into which he put what remained from the wreck of his estate. Caesar has now appointed him a member of the Senate, a rank which he can scarcely support if he loses this property. It is very hard that, having been raised in station, he should be at a disadvantage in fortune; and it is highly incongruous that a Senator by Caesar's favour should be evicted from land which is under distribution by Caesar's orders. However, I do not care to dwell on the rights of the matter, or I might seem to have prevailed with you in virtue of a strong case rather than by my personal influence. So let me particularly request you to regard C. Curtius' estate as mine, to do for C. Curtius' sake whatever you would do for mine, and, having done it, to consider that whatever comes to him through my intervention is a gift from you to me. This I most earnestly beg of you.

320 (XIII. 7)

CICERO TO C. CLUVIUS[813]

Rome, autumn 45

From Cicero to Cluvius greetings.

When you called upon me at my house just before you left for Gaul (a token of our friendship and an example of your unfailing attentiveness to me), I spoke to you about the leased land in Gaul belonging to the town of Atella, and made my deep concern for the town plain to you. Bearing in mind your

813. Evidently in charge of land assignments in Cisalpine Gaul.

particularly friendly disposition towards myself, I think it incumbent upon me to write to you after your departure in greater detail, since the matter involves both a major financial interest of a highly respected township with which I have close ties, and an imperative obligation on my side – although I am not unaware of the nature of the present situation and the extent of your powers, and perfectly understand that C. Caesar has assigned you a piece of business, not asked you to exercise your discretion. I am therefore requesting of you only so much as I think you can perform, and will gladly perform for my sake.

And first I would ask you to believe, what is the fact, that the finances of the municipality depend entirely on this rent, and that in these days they are labouring under very heavy burdens and are involved in serious difficulties. Many others seem to be in a similar situation, but I do assure you that this particular town has been exceptionally unfortunate. I do not go into details for fear I might seem to be casting aspersions on persons whom I have no wish to offend when I complain of the distresses of those connected with me. If I was not very hopeful that we shall establish the town's case to C. Caesar's satisfaction, there would be no reason for me to trouble you at present. But I am confidently persuaded that he will take into account the high standing of the community, the equity of their cause, and also their disposition towards himself. Therefore I do not hesitate to urge you to leave the case open for him to determine.

I should make this appeal to you even if I had not heard that you had so acted in another case, but I became more hopeful of your granting it after I was told that you had made the same concession to the people of Regium. Even though they have a certain connection with you, your affection for me constrains me to hope that what you do for your own connections you will do for mine – especially as I am asking this only for Atella, though several communities connected with me are in similar trouble. I do not think you will suspect me of so proceeding without good reason, or of soliciting you from a trivial desire to increase my popularity. Still, I hope you will believe me when I give you my word that I am under a great debt to this municipality. In my advancements as in my tribulations their devotion towards me has on every occasion been quite outstanding.

Accordingly, let me beg you most earnestly, in virtue of the intimate bond between us and your signal and unfailing good-will towards me, to grant what I ask, realizing that the finances of a municipality with which I am closely linked by mutual relations, services, and good-will are here at stake. You may take it that, if we get what we hope from Caesar, we shall regard ourselves as owing it to your kindness; and if not, that we shall take the will for the deed, considering that you will have done your best to get it for us. I myself shall be deeply grateful, and an excellent and highly respected body, one too that well knows the meaning of gratitude and is thoroughly worthy to be connected with you, will be bound to you and yours for all time by a signal benefaction.

321 (XIII. 8)

CICERO TO M. RUTILIUS[814]

46–44

From M. Cicero to M. Rutilius greetings.

Conscious of my regard for you and aware by experience of your good-will towards myself, I do not hesitate to lay before you the request I have to make.

How highly I regard P. Sestius is best known to myself; how highly I ought to regard him is known to you and all the world.

814. Evidently another land commissioner. The area in which he operated is unknown.

Learning from other sources of your eagerness to be of service to me, he has requested me to write to you most particularly about a matter concerning Senator C. Albanius, whose daughter was the mother of that excellent young man L. Sestius, P. Sestius' son. I mention this to let you know that, besides my obligation to concern myself on Sestius' behalf, Sestius has a like obligation towards Albanius.

The affair in question is as follows: C. Albanius received certain properties at valuation from M. Laberius, which properties had been purchased by Laberius from Caesar out of Plotius' estate. If I were to say that it is contrary to public interest that those properties should be brought under assignment, it would look as though I were not asking a favour but giving you instruction. All the same, I may point out that Caesar wishes the Sullan sales and assignments to be valid in order that his own may be thought more secure. If properties sold by Caesar himself are to be brought under assignment, what sort of title will his sales carry in future?

But you in your wisdom will consider that aspect of the matter. *I* am simply making a request of you (and I could make none with more earnestness and sincerity, or in a juster cause) to spare Albanius and not to touch the properties formerly belonging to Laberius. You will make me not only very happy but also rather proud to have been the means of enabling P. Sestius to meet the needs of a close connection, owing him as I do more than any other man. Allow me to ask you most pressingly so to do. You can confer upon me no higher favour, and you will find me most grateful.

322 (VI. 15)

CICERO TO MINUCIUS BASILUS

Date uncertain[815]

From Cicero to Basilus greetings.

Congratulations. I am delighted on my own account. Be sure of my affection and active concern for your interests. I hope I have *your* affection, and want to hear what you are doing and what is going on.

323 (VI. 16)

POMPEIUS BITHYNICUS[816] TO CICERO

Sicily, c. end of March(?) 44

From Bithynicus to Cicero greetings.

If my friendship with you did not rest on many good grounds peculiar to ourselves, I should go back to its origins and speak of our parents. But that I take to be appropriate when family friendship has not been followed up by personal good offices. Therefore I shall be content with our personal friendship, and relying thereupon would ask you to defend my interests during my absence, wherever there may be need, in the persuasion, I hope, that no service you render will ever lose its freshness in my memory.

Goodbye.

815. There are serious objections to the common view that this evidently hasty note refers to Caesar's assassination.
816. See Glossary of Persons.

324 (VI. 17)[817]

CICERO TO POMPEIUS BITHYNICUS

c. May(?) 44

From Cicero to Bithynicus greetings.

There are all manner of reasons why I am anxious to see the commonwealth settled at long last, but, believe me, the promise you make in your letter adds one to their number, causing me to long for that event yet the more. For you write that, if it comes about, you will be much in my society. Your wish is most gratifying to me, and you express it in the spirit of our friendship and of the opinion which that fine man, your father, held of me. You may be assured that, although those whom events made, or make, powerful are more closely attached to you than I in respect of the magnitude of what they have conferred upon you, none stands nearer in friendship. I am therefore gratified by your mindfulness of our connection and your wish to strengthen it still further.

325 (XI. 1)

D. BRUTUS TO M. BRUTUS AND CASSIUS

Rome, c. 22(?) March 44[818]

From D. Brutus to his friend Brutus and to Cassius greetings.

Let me tell you how we stand. Yesterday evening Hirtius was at my house. He made Antony's disposition clear – as bad

817. Evidently not a reply to the preceding, though probably belonging to the same period.

818. At least half-a-dozen dates have been assigned to this letter, of

and treacherous as can be. Antony says he is unable to give me my province,[819] and that he thinks none of us is safe in Rome with the soldiers and populace in their present agitated state of mind. I expect you observe the falsehood of both contentions, the truth being, as Hirtius made evident, that he is afraid lest, if our position were enhanced even to a moderate extent, these people would have no further part to play in public affairs.

Finding myself in so difficult a predicament, I thought it best to ask for a Free Commission[820] for myself and the rest of our friends, so as to get a fair excuse for going away. Hirtius promised to get this agreed to, but I have no confidence that he will, in view of the general insolence and vilification of us. And even if they give us what we ask, I think it won't be long before we are branded as public enemies or placed under interdict.

You may ask what I advise. I think we must give way to fortune, leave Italy, go to live in Rhodes or anywhere under the sun. If things go better, we shall return to Rome. If moderately, we shall live in exile. If the worst happens, we shall take any and every means to help ourselves. Perhaps one of you will wonder at this point why we should wait till the last moment instead of setting something on foot now. Because we have nowhere to base ourselves, except for Sex. Pompeius[821] and Caecilius Bassus – I imagine their hands will be strengthened when this news about Caesar gets through. It will be time enough for us to join them when we know what their power amounts to. I shall give any undertaking you and Cassius wish on your behalf. Hirtius demands that I do this.

Please let me have your reply as soon as possible. I don't doubt that Hirtius will inform me on these points before ten

which Cicero no doubt received a copy from the recipients. I accept the view that it was written soon after the disturbances which followed Caesar's funeral on 20 March.

819. Cisalpine Gaul according to Caesar's assignment.
820. See Glossary of Terms under 'Legate'.
821. Pompey's younger son, still fighting in Spain.

o'clock. Let me know where we can meet, where you wish me to come.

After Hirtius' latest talk I have thought it right to demand that we be allowed to stay in Rome with a public bodyguard. I don't suppose they will agree – we shall be putting them in a very invidious light. However, I think I ought not to refrain from demanding anything that I consider fair.[822]

326 (IX. 14)[823]

CICERO TO DOLABELLA

Pompeii, 3 May 44

From Cicero to his friend Dolabella, Consul, greetings.

Content as I am, my dear Dolabella, with *your* glory, and finding as I do sufficient cause in that for delight and rejoicing, yet I cannot but confess that my cup of happiness is filled to overflowing by the popular opinion which makes me a sharer in your laurels. Every single person I have met (and I meet a great many every day, for a large number of the best people come hereabouts for their health, and I have many visits in addition from friends in the neighbouring towns) has first praised you sky high in the most glowing terms and then in the same breath expressed deep gratitude to me, not doubting, so they say, that it is in conformity with my precepts and advice that you are showing yourself so admirable a citizen and so outstanding a Consul.

822. This paragraph is probably not, as generally supposed, a postscript added after Hirtius' return, since it does not say what answer Hirtius brought back.

823. This letter is also found in the Atticus series, 371A (XIV.17A). Dolabella, who became Consul after Caesar's death, had drastically repressed some pro-Caesarian demonstrations in Rome.

I can reply with perfect truth that what you do you do by
your own judgement and volition, needing nobody's advice.
In fact, however, I neither give a direct assent, in case I might
detract from your credit by letting it appear to have proceeded
entirely from my counsels, nor yet a very vigorous disclaimer,
for I am fond, perhaps too fond, of glory. And yet it detracts
nothing from your prestige to have a Nestor to consult, as did
the King of Kings, Agamemnon himself, without any loss of
dignity. As for me, it is a proud thing that a young Consul
should win such laurels as, so to speak, a pupil from my school.

I visited L. Caesar on his sick bed at Naples. His whole body
racked with pain though it was, he had scarcely greeted me
before he exclaimed 'Oh my dear Cicero, congratulations! If I
had as much influence with my nephew[824] as you have with
Dolabella, we might now be out of our troubles. As for your
Dolabella, I congratulate him and thank him. He is the first
Consul since yourself who deserves the name.' Then he went
on to speak at large of your action and achievement, which he
called as magnificent, distinguished, and publicly salutary as
any in history. And this is the sentiment expressed by all.

Now please allow me to accept this counterfeit inheritance,
so to speak, of an acclaim which does not belong to me, and
admit me to some small partnership in your triumph. Not but
what, my dear Dolabella – for I have written the above only in
jest – I would sooner transfer to you all the credit for my own
achievements, if any such there be, than divert any part of
yours. You cannot but know how deep my regard for you has
always been; but your recent exploits have kindled in me such
enthusiasm that no affection was ever more ardent. Nothing,
believe me, is more beautiful, fair, and lovable than manly
virtue. As you are aware, I have always loved M. Brutus for his
fine intellect, the charm of his manners, and his outstanding
uprightness and reliability. Yet the Ides of March added so
much to my love for him that I was astonished to find room for

824. Mark Antony, the other Consul.

95

increase where I had long believed all was full to overflowing. Who would have thought that the love I bore you admitted of any accession? Yet the accession is such that it seems to me as though I only now feel love where formerly I felt affectionate regard.

There is no need for me to urge you to cherish the high standing and glory you have won. Why should I, in hortatory fashion, remind you of famous names? I can quote none more famous than your own. You yourself should be your model, it is yourself you have to emulate. After such exploits you no longer have the *right* to fall below your own standard. Exhortation is therefore superfluous, felicitation rather is called for. In your case, and I dare say in yours only, the extreme of penal rigour has brought not merely no odium but actual popularity, delighting the lower orders as well as all honest folk. If this had come to you by a stroke of luck, I should congratulate you on your good fortune; but you owe it to your generous courage and, no less, to your ability and sound judgement. I have read your speech, an excellently conceived performance. How cautiously you felt your way towards the issue, now approaching, now drawing back, so that by common consent the simple facts of the case showed the time to be ripe for your punitive action!

So you have rescued Rome from danger and her inhabitants from fear. You have done a vast deal of good, not only for the present occasion, but as a precedent for the future. Having done that, you should understand that the commonwealth rests upon your shoulders, and that those men from whose initiative freedom has sprung are deserving, not only of your protection, but of your favour. But on these matters more when we meet; soon, I hope. Lastly, my dear Dolabella, as the commonwealth's guardian and mine, see that you take the utmost care for your own safety.

327 (XII. 1)

CICERO TO CASSIUS

Pompeii, 3 May 44

Cicero to Cassius greetings.

Believe me, Cassius, I never stop thinking about you and our friend Brutus, that is to say about the whole country, whose only hope lies in you both and in D. Brutus. I myself now feel more optimistic after the splendid performance of my dear Dolabella. The rot in Rome was spreading and getting more virulent every day, so that I for one was alarmed for the city and for public order inside it. But this has been so effectually suppressed that I think we may now reasonably consider ourselves safe for all time to come from that most squalid of threats at any rate.

The tasks that remain are many and serious, but all depends on you three. However, let me set out the position item by item.[825] As things have gone so far, it appears that we are free of the despot, but not of the despotism. Our king has been killed, but we are upholding the validity of his every regal nod. And not only that, but we sanction measures which he himself would not be taking if he were alive on the pretext that he had them in mind. I see no end to the business. Laws are posted up, exemptions granted, large sums of money assigned, exiles brought home, decrees of the Senate forged – it seems we are merely rid of the disgust we felt for an abominable individual and of the mortification of slavery, while the state still lies in the chaotic condition into which he flung it.

You and your friends must straighten out the whole tangle. You must not think that you have done enough for your

825. With what follows cf. *Letters to Atticus* 368 (XIV.14).2.

country already. She has indeed had more from you than it ever entered my mind to hope, but she is not satisfied; she wants great things from you, proportionate to the greatness of your hearts and service. So far she has avenged her injuries by the death of the tyrant at your hands, nothing more. What of her dignities? Which of them has she recovered? The right to obey a dead man, whom she could not tolerate alive? Are we defending the paper memoranda of one whose laws graven on bronze we ought to annul? Oh yes, we have so decreed.[826] When we did that, we bowed to circumstances, which in politics count for a great deal. But some people are abusing our facility without restraint or gratitude.

But of this and much else when we meet, soon. Meanwhile, please believe that I have your public standing very much at heart, both for the sake of the commonwealth, which has always been dearer to me than anything else in the world, and for that of our mutual affection. Take care of your health.

Goodbye.

328 (XII. 16)

TREBONIUS TO CICERO

Athens, 25 May 44

From Trebonius to Cicero greetings.

I trust you are well.

I arrived in Athens on 22 May,[827] and there saw what I most desired to see, your son devoting himself to liberal studies and bearing an exemplary character. How much pleasure this gave

---

826. In the temple of Tellus on 17 March, when the Senate confirmed Caesar's 'acts'.

827. Trebonius was on his way to take over the province of Asia.

me you can appreciate even without my telling you. You are not unaware how much I think of you and how warmly I welcome any gratification that comes your way, even the most trifling, let alone such a blessing as this. Such is the long-standing and sincere affection between us. Do not suppose, my dear Cicero, that I tell you this because it is what you want to hear. This young man of yours (or rather ours, for you can have nothing I do not share) could not be more popular with everybody in Athens, nor more enthusiastically attached to the studies for which you care most, that is to say, the highest. And so I am delighted to congratulate you, as I can sincerely do, and myself no less, upon the fact that in him we have a young man for whom it is a delight to care, since care for him we must however he had turned out.

When he let fall in conversation with me that he would like to visit Asia, I not only invited but requested him to do so during my term as governor of the province. You should have no doubt that I shall stand towards him in your stead with a father's care and affection. I shall also see that Cratippus comes with him, so you need not think that in Asia he will be taking a vacation from the studies to which he is spurred by your encouragement. He is evidently a willing student, advancing at the double. I shall be continually encouraging him to further progress through daily study and practice.

As I write this letter, I do not know how you at home are faring politically. I hear some reports of unrest. Naturally I hope they are untrue, and that we can at last enjoy freedom in peace and quiet. Up to date I have been very far from that good fortune. However, I got a modicum of relaxation during the voyage, and have fitted together a little present for you after my fashion – I have cast a *bon mot* of yours, one very complimentary to myself, into verse, and written it down for you below. If you think certain words in this little piece rather *risqués*, the turpitude of the figure[828] I am somewhat freely

828. Probably Antony.

assailing will be my excuse. You will also make allowance for my irascibility, which is justified against persons and citizens of this type. And then, why should I not be allowed as much licence as Lucilius? Even granted that he hated his targets as much as I, it certainly cannot be claimed that the people he attacked with such licence of language deserved it more.

As you have promised me, you will give me a place in your conversation-pieces as soon as possible. I am sure that, if you write anything on Caesar's death, you will not let me take the smallest share of the event, and of your affection.

Goodbye, and consider my mother and family as commended to your care.

Dispatched 25 May, from Athens.

329 (XI. 2)

M. BRUTUS AND CASSIUS TO ANTONY

Lanuvium, May (end) 44

From Brutus and Cassius, Praetors, to M. Antonius, Consul.

Were we not convinced of your good faith and friendly intentions towards us, we should not write you this letter, which, since you are in fact thus disposed, you will doubtless take in the best of part. We are informed by letters that a large number of veterans has already gathered in Rome, and that a much larger number is expected before the Kalends of June. It would be out of character for us to entertain any doubt or apprehension concerning yourself. But having placed ourselves in your hands and dismissed our friends from the municipalities on your advice, having done that moreover not only by edict but in private letters, we surely deserve to share your confidence, particularly in a matter which concerns us.

Therefore we request you to inform us of your disposition towards us, whether you think we shall be safe among such a multitude of veteran soldiers, who are actually thinking, so we hear, of replacing the altar.[829] It is not easy to believe that anyone who desires our security and dignity can desire and approve of that.

The event shows that peace has been our aim from the beginning, and that we have had no object in view but the freedom of the community. Nobody can deceive us except yourself, a thing surely abhorrent to your manly and honourable spirit. Still, no other man has the means to trick us, for we have trusted, and shall continue to trust, only you. Our friends are deeply anxious on our behalf. They have every confidence in your good faith, but it is in their minds that the crowd of veterans can more easily be impelled by others in any direction they please than held in check by you.

We request you to give us your reply on all points. As for the allegation that the veterans were summoned because you intended to bring matters to their advantage before the Senate in June, it is a quite frivolous and nugatory excuse. Who do you suppose is likely to be obstructive, since, as for ourselves, it is certain that we shall hold our peace? None should believe us over-anxious to preserve our lives, for nothing can happen to us without universal ruin and chaos.

829. A funeral monument to Caesar in the Forum which became an object of popular cult until it was demolished by Dolabella.

330 (XVI. 23)

CICERO TO TIRO

Tusculum, May (end) 44

From Cicero to Tiro greetings.

Yes, please get the declaration[830] done if you can, though with a sum of this sort no declaration is necessary – but do it all the same. Balbus writes to me that he has had an attack, so severe that he can't talk. Antony can do as he likes about the law,[831] so long as I am allowed to stay in the country. I have written to Bithynicus.[832]

Servilius I leave to you, since you think old age worth having.[833] To be sure our good Atticus, having found me susceptible to scares in the old days, still thinks it is so and doesn't see my proof-armour of philosophy. And, truth to say, being a nervous fellow himself he plays alarmist. However, I certainly want to keep my old-established friendship with Antony – we have never had a quarrel – and shall write to him, but not till I have seen you. Not that I am taking you away from your bond[834] – charity begins at home.[835] I expect Lepta

830. Perhaps the public registration of a transfer of assets.

831. Perhaps a bill for the distribution of all available public lands among veterans and the poor.

832. Not necessarily Pompeius Bithynicus. The purpose of Cicero's letter is unknown.

833. The elder Servilius Isauricus had recently died at a great age. Tiro seems to have relayed a talk with Atticus, who was afraid that Cicero might take fright at some current 'scare'. Tiro may have added that Cicero ought not to worry and that he would very likely live to a ripe old age, like Servilius.

834. Some private business of Tiro.

835. Cicero quotes a Greek proverb meaning literally 'the knee is nearer than the shin'.

tomorrow and *.[836] I shall need the sweet of your conversation to counteract the bitter of his company.

Goodbye.

331 (VII. 22)

CICERO TO TREBATIUS

Rome, 44(?)

From Cicero to Trebatius greetings.

You made game of me yesterday over our cups for saying that it was a moot point whether an heir can properly take action for theft in respect of a theft previously committed.[837] So when I got home, though late and well in tipple, I noted the relevant section[838] and send you a transcript. You will find that the view which, according to you, has never been held by anybody was in fact held by Sex. Aelius, Manius Manilius, and M. Brutus.[839] However, for my part I agree with Scaevola and Testa.

836. The manuscripts are corrupt at this point, but the person concerned is probably either Q. Cicero senior or his son; cf. *Letters to Atticus* 404 (XV.26).1.

837. i.e. in the interval between the testator's death and the heir's taking possession. A theft committed during the testator's lifetime *was* actionable.

838. No doubt in Scaevola the Pontifex's great treatise on civil law.

839. Three eminent second-century jurists.

332 (VII. 21)

CICERO TO TREBATIUS

Tusculum, June (latter half) 44

From Cicero to Trebatius greetings.

I have given you an account of Silius' case.[840] Since then he has been at my house. When I told him that in your opinion we could safely make the stipulation ('if Q. Caepio,[841] Praetor, under his edict has given me possession of the estate of Turpilia'), he said that Servius does not agree that the will of a person not possessing testamentary capacity has any existence in law, and that Offilius says the same. He told me that he has not spoken to you, and asked me to commend to you himself and his case.

My dear Testa, there is no better man alive than P. Silius and no better friend to me, yourself however excepted. I shall therefore be deeply obliged if you will go to see him and promise your services. But if you love me, no delay! I ask this as a most particular favour.

333 (VII. 20)

CICERO TO TREBATIUS

Velia, 20 July 44

From Cicero to Trebatius greetings.

I have found Velia[842] all the more likeable a place because I

840. The legal details are too complicated to go into here.
841. i.e. M. Brutus, the City Praetor.
842. Cicero was on his way to Athens, though he got no further than Syracuse; cf. *Letters to Atticus* 415 (XVI.7).1. It is not clear that he stayed in Trebatius' house.

saw how much Velia likes you. But I need not talk of you, who are liked by all the world – your man Rufio[843] is as much missed, my word upon it, as if he were one of ourselves. But I don't blame you for taking him along to your building operations. Velia is as respectable a place as the Lupercal,[844] but still I prefer Rome to everything down here. But if you will take my advice, as you generally do, you will hold on to your paternal property (the good folk of Velia are somewhat apprehensive), and not forsake the noble river Hales and the house of the Papirii.[845] To be sure it contains a lotus, a plant which captivates even strangers[846] – though if you cut it down, you will see a long way further than your nose! But there is a great deal to be said, particularly in times like these, for having a refuge – a town full of people who care for you and a house and land of your own, that too in a retired, healthy, and pleasant locality. And I feel that I myself have some stake in the matter, my dear Trebatius. However, you must keep well and look after my affairs and expect me back, Gods willing, before mid-winter.

I have taken away a book, from Nico's[847] pupil, Sex. Fadius – 'Nico on Heavy Eating'. What a charming physician, and how docile a patient he would find me! But our friend Bassus told me nothing about that book – though he seems to have told you![848]

The wind is getting brisker. Take care of yourself.

27 July, Velia

843. A slave or freedman of Trebatius.

844. A grotto at the foot of the Palatine, where the she-wolf was supposed to have suckled Romulus and Remus. Presumably Trebatius was building in its vicinity.

845. Presumably Trebatius' house, called after its previous owners.

846. With allusion to the lotus-eaters in the *Odyssey*.

847. Prescriptions by a physician so called are cited by Celsus. Nothing else is known of Fadius or Bassus.

848. Perhaps with the implication that Trebatius knew all about 'Heavy Eating'.

334 (VII. 19)

CICERO TO TREBATIUS

Regium, 28 July 44

From Cicero to Trebatius greetings.

This will show how highly I regard you – as indeed I ought, for your affection is no less warm than my own; but anyhow, that request of yours to which to your face I said something a little like no, and at any rate did not say yes – in your absence I could not let it go unanswered. As soon as my boat left Velia, I set to work on writing up Aristotle's *Topics*.[849] The town itself, in which you are so well-loved a figure, reminded me of you. I am sending the book to you from Regium, written in as clear a style as the material admits.[850] If you find it in places hard to follow, you must remember that no technical subject can be acquired by reading, without an interpreter and a certain amount of practice. You will not have far to go for an illustration – can your Civil Law be learned from books? There are any number of them, but they need a teacher and experience. However, if you read and re-read carefully, you will understand everything correctly by your own efforts. But only practice will make the 'topics' present themselves to your mind automatically when a question is proposed. I shall keep you hard at it, if I get back safely and find all safe with you.

28 July, Regium

849. In fact Cicero's *Topics* (on the sources of proof, *topoi*) is not based on Aristotle's work of the same name, which he had perhaps never seen. He seems to have used Antiochus of Ascalon, who claimed to be following Aristotle.

850. A somewhat defensive qualification. The *Topics* is the most difficult of Cicero's works, the examples being taken from Roman law in compliment to Trebatius.

335 (XI. 29)

CICERO TO OPPIUS

Anagnia(?), July (beginning) 44

From Cicero to Oppius greetings.

As our friend Atticus knows, I have been hesitating about this whole project of going abroad, because many considerations occurred to me on either side. Your judgement and advice have now come massively into the scales to put an end to my indecision. You have written your opinion in plain terms and Atticus has reported to me what you said to him. I have always had the highest respect for your sagacity in framing advice and your honesty in giving it, which I experienced most notably when I wrote to you at the beginning of the Civil War to ask you what you thought I should do – join Pompey or stay in Italy. You recommended me to think of my reputation; from which I understood your opinion, and admired your scrupulous honesty as an adviser. For although you believed that your greatest friend[851] would have preferred it otherwise, you thought more of my duty than of his wishes.

For my part, I had a regard for you even before that time and have always felt that you had a regard for me. When I was away and in great danger, I remember how you cared for and protected my absent self and my family on the spot. To our familiar association since my return, and to my sentiments and public expressions about yourself, we can call everybody who notices such things to witness. But the weightiest tribute you paid to my good faith and consistency was after Caesar's death, when you gave me your friendship without reserve. If I do not justify your choice by the most hearty good-will towards you

851. Caesar.

and by all friendly offices in my power, I shall consider myself a poor creature indeed.

On your side, my dear Oppius, you will maintain your affection (I say this more as a conventional form than because I suppose you need any reminder), and give me your support in all my concerns. I have asked Atticus to make sure you don't lack information about them. Expect a more substantial letter from me as soon as I get a little time to spare.

Take care of your health – you can do me no greater favour.

336 (XI. 3)

M. BRUTUS AND CASSIUS TO ANTONY

Naples, 4 August 44

From Brutus and Cassius, Praetors, to Antonius, Consul, greetings.

We trust you are well.

We have read your letter. We find it very similar to your edict, offensive and menacing, a letter which ought never to have been sent by you to us. We, sir, have done nothing to provoke or annoy you, nor did we suppose that you would be surprised if, as Praetors and gentlemen of a certain station, we put forward in an edict a request to you as Consul. If you resent our venturing it, permit us to be sorry that you grudge even so small a licence to Brutus and Cassius.

You say that you have made no protest concerning our levies of troops and money, our tampering with the loyalty of the armed forces, and our dispatching of messengers overseas. We believe in the excellence of your motives, but at the same time we do not acknowledge any of these allegations; we also find it surprising that, having held your peace on these matters, you should not have been able to control your spleen so far as to refrain from throwing Caesar's death in our teeth.

One point we must ask you yourself to consider: is it tolerable that Praetors should not be permitted in the interests of concord and freedom to abate the rights of their office by edict[852] without a Consul threatening military violence? You must not count upon such a threat to intimidate us. It would be unworthy and unbecoming in us to be cowed by any personal danger; and you, sir, should not claim authority over those to whom you owe your freedom. Suppose we desired on other grounds to stir up civil war, your letter would have no effect. Free men are not impressed by threats. But you are perfectly well aware that we cannot be driven into any course, and it may be that your present menacing behaviour is designed to make our deliberate choice look like fear.

To summarize our position, we are desirous to see you an important and respected member of a free commonwealth. We are not fastening any quarrel upon you. At the same time, our freedom means more to us than your friendship. On your part, consider what you undertake and what you can sustain. Bear in mind, not only the length of Caesar's life, but the brevity of his reign. We pray heaven that your counsels may be salutary to the commonwealth and to you. If it should be otherwise, then we pray that they may bring you as little hurt as possible without detriment to the public safety and honour.

4 August.

852. Brutus and Cassius had put out an edict to the effect that they were inhibited from carrying out their duties as Praetors and were ready to retire into voluntary exile.

337 (XVI. 21)

M. CICERO JUNIOR TO TIRO

Athens, August(?) 44

From Cicero junior to his beloved Tiro greetings.

I was eagerly expecting couriers every day, and at last they have come, forty-five days after leaving home. I was delighted by their arrival. My kindest and dearest father's letter gave me great pleasure, and then your own most agreeable letter put the finishing touch to my happiness. I am no longer sorry to have made a break in our correspondence, rather the contrary, since as a result of my letters falling silent I am repaid by this example of your good nature. I am truly delighted that you have accepted my excuses without question.

I don't doubt that you are pleased with the reports you are hearing of me, dearest Tiro, and that they are such as you wished to hear. I shall make sure and work hard to see that this tiny new image of mine goes on getting bigger and bigger[853] as the days go by. So you can carry out your promise to be my publicity agent with every confidence. Young men make mistakes, and mine have brought me so much unhappiness and torment that I hate to think of what I did, or even hear it mentioned. Very well do I know that you shared my worry and unhappiness, as well you might, for you wanted all to go right for me not for my sake only but for your own too, because I have always wanted you to have a part in any good things that come my way. Well, since I gave you unhappiness then, I shall make sure to give you twice as much happiness now.

I can tell you that Cratippus and I are very close, more like

853. Literally 'is doubled more and more', a phrase of which Cicero senior would hardly have approved.

CICERO'S LETTERS TO HIS FRIENDS

father and son than teacher and pupil. I enjoy hearing him
lecture, and quite delight in his own pleasant company. I spend
all day with him and often part of the night, for I beg him into
dining with me as frequently as possible. Now that he has got
into the habit, he often drops in on us at dinner unawares, and
then he puts off the grave philosopher and jokes with us in the
most genial way. So you must try to meet him as soon as
possible – he is such a pleasant, excellent man.

As for Bruttius,[854] what can I say? I never let him out of my
sight. He lives simply and strictly, and he is the best of company
too. Fun goes hand in hand with literary study and daily
disputation. I have rented a lodging for him near mine, and as
he is a poor man, I help him as best I can out of my own meagre
funds. Also I have started regular declamation in Greek with
Cassius,[855] and I want to practise in Latin with Bruttius. Some
people whom Cratippus brought over from Mytilene, scholars
whom he entirely approves of, are my friends and daily associates. I see a lot of Epicrates too (a leading man in Athenian
society), and Leonides, and people of that sort. So as to myself –
voilà!

As for what you say about Gorgias,[856] he *was* useful to me in
declamation practice, but I have put obedience to my father's
directions above all other considerations. He had written telling
me *sans phrase* to get rid of Gorgias at once. I thought I had
better not boggle over it – if I made too much fuss, he might
think it suspicious. Also it came to my mind that I should be
taking a lot upon myself in judging my father's judgement. All
the same, I am very grateful for your concern and advice.

I quite accept your excuse about shortage of time. I know
how busy you generally are. I'm really delighted to hear that

854. Nothing more known, but no doubt an Italian.
855. Another unknown professor of rhetoric.
856. Later a noted rhetorician in Rome, he is said by Plutarch ('Life of
Cicero', 24) to have led M. Cicero junior into bad ways and to have
received an angry letter (in Greek) from his father.

you have bought a property, and hope it turns out a successful investment. Don't be surprised at my congratulations coming at this stage in my letter – that was about the point where *you* put the news of your purchase. Well, you are a landed proprietor! You must shed your town-bred ways – you are now a Roman squire! How amusing to picture the delightful sight of you now! I imagine you buying farm tackle, talking to the bailiff, hoarding pips at dessert in your jacket pockets! But seriously, I am as sorry as you that I was not there to lend you a hand. However, dear Tiro, I *shall* help you, provided luck helps me, especially as I know you have bought the place to share with us.

Thank you for attending to my commissions. But do please get a clerk sent out to me, preferably a Greek. I waste a lot of time copying out my notes.

Take care of your health first and foremost, so that we can be students together. I commend Anterus[857] to you.

338 (XVI. 25)

M. CICERO JUNIOR TO TIRO

Athens, autumn(?) 44

From Cicero junior to his dear Tiro greetings.

Your excuse for letting your correspondence with me lapse is fair and sufficient, but I beg of you not to do this often. Even though I am kept informed of political rumours and reports and my father constantly writes to me about his sentiments towards me, a letter from you, no matter what or how trivial the topic,

857. Presumably the slave who carried the letter. The form *Anterum* here seems to come from a hybrid form 'Anterus' (instead of 'Anterōs'), which is also found in inscriptions.

has always been most welcome to me. So since I miss your letters above all things, don't let your obligation to write be fulfilled in the making of excuses, but by a steady stream of letters.

Goodbye.

339 (XII. 20)

CICERO TO CORNIFICIUS

Rome, 2 September 44(?)[858]

From Cicero to Cornificius.

Thank you for your letter – but you should not have been so rude to my little lodge at Sinuessa.[859] The insult will rankle with my poor little house, unless you make an *amende honorable* at Cumae or Pompeii. So that is what you must do; also you must remember me kindly, and prod me with a literary effort. I find it easier to answer a challenge than to issue one. However, if you drag your feet (a tendency of yours), I shall be the one to prod. Your laziness will not make an idler of *me*. More when I have time to spare – I scribbled this in the Senate.

858. Perhaps written at a sitting of the Senate on that day, after Cornificius had set out for his province of Africa.
859. Perhaps acquired from Lepta; cf. Letter 262 (VI.19). Evidently Cornificius had declined an invitation to use it on his way south.

340 (X. 1)

CICERO TO PLANCUS

Rome, September 44

From Cicero to Plancus.

I have been away, *en route* for Greece; and ever since the voice of the commonwealth called me home half way through my journey, Mark Antony has not left me a quiet moment. His insolence – but that is a common fault, say rather his atrocity – has reached such proportions that he cannot bear anybody to look like a free man, let alone speak like one. My greatest concern is not for my own life. As for that, I have run my race, whether in respect of years or achievements or (if that too be relevant) glory. But the thought of my country, and above all the prospect of your Consulship,[860] my dear Plancus, makes me anxious – it is so far away that I must pray rather than hope to be granted breath until that time comes for the commonwealth. For what hope can there be in a commonwealth where all lies crushed by the armed force of a violent, licentious individual, where neither Senate nor People has any power, where neither laws nor law-courts exist, nor any semblance or trace whatsoever of a free community?

Well, I imagine you are sent all the news of the day, so there is no point in my going into details. But the steadfast and indeed increasing affection I have entertained for you ever since you were a boy prompts me to urge and admonish you to consecrate all your thoughts and care to the commonwealth. If it lasts until your time comes, its guidance will be easy; but to make it last great fortune as well as great pains is required.

However, I hope we shall see you back some considerable

860. By Caesar's appointment Plancus and D. Brutus were to hold the Consulship in 42.

time before then. Apart from my obligation to think of the commonwealth I also take a strong and sympathetic interest in your future dignity. My advice and zeal, my time and service, my effort and industry, are entirely devoted to your advancement. Thus I conceive I shall most easily render what is due both to the commonwealth, which is most dear to me, and to our friendship, which I hold us bound religiously to maintain.

I am not surprised, but I am happy, that you value our friend Furnius as highly as his own goodness and high standing deserve. Please believe that any good opinion or good office you bestow upon him is in my estimation bestowed upon myself.

341 (X. 2)

CICERO TO PLANCUS

Rome, c. 19 September 44

From Cicero to Plancus greetings.

As a friend I should not have failed to support the decree in your honour,[861] had I been able to enter the Senate in security and dignity. But it is dangerous for any man of independent political views to move about in public when swords are drawn with complete impunity; and it does not seem to comport with my dignity to make a speech in a House where men-at-arms would hear me better and at shorter distance than members.

In private matters you shall find me always zealous to serve you; and even in matters public, if there be some compelling occasion for me to take part, I shall never fail you in your career, even at risk to myself. But in matters which can just as well be settled in my absence I would ask you to wish me to consider my own safety and dignity.

861. Probably for a Supplication in honour of Plancus' military successes in Rhaetia.

342 (XI. 4)

D. BRUTUS TO CICERO

Cisalpine Gaul, September 44

From D. Brutus, Imperator, Consul-Elect, to Cicero greetings.

If I had any doubt of your sentiments towards me, I should use many words in requesting you to defend my public standing; but the fact surely is as I am convinced, that you have my interests at heart.

I marched against the Alpine tribes, not so much in quest of the title Imperator, as desiring to satisfy my men and make them firm for the defence of our concerns. I think I have succeeded; for they have had practical experience of my liberality and spirit. I have made war on the bravest warriors in the world, taken many strong places, laid many areas waste. My dispatch to the Senate is not unwarranted. Support me with your voice in the House. In so doing you will be serving the common cause in no small measure.

343 (XI. 6)

CICERO TO D. BRUTUS

Rome, September or October (beginning) 44

From M. Cicero to D. Brutus, Imperator, Consul-Elect, greetings.

Arriving in Rome five days after leaving Mutina, our friend Lupus had an interview with me the following morning, at which he set forth your message very carefully and delivered your letter. When you commend your public standing to my care, I feel that you are also commending my own, which is truly no more precious to me than yours. Therefore you will gratify me highly if you will rest assured that my counsel and support shall at no point be lacking to promote your credit.

344 (XII. 2)

CICERO TO CASSIUS

Rome, c. 25 September 44

From Cicero to Cassius greetings.

I am very glad to find that my vote and speech[862] meet with your approval. If I had been able to make such speeches often, the recovery of liberty and constitution would have been no problem. But a crazy desperado, far more wicked even than he whom you called the wickedest man ever killed, is looking for a starting-point for a massacre. In charging me with having instigated Caesar's slaying he has no other object than to incite the veterans against me (a risk which I am not afraid to take so long as he honours me with a share in the glory of your exploit). Accordingly, neither Piso, who was the first to make an (unsupported) attack on him, nor I, who followed Piso's example a month later, nor P. Servilius, who came after me, can enter the Senate in safety. The gladiator is looking for a massacre, and thought to make a start with me on 19 September. He came prepared for the occasion, having spent several days in Metellus' villa[863] getting up a speech. How could that be done in an orgy of drink and debauchery? So, as I wrote to

862. The First Philippic, Cicero's first public challenge to Antony, delivered on 2 September.
863. Metellus Scipio's villa at Tibur, bought by Antony after its confiscation.

you earlier, everyone thought he was not speaking but vomiting – according to habit![864]

You say you are confident that with my prestige and eloquence something can be achieved. Well, something *has* been achieved, if we allow for the deplorable state of affairs. The People of Rome realizes that there are three Consulars who cannot come to the Senate in safety because they felt as loyal citizens and spoke their minds. Beyond that you must expect nothing. Your relative[865] is delighted with his new connection, and so he is no longer interested in the Games, and is ready to burst at the endless applause they give your brother. Your other connection[866] likewise has been cajoled by new memoranda of Caesar's. Such things are tolerable, but it is surely not to be borne that a certain person[867] should expect the Consulship for his son in your and Brutus' year, and give out that he is this brigand's humble servant on that account. As for my good friend L. Cotta, to use his own phrase, he is in a state of fatalistic despair, and rarely comes to the Senate any more. L. Caesar, an excellent citizen and a brave man, is tied by ill health. Ser. Sulpicius has great prestige and loyal sentiments, but he is away. As for the rest,[868] the Designates[869] excepted, you'll forgive me[870] but I

864. Antony's tendency to vomit in public is featured in the Second Philippic and attested in Plutarch's life of him.

865. L. Aemilius Paulus, whose brother Lepidus was married to a sister of Cassius' wife Junia Tertia. Lepidus' son had recently been betrothed to a daughter of Antony. Presumably Paulus was generally fond of shows, but now avoided them for fear of popular demonstrations.

866. C. Marcellus, Consul in 50, whose mother was a Junia, perhaps Junia Tertia's aunt.

867. L. Marcius Philippus, Consul in 56. His son of the same name was Praetor in 44 and so would be eligible for the Consulate in 41, which would be the earliest possible year for M. Brutus and Cassius.

868. Men appointed under Caesar's régime or recalled by him from exile.

869. A. Hirtius and C. Vibius Pansa (for 43); also, but absent from Rome, D. Brutus, Plancus (for 42).

don't reckon them as Consulars. Such are the men to whom the country looks for guidance; even for good times an all too meagre number, but for desperate times – I say no more.

So all our hope lies in yourselves.[871] If you are keeping away for your safety's sake, even that hope fails. On the other hand, should you be planning something worthy of your glory, I hope I may be alive to see it; but if I am not, at any rate the state will soon regain its rights through you.

Your family can count on me now and in the future. Whether they consult me or not, my loyalty and good-will to you shall not be wanting.

Goodbye.

345 (XII. 3)

CICERO TO CASSIUS

Rome, early October 44

From Cicero to Cassius greetings.

Your friend[872] gets crazier every day. To begin with he has inscribed the statue[873] which he set up on the Rostra 'To Father and Benefactor' – so that you are now set down, not only as assassins, but as parricides to boot! I say 'you', but ought rather to say 'we', for the madman declares that I was the promoter of your noble enterprise. If only I had been! He would not be giving us any trouble then. But all that is your responsibility,

870. The judgement logically applied to Cassius' connection by marriage, Lepidus, though he was absent from Rome; as also to P. Servilius, married to another sister of Junia Tertia, though Cicero includes him as a Consular above.

871. M. Brutus and Cassius. Both were leaving, or had already left, Italy for the East.

872. Antony.

873. Of Caesar.

and now that it is past and gone, I only wish I had some advice to offer you. But I cannot even think what to do myself. What can be done against violence except by violence?

Their whole plan is to avenge Caesar's death. On 2 October Antony was brought before a public meeting by Cannutius. He came off ignominiously indeed, but still he spoke of the country's saviours in terms appropriate to her betrayers. Of myself he declared unequivocally that everything you and your friends did and Cannutius is doing was on my advice. As a specimen of their behaviour in general, take the fact that they have deprived your Legate[874] of his travelling allowance. What do you suppose they infer by that? Presumably that the money was being conveyed to a public enemy.

It is a lamentable picture. We could not tolerate a master, so we are in bondage to our fellow-slave. However, hope still remains in your valour (though for me it is a case of wishing rather than of hoping). But where are your forces? For the rest I prefer you to consult your own conscience rather than listen to words of mine.

Goodbye.

346 (XII. 22)

CICERO TO CORNIFICIUS

Rome, not long after 19 September 44

From Cicero to Cornificius greetings.

Here I have a fight on my hands with a most rascally gladiator fellow, our colleague[875] Antony. But it is no fair match – words

874. Cassius had been appointed governor of Cyrene. The names of his Legates are unknown.
875. As Augur.

against weapons. However, he also makes speeches to public meetings, about you! Not with impunity – he shall find to his cost what sort of people he has provoked! However, I suppose you get details of all that *has* happened from other correspondents; it is my business to inform you of what is going to happen, and that is hard to guess at present.

The whole country is under heel. The honest men have no leader, our tyrannicides are at the other end of the earth. Pansa's sentiments are sound, and he talks boldly. Our friend Hirtius is making a slow recovery. What will come of it I simply don't know, but the only hope is that the People of Rome will at last show themselves like their ancestors. I at any rate shall not fail the commonwealth, and shall bear with courage whatever may befall, provided that I am not to blame for it. Of one thing you may be sure – I shall protect your reputation and prestige to the best of my ability.

347 (XII. 23)

CICERO TO CORNIFICIUS

Rome, c. 10 October 44

From Cicero to Cornificius greetings.

Tratorius has given me a comprehensive picture of your situation as governor and the state of your province. Outrages everywhere! But the higher your standing, the less you should acquiesce in what has happened to you. What *your* lofty spirit and intellect bear equably *you* should not on that account let go unpunished, even though it need not cause you pain. But of this later.

I feel sure that the city gazettes are sent to you. If I thought otherwise, I should give you the particulars myself, especially about Caesar Octavian's attempt.[876] The general public thinks Antony has trumped up the charge because he wants to lay hands on the young man's money; but intelligent and honest men both believe in the fact and approve. In a word, high hopes are set on him. He will do anything, it is thought, for honour and glory. As for our friend Antony, he is so conscious of his unpopularity that after catching his would-be murderers in his house he does not dare to make the matter public. So on 9 October he set off for Brundisium to meet the four Macedonian legions.[877] He intends to buy their good-will, and then to march them to Rome and set them on our necks.

Such is the political situation in outline, if a political situation can exist in an armed camp. I often feel sorry for you, because you are too young to have sampled any part of a free state in sound working order. Formerly it was at least possible to hope, but now even that has been torn from us. What hope is left, when Antony dares to say in a public meeting that Cannutius is trying to make a place for himself with people who can have no place in the community so long as he, Antony, remains a member of it?[878]

For my part, I take all this and whatever else can happen to mortal man with profound thankfulness to philosophy, which not only diverts me from anxiety but arms me against all assaults of fortune. I recommend you to do the same, and not to reckon as an evil anything devoid of culpability. But you know all this better than I.

I always thought well of our friend Tratorius, and I have been particularly impressed by his thorough loyalty, conscientiousness, and good sense in your affairs.

Take good care of your health. You can do nothing to please me more.

876. To have Antony assassinated.
877. Legions sent to Macedonia to take part in Caesar's projected war against Parthia and recently brought to Italy by Antony.
878. Caesar's assassins.

348 (XI. 27)

CICERO TO MATIUS

Tusculum, mid October(?) 44

From M. Cicero to Matius greetings.

I have not yet quite made up my mind whether our good Trebatius, a zealous and affectionate friend to both of us, has brought me more vexation or pleasure. He paid me an early morning visit at my house at Tusculum, where I had arrived the previous evening, although his health was still not fully restored. On my scolding him for not taking proper care of himself, he answered that he had never felt more impatience for anything than for an interview with me. 'Why, has something happened?' I asked. And he laid before me your grievance.

Before replying to that, I will make a few observations. As far back into the past as my memory extends, no friend of mine is older than yourself. But length of acquaintance is something which many share in some degree, affection is not. I cared for you from the first day we met and believed that you cared for me. Your subsequent departure for a long period, together with my pursuit of a political career and the difference between our modes of life, debarred us from cementing our friendly feelings by constant intercourse. But I had fresh evidence of your disposition towards me many years before the Civil War, when Caesar was in Gaul. Through your efforts Caesar came to look upon me as one of his circle, the object of his regard and friendly attentions; a result which you considered highly advantageous to me and not disadvantageous to Caesar himself. I pass over our many familiar interchanges in those days by word of mouth and correspondence, for graver matters followed.

At the outset of the Civil War, when you were on your way to join Caesar at Brundisium, you paid me a visit in my house at Formiae.[879] That to begin with meant a good deal, especially at such a time. And then, do you suppose I have forgotten your kindly advice and talk? I remember that Trebatius was present during all this. Nor have I forgotten the letter[880] you sent me after you had met Caesar in the Trebula district, I think it was.

Then followed the time when, whether impelled by my sensitivity to criticism or by obligation or by fortune, I went to join Pompey. Your devoted service was never wanting either to me in my absence or to my family on the spot. In the judgement of them all, neither they nor I had a better friend.

I arrived in Brundisium. Do you think I have forgotten how swiftly, the moment you heard the news, you rushed over to me from Tarentum, how you sat beside me, talking and encouraging me in the dejection to which fear of the common calamities had reduced me?

At long last we took up residence in Rome. Our familiar friendship was now complete. In the most important matters, in determining how to conduct myself towards Caesar, I availed myself of your advice; in others, of your good offices. Was there any man but me, Caesar excepted, whose house you chose to frequent, and often spend many hours in the most delightful conversation? It was at that time, if you recall, that you prompted me to compose these philosophical works of mine. After Caesar's return I doubt if you had any object so much at heart as that I should be on the best possible footing with him. In that you had succeeded.

You may wonder where all this discourse (longer than I had envisaged) is tending. The truth is, I am astonished that you, who ought to know all this, should have believed me guilty of any action against the spirit of our friendship. For besides the well-attested and manifest facts which I have mentioned above,

879. Cf. *Letters to Atticus* 178 (IX.11).2.
880. Presumably *Letters to Atticus* 184 (IX.15 a).

I have many others of a less conspicuous nature in mind, such as I cannot easily express in words. All about you delights me, but your most notable characteristics attract me most: loyalty to friendship, judgement, responsibility, steadfastness on the one hand, charm, humanity, literary culture on the other.

And so, to revert to your grievance, in the first place I did not believe you cast a vote on that law;[881] and in the second, if I had believed it, I should never have supposed you to have acted without some legitimate reason. Your standing brings all you do into notice, and the malice of the world sometimes presents your actions as more uncompromising than they really were. If such things don't come to your hearing, I don't know what to say. For my own part, if ever I hear anything, I defend you as I know you are in the habit of defending me against *my* ill-wishers. This I do in two ways: there are some things I deny outright, as this very matter of the vote, others in which I claim you are acting out of loyalty and good nature, for example your superintendence of the Games.[882]

But a scholar like yourself will not be unaware that if Caesar was a despot, which seems to me to be the case, your ethical position can be argued in two ways. On the one side it can be maintained (and this is the line I take) that in caring for your friend even after he is dead you show commendable loyalty and good feeling. According to the other view, which is adopted in some quarters, the freedom of one's country should come before a friend's life. I only wish that my argumentations arising from such talk had been conveyed to you. At any rate no one recalls more readily and more often than I the two facts which above all others redound to your honour, namely, that yours was the weightiest influence both against embarking on a civil war and in favour of a moderate use of victory.

881. A recent law, possibly one of Antony's redistributing provincial commands (certainly not Caesar's law on debt, as sometimes supposed).
882. Celebrated by Octavian in memory of Caesar and in honour of his victory from 20 to 30 July; cf. *Letters to Atticus* 379 (xv.2).2.

In this I have found nobody who did not agree with me.

So I am grateful to our good friend Trebatius for giving me occasion to write this letter. If you do not believe in its sincerity, you will be setting me down as a stranger to all sense of obligation and good feeling. Nothing can be more grievous to me than such a verdict, or more uncharacteristic of yourself.

349 (XI. 28)

MATIUS TO CICERO

Rome, in reply to the foregoing

Matius to Cicero greetings.

Your letter gave me great pleasure, because it told me that you think of me as I had expected and desired. Although I was not in any doubt on this score, the high importance I attach to your good opinion made me anxious that it should remain unimpaired. My conscience assured me that I had not been guilty of any act which could give offence to any honest man. I was therefore all the less disposed to believe that a man of your great and many-sided attainments would let himself be persuaded of anything hastily, especially in view of my ready and never-failing good-will towards yourself. Now that I know this is as I hoped, I will make some reply to the charges which you, as befitted the singular kindness of your heart and the friendly relations between us, have often rebutted on my behalf.

I am well aware of the criticisms which people have levelled at me since Caesar's death. They make it a point against me that I bear the death of a friend hard and am indignant that the man I loved has been destroyed. They say that country should come before friendship – as though they have already proved that his death was to the public advantage. But I shall not make debating points. I acknowledge that I have not yet arrived at that philosophical level. It was not Caesar I followed in the civil conflict, but a friend whom I did not desert, even though I did not like what he was doing. I never approved of civil war or indeed of the origin of the conflict, which I did my very utmost to get nipped in the bud. And so, when my friend emerged triumphant, I was not caught by the lure of office or money, prizes of which others, whose influence with Caesar was less than my own, took immoderate advantage. My estate was actually reduced by a law of Caesar's,[883] thanks to which many who rejoice at his death are still inside the community. For mercy to our defeated fellow-countrymen I struggled as for my own life.

Well then, can I, who desired every man's preservation, help feeling indignant at the slaughter of the man who granted it – all the more when the very persons[884] who brought him unpopularity were responsible for his destruction? 'Very well,' say they, 'you shall be punished for daring to disapprove of our action.' What unheard-of arrogance! Some may glory in the deed, while others may not even grieve with impunity! Even slaves have always had liberty to feel hope or fear or joy or sorrow of their own impulse, not someone else's. That freedom the 'authors of our liberty', as these persons like to describe themselves, are trying to snatch from us by intimidation. But they are wasting their breath. No threats of danger shall ever make me false to obligation and good feeling. I never thought an honourable death a thing to shun, indeed I should often have welcomed it.

Why are they angry with me for praying that they may be sorry for what they have done? I want every man's heart to be sore for Caesar's death. But I shall be told that as a citizen I ought

883. On debt.
884. Such as D. Brutus, who had 'taken immoderate advantage' of their position as leading Caesarians.

to wish the good of the commonwealth. Unless my past life and hopes for the future prove that I so desire without words of mine, then I do not ask anyone to accept it because I say so. Therefore I earnestly request you to consider facts rather than words, and, if you perceive that it is to my advantage that things go as they should, to believe that I cannot have any part or lot with rascals.[885] Is it likely that in my declining years I should reverse the record of my youth (*then* I might have been pardoned for going astray) and undo the fabric of my life? Nor shall I give any offence, except that I grieve for the tragic fate of a great man to whom I was intimately bound. But if I were differently disposed, I should never deny what I was doing, and risk being thought a rascal for my misconduct and a cowardly hypocrite for trying to conceal it.

Well, but I superintended the Games for Caesar's Victory given by his young heir. That was a matter of private service, which has nothing to do with the state of the commonwealth. It was, however, an office which I owed to the memory and distinction of a dear friend even after his death, and one which I could not deny to the request of a most promising young man, thoroughly worthy of the name he bears. Also I have often called on Consul Antony to pay my respects; and you will find that those who think *me* a poor patriot are continually flocking to his house to make their petitions or carry off his favours. The presumption of it! Caesar never put any obstacle in the way of my associating with whom I pleased, even persons whom he himself did not like. And shall the people who have robbed me of my friend try to stop me with their carping tongues from liking whom I choose?

However, I don't doubt that the moderation of my career will be a strong enough defence against false reports in time to come; and I am equally confident that even those who do not love me because of my loyalty to Caesar would rather have

885. i.e. subversive elements. Matius is here asserting his loyalty to established order.

friends like me than like themselves. If my prayers are granted, I shall spend the remainder of my days quietly in Rhodes; but if some chance interferes with my plan, I shall live in Rome as one whose desire will ever be that things go as they should.

I am most grateful to our friend Trebatius for revealing the straightforward and amicable nature of your sentiments towards me, thus adding to the reasons why I ought to pay respect and attention to one whom I have always been glad to regard as a friend.

I bid you goodbye and hope to have your affection.

350 (XVI. 24)

CICERO TO TIRO

Arpinum, November (middle) 44

From Tullius to Tiro greetings.

I sent Harpalus to you this morning, but having a suitable bearer, though nothing new to say, I thought I would write to you again on the same subjects – not that I doubt your conscientiousness, but the thing is so important. The fore and aft (as the Greek saying has it) of my letting you go away was that you should put my affairs straight. Offilius and Aurelius must be satisfied at all costs. If you cannot extract the full amount from Flamma,[886] I hope you will get some part of it. Above all the payment on the Kalends of January must be cleared. Settle the assignment and use your judgement about the cash payment. So much for domesticities.

As for public affairs send me full, reliable reports – on Octavian, on Antony, on the state of public opinion, on what you think will happen. I can hardly stop myself hurrying up to

886. On these transactions see *Letters to Atticus* 294 (XII.52).I.

town, but I am waiting to hear from you. You may be interested to know that Balbus *was* at Aquinum when you were told so, and Hirtius the next day; both on their way to the waters, I suppose – but let them do what they like. See that Dolabella's agents get a reminder. You will also ask Papias for payment.

Goodbye.

351 (XVI. 26)

Q. CICERO TO TIRO

44(?)[887]

From Quintus to his dear Tiro best greetings.

A second packet has reached me with no letter from you, and my thoughts have drubbed you with reproaches, though I *say* nothing. You cannot hope to escape punishment for this offence if you conduct your own case. You must call Marcus in and see whether he can prove you innocent with a speech long pondered in the watches of many a night. I really do beg of you – I remember how our mother in the old days used to seal up the empty bottles, so that bottles drained on the sly could not be included with the empties – so you likewise write, even though you have nothing to write about, so that you are not suspected of having scraped an excuse to cover your idleness. Your letters always tell me things most true and agreeable.

Love me and goodbye.

887. The letter is usually assigned to 44, but may be much earlier, perhaps written during Quintus' service in Gaul.

352 (XVI. 27)

Q. CICERO TO TIRO

December(?) 44

From Q. Cicero to his dear Tiro best greetings.

By your letter you have given me a fine drubbing for my idleness. My brother wrote more charily, no doubt because he did not like to say too much and was pressed for time. You handle the same material, but give the naked truth without varnish, especially about the Consuls-Elect. I know them through and through. They are riddled with lusts and languor, utter effeminates at heart. Unless they retire from the helm, there is every risk of universal shipwreck. It is incredible the things they did to my knowledge on active service, with the Gauls encamped right opposite. Unless a firm line is taken, that bandit[888] will woo them over by comradeship in vice. The position must be fortified by the Tribunes or by private initiative. As for that precious pair, you would hardly trust one with Caesena or the other with the cellars of Cossutius' taverns.[889]

As I have said, you are the apple of my eye. I shall see you all on the 30th and smother *your* eyes in kisses, even though I first sight you in the middle of the Forum.

Love me. Goodbye.

888. Antony.
889. Caesena was a small town in Cisalpine Gaul south of Ravenna. Cossutius' taverns were probably in the same area, which produced a noted wine. Possibly Quintus was staying there. He seems to mean that Hirtius was feeble and incompetent, Pansa a drunkard; cf. *Letters to Atticus* 409 (XVI.1).4.

353 (XI. 5)

CICERO TO D. BRUTUS

Rome, 9 December (or shortly after) 44

From M. Cicero to D. Brutus, Imperator, Consul-Elect, greetings.

When our friend Lupus arrived from you and spent some days in Rome, I was where I thought I should be safest.[890] That is how it came about that Lupus went back without a letter from me, although he had seen to it that I received yours. I returned to Rome on 9 December and made it my first business to meet Pansa without delay. From him I received news of you such as I was most desirous to hear.

You stand in no need of encouragement, any more than you wanted it in your late exploit, the greatest in history. Yet I think I should briefly intimate that the People of Rome look to you to fulfil all their aspirations, and pin upon you all their hope of eventually recovering their freedom. If you bear in mind day and night, as I am sure you do, how great a thing you have accomplished, you will not be likely to forget how much remains for you still to do. If the personage[891] with whom you have to deal obtains a province (I was always his friend until I saw him waging war upon the state not only without conceal-ment but with relish), I see no further hope of survival.

Therefore I implore you (and I am echoing the entreaty of the Senate and People of Rome) to liberate the state forever from despotic rule. Let the end chime with the beginning. Yours is this task, yours the role. Our community, or rather all nations of the earth, expect this of you, indeed they demand it.

890. In Arpinum.

891. Antony, who had marched north in order to dispossess D. Brutus of Cisalpine Gaul.

But as I have already said, you need no encouragement, so I shall not spend many words in offering it. That which properly concerns me I will do, namely, promise you all my devoted service, all my care and consideration, in all that shall tend to your credit and glory. Therefore I hope you will believe that both for the sake of the commonwealth, which is dearer to me than my life, and also because I wish you well personally and desire your further advancement, I shall not fail at any point to support your patriotic designs, your greatness, and your glory.

354 (XI. 7)

CICERO TO D. BRUTUS

Rome, mid December 44

From M. Cicero to D. Brutus, Imperator, Consul-Elect, greetings.

Lupus asked myself, Libo, and your cousin Servius to meet him at my house. I think you will have heard the view I expressed from M. Seius, who was present at our colloquy. Other matters you will be able to learn from Graeceius, although he left just after Seius.

The main point, which I want you thoroughly to grasp and remember in the future, is that in safeguarding the liberty and welfare of the Roman People you must not wait to be authorized by a Senate which is not yet free. If you did, you would be condemning your own act, for you did not liberate the commonwealth by any public authority – a fact which makes the exploit all the greater and more glorious. You would also be implying that the young man, or rather boy, Caesar had acted inconsiderately in taking upon himself so weighty a public cause at his private initiative. Further, you would be implying that the soldiers, country folk but brave men and loyal citizens, had taken leave of their senses – that is to say firstly, the veterans,[892] your own comrades in arms, and secondly the Martian and Fourth Legions, which branded their Consul as a public enemy and rallied to the defence of the commonwealth. The will of the Senate should be accepted in lieu of authority when its authority is trammelled by fear. Lastly, you are already committed, for you have twice taken the cause upon yourself – first on the Ides of March, and again recently when you raised a new army and forces. Therefore you should be ready for every contingency. Your attitude must be, not that you will do nothing except on orders, but that you will take such action as will earn the highest praise and admiration from us all.

355 (X. 3)

CICERO TO PLANCUS

Rome, shortly after 9 December 44

From Cicero to Plancus greetings.

I was delighted to see Furnius for his own sake, and all the more so because as I listened to him I felt I was seeing *you*. He gave me an account of your military prowess, your rectitude in the administration of your province, and your good sense in all spheres. He spoke further of your agreeable personality in familiar intercourse, which was no news to me, and added that you had treated him most handsomely. All this I heard with pleasure, the last item with gratitude as well.

My friendly connection with your family, my dear Plancus, came into being some time before you were born. My affection towards yourself dates from your early childhood. When you

892. Settled in Caesar's Campanian colonies. They had rallied to Octavian early in November and were later joined by two of the four 'Macedonian' legions, the Martian and Fourth.

became a grown man, my desire and your choice established a familiar friendship. For these reasons I take the most lively interest in your standing in the world, which I hold to be mine also. Guided by ability and accompanied by good fortune you have achieved the highest success in everything you attempted, and you have gained these triumphs as a young man in the face of much jealousy, which you have overcome by capacity and energy. Now, if you will listen to me, your truly affectionate friend, who could allow no man pride of place with you in virtue of old association, you will derive all further advancement to the end of your days from the establishment of the best form of constitution.

You are of course aware, for nothing could escape you, that there was a time when the world thought you too much at the service of the times. I should have held that opinion myself, if I had taken acquiescence on your part for approval. But, perceiving your sentiments as I did, I considered that you took a realistic view of your power to influence events. Now the case is altered. You will form your own judgement on all questions, and it will be unconstrained. You are Consul-Elect, in the prime of life and the flower of oratorical talent, at a time when the commonwealth is so sorely bereft of men of such calibre. In heaven's name, throw your thoughts and solicitude into the channel which will bring you to the highest honour and glory. To glory there is only one path, especially now, when the body politic has so many years been torn asunder: good statesmanship.

Affection, rather than any notion that you were in need of admonition and advice, made me think fit to write to you in this strain. I know you drink in such ideas from the fountains at which I myself imbibed them. Therefore I will go no further. At this time I thought I ought to intimate that much, to advise you of my affection rather than to advertise my wisdom. Meanwhile I shall most zealously and faithfully attend to any matters which I judge to bear upon your personal standing.

356 (XI. 6a)

CICERO TO D. BRUTUS

Rome, 20 December 44

From M. Cicero to D. Brutus, Imperator, Consul-Elect, greetings.

The Tribunes summoned a meeting of the Senate by proclamation for 20 December with the intention of bringing the question of a bodyguard for the Consuls-Elect before the House. I had determined not to come to the Senate before the Kalends of January, but seeing that your proclamation[893] was published on that very day, I felt I should never forgive myself if the meeting passed without any reference to your immortal services to the state (which would have happened if I had not attended), or even if you did come in for honorific mention and I were not there.

Accordingly, I arrived at the House early. When my presence was noticed, members gathered in large numbers. Of my part in the Senate's proceedings concerning you[894] and my subsequent speech[895] before a large public meeting I prefer you to learn from other correspondents. But I hope you will believe that I shall always take up and maintain with the utmost enthusiasm whatever may tend to the advancement of your public standing, which is already of the highest. I know that I shall have many fellow-labourers in this field, but I shall strive for the foremost place among them.

893. In which D. Brutus declared that he would hold Cisalpine Gaul for the Senate and People (cf. *Phil*. III.8).

894. The Third Philippic was delivered at this meeting.

895. The Fourth Philippic.

357 (XII. 22a)

CICERO TO CORNIFICIUS

Rome, c. 21 December 44

From Cicero to Cornificius greetings.

On 20 December a well-attended meeting of the Senate accepted my·proposals on certain urgent and important matters, including one to the effect that provincial governors should remain at their posts and hand over authority only to successors appointed by senatorial decree. I made this motion in the public interest, but I assure you that I was also actuated in no small measure by concern for the preservation of your personal consequence. Accordingly, I would ask you for the sake of our affection and exhort you for the sake of the commonwealth to allow no person any jurisdiction in your province and always to make your own public standing your primary consideration – and no man could stand higher. I will be candid, as our friendship requires. In the matter of Sempronius[896] you would have gained a great deal of credit in all quarters if you had paid heed to my letter. But that is a thing of the past and of no great moment, this is really important: be sure to keep your province in the state's control.

I should have written more if your people had not been in a hurry. So please make my excuses to our friend Chaerippus.

896. Perhaps C. Sempronius Rufus. His matter is obscure (cf. Letters 373 (XII.25), 433 (XII.29)).

358 (x. 4)

PLANCUS TO CICERO

Gaul, December (end) 44

From Plancus to Cicero.

Very many thanks for your letter, which I notice you wrote as a result of your talk with Furnius. As for myself, I have an excuse to plead for the time I have allowed to go by – I heard you had set out, but did not know of your return much before I was apprised of it in your letter. I mention this because even the slightest failure in due attention to you could not but make me feel most deeply to blame. I have many reasons to be punctilious – your relations with my father, the respect I have paid you since childhood, your reciprocal affection for me.

Therefore, my dear Cicero, be assured that (as our respective ages allow) in cultivating your friendship I have invested you, and only you, with the sacred character of a father. Your counsels all appear to me full no less of sincerity, which I measure by my own conscience, than of the wisdom for which you are distinguished. If my disposition were otherwise, your admonition would assuredly suffice to check it; and if I were hesitating, your exhortation would be enough to urge me forward in pursuit of what *you* hold to be best. But as it is, what is there to draw me in a different direction? Your affection leads you to estimate such advantages as I possess (whether the gift of kindly fortune or the product of my own effort) beyond their worth; but even my worst enemy would admit that only the world's good opinion seems wanting.

Therefore rest assured of one thing: all that my strength can compass, my prudence foresee, and my counsel suggest, shall ever be at the service of the commonwealth. I am not unaware of your sentiments. If I could have you with me in person, as *I* should so much wish, I should never dissent from your policies; and as it is, I shall take good care not to let any of my actions give you fair ground for censure.

I am waiting for news of all manner of things – what is toward in Cisalpine Gaul, and what in Rome this January. Please send me word, so that I know. Meanwhile I have a heavy and anxious task on my hands here, to guard (while others misbehave themselves) against the danger that the peoples of this country may see their opportunity in our calamities. If I am as successful in this as I deserve, I shall assuredly not disappoint you, whom I am most especially anxious to content, or the whole body of honest men.

Keep well and remember me kindly, as I do you.

359 (X. 5)

CICERO TO PLANCUS

Rome, January (middle) 43

From Cicero to Plancus greetings.

I have received two letters from you, duplicates. That in itself showed me how punctilious you are. I appreciated your anxiety that the letter I so eagerly awaited should duly reach me. The letter itself gave me a two-fold satisfaction; and when I try to make a comparison, I find it hard to decide which I should esteem the more precious, your affection for me or your spirit of patriotism. To be sure (in my judgement at all events) love of country transcends all other sentiments; but affection and friendly attachment undeniably exercise a greater charm. And so your reminder of my relations with your father, of the good-will you have bestowed upon me since your childhood, and of other points relevant to the theme, made me a happier man than you can well believe. But, again, the declaration of your political attitude, now and in time to come, pleased me exceedingly. My happiness was all the greater because this came as an addition to what had gone before.

So I urge you, my dear Plancus, nay more, I *beg* you, as I did in the letter to which you have replied so kindly, to bend all your thoughts and mental energy upon public affairs. There is nothing that can so richly reward you or so redound to your glory; nor in the whole range of human activities is there one more splendid and excellent than service to the state. Hitherto (your admirable good nature and good sense allow me to put my thoughts freely into words) you appear to have won brilliant success with luck on your side. That would not, it is true, have been possible without merit. None the less, the greater part of your achievements is credited to fortune and circumstances. But if you come to the aid of the commonwealth in the very difficult circumstances of today, all you do will be properly your own. The universal hatred of Antony (bandits[897] excepted) is extraordinary. Great is the hope pinned upon you and the army under your command, great the expectancy. Do not, in the name of heaven, lose the opportunity to render yourself popular and renowned. I admonish you as a son, I hope for you as for myself, I urge you as one addressing a very dear friend in his country's cause.

360 (XI. 8)

CICERO TO D. BRUTUS

Rome, late January 43

From M. Cicero to D. Brutus, Imperator, Consul-Elect, greetings.

I have had word from your lady Polla to give the bearer a

897. Antony and his followers are often referred to as *latrones* ('brigands'), as being in arms against the public peace.

letter for you if I wished to send something, but at this particular time I have nothing to write. Everything is in suspense while we wait to hear the result of the embassy,[898] of which nothing is reported as yet. However, I think I should tell you to begin with that the Senate and People of Rome is much concerned about you, not only for their own safety's sake but for that of your prestige. The emotion your name inspires is extraordinary. The whole citizen community feels a peculiar affection towards you, hoping and believing that you will now free our country from tyranny as you have already freed her from a tyrant. The levy is proceeding in Rome and all over Italy, if 'levy' is the right word to use when the whole population is freely volunteering in a flush of enthusiasm inspired by craving for liberty and disgust of their long servitude. On other matters it is time for us to be expecting a letter from you with news of yourself and our friend Hirtius and my young friend Caesar. I trust it will not be long before you and they are united in the bond of a common victory.

I have only to add concerning myself something which I hope and prefer you learn from the letters of those near to you, that my support for your public standing is not and never shall be wanting on any occasion.

361 (XII. 24. 1–2)

CICERO TO CORNIFICIUS

Rome, late January 43

From Cicero to Cornificius greetings.

I do not (and in duty I should not) lose any opportunity of

898. Three Consulars, Ser. Sulpicius Rufus, L. Calpurnius Piso, and L. Marcius Philippus, had been sent by the Senate to convey its behests to Antony, now besieging D. Brutus in Mutina (Modena). They returned about 1 February, Sulpicius having died on the journey.

singing your praises and, what is more, of securing practical recognition for you. But I prefer you to learn of my efforts and good offices from the letters of your domestic correspondents rather than from mine. I would, however, urge you to throw your whole mind into the public service. That is worthy of your spirit and intellect, and of the hope of increased prestige which you ought to entertain.

But of this more at some other time. As I write, everything hangs in suspense. The envoys sent by the Senate (not to beg for peace but to give notice of war if he did not comply with their message) have not yet returned. However, on the first occasion that presented itself to defend the commonwealth in my old style I offered myself to the Senate and People of Rome as their leader,[899] and, since I first took up the cause of freedom, I have not let slip the smallest opportunity to champion our corporate existence and liberties. But of this too I would rather you learned from others.

362 (IX. 24)

CICERO TO PAPIRIUS PAETUS

Rome, January 43

Cicero to Paetus greetings.

I should assist your friend Rufus,[900] about whom you now write to me for the second time, to the best of my ability, even if he had done me an injury, seeing how concerned you are on his behalf. But understanding and concluding as I do both from your letters and from one he has sent me himself that he has been greatly exercised about my safety, I cannot but be his

899. In the Third Philippic, delivered on 20 December 44.
900. Otherwise unknown.

friend, not only because of your recommendation (which carries the greatest weight with me, as is right and proper) but from my personal inclination and judgement. For I want you to know, my dear Paetus, that my suspicions and diligent precautions all started with your letter, which was followed by letters to like effect from many other correspondents. Plots were laid against me both at Aquinum and at Fabrateria of which something evidently came to your ears. They[901] put all their energies into catching me unawares, as though they had a presentiment of what a thorn in their flesh I was to become. Unsuspecting as I was, I might have laid myself open but for your admonition. Therefore this friend of yours needs no recommendation to me. I only hope the Fortune of the commonwealth may be such as to enable him to discover that gratitude is a strong point with me. So much for that.

I am sorry to hear that you have given up dining out. You have deprived yourself of a great deal of amusement and pleasure. Furthermore (you will not mind my being candid), I am afraid you will unlearn what little you used to know, and forget how to give little dinner-parties. For if you made such small progress in the art when you had models to imitate, what am I to expect of you now? When I laid the facts before Spurinna and explained to him your former mode of life, he pronounced a grave danger to the supreme interests of the state unless you resume your old habits when Favonius[902] starts to blow; at the present time of year he said he thought it might be borne, if *you* could not bear the cold.

And really, my dear Paetus, all joking apart I advise you, as something which I regard as relevant to happiness, to spend time in honest, pleasant, and friendly company. Nothing becomes life better, or is more in harmony with its happy

901. Partisans of Mark Antony. We hear something of plots against Cicero's person by L. Antonius in the summer of 44; cf. *Letters to Atticus* 385 (XV.8).2, 390 (XV.12).2, *Phil.* XII.20.

902. The west wind, harbinger of spring.

living. I am not thinking of physical pleasure, but of community of life and habit and of mental recreation, of which familiar conversation is the most effective agent; and conversation is at its most agreeable at dinner-parties. In this respect our countrymen are wiser than the Greeks. They use words meaning literally 'co-drinkings' or 'co-dinings',[903] but we say 'co-livings',[904] because at dinner-parties more than anywhere else life is lived in company. You see how I try to bring you back to dinners by philosophizing!

Take care of your health – which you will most easily compass by constantly dining abroad.

But do not suppose, if you love me, that because I write rather flippantly I have put aside my concern for the commonwealth. You may be sure, my dear Paetus, that my days and nights are passed in one sole care and occupation – the safety and freedom of my countrymen. I lose no opportunity of admonition or action or precaution. Finally it is my feeling that, if I must lay down my life in my present care and direction of public affairs, I shall consider myself very fortunate in my destiny.

Once again, goodbye.

363 (XII. 4)

CICERO TO CASSIUS

Rome, 2 or 3 February 43

From Cicero to Cassius greetings.

A pity you did not invite me to dinner on the Ides of March! Assuredly there would have been no leavings! As it is, *your*

903. 'Symposia', 'syndeipna'.
904. *convivia*.

leavings are giving me plenty of trouble – yes, me in particular. True, we have an excellent pair of Consuls, but the Consulars are a shocking collection. The Senate is firm, but firmest in the lowest rank. As for the people, they are magnificently firm and loyal, so is the whole of Italy. The envoys Philippus and Piso have played a disgusting, scandalous role. They were sent to announce certain specific items to Antony according to the will of the Senate. After he had refused to obey any of these, they took it upon themselves to bring back a set of intolerable demands from him to us. Accordingly there is a rally to me, and I have now become a popular favourite in a good cause.

But what *you* are doing or going to do, or even where you are, I don't know. Rumour reports you in Syria, but nobody vouches for it. Reports of Brutus[905] appear more trustworthy in so far as he is nearer Italy. Dolabella is severely censured by persons with some claim to wit for relieving you in such a hurry, when you had been barely thirty days in Syria![906] It is accordingly agreed that he ought not to be let into the province. You and Brutus are highly commended because you are supposed to have raised an army, which nobody expected. I should write more if I knew the facts of the case. As it is, what I write is based on public opinion and rumour. I am eagerly waiting to hear from you.

Goodbye.

905. M. Brutus was now in Macedonia.

906. Under the lex Cornelia a governor must leave his province within thirty days of the arrival of his successor. Cassius, as it seemed, was not to be allowed thirty days from the *start* of his tenure. But the real point of the joke is not obvious. Cassius had no legal claim to Syria, which had been assigned to Dolabella.

364 (X. 28)

CICERO TO TREBONIUS

Rome, 2 February 43

From Cicero to Trebonius greetings.

How I wish you had invited me to that splendid feast on the Ides of March! We should then have had no left-overs! As it is, we are having so much trouble with these that the immortal service which you and your friends rendered the state leaves room for some criticism. And when I think that it was your excellent self who drew that noxious creature[907] aside and that he has you to thank that he is still alive, I sometimes grow half angry with you, which for me is almost sinful.[908] For you have left *me* with more trouble on my hands than everybody else put together.

As soon as the Senate was able to meet in freedom after Antony's ignominious departure, my old spirit returned to me, the spirit which you and that ardent loyalist, your father, always praised and admired. The Tribunes had summoned a meeting on 20 December and put another matter to the House. I then entered upon a comprehensive survey of the whole political situation. I did not mince my words, and, more by will-power than by oratorical skill, I recalled the weak and weary Senate to its old, traditional vigour. That day, and my energy, and the course I took, brought to the Roman People the first hope of recovering their freedom. And from that time forward I have used every possible moment, not only in thought but in action, on behalf of the commonwealth.

907. Antony, who was kept in conversation by Trebonius while the other plotters were disposing of Caesar.
908. Because of the obligations rehearsed in Letter 207 (XV.21).

If I did not suppose you to be receiving all the city affairs and official proceedings, I should recount them myself, although I am immersed in pressing business. But you will learn all that from others – from me, only a few items, and those in brief. We have a courageous Senate, but of the Consulars some are timid and others disloyal. Servius was a great loss. L. Caesar is thoroughly sound, but as Antony's uncle he does not speak very forcibly in the House. The Consuls are admirable, D. Brutus is splendid, young Caesar admirable – I for one have good hopes of him in the future. This much at any rate you may take as certain; if he had not rapidly enrolled veterans, if two of Antony's legions had not put themselves under his orders,[909] and if Antony had not been confronted with this menace, he would have stopped at no crime or cruelty.

Although I suppose you have heard all this, I wished you to know it better. I shall write further as soon as I have more leisure.

365 (XII. 5)

CICERO TO CASSIUS

Rome, early February 43

From Cicero to Cassius greetings.

I dare say it is the winter weather that has so far prevented us getting any certain news of you – your doings and, above all, your whereabouts. But everybody is saying (I imagine because they would like it to be so) that you are in Syria at the head of a force. This report gains the readier credence because it has a ring of probability. Our friend Brutus has won golden opinions. His achievements have been no less important than unexpected, so

909. Cf. n. 892.

that, welcome as they are intrinsically, they are enhanced by their rapidity. If you hold the areas we think you do, the national cause has massive forces at its back. From the shores of Greece down to Egypt we shall have a rampart of commands and armies in thoroughly patriotic hands.

And yet, if I am not in error, the position is that the decision of the whole war depends entirely on D. Brutus. If, as we hope, he breaks out of Mutina, it seems unlikely that there will be any further fighting. In fact the forces besieging him are now small, because Antony is holding Bononia with a large garrison. Our friend Hirtius is at Claterna, Caesar at Forum Cornelium, both with a strong army; and Pansa has got together a large force in Rome, raised by levy throughout Italy. The winter has so far prevented action. Hirtius seems determined to leave nothing to chance, as he intimates in frequent letters to me. Except for Bononia, Regium Lepidi, and Parma, all Gaul is in our hands, enthusiastically loyal to the state. Even your clients[910] beyond the Po are marvellously attached to the cause. The Senate is thoroughly resolute, except for the Consulars, of whom only L. Caesar is staunch and straight. With Servius Sulpicius' death we have lost a tower of strength. The rest are without energy or without principle. Some are jealous of the credit of those whose statesmanship they see gaining approval. But the unanimity of the People of Rome and of all Italy is quite remarkable.

That is about all I wanted you to know. I pray now that from those lands of the sunrise the light of your valour may shine.

Goodbye.

910. Why the Transpadanes are called clients of Cassius is unknown. They were indebted to Caesar the Dictator for Roman citizenship.

366 (XII. 11)

CASSIUS TO CICERO

Tarichea, 7 March 43

From C. Cassius, Proconsul, to M. Cicero greetings.

I trust you are well, as I am, and my army.

Let me inform you that I am leaving for Syria to join Generals L. Murcus and Q. Crispus. These gallant and loyal gentlemen, having heard of events in Rome, have handed their armies over to me, and are themselves discharging their public duties jointly with me in the most resolute spirit. I beg further to inform you that the legion commanded by Q. Caecilius Bassus has joined me, and likewise that the four legions which A. Allienus[911] led from Egypt have been handed over to me by him.

Affairs thus standing, I do not suppose you need any encouragement to defend us in our absence and the state also, so far as in you lies. I want you to know that you and your friends and the Senate are not without powerful supports, so you can defend the state in the best of hope and courage. On other matters my friend L. Carteius will speak to you.

Goodbye.

Dispatched Nones of March from camp at Tarichea.

911. As Dolabella's Legate he was sent to Egypt to bring four legions stationed there to Syria.

367 (XII. 7)

CICERO TO CASSIUS

Rome, 7 March 43

From Cicero to Cassius greetings.

How zealously I have defended your position both in the Senate and before the People I prefer you to learn from your domestic correspondents than from myself. My motion[912] in the Senate would have gone through with ease but for Pansa's strong opposition. After delivering my speech, I was presented to a public meeting by Tribune M. Servilius. I said what I could about you loudly enough to be heard all over the Forum, amid unanimous shouts of approval from the crowd.[913] I have never seen anything like it. I hope you will forgive me for doing this against your mother-in-law's[914] wishes. She is a nervous lady, and was afraid that Pansa might take umbrage. In fact Pansa told a public meeting that your mother and brother too had been against my making my motion. But all this did not affect me; I had other considerations more at heart. I was for the state, as always, and for your dignity and glory.

I hope you will redeem the pledge I gave in the Senate, at some length of discourse, and at the public meeting. I promised, indeed almost guaranteed, that you had not waited and would not wait for our decrees, but would defend the commonwealth on your own initiative in your wonted fashion. Although no news has yet reached us of your whereabouts and the forces at

912. That Cassius should be put in charge of operations against Dolabella. For the wording see *Phil.* XI.29 f. Pansa put through a decree assigning the war to himself and Hirtius after D. Brutus had been relieved.

913. This speech has not survived.

914. M. Brutus' mother, Servilia.

your disposal, I am resolved that all resources and troops in that part of the world are yours, and am confident that you have already recovered the province of Asia for the commonwealth. You must now surpass yourself in adding to your glory.

Goodbye.

368 (X. 31)

POLLIO TO CICERO

Corduba, 16 March 43

C. Asinius Pollio to Cicero greetings.

You must not think it at all strange that I have written nothing on public affairs since war broke out. The pass of Castulo, which has always held up my couriers, has become more dangerous than ever with increasing banditry. Even so, that does not cause nearly so much delay as the pickets posted everywhere by both sides, which examine couriers and stop them proceeding. Had not letters got through by sea, I should be totally ignorant of affairs in Rome. But now that the opening of navigation gives me the chance, I shall write to you most eagerly and as often as I can.

There is no danger of my being influenced by the talk of an individual[915] whom nobody wants in his sight, but who even so is by no means as unpopular as he deserves to be. My own dislike of him is such that anything in common with him would be disagreeable to me. Furthermore, my nature and pursuits lead me to crave for peace and freedom. The outbreak of the former civil war cost me many a tear. But since I could not remain neutral because I had powerful enemies on both sides,

915. Almost certainly the Quaestor (strictly Proquaestor) L. Cornelius Balbus the Younger; cf. Letter 415 (X.32).

I avoided the camp where I well knew I should not be safe from my enemy's[916] plots. Finding myself forced whither I would not, and having no wish to trail in the rear, I certainly did not hang back from dangerous work. As for Caesar, I loved him in all duty and loyalty, because in his greatness he treated me, a recent acquaintance, as though I had been one of his oldest intimates. Where I was allowed to manage as I thought best, my actions were calculated to win cordial approval in the most respectable quarters. Where I obeyed orders, it was at a time and in a manner which made it clear that I had received them with reluctance. The ill-will thereby incurred, highly unjust as it was, was enough to teach me how pleasant a thing is freedom and how miserable life under despotic rule.

If, therefore, we have an attempt to place supreme power once again in the hands of one man, I profess myself his enemy, whoever he is. There is no danger on behalf of freedom from which I shrink or seek to be excused. But the Consuls had not instructed me how to act, either by senatorial decree or by letter. I have finally received one letter, from Pansa, on the Ides of March, in which he urges me to write to the Senate that I and the army under my command will be at their disposal ★★★.[917] That would have been very unhelpful, since Lepidus was declaring in public speeches and in letters to all and sundry that he saw eye to eye with Antony. Where would I get provisions if I led my legions through his province against his will? Or even if I had passed the earlier stages, could I fly across the Alps, which are held by his troops? Add the fact that it was quite impossible for a letter to get through. Couriers are searched at any number of points, and then are actually detained by Lepidus. One thing nobody will question, that before a public meeting in Corduba I declared that I would hand over my province to none but an emissary of the Senate. There is no

916. He cannot be identified.
917. Something like 'which he intimates I should have done at an earlier stage' seems to have dropped out of the text.

need for me to describe the struggle I have had about handing over the Thirtieth Legion.[918] Had I done so, nobody can be unaware how greatly my power to aid the national cause would have been enfeebled. For I assure you that the keenness and fighting spirit of that legion is quite outstanding. So you must think of me as one who is, first, most eager for peace (I am unashamedly anxious that none of our fellow-countrymen should perish) and, second, ready to defend my country's freedom and my own.

I am more gratified than you imagine by your taking my friend[919] into your circle. But I envy him his walks and jests with you. You will ask how highly I value that privilege: if we are ever allowed to live in peace, you will find out by experience. I shall not stir a yard from your side.

What does very much surprise me is that you have not written to me whether I shall help the commonwealth more by staying in my province or by leading my own army to Italy. As for myself, although it is safer and easier for me to stay here, I perceive that at a time like this legions are needed much more than provinces, especially as the latter can be recovered without trouble. So I have decided, as matters stand, to march.[920]

Further, you will learn everything from the letter I have sent to Pansa – I am sending you a copy.

16 March, from Corduba.

918. To Lepidus.

919. Probably the poet C. Cornelius Gallus; cf. end of Letter 415 (x. 32).

920. Yet earlier in his letter Pollio represented that it was quite impossible for him to get to Italy through Lepidus' province without Lepidus' consent; and there is nothing to suggest that this would now be forthcoming. Perhaps he was thinking of a sea route. The letter to Pansa may have made matters clear.

369 (x. 27)

CICERO TO LEPIDUS

Rome, 20 March 43

From Cicero to Lepidus greetings.

The great good-will I bear you makes me very anxious for you to enjoy the highest measure of public esteem. For that reason I was pained by your omission to thank the Senate after having been signally honoured by that body.[921] I am glad that you are desirous of restoring peace between your fellow-countrymen. If you draw a line between peace and slavery, you will do a service to the state and your own reputation. But if the peace you have in view is one which is going to put unbridled autocratic power back into the hands of a desperado, then you should understand that all sane men are of a mind to prefer death to slavery. You will therefore, in my opinion at least, be wiser not to involve yourself in a kind of peacemaking which is unacceptable to the Senate, the People, and every honest man.

However, you will be hearing all this from others, or will be informed by your correspondents. Your own good sense will tell you what is best to do.

921. On Cicero's motion at the beginning of the year the Senate had passed a vote of thanks to Lepidus for his successful conclusion of negotiations with Sex. Pompeius and decreed the erection of a gilded equestrian statue on the Rostra, an extraordinary distinction. On 20 March the Senate considered letters from Lepidus and Plancus advocating peace. Cicero dealt with the former in his Thirteenth Philippic.

370 (x. 6)

CICERO TO PLANCUS

Rome, 20 March 43

From Cicero to Plancus.

Our friend Furnius' account of your political disposition was most agreeable to the Senate and warmly approved by the Roman People. But your letter,[922] which was read out in the Senate, appeared by no means in accordance with Furnius' statement. You wrote as an advocate of peace, at a time when your distinguished colleague[923] is under siege by a band of the foulest brigands. Either they ought to lay down their arms and sue for peace, or, if they demand it fighting, then peace must be had by victory, not by negotiation. However, you will be able to learn from your excellent brother[924] and from C. Furnius how letters about peace have been received, whether yours or Lepidus'. You are well able to think for yourself; and the good-will and loyal good sense of your brother and Furnius will be at your call. None the less, my affection for you prompts me to wish that a word of advice, to which the many ties between us ought to lend some weight, should also reach you from myself.

So, believe me, Plancus, when I say that all the stages of advancement which you have hitherto attained – and most splendid they are – will count but as so many official titles, not as symbols of public esteem, unless you ally yourself with the freedom of the Roman People and the authority of the Senate. At long last pray dissociate yourself from those to whom no choice of yours but bonds forged by circumstances have attached you. In this period of political turmoil a number of

922. See previous note.
923. D. Brutus.
924. L. Plotius Plancus.

persons have been called Consuls, none of whom has been considered a Consular unless he displayed a patriotism worthy of the office. Such a patriot you should show yourself: firstly, in dissociating yourself from all connection with disloyal citizens, persons utterly unlike you; secondly, in offering yourself to the Senate and all honest men as adviser, principal, leader; lastly, in judging peace to consist, not in the mere laying down of weapons, but in the banishment of the fear of weapons and servitude. If such are your acts and sentiments, you will be not only a Consul and a Consular, but a great Consul and Consular. If otherwise, there will be no honour in these splendid official designations; rather they will carry the direst disgrace.

Prompted by good-will, I have written rather gravely. You will prove the truth of my words by experience, in that path of conduct which is worthy of you.

Dispatched 20 March.

371 (X. 8)

PLANCUS TO THE MAGISTRATES, SENATE, AND PEOPLE

Gaul, March (middle) 43

From Plancus, Imperator, Consul-Elect, to the Consuls, Praetors, Tribunes of the Plebs, Senate, and People and Plebs of Rome.

Before I make any promise to any man as to my duty in time to come, it will, I think, be proper to offer my excuses to those, if any there be, who feel that I have kept public expectancy and the hopes of the commonwealth concerning my political sentiments too long in suspense. For I do not wish to appear to have made amends for past shortcomings, but rather to be enunciating in the fulness of time thoughts long pondered in a loyal heart.

I was not unconscious that at such a time of grave public anxiety and national upheaval the profession of loyal sentiments is highly rewarding, and I saw that a number of persons had gained signal honours by this means. Fortune, however, had placed me in a dilemma. I had to choose whether to make promises without delay and thereby create obstacles to my own possibilities of usefulness, or, if I restrained myself in that particular, to gain larger opportunities for service. I preferred to smooth the path of national deliverance rather than that of my personal glory. A man enjoying a position such as mine, after a life such as I think I am generally known to have led, and with such a prospect as I now see before me, is not likely to submit to anything degrading or entertain a mischievous ambition. But a certain amount of time, a great deal of effort, and substantial expenditure of money were requisite, if I was in the end to make good my promises to the state and to all honest men, and to bring to the national cause, not empty hands and loyal sentiments, but the means to aid. I had to confirm the loyalty of the men under my command, who had been repeatedly tempted by lavish offers, inducing them to look to the state for a moderate recompense rather than to an individual for unlimited bounty. I had to confirm the loyalty of a number of communities which during the previous year had been obligated by means of gifts and grants of privileges, inducing them to regard those concessions as void and to make up their minds to seek the same from those better qualified to bestow them. I had to elicit the sentiments of my fellow-governors and commanders in adjoining provinces; for I wished to join with many partners in a league for the defence of freedom, not to share with a few[925] the fruits of a victory disastrous to the world. I had

925. Not the Antonians. Plancus assumes that the Republic will triumph anyhow, but the more of his fellow-commanders who join its cause the less costly the victory. He is thinking of Lepidus and Pollio.

also to strengthen my own position by increasing the size of my army and the numbers of its auxiliary forces, so that, when I came to make open declaration of my views, there might be no danger in the cause I intended to support becoming common knowledge, even though the announcement might be unwelcome in certain quarters.

So I shall never deny that, in order to bring those plans into effect, I made many reluctant pretences and distressful concealments; for I saw from my colleague's[926] predicament how dangerous it was for a loyal citizen to proclaim himself without preparing the ground. That is why the greater part of the communication which I entrusted to my Legate C. Furnius, a gallant and energetic officer, was by word of mouth rather than in writing, in order that it might reach you with less publicity and that I might run less risk. Therein I gave advice as to the measures requisite for the protection of the common safety and for my own equipment, from which it can be seen that the defence of the supreme interests of the state has for a long time past been my vigilant concern.

Now, by the grace of heaven, I am in every way better prepared; and I wish my countrymen not only to entertain good hope of me, but to make up their minds in full assurance. I have five legions under the standards; their own loyalty and valour closely attach them to the state, and my liberality has secured their obedience to myself. My province is in full readiness; all its constituent communities are of one mind, and there is the keenest rivalry in rendering services. I have cavalry and auxiliary forces in such strength as these peoples can muster for the defence of their lives and liberties. As for my personal resolution, I am prepared to defend my province, or to go wherever the public interest may summon, or to hand over my army, auxiliaries, and province, or to turn the whole brunt of the conflict upon myself, if only by such personal hazard I can assure my country's safety or hold back the danger that threatens her.

926. D. Brutus, under siege in Mutina.

It may be that I make these professions when the clouds have already dispersed and national tranquillity has been restored. In that case my credit will be the less, but I shall rejoice in the public good. If, however, I come to take my share in dire and quite undiminished dangers, I commend the defence of my conduct from the malice of jealous tongues to equitable judges. For myself, I can look forward to the preservation of the state as an ample enough return for my services. But I think I ought to ask you to regard as recommended to your favour those[927] who, in deference to me and (what counts for much more) in reliance upon your good faith, have resisted all blandishments and defied all threats.

372 (X. 7)

PLANCUS TO CICERO

Gaul, March (middle) 43

From Plancus to Cicero.

I should be writing at greater length about my plans and rendering you a more extended account of all particulars, thus enabling you better to judge how faithfully I have rendered to the state all that I took upon myself at your instigation and to which I am pledged by my solemn word to you given – I have always wanted your approval no less than your affection, and if in you I have secured a defender when at fault, I have also wished you to be the herald of my good works: but two things make me comparatively brief; first, I have dealt with everything in an official dispatch; second, I have told M. Varisidius, a Roman Knight and my close friend, to come over to you in person, so that you can learn it all from him.

927. His soldiers.

I have felt no small chagrin, I give you my word, when others appeared to be staking out claims to glory ahead of me. But I made myself wait until I should have brought the situation to the point when I could achieve something worthy of my Consulship and the expectations of my friends in Rome. That aim, if fortune does not disappoint me, I hope to accomplish, so that contemporaries shall recognize and posterity remember me as one who has rendered signal service to the state at need.

Let me ask of you to support my public standing and to render me more ardent in the further pursuit of glory by the enjoyment of those rewards which you set before my eyes when you called me to that endeavour. That your power is no less than your will I am well assured. Take care of your health and remember me as affectionately as I do you.

373 (XII. 25)

CICERO TO CORNIFICIUS

Rome, c. 20 March 43

From Cicero to Cornificius greetings.

I received your letter on Bacchus' Day. Cornificius[928] handed it to me three weeks after dispatch, so he told me. There was no meeting of the Senate that day or the next. On Minerva's Day I pleaded your cause at a well-attended session, not without the Goddess' good-will[929] – my statue of her as Guardian of Rome[930] had been blown down in a gale, and that very day the Senate passed a decree to set it up again. Pansa read your dispatch. The House highly approved of it, to my great delight

928. Perhaps son of Cicero's correspondent.
929. *non invita Minerva*; see Letter 64 (III.1).1.
930. Just before leaving Rome for exile in 58 Cicero dedicated a small statue of Minerva Guardian of the City (=Athene Polias) in the temple of Jupiter Capitolinus.

and the discomfiture of the Minotaur (Calvisius and Taurus).[931] A decree in honorific terms was voted concerning you. There was a demand that *they* should be censured as well, but Pansa took a more lenient view.

For my part, my dear Cornificius, the day I first embarked upon the hope of liberty, that 20th of December on which I laid the foundations of a free state while all the rest hung back, that very day I looked carefully ahead and took account of your personal standing – the Senate acceded to my proposal about the provincial governorships' remaining in their present hands. Ever since then I have delivered blow after blow at the position of the person[932] who is acting as governor *in absentia* – an insult to yourself and a defiance of the state. My frequent, I might say daily, denunciations were too much for him. Unwillingly he returned to Rome, and was evicted not merely from the prospect of the province but from the actuality, the possession, by my most just and proper invective.

I am indeed delighted that you have held your distinguished post so ably and have received the highest honours the province has to offer. As for your apologia about Sempronius,[933] I accept it. In those days of slavery we lived in a land of mist. I myself, the inspiration of your conduct and the well-wisher of your public career, was letting myself be carried off to Greece in a mood of anger against the times and despair of freedom, when the Etesian winds, like loyal citizens, refused to escort a deserter of the commonwealth and a contrary southerly gale brought me back to your fellow-tribesmen of Regium. From there I hastened back to my country as fast as sail and oar could take

931. On 28 November 44 Antony had put through a senatorial decree reassigning provincial commands, under which Africa was given to its former governor C. Calvisius Sabinus, a former officer of Caesar's with a distinguished career ahead of him as a partisan of Octavian. Taurus may be T. Statilius Taurus, later to command Octavian's land forces at Actium. The nature of his association with Calvisius is unknown.

932. Calvisius.

933. Cf. n. 896.

me, and the day after my arrival I was the one free man in an assembly of abject slaves. I delivered an attack[934] upon Antony which was more than he could stand. So he poured out all his drunken fury on my single person, at one time trying to provoke me into giving him a pretext for bloodshed, at another laying traps to catch me. I flung the belching, vomiting brute into Caesar Octavian's toils. This extraordinary youngster has raised a force to defend himself and us in the first place and the supreme interests of the state in the second. But for him Antony's return from Brundisium would have been the downfall of Rome. The sequel I think you know. But to return: I accept your explanation about Sempronius. In such confusion you could not have any definite code.

'Now this day brings new life, demands new modes,' as Terence has it.[935] So, my dear Quintus, come aboard with us and stand at the poop. All honest men are now in the same boat. I am trying to keep her on course, and I pray we have a fair voyage. But whatever winds may blow, my skill shall not be wanting. What more can virtue guarantee? Do you keep a brave spirit and a lofty one. Remember that all your personal consequence should be bound up with the common weal.

374 (XII. 28)

CICERO TO CORNIFICIUS

Rome, March (latter part) 43

From Cicero to Cornificius greetings.

I agree with you that the individuals who you say are threatening Lilybaeum[936] ought to have been brought to book

934. The First Philippic.
935. In *The Girl from Andros* (189).
936. Apparently certain Antonian partisans in Africa had been detected in a plot to descend on Sicily.

in Africa. But you were afraid, so you say, of seeming too little inhibited in punitive proceedings; which means that you were afraid of seeming too responsible a citizen, too brave, too worthy of yourself.

I am glad you are reviving for yourself that partnership with me in the preservation of the commonwealth which you have inherited from your father. It will always remain in being between us, my dear Cornificius. I am also glad you feel that expressions of thanks to me on your part are out of place – you and I do not have to do that between ourselves. The Senate would have been reminded more often of what is due to your position but for the fact that in the absence of the Consuls it is only convoked in emergencies. So nothing can be done through the Senate at present either about the HS2,000,000 or the HS700,000. I advise you to levy a tax on the basis of the Senate's decree, or to raise a loan.

I expect you are kept informed of what is going on politically by your correspondents, who should be sending you details of public proceedings. I am hopeful. I am not behindhand with advice, solicitude, and hard work. I declare myself a deadly foe to all enemies of the state. In my view the situation is not a difficult one as it stands; it would have been a very easy one, if certain parties had not been to blame.[937]

375 (X. 10)

CICERO TO PLANCUS

Rome, 30 March 43

From Cicero to Plancus.

Although sufficiently apprised of your political sentiments

937. Probably a reflection on the Consuls; cf. *Letters to Marcus Brutus* I (I or II.I)I.

and intentions by our friend Furnius, I have reached a clearer assessment of your whole attitude after reading your letter.[938] The Fortune of the commonwealth is deciding all points at issue in a single battle (when you read these lines I expect its outcome will have been determined). None the less the widespread report of your sentiments has in itself redounded greatly to your credit. Had we had a Consul in Rome, the Senate would have declared its appreciation of your efforts and preparations and conferred high honours upon yourself. But the time for that has not gone by; indeed, in my judgement it was not yet ripe. For I always consider an honour to be really and truly such when offered and given, not in the expectation of future benefit, but to persons whose great services have made them illustrious.

And so, provided always that some form of free society exists wherein honours can shine, all the highest, trust me, shall be yours in abundance. But an honour truly so called is not an allurement offered at a crisis, but the reward of constant merit. Therefore, my dear Plancus, strive heart and soul for glory, bring aid to your country, succour to your colleague, support to the marvellous union of all nations banded together in spirit. In me you will find one to help your counsels and further your advancement, an ever loyal and loving friend in all things. For to the bonds of affection, good offices, and old acquaintance which link us to one another the love of country has been added, to make your life more precious to me than my own.

30 March.

376 (XII. 6)

CICERO TO CASSIUS

Rome, March (end) or April (beginning) 43

From Cicero to Cassius greetings.

938. Lost.

You will be able to find out the state of affairs at the time this letter was dispatched from C. Tidius Strabo,[939] a good man and an excellent patriot – that he is most anxious to serve you I need hardly say, seeing that he has left home and career expressly in order to join you. I do not even recommend him to you. His own arrival will be recommendation enough.

Of one thing I hope you are thoroughly convinced, that honest men can look for refuge solely to yourself and Brutus, should any reverse unfortunately take place. As I write, the ultimate crisis is upon us. Brutus[940] is hard put to it to hold out any longer at Mutina. If he is saved, we have won. If not, which heaven forfend, there is only one road for us all – to you. Your courage and preparations must be on the scale needed for the recovery of the whole commonwealth.

Goodbye.

377 (X. 12)

CICERO TO PLANCUS

Rome, 11 April 43

From Cicero to Plancus.

I must heartily rejoice for our country's sake that you have brought such large resources to her defence and aid at an almost desperate hour. And yet, as truly as I hope to embrace you victorious in a restored commonwealth, a great part of my happiness is in your prestige, which I know is already of the highest and will so remain. I assure you that no dispatch ever read in the Senate was more favourably received than yours,[941] an effect due not only to the peculiar importance of your public services

939. Cf. n. 793.
940. D. Brutus, distinguished from M. Brutus (above) by the context.
941. Letter 371 (X.8).

but also to the impressiveness of the words and sentiments. It was all no novelty to me, who knew you and remembered the promises you made in your letters[942] to me and had been thoroughly apprised of your intentions by our friend Furnius; but the Senate felt that their expectations had been surpassed – not that they ever doubted your good-will, but they were not altogether clear as to how much you could do or how far you wished to go.

Accordingly, when M. Varisidius gave me your letter on the morning of 7 April and I read it, I was transported with delight; and as I was escorted from my house by a large throng of loyal patriots, I lost no time in making all of them sharers in my pleasure. Meanwhile our friend Munatius[943] called on me as usual, so I showed him your letter – he knew nothing about it beforehand, because Varisidius had come to me first, on your instructions as he said. A little later the same Munatius gave me the letter you had sent him together with your official dispatch for me to read. We decided to lay the dispatch immediately before Cornutus, the City Praetor, who in the absence of the Consuls is discharging consular functions according to traditional practice. The Senate was convoked at once and met in large numbers, attracted by the report of your dispatch and their eagerness to hear it. After the dispatch had been read out, a religious scruple arose: Cornutus was apprised by the Keepers of the Chickens of an inadvertence in his taking of the auspices, and their representations were confirmed by our College.[944] Business was therefore deferred till the following day, on which I had a great struggle with Servilius so that you should get your due. By personal influence he managed to get his motion taken first, but a large majority of the Senate left him and voted

942. Or 'letter'; perhaps the lost letter referred to in Letter 375 (X.10)1.

943. Who this T. Munatius (cf. end of letter) was and how related to Plancus is unknown.

944. The Augurs.

against it. My motion, which was taken second, was gaining widespread assent, when P. Titius at Servilius' request interposed his veto. The matter was adjourned to the day following. Servilius arrived ready for the fray, 'wrath with Jove himself',[945] in whose temple the meeting was taking place. How I tamed him and how vigorously I put down Titius with his veto I prefer you to learn from other correspondents. One thing, though, you may learn from me: the Senate could not have been more responsible, resolute, and disposed to hear your praises than it was on that occasion; and the community at large is no less well disposed towards you than the Senate. Marvellous indeed is the unanimity with which the entire Roman People, and every type and order therein, has rallied to the cause of freedom.

Continue then in your present course, and hand down your name to eternity. Despise all these prizes that have only the semblance of glory, deriving from meaningless badges of distinction; hold them for brief, unreal, perishable things. True dignity lies in virtue; and virtue is most conspicuously displayed in eminent services to the state. Such you have a splendid opportunity to render. You have grasped it; do not let it slip. Make your country's debt to you no less than yours to her. You shall find me prompt not only to support but to amplify your standing. That I consider I owe both to the commonwealth, which is dearer to me than my life, and to our friendship. Let me add that in my recent endeavours for your credit I have had great pleasure in perceiving more clearly what I already knew well – the sound sense and loyalty of T. Munatius, shown in his truly remarkable good-will and devotion to yourself.

11 April.

945. Proverbial for violent anger or truculence; cf. *Letters to Atticus* 165 (VIII.15)2.

378 (X. 30) [946]

GALBA TO CICERO

Camp at Mutina, 15 April 43

Galba to Cicero greetings.

On 14 April, that being the day Pansa was to have joined Hirtius' camp (I was with him, having gone 100 miles to meet him and expedite his arrival), Antony led out two legions, the Second and Thirty-Fifth, and two praetorian cohorts, one his own and the other Silanus', together with part of his reservists. In this strength he advanced to meet us, thinking that we had only four legions of recruits. But the previous night Hirtius had sent us the Martian Legion, which used to be under my command, and the two praetorian cohorts for our better security on the march to his camp.

When Antony's cavalry came into sight, there was no holding the Martian Legion and the praetorian cohorts. We started to follow them willy-nilly, since we had not been able to hold them back. Antony kept his forces at Forum Gallorum, wanting to conceal the fact that he had the legions; he only showed his cavalry and light-armed. When Pansa saw the legion advancing contrary to his intention, he ordered two legions of recruits to follow him. Having traversed a narrow route through marsh and woodland, we drew up a battle-line of twelve cohorts; the two legions had not yet come up. Suddenly Antony led his forces out of the village, drew them up and immediately engaged. Both sides at first fought as fiercely as men could fight. But the right wing, where I was

946. An account of the battle of Forum Gallorum. On 27 April Antony suffered a second defeat (in which, however, the Consul Hirtius was killed) and was forced to raise the siege of Mutina.

placed with eight cohorts of the Martian Legion, threw back Antony's Thirty-Fifth at the first charge, and advanced more than half a mile from its original position in the line. The cavalry then tried to surround our wing, so I started to retire, setting our light-armed against the Moorish horse to stop them attacking our men in the rear. Meanwhile I found myself in the thick of the Antonians, with Antony some distance behind me. All at once I rode at a gallop towards a legion of recruits which was on its way up from our camp, throwing my shield over my shoulders. The Antonians chased me, while our men were about to hurl their javelins. In this predicament some providence came to my rescue – I was quickly recognized by our men.

On the Aemilian Way itself, where Caesar's praetorian cohort was stationed, there was a long struggle. The left wing, which was weaker, consisting of two cohorts of the Martian Legion and one praetorian cohort, began to give ground, because they were being surrounded by cavalry, which is Antony's strongest arm. When all our ranks had withdrawn, I started to retreat to the camp, the last to do so. Having won the battle, as he considered, Antony thought he could take the camp, but when he arrived he lost a number of men there and achieved nothing.

Having heard what had happened, Hirtius with twenty veteran cohorts met Antony on his way back to his camp and completely destroyed or routed his forces, on the very ground of the previous engagement near Forum Gallorum. Antony withdrew with his horse to his camp at Mutina about 10 o'clock at night. Hirtius then returned to the camp from which Pansa[947] had marched out and where he had left two legions, which had been assaulted by Antony. So Antony has lost the greater part of his veteran troops; but this result was achieved at the cost of some losses in the praetorian cohorts and the Martian Legion.

947. Pansa had been taken to Bononia (Bologna), fatally wounded. Galba had evidently not heard of this.

Two eagles and sixty standards of Antony's have been brought in. It is a victory.

16 April, from camp.

379 (x. 9)

PLANCUS TO CICERO

Near Vienne in Gallia Narbonensis, c. 27 April 43

From Plancus to Cicero greetings.

I am happy to feel that the pledges I made to you were not hasty, and that those you gave to others concerning me have not proved idle. At any rate, the earlier I wished you to know my plans before anyone else the greater evidence you have of my affection.[948] I hope you observe how the tale of my services lengthens every day; that you will learn of them in the future I do not hope so much as guarantee.

As for myself, my dear Cicero (so may the state be relieved with my assistance from impending evils), I prize the honours and rewards which you and those with you have to bestow as gifts surely no less precious than immortality itself; at the same time my zeal and perseverance will be no whit relaxed without them. Only if amid the throng of good patriots *my* enthusiasm and exertions shine conspicuous do I wish my standing to be enhanced by your collective support. For myself I covet nothing – that[949] is exactly what I am fighting against. When and what are questions which I am well content to leave to your discretion. No gift that a man receives from his country can appear tardy or trivial.

948. Or (reading *quod* for *quo*) 'you have so much the greater evidence of my affection in that I wished . . .'

949. i.e. personal ambition like Antony's.

By dint of forced marches I have taken my army across the Rhône this 26th of April, and have sent a thousand horse ahead to Vienne by a shorter route. I myself shall not fail in the matter of speed, if I am not held up by Lepidus; but if he blocks my way, I shall act as circumstances suggest. The forces I am bringing are very strong in numbers, character, and loyalty. I ask you to remember me affectionately, if you know that I shall do the like for you.

Goodbye.

380 (XI. 9)

D. BRUTUS TO CICERO

Regium Lepidum, 29 April 43

From D. Brutus to M. Cicero greetings.

How serious a loss the state has sustained in Pansa you doubtless appreciate. It now behoves you to apply your authority and foresight to ensuring that the removal of the Consuls does not give rise to hopes of possible recovery among our enemies. For my part, I shall try to see that Antony is unable to maintain himself in Italy. I shall be after him immediately. I trust I can stop Ventidius[950] slipping away on the one hand, and Antony remaining in Italy on the other. Let me especially ask you to send word to that arrant weathercock Lepidus, so that he does not let Antony join him and perhaps make us fight the war all over again. As for Asinius Pollio, I expect you see well enough what he is likely to do.[951] The legions under Lepidus and Asinius are good and strong, and there are many of them.

950. He was bringing up three legions from Picenum in support of Antony whom he eventually joined at Vada Sabatia (cf. Letter 385 (XI.10)).

951. i.e. join Antony if he got the chance.

I do not write to you thus because I am not sure that these same points have occurred to yourself, but because I am firmly convinced that Lepidus will never behave well, in case you people in Rome feel any doubt about the matter. I also beg you to stiffen Plancus. After Antony's defeat I trust he will not fail the public cause. If Antony gets over the Alps, I have decided to station a force there and to inform you on all points.

29 April, from camp at Regium.

381 (XI. 13b)

D. BRUTUS TO CICERO

Parma, 30 April 43

From D. Brutus, Consul-Elect, to M. Cicero greetings.

The unfortunate people of Parma ★ ★ ★[952]

382 (X. 11)

PLANCUS TO CICERO

Country of the Allobroges, April (end) or May (beginning) 43

From Plancus to Cicero.

Thank you a thousand, thousand times.[953] As long as I live I shall thank you.– as for repaying you, I cannot promise. I feel incapable of matching such services as yours – unless, perchance,

952. The rest is lost. Parma, which must have passed into the hands of the republicans (cf. Letter 365 (XII.5)), had been captured and sacked by L. Antonius.
953. Plancus is answering Letter 377 (X. 12).

as you have so movingly and eloquently written, you will consider yourself repaid so long as I hold them in remembrance. If your own son's standing had been in question, assuredly you could have shown no warmer affection. Your earlier motions in the Senate heaping all imaginable favours on my head, those more recent adapted to the occasion and the wishes of my friends, your unremitting series of speeches concerning me, your altercations with detractors for my sake – how well I know it all! I must study, no light matter, to show myself a patriot worthy of your eulogies and a friend whose gratitude is undying. For the rest, act in the spirit of your bounty, and if in the actual event you find me the man you wished me to be, take me under your protection and patronage.

After taking my forces across the Rhône, I sent my brother ahead with 3,000 horse and myself advanced along the road to Mutina. While on the march, I heard the news of the battle and of Brutus' and Mutina's liberation from siege. It was apparent to me that Antony and the remnants accompanying him had no refuge except in these areas; also that he had two hopes before him, one in Lepidus himself, the other in Lepidus' army, since part of that army is no less rabid than the men who were with Antony. I recalled the cavalry and have myself halted in the Allobrogian country to be ready for anything as circumstances may suggest. If Antony comes here without a following, I believe I can easily cope with him by myself and handle the situation to your and your friends' satisfaction, even though Lepidus' army takes him in. On the other hand, if he brings some force with him and if the veteran Tenth Legion,[954] which I recalled to its duty along with the others, reverts to its former infatuation, I shall still do my best (and I hope with success) to see that no harm comes until forces are sent over from Italy. United we shall have less difficulty in crushing the desperados.

954. Despite Appian's statement (*Civil Wars*, III.83) that this famous legion was under Lepidus' command it seems to have been under Plancus. How otherwise could he have recalled it to its duty?

This I guarantee you, my dear Cicero, that neither courage nor pains shall be lacking on my part. I most earnestly hope that there is no further reason for anxiety. But if any there should be, my spirit, good-will, and endurance on your collective behalf shall be second to no man's. I am doing my best to urge Lepidus too to come into the fold, and am promising him all manner of compliance, if only he chooses to remember his patriotic duty. As coadjutors and intermediaries in this matter I am employing my brother, Laterensis, and our friend Furnius. No private quarrels shall prevent me from co-operating with my worst enemy for the safety of the commonwealth. If these efforts turn out fruitless, none the less I am in excellent heart and perhaps I shall content you all with greater glory to myself.[955]

Take care of your health and remember me kindly, as I do you.

383 (XII. 25a)

CICERO TO CORNIFICIUS

Rome, May (beginning) 43

From Cicero to Cornificius greetings.

You recommend to me P. Luccius, one of my own circle. I shall spare no pains to help him in any way I can.

We have lost our colleagues Hirtius and Pansa at a very unfortunate moment. In their Consulship they gave good service to the state, which is now rid of Antony's brigandage, but not yet completely out of the wood. If permitted, I shall fight the good fight as ever, though I am now very tired. But no weariness should stand in the way of duty and loyalty. Well, enough

955. If Lepidus took the wrong side after all, Plancus would not have to share the credit of victory.

of that. I would rather you heard about me from others than from myself.

Of you we hear what we should most have wished to hear. There are some sinister rumours abroad about Cn. Minucius, whom you praised to the skies in one of your letters. I should be glad if you would let me know the facts, and how things are going over there in general.

384 (X. 14)

CICERO TO PLANCUS

Rome, 5 May 43

From Cicero to Plancus greetings.

Most welcome the report that arrived two days before the victory about the aid you are bringing – your devotion, your speed, your forces! Even after the rout of the enemy all our hopes are pinned on you. The foremost rebel leaders are said to have escaped from the field of Mutina. Now to wipe out the last remnants of mischief is no less thankworthy an achievement than to drive off its beginnings.

For my part I am already awaiting a dispatch from you, as are many others. I hope that Lepidus too will pay heed to the national emergency and co-operate with you in the national interest. Therefore bend your energies, my dear Plancus, to the end that not a spark of this abominable war is left alive. If that is accomplished you will have conferred a superhuman benefit upon the state and will yourself reap immortal glory.

Dispatched 5 May.

385 (XI. 10)

D. BRUTUS TO CICERO

Dertona, 5 May 43

From D. Brutus to M. Cicero greetings.

I think the country owes me no more than I owe you. Be sure that I can be more grateful to you than those ill-natured folk are to me. But if you should think I am saying this for expediency's sake, then have it that I prefer your good opinion to that of the whole lot of them put together. For your judgement of me starts from a sure and true perception. *They* cannot judge so, because they are handicapped by vicious malice and jealousy. Let them interfere to block the conferment of honours upon me, so long as they do not interfere with my ability to do my job to the advantage of the country. Let me set out as briefly as I can the danger in which she stands.

To begin with, I do not have to tell you of the confusion into which the death of the Consuls has plunged affairs in Rome, or of the greedy spirit aroused by the official vacuum.[956] I think I have written enough – as much as can be committed to a letter. After all, I know to whom I am writing.

Now to come back to Antony. He fled with a petty little band of unarmed foot-soldiers, but by throwing open the slave-barracks and laying hands on every sort of manpower he seems to have made up a pretty sizable body. This has been joined by Ventidius' band, which after a very difficult march across the Apennines reached Vada and linked up with Antony there. There is a pretty considerable number of veterans and armed troops with Ventidius.

956. Octavian may already have given signs of his ambition to take one of the vacant Consulships.

Antony must choose between the following plans: (a) He may go to Lepidus if Lepidus is receiving him. (b) He may keep to the Apennines and Alps and use his cavalry, with which he is well provided, in raids to devastate the areas he invades. (c) He may come back to Etruria, because there is no army in that part of Italy. If Caesar had listened to me and crossed the Apennines, I should have put Antony in so tight a corner that he would have been finished by lack of supplies rather than cold steel. But there is no giving orders to Caesar, nor *by* Caesar to his army – both very bad things.

In this situation, as I have said above, if people want to interfere with what concerns me personally, let them. What alarms me is how this situation can be straightened out, or that, when you are in process of straightening it, others may tangle it up. I cannot any longer feed my men. When I put my hand to the work of liberation, I had a fortune of over HS40,000,000. Now my whole estate is encumbered; not only that, but I have involved all my friends in debt. I am maintaining seven legions, you may imagine with what difficulty. If I had Varro's treasure-vaults,[957] I could not stand against the expense.

As soon as I know for certain about Antony I shall send you word. Let me have your kind regard, provided you find a corresponding sentiment on my side.

5 May, from camp at Dertona.

957. Possibly with reference to a fragment of one of Varro's Menippean Satires (ed. Riese, p. 103): 'not by treasure-vaults (*thesauris*) nor by gold is the heart freed of bondage; not the mountains of Persia nor the halls of wealthy Crassus take care and superstition from men's minds'.

386 (XI. 11)

D. BRUTUS TO CICERO

Borders of the Statiellenses, 6 May 43

From D. Brutus, Imperator, Consul-Elect, to M. Cicero, greetings.

A duplicate of the letter which my boys brought from you has been delivered to me. I consider that I owe you a great debt, which it is difficult to pay in full.

I am writing to tell you what is going on here. Antony is on the march, he is going to Lepidus. He has not yet given up hope even of Plancus, as I have perceived from some papers of his which have come my way, in which he entered the names of his various emissaries to Asinius, Lepidus, and Plancus. However, I entertained no misgivings, and sent word to Plancus straight away. And in a couple of days I expect envoys from the Allobroges and the whole of Gaul. I shall send them back home in good heart.

Please look to future action in Rome, so that any necessary steps may be taken in accordance with your views and the public interest. You will counter the world's malice towards me if you can. If that is beyond your power, you will have the consolation of knowing that they cannot by any indignities turn me away from the position I have taken up.

6 May, from camp on the borders of the Statiellenses.

387 (XII. 12)

CASSIUS TO CICERO

Syria, 7 May 43

From Cassius, Proconsul, to his friend M. Cicero, greetings.

I trust you are well, as I am, and my army.

I have read your letter,[958] in which I find evidence once again of your singular regard for me. You would appear not only to wish me well, as you have always done both for my sake and the country's, but to have taken a grave responsibility upon yourself and to be very anxious on my account. Because I felt you were persuaded that I could not stand idly by while freedom was stifled, and because I felt that, suspecting me to be at work, you were anxious about my safety and the outcome of the enterprise, I wrote to you and sent a number of couriers to Rome as soon as I took over the legions which A. Allienus had led from Egypt. I also wrote a dispatch to the Senate, with orders that it should not be delivered until it had been read to you – if my people have seen fit to comply with my instructions. If the letters have not been delivered, I can only suppose that Dolabella, who has villainously put Trebonius to death and seized Asia, has caught my couriers and intercepted the letters.

All the armies that were in Syria are at my orders. I was held up for a short time pending discharge of promises given to the men. Now my hands are free. May I ask you to regard my public standing as entrusted to your care, if you recognize that I have declined no risk or labour for the country's sake? On your encouragement and advice I have taken up arms against a set of savage brigands, and have not only raised armies for the defence of commonwealth and liberty but wrested them from

958. Doubtless Letter 367 (XII.7).

the grip of cruel tyrants. Had Dolabella seized upon these troops before me, he would have strengthened Antony's hands, not only by the arrival of his army on the scene but by the report and expectation of it.

In view of these facts take the soldiers under your protection, if you perceive that they have deserved wonderfully well of the state, and see to it that no man of them regrets having chosen to follow the national cause rather than the hope of spoil and plunder. Likewise defend the standing of Generals Murcus and Crispus, so far as in you lies. As for Bassus, he was sorely reluctant to hand over his legion to me, and if the troops had not sent me their representatives against his will, he would have shut the gates and held Apamea[959] until it was taken by storm. I make these requests of you not only for the sake of the commonwealth, which has always been most dear to your heart, but also in the name of our friendship, which I am confident counts for a great deal with you. Believe me, this army under my command is devoted to the Senate and the loyalists, and most of all to you. By dint of constantly hearing about your friendly sentiments they have developed an extraordinary regard and affection for you. Once they realize that you have their interests at heart, they will feel unbounded gratitude as well.

P.S. I hear that Dolabella has entered Cilicia with his force. I shall set out for Cilicia. I shall try to let you know quickly how I get on. And I hope that luck will be on my side in so far as I deserve well of the commonwealth. Take care of yourself and your affection for me.

Nones of May, from camp.

959. On the Orontes, south of Antioch.

388 (XI. 13)

D. BRUTUS TO M. CICERO

Pollentia, c. 9 May 43

From D. Brutus, Imperator, Consul-Elect, to M. Cicero, greetings.

I have given up thanking you. There is no making adequate return in words to one whom I can scarcely repay in deeds. I want you to concentrate on the matters in hand – nothing will escape your perspicacity if you read my letter carefully.

The reasons why I was unable to pursue Antony at once, my dear sir, were these: I had no cavalry, no pack-animals; I did not know of Hirtius' death, but I did know of Aquila's; I did not trust Caesar until I had met and talked to him. So the first day passed. Early on the next I had a message from Pansa summoning me to Bononia. As I was on my way I received the report of his death. I hastened back to my own apology for an army, as I can truly call it; it is most sadly reduced, and in very bad shape through lack of all things needful. Antony got two days' start of me and made far longer marches as the pursued than I as the pursuer, for he went helter-skelter, while I moved in regular order. Wherever he went he opened up the slave-barracks and carried off the men, stopping nowhere until he reached Vada. I want you to know this place. It lies between the Apennines and the Alps, and its approach offers the greatest difficulties.

When I was thirty miles away from Antony and Ventidius had already joined up with him, a speech of his was brought to me in which he now asked his troops to follow him across the Alps and told them that he had an understanding with Lepidus. There was a shout (coming in volume from Ventidius' men, for Antony has precious few of his own) of 'death or victory in

Italy', and they started begging him to let them march on Pollentia. Unable to hold out against them, he fixed his march for the following day.

On receiving this report I immediately sent five cohorts in advance to Pollentia, and myself set out for the town. My detachment arrived there an hour ahead of Trebellius and a squadron of horse.[960] I felt no small satisfaction, for I think victory depends upon ★★★.

389 (X. 13)

CICERO TO PLANCUS

Rome, c. 11 May 43

From Cicero to Plancus.

As soon as the opportunity to enhance your standing came my way, I left nothing undone to your honour – no recompense of merit, no verbal accolade. That you will be able to see from the terms of the Senate's decree. They are exactly those of my motion, which I delivered from a script and which a well-attended House adopted with remarkable enthusiasm and unanimity. It was indeed clear to me from the letter you sent me that you find greater satisfaction in the judgement of honest men than in badges of glory. None the less, I felt it incumbent upon us to consider what was due to you from the state, even though you asked for nothing. It is for you to match the end with the beginning. The man who crushes Mark Antony will have won the war. It was Ulysses whom Homer called 'sacker of cities', not Ajax or Achilles.[961]

960. The evidence does not support the view that D. Brutus was deceived by a feint.

961. The passages in the *Iliad* in which Achilles is so called were held by Aristarchus to be spurious.

390 (X. 15)

PLANCUS TO CICERO

Camp on the Isara, 11(?) May 43

From Plancus to Cicero.

After writing the above,[962] I thought that in the public interest you should know the sequel. My assiduity has, I hope, borne fruit both for the state and for myself. Through intermediaries frequently passing to and fro I urged Lepidus to lay aside all quarrel, be reconciled with me, and collaborate in aiding the commonwealth. I exhorted him to think more of himself, his children, and his country than of one ruined, desperate bandit, and told him that if he did so my compliance in all things was entirely his to command.

My representations took effect. Lepidus gave me his word through Laterensis to make war on Antony, if he was unable to bar him from his province. He requested me to come and join forces, particularly as Antony is said to be strong in cavalry, while Lepidus has not even a second-class cavalry force. Even of the few he had, six hundred – the pick of them – had come over to me not long beforehand.

On receiving this intelligence I lost no time, reckoning that Lepidus should be assisted in the flowing tide of his good intentions. I saw the salutary effects to be expected from my arrival on the scene. I should be able to pursue Antony and crush his cavalry with mine, and at the same time the presence of my troops would serve to reform and coerce that portion of Lepidus' army which is tainted with disaffection. I therefore constructed in one day a bridge across the great river Isara on the border of the Allobrogian territory, and led my army

962. The letter to which this is a postscript seems to have been lost (it can hardly be 382 (X.11), written about thirteen days earlier).

across on 9 May. On 11 May, receiving a report that L. Antonius had been sent ahead with some cavalry and cohorts and had reached Forum Julii, I dispatched my brother with 4,000 horse to block him. I shall follow myself by forced marches with four legions without baggage and my remaining horse. Aided, even to a moderate degree, by the fortune of the commonwealth, we shall here find an end to the audacity of the desperados and our own anxiety. If, however, the bandit hears that I am on my way and beats a retreat back to Italy, it will be Brutus' duty to block him. I am sure that Brutus will lack neither skill nor courage. None the less, I shall in that event send my brother with the cavalry in pursuit and for the defence of Italy from devastation.

Take care of your health and remember me kindly, as I do you.

391 (X. 21)

PLANCUS TO CICERO

Camp on the Isara, 13(?) May 43

From Plancus to Cicero.

I should be ashamed to chop and change in my letters, were it not that these things depend on the fickleness of another person. I did everything in my power to combine with Lepidus for the defence of the commonwealth, so that I could oppose the desperados on terms which would leave you at home less cause for anxiety. I pledged myself to all he asked and made other promises voluntarily. The day before yesterday I wrote to you that I was confident of finding Lepidus amenable and of conducting the war in concert with him. I relied on letters in his handwriting and on the assurance given in person by Laterensis, who was with me at the time, begging me to make up my quarrel with Lepidus and to trust him. It is now no longer possible to augur well of him. But at least I have taken, and shall continue to take, good care that the supreme interests of the state are not betrayed by my credulity.

After constructing in one day a bridge over the river Isara, I led my army across in all haste, as the importance of the emergency demanded, since Lepidus himself had requested me in writing to make all speed to go to him – only to be met by his orderly with a letter enjoining me not to come. He wrote that he could settle the business himself, and asked me in the meanwhile to wait on the Isara. I will tell you the rash plan I formed. I decided to go none the less, supposing that Lepidus did not want to share the glory. I reckoned that without in any way detracting from this paltry personage's credit I could be at hand somewhere in the vicinity, so as to come rapidly to the rescue if anything untoward should occur.

That was how in my innocence I gauged the situation. But Laterensis, who is a man of complete integrity, now sends me a letter in his own hand utterly despairing of himself, the army, and Lepidus' good faith, and complaining that he has been left in the lurch. He warns me in plain terms to beware of treachery, says that he himself has kept faith, and urges me not to fail the commonwealth. I am sending a copy of his letter to Titius.[963] All the autograph originals (both those which I believed and those which I considered untrustworthy) I shall give to Cispius Laevus, who has been privy to all these transactions, for him to take to Rome.

There is a further item. When Lepidus was addressing his soldiers, who are disloyal by inclination and have been further corrupted by their officers such as Canidius, Rufrenus, and others whose names you will know when the time comes, these honest patriots roared out that they wanted peace, that they would fight nobody now that two excellent Consuls had

963. Probably Plancus' brother-in-law L. Titius, not the Tribune mentioned in Letter 377 (x.12).

CICERO'S LETTERS TO HIS FRIENDS

been killed and so many Romans lost to the fatherland, branded wholesale moreover as public enemies and their goods confiscated. Lepidus neither punished this outburst nor remedied the mischief.

For me to go this way and expose my thoroughly loyal army with its auxiliaries and the Gaulish chiefs and the whole province to two combined armies, would clearly be the height of folly and temerity. If I was overwhelmed and had sacrificed the state along with myself, I could expect no pity, much less honour, for such a death. Therefore I intend to go back, and shall not let these desperate men be presented with the possibility of such advantages.

I shall take care to keep my army in suitable locations, to protect my province even if Lepidus' army defects, and to preserve the whole position uncompromised until you send armies to my support and defend the commonwealth here as successfully as you have done in Italy. On behalf of you all I am ready, no man has ever been more so, either to fight it out if I get a fair opportunity, or to stand a siege if it prove necessary, or to die if chance so fall. Therefore I urge you, my dear Cicero, to do your utmost to get an army across the Alps here as soon as possible, and to make haste before the enemy's strength grows further and our men become unsettled. If speed is used in this operation, the state will remain in possession of its victory and the criminals will be destroyed.

Take care of your health and remember me kindly.

392 (X. 21a)

PLANCUS TO CICERO

Camp on the Isara, c. 15 May 43

Would you have me offer you apologies for my brother in a letter – the most gallant of gentlemen and the most forward in every patriotic endeavour? As a result of his exertions he has contracted a slight fever, continuous and pretty troublesome. As soon as he can manage it he will hasten back to Rome without question, so that the state may not lack his services wherever he may be.

Let me ask you to regard my public standing as entrusted to your care. There is no need for me to be covetous, for in you I have a most affectionate friend and (as I prayed you would be) a most influential one. The magnitude and timing of any benefaction you may wish me to owe you will be yours to determine. All I ask is that you take me as Hirtius' successor both in affection on your side and respect on mine.

393 (X. 19)

CICERO TO PLANCUS

Rome, mid May 43

From Cicero to Plancus.

I felt no need for words of thanks from you, knowing how grateful you are in truth and heart. But I must acknowledge that they gave me deep pleasure. I saw your affection for me plain as I see what is in front of my eyes. 'And before?' you may ask. Yes indeed, always, but never more clearly.

Your dispatch[964] made an extraordinarily favourable impression on the Senate, both from the great and momentous news it contained, magnificent evidence of your courage and judgement, and from the impressive quality of sentiments and style. Forward now, my dear Plancus, to finish the last remnants of the war! That will be a most grateful and glorious achievement. I am heart and soul devoted to the commonwealth; yet, truth to tell, I have grown weary in its preservation

964. Not preserved.

and my zeal for my country is not much greater than that which I feel for your glory. The Immortals have given you, as I trust, a golden opportunity to earn it. Grasp that opportunity, I beg of you. The man who crushes Antony will have finished this ghastly and perilous war.

394 (XI. 12)

CICERO TO D. BRUTUS

Rome, c. 13 May 43

From M. Cicero to D. Brutus, Imperator, Consul-Elect, greetings.

I have received three letters[965] from you on the same day: a short one, which you sent by Volumnius Flaccus, and two of more substance, one brought by T. Vibius' couriers, the other sent to me by Lupus.

From what you write and from what Graeceius says, the flames of war, so far from having been extinguished, seem to be blazing higher. Knowing your exceptional perspicacity, I do not doubt you realize that if Antony acquires a position of any strength all your splendid services to the state will be brought to nothing. According to reports reaching Rome and to the universal persuasion here Antony had fled in despair with a few unarmed and demoralized followers. If in fact his condition is such that, as I hear from Graeceius, a clash with him will be a dangerous matter, I do not regard him as having fled from Mutina but as having shifted the war to another theatre. Accordingly, the public mood has changed. There are even those who criticize you men in the field for having failed to pursue Antony. They think that with prompt action he might

965. Letters 380 (XI.9), 385 (XI.10), and 386 (XI.11).

have been overwhelmed. No doubt it is a characteristic of the masses, those of Rome in particular, to exercise their liberties upon the one person of all others through whose agency they have gained them. Even so, care must be taken not to give just grounds for complaint. The case stands thus: the man who crushes Antony will have finished the war. What this means I would rather leave you to consider than put it in plainer language myself.

395 (x. 18)

PLANCUS TO CICERO

Camp on the Isara, 18 May 43

From Plancus to Cicero.

What I had in mind when Laevus and Nerva took their leave you will have learned from the letter I gave them and from their own report – they have been privy to all my actions and plans. I find myself, as a man of honour anxious to do his duty to the state and all honest citizens is apt to find himself, following a dangerous course in earning approval rather than a safe one which might be censurable.

After the departure of my envoys I received two letters in quick succession, one from Lepidus urging me to go to him, the other in still more pressing terms from Laterensis, almost begging and imploring me. His one fear is exactly my own – the fickle and disloyal disposition of Lepidus' troops. I felt I must not hesitate to go to his assistance and face the common peril. No doubt I should be acting more cautiously if I waited on the Isara till Brutus brought his army across the Alps, and then advanced against the enemy with a like-minded colleague and a united and patriotic army (as my men are). But I can see that if Lepidus came to any harm in the right cause, all would be

CICERO'S LETTERS TO HIS FRIENDS

blamed on my obstinacy in not going to the relief of a friend to the public with whom I had a personal quarrel, or on my pusillanimity in deliberately withdrawing myself from the clash in so necessary a conflict.

Accordingly, I have chosen to take a chance, in the hope that my presence will bolster up Lepidus and improve the morale of his army, rather than to be considered over-cautious. I really believe no man was ever in greater anxiety through no fault of his own. If Lepidus' army were elsewhere, it would be plain sailing; but as matters stand, there is great cause for anxiety and great risk. If I had had the luck to meet Antony first, I give you my word he would not have lasted an hour – I have enough self-confidence and enough contempt for his battered forces and that muleteer[966] Ventidius' army to say so much. But I cannot help trembling at the thought of a wound beneath the skin which may do mischief before it can be diagnosed and treated. But if I stayed where I am, it is certain that Lepidus himself and the loyal section of his troops would be in deadly peril. The enemy ruffians too would have gained much in strength if they had drawn forces over from Lepidus. If my arrival dispels these threats, I shall thank my stars and my own resolution, which has spurred me on to this adventure.

Accordingly, this 18th of May I am striking camp on the Isara. I am, however, leaving the bridge which I constructed over the river and two forts at either bridgehead strongly garrisoned, so that when Brutus and his army arrive they will find free passage. I hope myself to effect a junction with Lepidus' forces within eight days of dispatching this letter.

966. Ventidius had at one time made money by contracting for the supply of mules and carts for provincial governors.

396 (X. 34)

LEPIDUS TO CICERO

Pons Argenteus, c. 19 May 43

Lepidus, twice Imperator, Pontifex Maximus, to M. Tullius Cicero, greetings.

I trust you are well, as I am, and my army.

On hearing that M. Antonius was on his way with his forces into my province and had sent L. Antonius ahead with part of his cavalry, I struck my camp at the confluence of the Rhône and the ⋆ and started to advance against them with my army. Marching every day, I reached Forum Voconium and took up a position against the Antonii east of the town on the River Argenteus. P. Ventidius joined him with his three legions, and pitched his camp to the east of me. Previously Antony had the Fifth Legion and a great number of men from his other legions, but these latter are unarmed. His cavalry is very strong; the whole of it withdrew without loss from the battle, amounting to more than 5,000 troopers. Numbers of foot and horse have deserted him to join me, and his forces are dwindling every day. Silanus and Culleo have left him. Although they had committed a grave offence against me in going to Antony against my will, yet for mercy and friendship's sake I have spared their lives; but I do not employ them or have them in camp, nor have I given them any charge.

As for this war, I shall not fail the Senate or the commonwealth. I shall keep you informed of my further activities.

397 (XI. 18)

CICERO TO D. BRUTUS

Rome, 19 May 43

From M. Cicero to D. Brutus, Imperator, Consul-Elect, greetings.

From the messages you sent to the Senate by Galba and Volumnius we suspect the nature of the dangers you envisage; but those messages seem apprehensive to a degree unworthy of your and the Roman People's victory. The Senate, my dear Brutus, is brave and has brave leaders; and so they are vexed to be set down by you, whom they judge the bravest man that ever was, as a body of nervous faint-hearts. And really, considering that when you were shut up in the town everybody placed the highest hopes upon your valour, though Antony was flourishing, who could be afraid of anything after his overthrow and your liberation? Nor are we afraid of Lepidus. After declaring his desire for peace when the war was at its height, could anyone suppose him mad enough to declare war on the state when peace, the peace we prayed for, reigned?

At the same time I don't doubt that you see further than we. All the same, this renewal of alarm, following so swiftly upon the thanksgivings which we offered upon your account at every temple, is causing great vexation. So for my part, my wish and hope is that Antony is really down and out. If, however, he manages to collect some sort of power, he shall find that the Senate does not lack for counsel, nor the People of Rome for valour, nor the commonwealth, while you live, for a general.

19 May.

398 (x. 17)

PLANCUS TO CICERO

En route *to Forum Voconii, c. 21 May 43*

From Plancus to Cicero.

On the Ides of May Antony arrived at Forum Julii with his advance guard. Ventidius is two days' march away from him. Lepidus is encamped at Forum Voconii, twenty-four miles from Forum Julii, and has decided to wait for me there, as he has written to me himself. If he and fortune leave me a clear field, I guarantee that I shall quickly finish the job to your collective satisfaction.

I have already told you that my brother has been seriously ill, worn out by the fatigue of continual hurrying to and fro. None the less, as soon as he was able to walk, he was ready to be foremost in every dangerous work, regarding his recovery as for the state's benefit as much as his own. However, I have urged, in fact compelled, him to leave for Rome, on the ground that in his present state of health he would be more likely to wear himself out than to help me in camp; and I thought that a man of his calibre would be needed as Praetor in city affairs, now that the state has been left denuded by the lamentable loss of the Consuls. If anyone at home disapproves of this, let him know that there has been a failure of judgement on my part, not any lack of patriotic loyalty on my brother's.

To resume, Lepidus has complied with my desire that he should send me Apella[967] as a hostage for his good faith and collaboration in the public service. In this connection, I have found L. Gellius, one of the three brothers from Segovia,[968]

967. Presumably a confidential freedman of Lepidus.

968. The reading is very doubtful. If 'Segovia' is wrong, this Gellius may be a son of Gellius Poplicola (see Glossary of Persons) who later served with Brutus and Cassius in the East.

very ready to help. He has been my latest go-between with Lepidus. I think I can say that he has proved himself a good patriot and I am glad to testify accordingly, as I shall readily do for all who deserve it.

Take care of your health and remember me kindly, as I do you. Stand up for me in public (if I deserve it), as you have done hitherto with such notable good-will.

399 (XI. 19)

D. BRUTUS TO CICERO

Vercellae, 21 May 43

From D. Brutus, Imperator, Consul-Elect, to M. Cicero greetings.

Will you be good enough to read beforehand the dispatch I am sending to the Senate and make any alterations you think proper? You will see for yourself that I had no choice but to write it. When I thought I should have the Fourth and Martian Legions with me, as proposed by Drusus and Paulus with the assent of yourself and the rest, I saw less reason for anxiety as to future operations. But now that I am left with a wretchedly appointed body of recruits, I must needs be gravely apprehensive on my own account and that of you all.

The Vicetini show myself and M. Brutus particular attention. May I beg of you not to let any injury come to them in the Senate for the sake of a pack of slaves?[969] They have an excellent case, and are eminently loyal to the commonwealth; and their opponents are a disorderly, thoroughly untrustworthy set.

21 May, from Vercellae.

969. Perhaps contemptuously for freedmen. But they may have been slaves belonging to the municipality, which denied the validity of their manumission.

400 (X. 34a)

LEPIDUS TO CICERO

Pons Argenteus, 22 May 43

M. Lepidus, twice Imperator, Pontifex Maximus, to M. Tullius Cicero greetings.

You and I have always vied in the eagerness of our mutual zeal to do one another service in virtue of the friendship between us, and both of us have been careful to maintain our practice accordingly. At the same time I have no doubt that in the present violent and unexpected political disturbance my detractors have brought you false and unworthy reports concerning me, calculated to give your patriotic heart no small disquiet. My agents have informed me that you have not allowed these rumours to upset you or thought it right to give them hasty credence. For that I am deeply and duly grateful. I also remember your earlier friendly efforts to promote and enhance my standing; they will ever remain firmly rooted in my mind.

I have one earnest request to make of you, my dear Cicero. If in time past my life and endeavour, my diligence and good faith in the conduct of public affairs, have to your knowledge been worthy of the name I bear, I beg you to expect equal or greater things in time to come, and to regard me as deserving the protection of your public influence in proportion as your kindness places me further and further in your debt.

Goodbye.

Dispatched 22 May from camp, Pons Argenteus.

401 (XI. 20)

D. BRUTUS TO CICERO

Eporedia, 24 May 43

From D. Brutus to M. Cicero greetings.

My affection for you and your services to me make me feel on your account what I do not feel on my own – fear. Here is something I have often been told and have not thought negligible – my latest informant is Segulius Labeo (he never acts out of character), who tells me that he has been with Caesar and that a good deal of talk about you took place. Caesar, he says, made no complaints about you to be sure, except for a remark which he attributed to you: 'the young man must get praises, honours, and – the push.'[970] He added that he had no intention of letting himself get the push. I believe that the remark was repeated to him (or invented) by Labeo, not produced by the young man. As for the veterans, Labeo would have me believe that they are grumbling viciously, and that you are in danger from them. He says they are particularly indignant that neither Caesar nor I have been put on the Commission of Ten,[971] and that everything has been placed in the hands of you gentlemen.

When I heard all this, though I was already on the march, I thought it would be wrong for me to cross the Alps yet, before I knew what was going on in Rome. As for the danger to yourself, believe me, they are hoping to gain larger gratuities by talking at large and threatening trouble – they mean to terrorize you and instigate the young man. This whole rigmarole has one origin – they want to make as much profit for themselves as

970. *laudandum, ornandum, tollendum.* The last verb seems to be used with a double meaning, 'exalt' and 'get rid of'.

971. Appointed by the Senate after the battle of Mutina to review Antony's 'acts' as Consul. Decimus seems to have thought that land and gratuities for the republican army were involved, but cf. Letter 411 (XI.21), last paragraph but one.

possible. At the same time I don't want you to be other than circumspect and wary of plots; I can have no greater source of pleasure, nothing more precious, than your life. Only you must be careful that fearing does not give you further cause for fear; and at the same time you should meet the veterans where you can. First, do what they want about the Commission of Ten. Second, with regard to gratuities, you should propose, if you think fit, that the lands of the veteran soldiers who were with Antony be assigned them by the two of us, and, as regards cash, say that the Senate will take time to decide in the light of the financial situation. It occurs to me that the four legions for whom the Senate has voted grants of land can be provided for out of the ★ lands and the Campanian land. I think the lands should be assigned to the legions in equal portions, or by lot.

It is not my perspicacity that impels me to write all this, but my affection for you and my desire for public tranquillity, which cannot subsist without you. Unless it is really necessary, I shall not leave Italy. I am arming and equipping my troops. I hope I shall have a not wholly contemptible army to meet all contingencies and attacks. Caesar is not sending me back the legion from Pansa's army.

Please answer this letter at once, and send one of your own people if there is anything especially confidential which you think I ought to know.

24 May, from Eporedia.

402 (XI. 23)

D. BRUTUS TO CICERO

Eporedia, 25 May 43

From D. Brutus to M. Cicero greetings.

We are in good shape here and shall try to be in better.

Lepidus' sentiments seem to me satisfactory. We must put all fear aside and take measures for the public interest without inhibition. But even if everything were against us, with three such large and powerful armies[972] dedicated to the public service you ought to keep your spirit high – high you have always kept it, and now with fortune's help you can raise it higher. As for what I wrote in my own hand in my earlier letter, people talk like this to scare you. Just take the bit between your teeth, and I'll be hanged if the whole pack of them will be able to stand against you when you open your mouth.[973]

As I wrote to you in my earlier letter, I shall stay in Italy till I hear from you.

25 May, from Eporedia.

403 (x. 25)

CICERO TO FURNIUS

Rome, May 43

From Cicero to Furnius greetings.

If, as is generally supposed, it is in the public interest for you to continue as you have begun, still taking an active part in the vitally important operations directed to stamping out the remnants of the war, I think that no course could be better or redound more to your credit and honour; and I consider that your activity, energy, and patriotic spirit should be of more account than a swift attainment of the Praetorship. For I would not have you unaware how much credit you have already won. Believe me, it is second only to Plancus', and that by Plancus' own testimony as well as by report and universal opinion. So if

972. Those of Decimus himself, Plancus, and Octavian.

973. For the singular infelicity of the metaphor Decimus is responsible.

you have any further work to do, I consider it most important that you should go ahead with it. Surely that is the most honourable course, and surely honour must come first. On the other hand, if you think you have done enough for duty and enough for your country, I advise you to lose no time in returning for the elections, since they will be held early; always provided that such haste in the furtherance of your career does not in any degree detract from the reputation we[974] have won. Many famous men, while engaged on public service, have not stood for office in the normal year.[975] That course is all the easier for us because this is not your appointed year in the way that, had you been Aedile, your time would have come two years later. As things stand, you will be looked upon as not letting slip any of the customary, quasi-legal period of candidacy.[976] It also occurs to me that your candidacy will have more *éclat* when Plancus is Consul (though you would have nothing to worry about even without him), if only matters in Gaul have been brought to a satisfactory conclusion.

To be sure, I do not think there is much need for me to write at length to a man of such sense and judgement as yourself. However, I would not have you ignorant of my opinion, the long and short of which is that I should like you in all things to make prestige rather than ambition for office your criterion, and to look for reward in lasting reputation rather than swift attainment of the Praetorship. I asked your very good friends

974. As often, Cicero politely affects to consider his correspondent's affairs as his own.

975. Literally 'the year of their candidature', i.e. in which they attained the qualifying age for this or that office. Since Furnius had been Tribune in 50 he will already have been past the normal minimum age for praetorian candidacy.

976. In common parlance (though not technically) candidacy began long before the official declaration (*professio*). If Furnius stood in 43 he would be a candidate in this customary sense for a much shorter time than was normal, whereas if he waited till the following year he would be regarded as giving himself the benefit of the full period.

my brother Quintus, Caecina, and Calvisius[977] to my house, and said the same to them in the presence of your freedman Dardanus. My words seemed to find favour with them all. But you will judge best.

404 (X. 16)

CICERO TO PLANCUS

Rome, c. 26 May 43

From Cicero to Plancus.

I know of nothing in history, my dear Plancus, more glorious than your dispatch.[978] No happening in my experience has ever been more welcome, more fortunate too in its moment. It was delivered to Cornutus during a well-attended meeting of the Senate, after he had read out a distinctly cold, shuffling communication from Lepidus. Yours was read immediately after, and to loud cheers. The facts themselves and your patriotic zeal and services gave the most lively satisfaction; and furthermore, words and sentiments alike were deeply impressive. The House began to importune Cornutus for an immediate debate on your dispatch. He said he wanted time to consider. There was a great outcry from the entire House, and finally five Tribunes put the question. Servilius, when called upon, proposed an adjournment. I put forward a motion which received unanimous assent. You will learn its terms from the Senate's decree.

You stand in no need of counsel, or rather you have it in abundance. Still, you should make up your mind not to refer any decision to Rome and not to consider yourself obliged to seek the Senate's advice in a situation so fraught with surprises

977. Surely to be distinguished from the obnoxious C. Calvisius Sabinus; cf. Letter 373 (XII.25).

978. Its contents will have corresponded to Letter 390 (X. 15).

and with so little margin for error. You must be your own
Senate, and follow wherever the national interest leads you.
Let us hear of some fine achievement on your part before we
think that it is coming. One thing I promise you: whatever you
do will meet with the Senate's approval as not only loyally, but
wisely done.

405 (XII. 14)

LENTULUS SPINTHER THE YOUNGER TO CICERO

Perge, 29 May 43

Lentulus to his friend Cicero cordial greetings.

After meeting our friend Brutus and perceiving that his
arrival in Asia was likely to be somewhat delayed, I returned to
the province to tie up the loose ends of my work[979] and dispatch
the money to Rome at the earliest possible moment. Meanwhile I learned that Dolabella's fleet was in Lycia together with
more than a hundred freighters in which his army might be
embarked. He was reported to have got them together in case
his hopes of Syria were disappointed, with a view to going
aboard and making for Italy, there to join forces with the
Antonii and the other bandits.

This news alarmed me so much that I dropped all else and
set out to meet them with a squadron of vessels inferior in
number and size. Had I not been obstructed by the Rhodians,
perhaps the whole business would be out of the way. Even as it
is, the back of it has been nearly broken. Their fleet scattered in
alarm at my coming, commanders and men took to flight, and
all the freighters without exception fell into our hands. I think
I can at least say that I have prevented Dolabella from getting

979. i.e. tax-collecting.

to Italy and reinforcing his associates, so as to make your task the harder – which was my principal fear.

The contempt which the Rhodians have displayed for me and for the state you will see from my official dispatch. Actually I wrote in terms much less emphatic than their infatuation, as I found it, really warranted. That I *did* write something about them you must not be surprised. Their folly is extraordinary. My private injuries have at no time influenced me, but their hostility to our welfare, their partiality to the other side, their obstinate contempt for our leading men, were more than I could tolerate. Not that I regard the whole community as hopelessly depraved. But by a strange fatality the same individuals who formerly refused to admit my father in his flight, and L. Lentulus, Pompey, and other exalted personages likewise, now again either hold magistracies themselves or have the magistrates under their thumb. Accordingly they are behaving with the same arrogant perversity. It is not only desirable in our national interest, it is necessary that their evil disposition should at last be checked and not allowed to flourish with impunity.

As for my own standing, I hope you will always make it your concern, and lend your support to anything tending to my credit whenever you find occasion, both in the Senate and in other contexts. Since Asia has been assigned by decree to the Consuls with licence to appoint a deputy to govern the province pending their arrival, I would ask you to request them to confer this distinction upon me rather than another, and to appoint me as their deputy to govern Asia until one or other of them arrives. They have no cause to hurry out here during their term of office or to send an army. Dolabella is in Syria, and, as you with your prophetic instinct foresaw and publicly foretold, Cassius will crush him while these gentlemen are still on their way. Antioch shut its gates against him and gave him a rough reception when he tried an assault; so, having no other town he could rely on, he betook himself to Laodicea on the Syrian coast. There I trust he will soon be brought to book. He has nowhere to retreat, and he cannot hold out for long against an army the size of Cassius'. Indeed I trust that Dolabella has already been finally crushed.

Thus I do not expect Pansa and Hirtius to leave Rome and hurry to their provinces during their Consulship, but rather to serve their term of office in Rome. And so, if you ask them to put me in charge of Asia in the meantime, I imagine you can gain your point. Furthermore, Pansa and Hirtius promised me in person and wrote to me after I left, and Pansa confirmed to our friend Verrius that he would see that I was not relieved during their Consulship. As for myself, I do assure you that I don't want my tenure extended because I covet provincial office; it has brought me abundance of work, risk, and financial loss. I *am* much concerned that I shall not have undergone all this for nothing, nor be compelled to leave before I have reaped the remaining harvest of my efforts. Had I been able to send the whole of the money I raised, I should be asking to be relieved. As it is, I want to collect and make good the sums I gave Cassius and lost by Trebonius' death, also by Dolabella's ruthlessness or the bad faith of those who broke their word to me and to the state. This cannot be done unless I have time. I hope you will gain it for me, with your usual solicitude.

I conceive my public deserts to be such that I may legitimately expect not only the favour of this assignment but as much as Cassius and the two Bruti, in virtue both of my association in the great deed and danger[980] and of my current zeal and activity. After all, I was the first to break Antony's enactments, the first to bring Dolabella's cavalry over to the national cause and hand them over to Cassius, the first to levy troops for the defence of the whole community against a criminal conspiracy. I alone brought Syria and the armies there to Cassius' side; for

980. Lentulus was one of several who, though not party to the plot against Caesar, joined the assassins immediately and claimed to have been of their number.

if I had not so promptly furnished Cassius with money and troops on so considerable a scale, he would not even have ventured to go to Syria, and Dolabella would now constitute no less serious a threat to the commonwealth than Antony. And I, who have done all this, was Dolabella's familiar friend and companion, closely related by blood to the Antonii, to whose favour moreover I owed my provincial post. But, 'loving my country more', I took the lead in declaring war on all those near to me. Although I do not observe that my conduct has so far brought me any very notable return, I do not give up hope, nor shall I grow tired of persevering in zeal for liberty and in toil and danger as well. At the same time, if I am challenged to further effort by some just and well-merited distinction through the good offices of the Senate and leading loyalists, I shall carry more weight with others and my power to serve the state will be all the greater.

I was unable to see your son when I visited Brutus, because he had already left for winter quarters with the cavalry. But upon my word I am delighted both for your sake and his, and not least for my own, that he should be so well thought of. As a son of yours, and worthy of you, he is like a brother to me.

Goodbye.

Dispatched 29 May, at Perge.

406 (XII. 15)

LENTULUS SPINTHER THE YOUNGER TO THE MAGISTRATES, SENATE, AND PEOPLE

Perge, 29 May and 2 June 43

From P. Lentulus, son of Publius, Proquaestor *pro praetore*, to the Consuls, Praetors, Tribunes of the Plebs, Senate, and People and Plebs of Rome greetings.

CICERO'S LETTERS TO HIS FRIENDS

I trust you and your children are well, as I am.

After Dolabella's criminal seizure of Asia I made my way to the adjacent province of Macedonia and the national forces under our illustrious fellow-citizen, M. Brutus. From there I worked for the restoration of your authority over the province of Asia and its revenues through the agency of those best able to achieve the same with speed. Dolabella took alarm at this prospect, and evacuated the province before troops could be brought against him, having laid it waste, seized the revenues, and ruthlessly stripped and sold the goods of all and sundry, especially Roman citizens. It appeared to me unnecessary to delay any longer or to wait for troops; and I considered it my duty to return to my post as soon as possible in order to levy the remaining taxes and collect the money I had deposited, also to discover as soon as possible how much of it had been carried off and by whose fault this had occurred, and to inform you of the whole transaction.

Meanwhile, as I was sailing through the islands to Asia, it was reported to me that Dolabella's fleet was in Lycia and that the Rhodians had a number of ships afloat equipped and ready. With a squadron consisting of the vessels which I had brought with me and those collected by Proquaestor Patiscus (an officer with whom I have close ties of political sentiment as well as of personal friendship) I changed course and made for Rhodes. In so doing I relied upon your authority and the Senate's decree pronouncing Dolabella a public enemy, as well as the treaty with Rhodes renewed in the Consulship of M. Marcellus and Servius Sulpicius, under which the people of that island bound themselves to regard as enemies the enemies of the Senate and People of Rome.

I was much deceived in my expectation. So far from our reinforcing our fleet with a Rhodian contingent, our troops were actually refused access to the town, the harbour, and the roadstead outside the town, as also supplies and even water. I myself gained admittance with difficulty, in one little boat on each

occasion. I put up with this unseemly treatment and the derogation to the majesty, not merely of my official prerogative,
but of the Empire and People of Rome, because an intercepted
letter had apprised me that, if Dolabella gave up hope of Syria
and Egypt (as he must), he was ready to embark with his entire
band of ruffians and all his money, and make for Italy; for
which purpose he had requisitioned freighters, none of less than
2,000 amphorae,[981] and kept them in Lycia under guard with
his fleet.

Alarmed at such a prospect, Fathers Conscript, I preferred to
swallow insults and try every means of prevention, even at the
cost of my dignity. I was accordingly admitted into their town
and Senate in the manner of their choice, and there I pleaded the
national cause to the best of my ability, and gave a full exposition of the impending danger, should that bandit embark
with all his following. But I found the Rhodians utterly wrongheaded, convinced that preponderance of force lay anywhere
but with the honest men, refusing to believe that the present
union and concert of all classes for the defence of freedom had
come about spontaneously, confident that the apathy of the
Senate and its supporters still continued and that nobody could
have dared to pronounce Dolabella a public enemy. In short,
they gave more credence to every rascally fabrication than to
the true facts as presented by myself.

This attitude had been in evidence even before my arrival.
After the shocking murder of Trebonius and all his other
heinous crimes a couple of Rhodian delegations set out to meet
Dolabella – contrary to precedent, moreover, and their own
laws, and against the orders of the magistrates then in office.
Whether their conduct is due to apprehensions for their possessions on the mainland, as they like to allege, or to mental
aberration, or to the domination of a clique who similarly
insulted exalted personages on a former occasion and hold the
principal offices just at this time, the fact is that, without

981. About 52.4 tons.

precedent and with no provocation on my part, they have refused the assistance they might easily have rendered in my own immediate danger and in that which hung over Italy and Rome, should the traitor and his rebel following have sailed for Italy after his expulsion from Asia and Syria.

In some quarters the magistrates themselves were suspected of having deliberately detained us so as to give time for news of our approach to reach Dolabella's fleet. Some subsequent events lent colour to this suspicion, especially the fact that Dolabella's Legates, Sex. Marius and C. Titius, suddenly left the fleet and took flight from Lycia in a warship, abandoning the freighters which they had collected at no small expense of time and trouble. Accordingly, when I arrived in Lycia from Rhodes with the squadron I already had, I took over the freighters and returned them to their owners. My principal fear, that Dolabella and his ruffians might get to Italy, was thus at an end. I pursued the fleet in its flight as far as Side, which district forms the border of my province.

There I learned that part of Dolabella's ships had fled in various directions and the remainder made for Syria and Cyprus. After their dispersal, knowing that a very large naval force under the orders of our distinguished fellow-citizen and general, C. Cassius, would be to hand in Syria, I returned to my post. I shall take good care that my zeal and diligence shall be forthcoming in your service, Fathers Conscript, and the state's, and shall collect as large a sum as I can with all possible speed, and forward it to you with complete accounts. As soon as I have made a rapid tour of the province and found out who has kept faith with me and the state in preserving intact the funds I deposited, as well as the villains who went to Dolabella with the public money in their hands as an offering with which to buy their way into a partnership of crime, I shall apprise you accordingly. If of your good pleasure you take drastic measures with the latter as they have deserved and strengthen my position by your authority, it will be easier for me to levy the taxes still due and to keep safe those levied already. In the meanwhile, I have raised a necessary guard on a voluntary basis, thus enabling myself to look after the revenues with less trouble and to defend the province from any harm.

After this dispatch was written, about thirty soldiers recruited by Dolabella in Asia arrived in Pamphylia in flight from Syria. They reported as follows: Dolabella went to Antioch in Syria. Refused admittance, he made several attempts to enter by force, but was repulsed every time with heavy casualties. After losing about 600 men and abandoning his disabled, he fled from Antioch at night in the direction of Laodicea. Almost all his Asiatic troops deserted that night. About 800 of them returned to Antioch and surrendered to the officers left by Cassius in charge of the city, while the rest crossed the Amanus into Cilicia (they themselves claimed to be part of this body). Cassius and his entire force were reported to be four days' march from Laodicea when Dolabella was moving towards the place.

In the light of this news I am confident that the nefarious bandit will be brought to book sooner than was anticipated.

2 June, at Perge.

407 (X. 20)

CICERO TO PLANCUS

Rome, 29 May 43

From Cicero to Plancus.

Reports coming in from Gaul are so uncertain that what to write to you I cannot tell. Sometimes we get satisfactory accounts of Lepidus, sometimes the reverse. As for yourself, rumour speaks with one tongue to the effect that you can be neither tricked nor overcome. Fortune has some part in the latter; for the former your own prudence is alone responsible.

However, I have received a letter from your colleague dispatched on the Ides of May in which he says you have written to him that Lepidus is not letting Antony in. I shall be better assured of that if you write the same to me. Perhaps you do not much care to do so because the optimism of your earlier letter[982] turned out to be unfounded. My dear Plancus, you could make a mistake like everybody else; but anyone can see that you are not to be tricked. But *now* there can be no excuse even for a mistake. There's a common proverb scolding people who trip twice over the same stone. If, however, the fact is as you have written to your colleague, then all our worries are over; but they will not be until you have told us that it is so.

My view is, as I have often told you, that the man who crushes its remnants will be the winner of the entire war. I pray you are that man, and believe you will be. That you appreciate my efforts on your behalf (which certainly could not have been greater) as highly as I expected you would does not in the least surprise me, but makes me very happy. If all goes well in your quarter, you will find them greater and more effective.

29 May.

408 (x. 35)

LEPIDUS TO THE MAGISTRATES, SENATE, AND PEOPLE

Pons Argenteus, 30 May 43

M. Lepidus, twice Imperator, Pontifex Maximus, to the Praetors, Tribunes of the Plebs, Senate, and People and Plebs of Rome greetings.

982. Letter 390 (x.15).

I trust you and your children are well, as I am and my army.

I call Gods and men to witness, Fathers Conscript, how my heart and mind have ever been disposed towards the commonwealth, how in my eyes nothing has taken precedence of the general welfare and freedom. Of this I should shortly have given you proof, had not fortune wrested my decision out of my hands. My entire army, faithful to its inveterate tendency to conserve Roman lives and the general peace, has mutinied; and, truth to tell, has compelled me to champion the preservation in life and estate of so vast a number of Roman citizens.

Herein, Fathers Conscript, I beg and implore you to put private quarrels aside and to consult the supreme interests of the state. Do not treat the compassion shown by myself and my army in a conflict between fellow-countrymen as a crime. If you take account of the welfare and dignity of all, you will better consult your own interests and those of the state.

Dispatched 30 May from Pons Argenteus.

409 (X. 33)

POLLIO TO CICERO

Corduba, early June 43

From Pollio to Cicero best greetings.

I trust you are well, as I am and my army.

News of the battles at Mutina reached me later than it should thanks to Lepidus, who held up my couriers for nine days. To be sure, it is desirable to hear of so grievous a public calamity as late as may be; that is to say, for those who can do nothing to help or remedy. I only wish you and your colleagues had ordered me back to Italy in the same decree in which you summoned Plancus and Lepidus. Surely the state would not then have suffered this blow. Some may be rejoicing at the moment, because the leaders and veterans of Caesar's party appear to have perished, but they must needs be sorry ere long, when they contemplate the desolation of Italy. For the flower of our soldiers, present and to come, has perished, if there is any truth in the reports.

I did not fail to realize how useful I could have been to the state if I had joined Lepidus. I should have dispelled all his hesitation, especially with Plancus to help me. But when he wrote me letters of the kind you will read, similar no doubt to the speeches which he is said to have delivered at Narbo, I had to stroke him the right way if I wanted to get provisions on my way through his province. I was also afraid that if the decisive battle took place before I had completed my intention, detractors of mine might put the opposite construction on my patriotic purpose, because of my former friendship with Antony – though no closer than Plancus had with him.

Accordingly, in April I dispatched two couriers in two ships from Gades with letters to yourself, to the Consuls, and to Octavian, asking to be informed how I could best help the commonwealth. But according to my reckoning the ship left Gades on the same day that Pansa joined battle; for before that day there had been no navigation since last winter. Far removed as I certainly was from any suspicion of a coming civil upheaval, I had stationed my legions in winter quarters in the interior of Lusitania. And both sides were in such a hurry to come to grips, one might think their worst fear was of a settlement to the war without maximum loss to the commonwealth. However, if haste was called for, Hirtius evidently showed the highest qualities of generalship throughout.

According to letters and reports coming in to me from Lepidus' part of Gaul, Pansa's army has been cut to pieces, Pansa is dead of his wounds, the Martian Legion has been destroyed in the same battle together with L. Fabatus, C. Peducaeus, and D. Carfulenus. In Hirtius' battle I hear that the Fourth Legion and all Antony's legions alike have suffered severely, as also Hirtius', and that the Fourth was cut to pieces by the Fifth after capturing Antony's camp; that Hirtius too lost his life there, and Pontius Aquila; and that Octavian also is said to have fallen. If these reports are true, which heaven forfend, I am sorry indeed. I further hear that Antony has ignominiously abandoned the siege of Mutina, but that he has 5,000 horse and three well-armed legions under the standards and one under P. Bagiennus, along with a considerable number of unarmed men; that Ventidius too has joined him with the Seventh, Eighth, and Ninth Legions; that, if he has nothing to hope for from Lepidus, he will go to all lengths and stir up the native tribes, even the slaves; that Parma has been sacked; and that L. Antonius has occupied the Alps.

If these reports are true, then none of us must lose time or wait for what the Senate decrees. The nature of the case compels all who wish the survival of the empire, or even the very name, of the Roman People to rush to quench the devouring flames. I hear that Brutus[983] has seventeen cohorts and two legions of recruits, not up to strength, which Antony had raised; though I make no doubt that all the survivors of Hirtius' army will flock to join him. I see little hope in a levy, especially as the most dangerous thing of all would be to give Antony time to recover. The season of the year, moreover, gives me greater freedom of action because the grain is now in the fields or on the farms. So I shall explain my plans in my next letter. I do not wish to fail the commonwealth, nor to survive it. But what irks me most is that the distance to my whereabouts is so long and the route so unsafe that all news reaches me forty days, if not more, after it has happened.

983. i.e. D. Brutus.

410 (XI. 26)

D. BRUTUS TO CICERO

Camp in the Alps, 3 June 43

From D. Brutus to M. Cicero greetings.

Greatly as I am distressed by what has happened, I take some comfort in the general realization that my fears of it were not idle. Let them deliberate whether to bring over the legions from Africa and Sardinia or not, whether to summon Brutus or not, whether to give me pay for my troops or decree it! I am sending a dispatch to the Senate. Believe me unless all these steps are taken as I say, we shall all find ourselves in great danger. I beg of you, let the Senate be careful in choosing the men for the job of conducting the legions to me. Both loyalty and speed are needful.

3 June, from camp.

411 (XI. 21)

CICERO TO D. BRUTUS

Rome, 4 June 43

From M. Cicero to D. Brutus, Imperator, Consul-Elect, greetings.

Confound that Segulius,[984] the most arrant scoundrel alive or dead or yet to be! Do you really suppose that he talks only to you or to Caesar? He has told the same tale to every person he could find to listen to him. But I am properly grateful to you,

984. Cf. Letter 401 (XI.20).

my dear Brutus, for wanting me to know of this piece of tittle-tattle, such as it is – a notable mark of your affection.

As for this same Segulius' story that the veterans are grumbling because you and Caesar are not on the Commission of Ten, I only wish *I* was not on it! A most tiresome business! However, I did move that a vote should be taken on generals in command of armies, but was met by an outcry from the usual quarters. So you two were actually excluded specifically, against my strong opposition. Let us then pay no attention to Segulius. He's out for news and a new deal – not that he squandered his share (which was nil) in the old deal, but he *has* wolfed down what he got out of this latest new one![985]

You say that you have some fears on my account, feeling for me what you do not feel for yourself. Excellent and dearest Brutus, I hereby absolve you of all fear concerning me. As regards foreseeable dangers, I shall not be caught napping; and as for those which will not admit of precaution, I am not worrying so very much about them. After all, I should be presumptuous if I claimed more than can be granted to humanity by the nature of things.

You advise me to have a care lest fearing give me further cause for fear, a wise and friendly precept. But as you are generally admitted to be an outstanding example of the courage that is never frightened or discomposed, I should like you to believe that I am not far your inferior in this quality. Therefore I fear nothing and shall beware of everything. But you must take care, my dear Brutus, that the fault be not yours in future, if I should have any fears. Even if I were a timid man, I should cast all fear aside when I thought of your resources and your Consulship, especially as everyone (and I myself above all) is persuaded that you have a singular regard for me.

I emphatically agree with your advice in what you write about the four legions and the assignment of lands by the two

985. i.e. Segulius, a poor man before the Civil War, had profited from the Caesarian victory, but squandered his gains.

of you. For that reason, when certain of my colleagues were nibbling at the agrarian business, I thwarted it and reserved the whole matter for your two selves.

If anything of a secret and, as you say, 'recondite' nature arises, I shall send you a letter by one of my own people for more trustworthy delivery.

4 June.

412 (XI. 24)

CICERO TO D. BRUTUS

Rome, 6 June 43

From M. Cicero to D. Brutus, Imperator, Consul-Elect, greetings.

Take note: I used to be a trifle irritated by the brevity of your letters. Now I look upon myself as a chatterbox, so I shall follow your example. How much you have said in a few words![986] – that you are in good shape and trying to be in better every day, that Lepidus' sentiments are satisfactory, that we ought to place unlimited confidence in the three armies. Even if I were a timid man, this epistle of yours would have swept all apprehensions out of my mind; but, as you advise, I have taken the bit between my teeth. After all, I placed my entire hopes in you when you were a prisoner, so you can imagine my feelings now. I long to hand over my patrol to you, dear sir, but only if I can do so while remaining true to my own resolution.

You say you will stay in Italy until you hear from me, if the enemy allows. You will not be doing wrong, for there is much afoot in Rome. But if the war can be finished by your advent, let nothing come before that. You have been decreed the funds

986. In Letter 402 (XI.23).

most immediately available. Servius[987] is devoted to you. I am not behindhand.

6 June.

413 (XI. 14)

CICERO TO D. BRUTUS

Rome, 7 June 43

From M. Cicero to D. Brutus, Consul-Elect, greetings.

I am wholeheartedly delighted, my dear Brutus, that you approve of my views and proposals on the Commission of Ten and the honours for the young man.[988] And yet, what is the use? Believe me, Brutus, as one not given to self-depreciation, I am a spent force. The Senate was my right arm, and it has lost its cunning. Your splendid break-out from Mutina and Antony's flight with his army cut to pieces had brought such high hopes of assured victory that there was a universal slackening of energy, and those vehement harangues of mine look like so much shadow-boxing.

However, to come back to the business in hand, those who know the Martian and Fourth Legions say that they cannot be brought to join you on any terms.[989] The money you require *can* be looked to, and will be. As regards sending for Brutus and keeping Caesar to protect Italy, I entirely agree with you. But, as you say, you have your detractors – I withstand them very easily, but still they hold things up. The legions from Africa are expected.

987. Ser. Sulpicius Rufus, son of the Consul of 51. He was D. Brutus' cousin.
988. Octavian. D. Brutus' letter to which Cicero refers is lost.
989. They put themselves under Octavian.

But there is general amazement at the revival of the war in the north. Nothing was ever so unexpected. When the victory was announced on your birthday,[990] we looked to the re-establishment of freedom for centuries to come. Now these new alarms undo all that was done. You wrote to me in the letter you dispatched on the Ides of May that you had recently heard from Plancus that Lepidus is not harbouring Antony.[991] If that is so, all will be easier; if otherwise, we have a big job on our hands, but I am not afraid of the outcome. That is your part. I can do no more than I have done. But I am anxious to see you the greatest and most famous of us all, as I expect I shall.

414 (X. 23)

PLANCUS TO CICERO

Culoro, 6 June 43

From Plancus to Cicero.

Never, my dear Cicero, shall I regret the grave risks I am taking for my country's sake, provided that I am free of the reproach of rashness if anything happens to me. I should confess to a mistake due to imprudence if I had ever in my heart trusted Lepidus. After all, credulity is an error rather than a sin, and one which slides into an honourable mind with peculiar ease. But it was not through any such tendency that I was almost hoodwinked, for I knew Lepidus only too well. The truth is that sensitivity to criticism, a most dangerous proclivity in military operations, impelled me to take this chance. I was afraid that, if I stayed where I was, some detractor might think I was too obstinately holding a grudge against Lepidus, and

990. The date is uncertain, perhaps 26 April.
991. Cf. Letter 407 (X.20).

even that my inertia was responsible for the enlargement of the conflict.

Accordingly, I led my forces almost within sight of Lepidus and Antony, and took up a position at a distance of forty miles from which I could either make a rapid approach or a successful retreat. Further, I chose a position with a river to my front which would take time to cross, hard by the Vocontii, through whose territory I could count on a free and trustworthy passage. Lepidus made strenuous efforts to lure me on, but finally giving up hope of success he joined forces with Antony on 29 May, and they advanced against me on the same day. This intelligence reached me when they were twenty miles away. I took good care, under providence, to retreat rapidly, but without letting my departure look in any way like a flight, so that not a soldier nor a trooper nor an item of baggage was lost or intercepted by those red-hot rebels. So on 4 June I recrossed the Isara with my entire force and broke the bridge which I had constructed, so as to give people time to readjust while I myself effect a junction with my colleague. I am expecting him three days after the dispatch of this letter.

I shall always acknowledge the good faith and conspicuously patriotic spirit of our friend Laterensis. But his over-tenderness towards Lepidus undeniably made him less alert to perceive the dangers in which we stood. When he saw that he had been the victim of a deception, he tried to turn against himself the weapon which he might with greater justice have used to destroy Lepidus, but he was interrupted in the act. He is still alive, and is said to be likely to live.[992] However, I have no certain information on the latter score.

The traitors are deeply chagrined at my escape from their clutches. They came at me with the same fury that stirred them against their country, angry besides on several recent counts arising from these transactions: namely, that I had continually taken Lepidus to task and urged him to stamp out the war, that

992. He died.

I censured the talks that were going on, that I refused to allow envoys sent to me under safe conduct from Lepidus into my sight, that I arrested C. Catius Vestinus, Military Tribune, carrying a letter to me from Antony, and treated him as an enemy. It gives me some satisfaction to think that at any rate their disappointment will annoy them in proportion to the viciousness with which they attacked me.

For your part, my dear Cicero, continue as hitherto to furnish us here in the front line with vigilant and energetic support. Let Caesar come with the very dependable force under his command, or, if he is personally prevented for some reason, let his army be sent. He is himself perilously[993] involved. All the elements that were ever likely to appear in the camp of the desperados to fight against their country have now joined forces. Why should we not use every means we possess to save Rome? As for me, if you at home do not fail me, I need hardly say that I shall do my patriotic duty to the very uttermost.

Of yourself, my dear Cicero, I do assure you I grow fonder daily; and every day your good offices sharpen my anxiety not to forfeit one jot of your affection or esteem. I pray that I may be able in person to add by my devoted services to the pleasure you take in your benefactions.

6 June, from Cularo, on the border of the Allobrogian territory.

415 (X. 32)

POLLIO TO CICERO

Corduba, 8 June 43

From C. Asinius Pollio to Cicero.

My Quaestor Balbus has taken himself off from Gades, and

993. This can hardly refer to plots by Antony against Octavian's life. Plancus is merely pointing out incidentally that Octavian had a personal interest in doing everything possible to achieve victory.

after three days' hold-up off Calpe due to weather has crossed over into King Bogud's territory[994] with his pockets very nicely lined – a large sum in cash, a mass of gold, and a bigger mass of silver, all collected from the public revenues – without even giving the troops their pay. With the rumours that are coming in, I don't yet know whether he will be returning to Gades or going to Rome – he changes his plans on every new report in the most contemptible fashion.

The following exploits, on the model of C. Caesar as he himself boasts, are in addition to his pilferings and robberies and floggings of provincials: At the games which he gave at Gades he presented a gold ring[995] to an actor, one Herennius Gallus, on the last day of the show, and led him to a seat in the fourteen rows (that being the number he had assigned to the Knights). He extended his own term of office on the Board of Four.[996] He held elections, that is to say he returned his own nominees, for two years in two days. He brought back exiles, not those of recent years but agitators responsible for the massacre or expulsion of the Senate during Sex. Varus' Proconsulate.[997]

For other proceedings he could not even quote Caesar's precedent. He put on a play at the show about the journey he made to persuade Proconsul L. Lentulus to change sides,[998] and what is more, burst into tears during the performance at the poignant memory of his adventures. At the gladiators a Pompeian soldier called Fadius, who had been forced to join the troop, twice fought to a finish without pay. Being unwilling to bind himself over as a gladiator, he besought the people to protect him. Balbus had his Gaulish horse charge the crowd (some stones had been flung at him when Fadius was

994. Mauretania.
995. The badge of a Knight.
996. The governing magistrates of the town.
997. In 56 or 55. Nothing is known of this incident.
998. Shortly before the battle of Pharsalia the younger Balbus secretly entered Pompey's camp and talked to Lentulus Crus.

being hauled off), and then carried the man off to the Gladiator School, where he had him buried in the ground and burned alive. While this was going on, Balbus walked up and down after lunch barefoot, his tunic loose and his hands behind his back. The poor fellow kept crying out pitifully that he was a Roman citizen born. 'Off you go then!' said Balbus. 'Appeal to the People!'[999] He even threw Roman citizens to the wild beasts, among them a certain pedlar who went round auction-sales, a very well-known character in Hispalis – because he had a deformity! Such is the monster I have had to deal with!

More of him, however, when we meet. What is of greater importance at the moment, you gentlemen must decide what you want me to do. I have three reliable legions. One of them, the Twenty-Eighth, was summoned by Antony at the start of the war with a promise that the day they arrived in his camp he would give them 500 denarii per man; further, that when he had won, they should have the same bounties as his own legions – and these, as anyone may guess, would be absolutely unbounded. The men were much excited, and I give you my word I had a hard job of it to hold them in check. I should not have succeeded, if I had kept them together – certain cohorts mutinied individually. He has been continually inciting the other legions too with letters and unlimited promises. Lepidus has been no less insistent, urging me by letters (his own and Antony's) to send him the Thirtieth.

You must then consider this army, which I have refused to sell for any rewards or to reduce out of fear of the dangers held over my head in the event of these people winning the war, as kept and preserved for the commonwealth. On the evidence of my obedience to the orders you have actually given you must believe that I should have obeyed any I had received. I have kept this province free of disturbance and the army under my control, I have not stirred outside my province borders,

999. A Roman citizen had the right of appeal to the People against a sentence of death or flogging.

have dispatched not a single legionary or even auxiliary to any destination, and have punished any troopers I found leaving. For all of which I shall feel sufficiently recompensed if the commonwealth is saved. But had the commonwealth and the majority of the Senate known me better, they would have gained more from me.

I am sending you for your perusal a letter I wrote to Balbus when he was still in the province. If you want to read the play too, ask my friend Cornelius Gallus for it.

8 June, from Corduba.

416 (XII. 8)

CICERO TO CASSIUS

Rome, c. 9 June 43

From Cicero to Cassius greetings.

I expect you have learned from the gazette, which I am sure is sent to you regularly, of the criminal behaviour of your relative Lepidus, his egregious faithlessness and fickleness. After the war had been finished, as we thought, we find ourselves waging it afresh, and pin all our hopes on D. Brutus and Plancus, or, if you will have the truth, on you and M. Brutus – not only for immediate refuge, should some reverse unfortunately occur, but for the assurance of freedom in perpetuity.

Satisfactory reports concerning Dolabella are reaching us here, but without reliable authority. You are in grand repute, let me tell you, both on present estimate and in expectation of things to come. Set that thought before you, and strive on to the heights! There is nothing that the People of Rome does not judge you capable of achieving and maintaining.

Goodbye.

417 (XII. 30)

CICERO TO CORNIFICIUS

Rome, c. 9 June 43

From Cicero to Cornificius greetings.

So! Nobody brings you a letter of mine except people with lawsuits! Such letters, to be sure, you get in plenty – it is your own doing that nobody thinks himself recommended to you without a letter from me. But has there been a single occasion when one of your people told me of a bearer and I did not write? Now that I cannot talk to you face to face, what could I like better than writing to you or reading your letters? My trouble is rather that I have such a press of matters to keep me occupied that I am given no chance of writing to you at will, or I should be bombarding you with letters, or rather with pamphlets. *You* should be the challenger, for, busy as you are, you have more time to call your own than I – or if you too have none, don't have the effrontery to nag me and dun me for letters when you write so few yourself. Even earlier on I was under very heavy pressure of work, because I felt it my duty to give my whole mind to the national struggle, but at the present time the pressure is far greater. We are like relapsed invalids, who get much worse after an apparent recovery. Our troubles weigh heavier now that we have to set about fighting a resurrected war after the old one had been all but finished and done with.

Well, so much for that. Now please assure yourself, my dear Cornificius, that I am not so poor-spirited, not to say unfeeling, as to be capable of letting you outmatch me either in friendly services or in affection. Of your affection I had no doubts before, but thanks to Chaerippus I know it far better than I did. What a good fellow he is! I always liked him, but now I find him absolutely charming. Upon my word, he made me see your every look to the life, let alone conveying your mind and words. So don't be in any apprehension as to my feeling irritated at your sending me the same letter you sent to others. True, I should have liked a special letter to myself individually, but it was not a very strong reaction and it was an affectionate one.

As regards the expenses to which you say you are being put, and have already been put, for military purposes, I am afraid I cannot help you. The Senate is bereaved, both Consuls lost; and the Treasury is in terribly low water. Efforts are being made to raise money from all sources in order to discharge promises given to the soldiers who have deserved so well. I don't think it can be done without a special levy.

With regard to Attius Dionysius, I imagine there is nothing in it since Tratorius said nothing to me about it. As for P. Luccius, I won't allow that you are any more anxious to help him than I am – he is a friend of mine. But when I pressed the receivers for a postponement, they explained to my satisfaction that the arbitration agreement and their oath would not allow them to do it. So I think Luccius had better come over. To be sure, if he has paid attention to my letter, he should be in Rome by the time you read this.

You write on other points, especially money, which you thought you might be able to obtain from Pansa (not knowing of his death) through my mediation. Had he lived, you would not have been disappointed, for he had a high regard for you. But now that he is dead, I do not see what can be done.

As regards Venuleius, Latinus, and Horatius,[1000] I emphatically approve of your decision. On one point I am not too happy – you say that to spare these people's feelings you have also withdrawn lictors from your own Legates. Persons deserving respect ought not to have been put on a par with

1000. Apparently three Legates left in the province by the previous governor Calvisius Sabinus.

those deserving the opposite. And I think that if the latter do not leave the province in accordance with the Senate's decree, they should be compelled to do so.

The above more or less answers the letter which I have received in two copies. As for all else, please rest assured that my own public standing is not more precious to me than yours.

418 (XI. 13a)

D. BRUTUS AND PLANCUS TO THE MAGISTRATES, SENATE, AND PEOPLE

Cularo, c. 10 June 43

★ ★ ★ had come to hope, thinking Plancus' four legions no match for their total force and not believing that an army could be brought over from Italy at such speed. But so far the Allobroges and our entire cavalry, which had been sent there in advance, are holding them presumptiously enough, and we are confident that they can be held more easily when we arrive. All the same, even if by some chance they cross the Isara, we shall take very good care that they do the state no damage.

We would have you be of good courage and in the highest hopes for the national cause, seeing as you do that we and our armies stand shoulder to shoulder, notably united and ready for any sacrifice on your behalf. Even so, you should by no means relax your efforts, and should take care that in military force and all other respects we are as well equipped as possible to join battle in your defence against a criminal combination of enemies, who have suddenly turned to threaten their country with the forces which they have for long been assembling under cover of the public interest.

419 (XII. 13)

CASSIUS PARMENSIS TO CICERO

Crommyacris, 13 June 43

C. Cassius, Quaestor, to M. Cicero greetings.

I trust you are well, as I am.

I am rejoicing not only at the national salvation and victory, but at the renewal of your glory. You have excelled yourself; Rome's greatest Consular has surpassed her greatest Consul. My joy and admiration know no bounds. Surely a mysterious blessing of providence rests upon your valour, as we have often found; your gown is more fortunate than the arms of any other man – in which garb you have once again snatched our almost vanquished country from the hands of her enemies and restored her to us. So now we shall live as free men. I shall now have your testimony – the word of the greatest of Romans and to me (as you came to know in our country's darkest hours) the dearest – your testimony to my affection for yourself and for the commonwealth, with which you are identified. There are words concerning me which you often promised not to say while our bondage continued, but to pronounce when they should be to my benefit. For my part, I do not so much desire to have them now spoken aloud as to know that you feel them in your heart. I would rather myself be recommended to your good opinion according to my just deserts than be recommended by you to the good opinion of the world. I want you to set down my latest actions as no sudden or incongruous departure, but as conformable to the ideas which you are witness that I entertained; and to think me deserving of advancement to a fine prospect of service to my country and a prospect not negligible of service to you.

You have children,[1001] dear sir, and blood-relations who do you credit and of whom you are deservedly very fond. Next to them in your affections should stand those who emulate your patriotic ideals. I wish you to have many such, and yet I do not think I am shut out by a vast crowd. You will, I trust, find time to take my outstretched hand and advance me to such stations as you may wish and think proper. My spirit you have perhaps seen reason to approve. As for my talents, however humble, it can at least be claimed that the long years of servitude let them seem less than they really were.

Having launched all available ships from the coast of the province of Asia and the islands, and held a levy of rowers fairly quickly despite the stubbornly uncooperative attitude of the communes, I went in pursuit of Dolabella's fleet, which was under the command of L. Figulus. While often holding out hopes that he might change sides, he kept drawing away all the time until he finally betook himself to Corycus, where he blocked the harbour and shut himself inside. I left them there, because I thought it better to join the land army, and because another fleet, raised in Bithynia last year by Tillius Cimber, was sailing up behind me under the command of Quaestor Turullius. I therefore made for Cyprus, and have thought proper to write to Rome as soon as possible with information of what I learned there.

Like our treacherous allies the people of Tarsus, the Laodiceans, who are far more wrongheaded than they, have called in Dolabella of their own motion. From these two communes he has raised the semblance of an army with a quantity of native troops. He is encamped in front of the city of Laodicea, and has demolished part of the wall, thus joining camp and town. Our friend Cassius has pitched camp with ten legions, twenty auxiliary cohorts, and 4,000 horse about twenty miles away at Paltus. He reckons to win a bloodless victory, for the price of grain with Dolabella has gone up to twelve drachmae. Unless

1001. In fact only one, but the plural is often so used.

227

he brings in a supply in Laodicean ships, he must starve to death before long; and Cassius' very sizable fleet, commanded by Sextilius Rufus, and the three others which I myself, Turullius, and Patiscus have brought to join him, will have no trouble in preventing Dolabella from importing. So you may be of good cheer, confident that, following your example in Italy, we for our part shall soon succeed in solving the commonwealth's problems.

Goodbye.

Dispatched Ides of June, from Crommyacris, Cyprus.

420 (XI. 25)

CICERO TO D. BRUTUS

Rome, 18 June 43

From M. Cicero to D. Brutus greetings.

I have been waiting to hear from you every day. All of a sudden our friend Lupus has given me notice to write to you if I have anything I want to say. In point of fact I haven't – I know that the news of the day is sent to you, and perceive that empty chat in correspondence is not to your liking – but I did not want to write nothing at all. But I study to be brief, as your pupil.

Let me tell you then that all hopes rest on you and your colleague. Of Brutus there is no certain news as yet. As you recommend, I am continually urging him in private letters to join the common fight. I only wish he were here now. I should then be less apprehensive about the internal mischief in Rome, which is no light matter. But what am I doing? I am not copying your laconism – here is the second little page on its way! Victory and goodbye!

18 June.

421 (XII. 9)

CICERO TO CASSIUS

Rome, June (middle or end) 43

From Cicero to Cassius greetings.

The brevity of your letters makes me too write more briefly; and, to tell the truth, nothing very much occurs to me to write about. I am sure our news reaches you in the gazette, and of yours I know nothing. It is as though Asia were sealed off. Nothing gets through to us except rumours that Dolabella has been crushed – consistent enough, but so far unvouched for.

As for us, just when we thought the war was finished, we have suddenly been plunged into grave anxiety by your connection Lepidus. You must therefore realize that the state's best hope lies in you and your men. True, we have strong armies, but though all goes well, as I trust it may, it is highly important that you should come. The hope for a free constitution is meagre (I do not like to say non-existent), but, such as it is, it is bound up with the year of your Consulship.

Goodbye.

422 (XI. 15)

CICERO TO D. BRUTUS

Rome, late June 43

From M. Cicero to D. Brutus, Consul-Elect, greetings.

Although your letters give me great pleasure, your asking your colleague Plancus to write to me and make your excuses in the midst of your heavy preoccupations gave me more. He did so faithfully. I am deeply touched by your attention and thoughtfulness. The full and friendly co-operation between you and your colleague, as declared in your joint dispatch, has been warmly welcomed by the Senate and People of Rome.

As for the future – carry on, my dear Brutus, and try now to excel, not others, but yourself. I ought not to write any more, especially to you from whom I plan to take lessons in brevity. I eagerly await a letter from you – one such as I most pray for. Goodbye.

423 (X. 22)

CICERO TO PLANCUS

Rome, late June 43

From Cicero to Plancus.

In you and your colleague lie all our hopes, with the favour of heaven. Your concert, declared to the Senate in your joint letters, has given the liveliest pleasure both to the Senate and the community at large.

As for what you wrote to me with reference to the agrarian matter,[1002] if the Senate had been consulted, it would have followed the proposer of the motion most complimentary to you – and no doubt he would have been none other than I myself. But the speeches dragged on and business was held up, so that the matters submitted to the House never came to an issue. Therefore your brother Plancus and I think it best to make do with the Senate's decree as it stands – who[1003] pre-

1002. The distribution of land to Plancus' troops. His letter on the subject has not survived.
1003. Perhaps Servilius Isauricus; cf. Letter 377 (X.12).

vented its being drafted as we desired, you will, I suppose, have learned from your brother's letter.

However, if you have any further desires in respect to the Senate's decree or any other matter, the attachment which all honest men feel for you is such (rest assured of it) that every conceivable distinction, of whatever type or eminence, is yours for the asking.

I eagerly await a letter from you – one such as I most pray for. Goodbye.

424 (x. 26)

CICERO TO FURNIUS

Rome, June (end) 43

M. Cicero to C. Furnius greetings.

When I read your letter in which you declared that the choice lay between giving up Narbonese Gaul and fighting a risky battle, I found the former alternative the more alarming. I am not sorry it has been avoided. You write of the good understanding between Plancus and Brutus; therein lies my greatest hope of victory. As for the loyal spirit of the Gauls, we shall know one day, as you say, who has done most to evoke it – but, take my word for it, we know already. And so the final passage in your most agreeable letter put me out of humour. You write that if the elections are put off till August, you will soon be here, and if they have already taken place, sooner still, since you have been a fool at the risk of your neck long enough.

Oh my dear Furnius, for one so adept in getting up other people's cases, how little you know of your own! Do you at this moment regard yourself as a candidate? Are you thinking of hurrying back for the elections, or staying in your own house if they have taken place already – so as not to be an idiot and risk your life into the bargain, as you put it? I do not believe that these are your true sentiments. I know all your impulses to glory. But if you really feel as you write, then I do not blame *you* so much as the opinion I formed of you. Will you allow precipitate impatience to gain an insignificant office (if you were to come by it in the ordinary way), vulgarized as it is,[1004] to draw you away from the shining honour with which all men are rightly and properly gilding your name? As though what signifies is whether you become Praetor this year or next, not that you should deserve so well of the state as to be judged most worthy of every distinction! Don't you know how high you have climbed or don't you think it of any consequence? If you don't know, I forgive you, the fault is ours. But if you do realize it, is any Praetorship sweeter to you than duty, the goal of the few, or glory, the goal of all mankind? I and Calvisius,[1005] a man of the soundest judgement with a great affection for you, scold you every day over this. However, since the elections are keeping you on tenterhooks, we are doing our utmost to stave them off till January, which we consider would be in the public interest for many reasons.

I wish you victory then, and goodbye.

425 (XII. 10)

CICERO TO CASSIUS

Rome, c. 1 July 43

From Cicero to Cassius greetings.

Lepidus, your relation[1006] and my friend, was declared a

1004. Caesar had increased the number of Praetors from eight to sixteen. The competition in 43 was keen, however (cf. Letter 435 (XI.17)).
1005. Cf. n. 977.
1006. The wives of Lepidus and Cassius were sisters, half-sisters to M. Brutus.

CICERO'S LETTERS TO HIS FRIENDS

public enemy by unanimous vote of the Senate on 30 June, as also those who defected from the commonwealth along with him. They have, however, been given until the Kalends of September to come to their senses. The Senate is in stout heart to be sure, but principally because they expect succour from you. At the time of writing we have a major war on our hands through Lepidus' criminality and fickleness.

Satisfactory reports come in every day about Dolabella, but still without known source or authority – just hearsay. Even so, your letter[1007] dispatched from camp on the Nones of May has produced a universal conviction in the community that he has already been crushed, and that you are on your way to Italy with your army, so that we shall rely upon your advice and prestige, if operations here have by then been satisfactorily concluded, or upon your army, if anything goes awry, as is apt to happen in war. As for that army, I shall give it every subvention I can. The time for that will arrive when it becomes clear to what extent this army will assist the national cause, or has already done so. Hitherto we hear only of enterprises – fine and splendid to be sure, but we are waiting for results; some I am confident have already materialized or soon will. Your vigour and generous courage are indeed admirable. We pray therefore to see you in Italy as soon as possible. We shall think we have a free constitution, if we have you two.

We had won a splendid victory, if Lepidus had not harboured Antony as he fled, stripped of his power and unarmed. Hence Lepidus is more hated in the community than ever Antony was; for whereas Antony stirred up war in a country that was already in turmoil, Lepidus has done so in time of peace and victory. Our Consuls-Elect stand against him, and we have great hopes of them, but suspense and anxiety too, since the results of a battle are never certain beforehand.

Believe then that all depends on you and your brother-in-law, that you are expected – Brutus indeed from day to day.

1007. Letter 387 (XII.12).

Even if, as I hope, you arrive after our enemies have been defeated, the commonwealth will rise again and settle down in some tolerable shape under your leadership. There are a great many evils that will call for remedy, even if the commonwealth shall come to seem pretty well emancipated from the villainies of its enemies.

Goodbye.

426 (X. 29)

CICERO TO APPIUS PULCHER MAJOR

Rome, 6 July 43

Cicero to Appius greetings.

Of my zeal for your welfare and restitution I believe your relatives' letters will have told you. I am sure that I have more than contented them; and signal as is their good-will towards you, I cannot admit that any one of them is more anxious for your welfare than I. *They* must grant that at the present time I have more power than themselves to serve you, as I have never ceased and shall continue to do, and have already done in a matter of the greatest consequence,[1008] thereby laying the foundations of your welfare. On your side, be of good cheer and courage, and be confident that you may count on me in all matters.

6 July.

1008. Just what this was cannot be determined.

427 (XI. 22)

CICERO TO D. BRUTUS

Rome, June or July 43

From M. Cicero to D. Brutus greetings.

I have the closest relations with Appius Claudius, son of Gaius, established by our many services to one another, rendered and received. May I particularly request you, whether for the sake of your own kindly nature or for my sake, to use your weighty public influence for his preservation? You are well known as a very brave man, and I want you to be considered a very merciful one. It will be a fine feather in your cap that a young man of the highest family should owe his civic existence to your kindness. His case ought to be improved by the fact that he joined Antony from a motive of filial affection on account of his father's restoration. So you will be able to put forward *some* excuse, even if you do not think it entirely convincing.

A nod from you can retain in the community a man of the highest birth, abilities, and character, one moreover with a strong sense of obligation and gratitude. Let me request you to do so in all possible earnestness and sincerity.

428 (X. 24)

PLANCUS TO CICERO

Camp in Gaul, 28 July 43

Plancus, Imperator, Consul-Elect, to Cicero greetings.

I cannot refrain from thanking you with respect to your

services in this matter or that, but I assure you I do so with a sense of shame. The intimate friendship which by your choice binds you and me does not seem to require expressions of gratitude. And it goes against the grain to acquit myself of your splendid benefactions with so cheap a commodity as words. I prefer to prove myself grateful in person by diligent and assiduous observance. If life is granted me, my devotion to you will transcend all gratitude of friends, all duteous observance of kin. For I should be hard put to it to say whether your affection and esteem will tend more to my lasting honour or to my pleasure from day to day.

You have been attending to my soldiers' interests. It was not for the sake of personal power (for I know that none but patriotic thoughts are in my mind) that I wished them to be provided for by the Senate, but, firstly, because I considered they deserved it; secondly, because I wished to strengthen their attachment to the commonwealth against all contingencies; and lastly, to enable me to guarantee you that their future behaviour will correspond to their past, proof against all solicitations from any quarter.

So far we have maintained the situation here entirely uncompromised. I trust that this course meets with approval from you and your fellows, although I know the general and understandable impatience for a victory so much to be prayed for. If these armies meet with a reverse, the state has no large reserves in readiness to withstand a sudden onslaught by those rebels and traitors. I think you know our forces. There are three veteran legions in my camp and one of recruits – a very fine one, the best of the lot.[1009] In Brutus' camp there is one veteran legion, one of two years' service, and eight of recruits. The combined army is therefore very strong numerically, but meagre from the standpoint of reliability. We have seen only too often how much reliance can be placed on raw troops in battle.

If the power of our armies were augmented by the veteran

1009. i.e. of the recently recruited legions.

African army or by Caesar's army, we should have no misgivings in staking the fate of the commonwealth on a decision.
And we observe that in Caesar's case the distance is considerably
less. I have continually urged him by letter, and he has never
stopped affirming that he is coming without delay; but in the
meanwhile I perceive that his mind has been diverted from that
intention and shifted to other projects. However, I have sent
our friend Furnius to him with a letter and an oral message in
the hope that he may possibly be able to achieve something.

You are well aware, my dear Cicero, that so far as affection
for Caesar is concerned you and I are partners. Even during the
late Caesar's lifetime, as an intimate of his, I was bound to have
a care and regard for the young man. So far as I could tell, his
disposition was eminently moderate and gentle. By Caesar's
decision and that of you all he has been given the place of
Caesar's son, and I think it would be to my discredit, considering the conspicuously friendly relations between Caesar and
myself, if I did not look upon him as such. At the same time (and
whatever I write to you, believe me, is written more in sorrow
than in any spirit of ill-will), the fact that Antony is alive today,
that Lepidus is with him, that they have armies by no means
contemptible, that their hopes and audacity run high – for all
this they can thank Caesar. I will go no further back than the
time when he himself professed to me to be coming: if he *had*
chosen to come, the war would by now have been either
quashed altogether or thrust back into Spain (a province
thoroughly unfriendly to them) with heavy loss on their side.
What he can be thinking of or whose advice has turned him
away from so glorious a course, so necessary moreover and
salutary to himself, and diverted him to this notion of a six-
months' Consulship, which to the general consternation he is
pushing with such tasteless persistence, is more than I can
fathom. I imagine his connections can do a good deal in this
matter, for the commonwealth's sake and his own; but you
too, I think, can do most of all, since you have done more for

him than for anyone in the world except myself – for I shall never forget the magnitude and number of my obligations to you. I have charged Furnius to go into these matters with him. If he pays as much attention to me as he ought, I shall have done *him* a great service.

Meanwhile we are bearing the brunt of the war in a situation of considerable difficulty. We do not see our way quite clear to a decisive engagement, and on the other hand we have no intention of risking further damage to the national cause by taking to our heels. If Caesar considers his own best interests, or if the African legions come up quickly, we shall free you from anxiety on this side.

Please maintain your regard for me, and be sure that I am thoroughly yours.

28 July, from camp.

429 (XII. 21)

CICERO TO CORNIFICIUS

Rome(?), 44–43

From Cicero to Cornificius.

My friend C. Anicius, a man of quality in every sense of the word, has been appointed to a Free Commissionership to Africa for purposes of private business. I shall be grateful if you will give him every assistance, and do all you can to facilitate the smooth transaction of his affairs. In particular (something he has very much at heart) I would ask you to look after his personal dignity, and to do for him what I myself used to do for all Senators in my province without being asked – I granted them lictors, having received the same privilege myself and knowing it had been commonly done by persons of the highest eminence. So please do this as a friend, my dear Cornificius, and have regard for his prestige and material interests in all other respects. I shall take it very kindly.

Take care of your health.

430 (XII. 24.3)

CICERO TO CORNIFICIUS

44 or 43

I should like to recommend to you in the strongest possible way a very good friend of mine, T. Pinarius. I have a very warm regard for him, both for his generally admirable character and because of the pursuits we have in common. He is acting as accountant and general agent for our friend Dionysius,[1010] for whom you have a considerable, and I a very special, affection. I ought not to recommend his affairs to *you*, but I do. So please see that Pinarius' letters (he is a very grateful sort of person) give me evidence of your interest both in him and in Dionysius.

431 (XII. 26)

CICERO TO CORNIFICIUS

Rome, spring of 43

From Cicero to Cornificius greetings.

Q. Turius, an honest and respectable gentleman who had business affairs in Africa, left as his heirs Cn. Saturninus, Sex. Aufidius, C. Anneus, Q. Considius Gallus, L. Servilius Pos-

1010. Cf. Letter 417 (XII.30).

tumus, and C. Rubellinus – men of his own stamp. From what they tell me I gather that an expression of thanks would be more to their purpose than a recommendation. They are so loud in praise of the handsome way you have treated them as to make it evident to me that you have done more for them than I should dare to ask. Dare, however, I shall, knowing how much weight my recommendation will carry. Let me therefore request of you that your generosity, shown in ample measure without any letter of mine, may be increased as substantially as possible by what I now write. The main point of my recommendation is that you should not allow Q. Turius' freedman, Turius Eros, to appropriate the estate, as he has done hitherto, and that in all other respects you regard the heirs as specially recommended by me. You may expect much gratification from the attentions of such distinguished persons. Let me again ask you very particularly to be good enough to act accordingly.

432 (XII. 27)

CICERO TO CORNIFICIUS

Rome, spring of 43

From Cicero to Cornificius greetings.

Sex. Aufidius is most attentive to me – my nearest intimates hardly more so – and there is no more distinguished member of the equestrian order. His personality is a singularly judicious blend of moral strictness and unselfish courtesy. Let me recommend to you his affairs in Africa in all earnestness and sincerity. I shall be deeply obliged if you make it apparent to him that my letter has carried great weight with you. My dear Cornificius, I ask this as a particular favour.

433 (XII. 29)

CICERO TO CORNIFICIUS

Rome, spring(?) of 43

From Cicero to Cornificius greetings.

To say nothing of yourself, who are thoroughly familiar with all that concerns me, I suppose there is no man in all Rome who is ignorant of my friendship with L. Lamia. It came before the public eye on a grand stage when he was banished from Rome by Consul A. Gabinius for his free and intrepid defence of my status as a citizen. That was not the origin of our affection; on the contrary, he was ready to face any risk on my behalf just because of its strength and long standing. Besides these acts of friendship, or rather these benefactions, a most agreeable intimacy exists between us, and Lamia's society really gives me as much pleasure as that of anyone in the world.

After all this you will not be waiting to see what terms I use in recommending him. Where such affection exists, you know what terms are appropriate, and you are to suppose that I have used them all. I would only ask you to believe that if you protect Lamia's interests and assist his agents, freedmen, and household as occasion may require, I shall be more beholden to you than if your generosity had to do with my own finances. Knowing what a good judge of men you are, I do not doubt that you would do your utmost for Lamia's own sake without any recommendation from me. To be sure, I have been told that you are under the impression that Lamia witnessed the drafting of a certain decree derogatory to yourself. In fact, he never on any occasion witnessed a drafting that year;[1011] further-

1011. Literally 'when they (i.e. Antony and Dolabella) were Consuls', i.e. from 15 March 44 to the end of the year.

more, all manner of forged decrees were registered at that time. You might as well suppose that I was present at the drafting of that decree about Sempronius,[1012] whereas in fact I was not even in Rome, as I wrote to you at the time just after the event.

But enough of that. Let me ask you again, my dear Cornificius, to look upon all Lamia's affairs as though they were mine, and to make sure that he realizes that this recommendation has been of the greatest service to him. You can do nothing to oblige me more.

Take care of your health.

434 (XI. 16)

CICERO TO D. BRUTUS

Rome, May or June 43

From M. Cicero to D. Brutus, Consul-Elect, greetings.

A great deal depends on *when* this letter is delivered to you – whether at a time when you have something on your mind or when you are quite free from anxiety. I have accordingly instructed the bearer to watch for the right moment to hand you his charge, for a letter delivered unseasonably often annoys us like an inopportune visitor. But if, as I hope, you have nothing to worry and distract you and my messenger chooses a sufficiently tactful and convenient time to make his approach, I am confident that the request I have to put to you will be readily granted.

L. Lamia is standing for the Praetorship. He is the most familiar friend I have. Our intimacy goes back a long way, and we have had a great deal to do with one another; but what counts most is that his friendship gives me as much pleasure as

1012. Cf. n. 896.

anything in life. Furthermore, I am indebted to him for a great kindness and service. In Clodius' time, when he was a leading member of the Order of Knights and took a most active part in the campaign for my restoration, he was banished from town by Consul Gabinius, something that had never previously happened to a Roman citizen in Rome. The people of Rome remembers this; for *me* not to remember it would be shameful indeed.

Therefore, my dear Brutus, I want you to believe that *I* am standing for the Praetorship. To be sure, Lamia is a most distinguished and influential figure, with a splendid aedilician show to his credit. But I have taken the whole business upon myself, as though none of that were in the case. Now you control the Centuries of Knights[1013] and reign supreme in them. If you think as much of me as I know you do, send to our friend Lupus and tell him to make certain of these Centuries for us. I shall not keep you with further words. Let me just put down in conclusion what I feel. Though I expect of you any and every service, there is nothing, dear sir, that you could do to please me more.

435 (XI. 17)

CICERO TO M. BRUTUS

Rome, May or June 43

From M. Cicero to M. Brutus[1014] greetings.

L. Lamia is my most intimate friend. He has rendered me

1013. i.e. 'Knights with public horse', consisting of young aristocrats and distinguished members of the *ordo equester*.

1014. The manuscripts say 'Decimus Brutus'; but this and the preceding letter could not have been written to the same person.

great services, I will not say as a friend but as a benefactor, and they are very well known to the People of Rome. Having fulfilled his duty as Aedile with a splendid show, he is standing for the Praetorship, and everyone is aware that he lacks neither public respect nor popularity. But the competition for the office seems to be becoming so unbridled that I fear anything may happen and feel I must take the whole business of Lamia's candidature upon myself.

How substantially you can help me in this matter I can easily perceive, nor do I doubt your good-will towards me. Please believe then, my dear Brutus, that I have nothing to ask of you with greater urgency, and that you can do nothing to please me more than if you assist Lamia in his candidature with all your power and zeal. And I earnestly request you so to do.

INTRODUCTION TO CICERO'S LETTERS TO HIS BROTHER QUINTUS

Marcus Cicero's only brother, Quintus, was about two years his junior. They grew up together, and when Marcus went on his eastern travels in 79 Quintus accompanied him. Some ten years later he married the sister of Marcus' closest friend, T. Pomponius Atticus. The marriage, which M. Cicero is said on good authority to have engineered, was a failure, although it lasted nearly a quarter of a century and produced a son. Pomponia was somewhat older than her husband and they made a cantankerous pair from the first.

Following in his elder brother's wake, Quintus embarked on a political career, although he had no taste for public speaking, and stood successfully for Quaestor, Aedile, and Praetor (the last during Marcus' Consulship in 63). In 61 he went out to the province of Asia as Proconsul, a post which he held for the exceptional period of three years. It says much for his integrity as a governor that he was genuinely annoyed when the Senate extended his term a second time. His return from Asia in 58 coincided with his brother's journey into exile. Back in Rome, Quintus was for some time anxious about a threatened prosecution for maladministration in his province, perhaps to be conducted by a nephew of P. Clodius. When nothing came of it, he was able to devote himself wholeheartedly to the campaign for Marcus' restoration. On one occasion his efforts nearly cost him his life, when he was left for dead on the scene of a riot.

After Marcus' return in 57, Quintus remained for nearly two more years in Italy, with a brief interval of overseas employment in 56, when Pompey stationed him in Sardinia to supervise grain supplies. In the spring of 54 he joined Caesar's staff in Gaul as Legate, where he distinguished himself by a heroic defence of his camp against a rebel tribe. Caesar congratulated him publicly and gives the episode handsome recognition in his *Commentaries*, qualified however by criticism of a subsequent piece of negligence on Quintus' part, which nearly led to a disaster. With his later career down to his death in the Proscriptions of 43 we are not here concerned.

Quintus shared his brother's and brother-in-law's interest in Hellenic culture and was himself a prolific versifier, whiling away inactive spells in Gaul by translating Sophocles' plays into Latin. Twenty uninspired hexameters about the signs of the zodiac, taken from an unknown poem, are attributed to him. We also have four short letters from him in the collection *ad Familiares* (44, 147, 351, 352) and a tract on electioneering couched in the form of a letter of advice to his brother on his consular candidature in 64, generally known as *Commentariolum Petitionis* ('A Short Memorandum on Standing for Office'). But the authenticity of this last is in serious doubt.

Down to the closing years of their lives the relationship between the brothers remained on the whole close and affectionate, though indications of friction and latent resentments on Quintus' part are not lacking. For details I must refer to my biography, from which I quote the following summary: 'The deplorable marriage, which Marcus Cicero had made and striven to keep in being for his own reasons, friction over Statius, disappointments in Gaul, untoward incidents in Cilicia, Quintus' strange passivity in the early months of the Civil War – all this and much more of which we are not informed may have gone to nourish an ulcer in Quintus' mind: the mind of a small man, irritable, querulous, and weak; a severe magistrate, who spoiled his son and let himself be run by a slave; a good man in a battle or a riot, but a rabbit in front of his wife; ambitious, but inhibited by a distrust of his talents, which were not of the first order, and handicapped by the unlucky accident of birth, which had made him a bigger man's younger brother.' The outcome was a prolonged and bitter quarrel during the

Civil War, which was never more than superficially patched up.[1]

The three 'Books' of Cicero's letters to Quintus may well have been published by Tiro, like the *Letters to Friends*. The first in the series is no ordinary letter but a tract, presumably meant for at least private circulation, which might have been entitled 'Advice to a Governor' and could be regarded as a *quid pro quo* for the *Commentariolum*, if the latter were certainly authentic. A second, genuinely private letter belongs to this period. Then come two letters from exile, followed by the remaining nineteen, which date from the end of 57 to the end of 54.

The text on which my translation is based that is of W. S. Watt (Oxford Classical Text series, 1958). A few significant departures are mentioned in footnotes.

1. The orthodox view, at least until 1971, that the reconciliation between the brothers was genuine and complete cannot be entertained by anyone who has read the contemporary letters to Atticus with attention and without sentimental prejudice.

CICERO'S LETTERS TO HIS BROTHER QUINTUS

I (I. I)

CICERO TO HIS BROTHER

End of 60 or beginning of 59

From Marcus to his brother Quintus greetings.

I don't doubt that this letter will be outpaced by many messengers, indeed by Rumour herself with her well-known speed, and that you will hear from others beforehand that our loss and your labour[1] have been extended for a third year. Still, I thought it proper that this tiresome news should reach you from me as well as others. After all, in writing to you previously, not once but a number of times, I have held out to you the hope of an early homecoming after others had already despaired of it. That was not just to amuse you as long as possible with a pleasant notion but because the Praetors and I were both working so hard for it that I felt sure the thing could be done.

Well, unfortunately, neither the Praetors' influence nor my own zeal has had any success. It is hard not to feel irked. However, we have had too long a training in the conduct of great affairs and the bearing of great responsibilities to lose heart and strength in our vexation. And in one respect I should be taking it harder than you, since it is the misfortunes for which they are ourselves to blame that ought to distress people the most. It *was* my fault that, against your urgings before you set out and later by letter, you were not relieved the previous year. Thinking of the welfare of the provincials, opposing the effrontery of certain businessmen, and seeking to add to our prestige by your abilities, I acted unwisely, all the more so as I ran the risk of that second year entailing a third.

1. As Proconsul in Asia.

I acknowledge my error. Now it is for you, with your great good sense and your kind heart, to take good care to correct my lack of foresight by your pains. If you gird up your loins to the business of gaining approval all round and try to excel, not others, but yourself; if you urge your whole mind and concern and thought into one ambition – to do yourself the utmost credit in all things: then take my word for it, a single added year of work will bring us happiness for many years ahead and glory to those who come after us as well.

Well then, this is the first thing I ask of you: let there be no inner withdrawal or discouragement. Don't allow yourself to be submerged beneath the flood of a great responsibility. Stand up and face it, contend with business as it comes or even go out to meet it. Success in your sphere of public service is not in the hands of chance, it mainly depends on thought and application. If you were conducting some big, dangerous war and I saw your command extended, I should be alarmed, because I should realize that it also meant an extension of fortune's power over ourselves. But as matters stand, fortune has no part, or only a very small part, in the public responsibility which has been entrusted to you. It seems to me to lie wholly in your own ability and discretion. We do not, I think, have to fear a hostile ambuscade or a pitched battle or the desertion of allies or want of means to pay and feed our troops or a mutiny. Such things have happened time and time again to very wise men; they could not overcome fortune's onset any more than the best of seamen can master a violent storm. *Your* portion is perfect peace and calm; and yet if the helmsman falls asleep he could go to the bottom in such weather, while if he keeps wide awake he may actually enjoy it.

Your province consists of a native population the most highly civilized in the world and of Romans who are either tax-farmers, and thus very closely connected with us, or wealthy businessmen who think they owe the safety of their money to my Consulship. Ah, but they get into disputes among themselves, often do each other harm leading to mighty contentions. Well, I am not under the impression that you have no responsibilities at all! I do realize that you have a very great responsibility, calling for the highest qualities of judgement. But remember that in my opinion it is a good deal more a matter of judgement than of luck. After all, it is not too difficult to control the people under you if you control yourself. Self-control may be a great and difficult achievement for others, is so indeed, most difficult; but for you it has always been quite easy, and why not? You have a nature which would surely have tended to gentleness even without instruction; and instruction such as yours might lend some grace even to the most faulty of natures. In the future, as now, you will resist the temptations of money, pleasure, and every sort of appetite. Small fear then of your finding yourself unable to restrain a crooked businessman or an over-acquisitive tax-farmer! As for the Greeks, when they look at you leading the life you do, they will think you are a character from an ancient story or a divine being come down from heaven into the province.

I do not write all this to tell you how to behave, but to make you glad of your behaviour, past and present. It is a fine thing to have spent two[2] years in Asia in supreme authority without letting any of the commodities in which your province abounds draw you away from the strictest uprightness and integrity – neither statue nor painting nor cup nor fabric nor slave, neither beauty of person nor financial arrangement. And it is a rare and enviable piece of good fortune that your ability, discretion, and self-restraint are not hidden away in some dark corner but placed in the full light of Asia, for the most brilliant of provinces to see and for all peoples and nations to hear tell of: how no man is afraid of your progresses or put to crushing expense or disturbed by your arrival; how there is hearty rejoicing in public and private wherever you go, for you enter

2. 'Three' according to the manuscripts.

a city as a protector, not a tyrant, and a house as a guest, not a looter.

However, experience has doubtless taught you that in these matters it is not enough for you to have such virtues yourself; you must look carefully around you, so that as guardian of your province you are seen to take responsibility to the provincials, the Romans, and the commonwealth not only for your individual self but for all your subordinate officials. To be sure you have Legates who of their own volition will pay regard to your good name. Tubero is first among them in official rank, personal consequence, and age. I imagine that as a historian he can choose many a figure from his own chronicles whom he is wishful and able to imitate. Allienus is ours in spirit and goodwill, and in the way he takes our lives as models for his own. As for Gratidius[3] what shall I say? I am sure that his brotherly affection for us will prompt concern for our reputation along with the concern he feels for his own. You have a Quaestor[4] whom you did not choose of your own judgement but acquired by the luck of the draw. It behoves him to exercise discretion of his own accord and to defer to your rules and advice. If it were by any chance the case that the moral standards of one or other of these gentlemen left something to be desired, you would put up with his disregard of regulations which apply to him as an individual, but not allow him to use for profit the authority which you confer upon him as appropriate to his rank. Now that our modern ways have leaned so far in the direction of excessive lenity and popularity-mongering, I would not really have you examine every dark patch and search their pockets man by man; better to assign to each one an amount of responsibility commensurate with the trust he inspires.

Very well, you will answer for the officers whom the state itself gives you as your companions and assistants within the

3. M. Gratidius, a relative of the Ciceros.
4. His name is unknown.

limits I have just laid down, and no further. What of those whom you have chosen to be with you as part of your household entourage or to do necessary jobs – members of the Governor's Staff, as they are usually called? In their case we have to answer not only for everything they do but for everything they say. However, the people with you are people of whom you can easily be fond if they behave well and whom you can even more easily check if they don't pay enough regard to your reputation. When you were new to the job, they could perhaps have taken advantage of your generous instincts – the better a man is, the harder he finds it to suspect rascality in others. Now a third year is opening; let it show the same integrity as the two that preceded it with an even greater measure of watchfulness and care. Let men think of your ears as hearing what they hear, not as receptacles for false, deceitful, profit-seeking whispers. Let your seal-ring be no mere instrument but like your own person, not the tool of other men's wills but the witness of your own. Let your orderly be what our forbears meant him to be. Except for some good reason they gave this function to none but their own freedmen, and that not as a favour but as a task and duty; and their authority over their freedmen differed little from their authority over their slaves. Let your lictor be the servant of *your* clemency, not of his own; let the rods and fasces bear before you insignia of rank rather than power. In a word let the whole province know that the lives, children, reputations, and property of all over whom you rule are most precious to you. Finally let it be believed that, if you get to know of a bribe, you will be the enemy of the giver as well as of the taker. Nor will anybody give a bribe once it becomes clear that as a rule nothing is obtained from you through the agency of people who pretend to have much influence with you. Mind you, what I have been saying does not mean that I want you to be over-austere or suspicious towards your entourage. If any of them in the course of two years has never given you cause to suspect him of money-grubbing, as I hear to be true of Caesius and Chaerippus and Labeo and so judge from my own knowledge of them, I should think it entirely proper to place unlimited trust and confidence in them and in anyone else of the same stamp. But if you find something wrong with a man or scent corruption, don't trust him an inch or put any part of your good name in his keeping.

If, however, you have met someone in the province itself, not previously acquainted with us, who has found his way into your closer intimacy, take care how far you trust him. I don't say that many residents in the provinces are not honest men; but this is something which it is allowable to hope but dangerous to decide. Each man's nature lies hidden under a mass of enveloping pretence, like veils stretched to cover it from sight. Countenance, eyes, expression very often lie, speech yet oftener. These people out of desire for money go without all those amenities from which we cannot bear to be parted.[5] Are you likely to find any man among them to love you, a stranger, sincerely, not just pretending it for his own advantage? That would be most extraordinary in my opinion, especially if these same persons love hardly anybody in a private station but are always fond of every governor. If you have come to know someone in this category as caring more for you than for your temporary position (it is not impossible), by all means write him down as your friend. But unless you see this clearly, there is no class of men with whom as intimates you should be more on your guard. They know all the paths that lead to money, everything they do is for money's sake, and they are not concerned to guard the reputation of someone who will not be with them indefinitely.

Furthermore, much caution is called for with respect to friendships which may arise with certain among the Greeks themselves, apart from the very few who may be worthy of the Greece of old. A great many of these people are false, unreliable,

5. The amenities of life in Italy.

and schooled in over-complaisance by long servitude. My advice is to admit them freely to your company in general and to form ties of friendship and hospitality with the most distinguished; but too close intimacies with them are neither respectable nor trustworthy. They do not dare to oppose our wishes and they are jealous not only of Romans but of their fellow-countrymen.

If I am for watchfulness and care in relationships as to which I fear I may actually be taking too austere a view, how do you think I feel about slaves? We ought to keep them firmly in hand wherever we are, but most especially in the provinces. A great deal can be said by way of advice upon this subject, but the shortest rule and the easiest to follow is this: let them conduct themselves on your journeyings in Asia as though you were travelling down the Appian Way, let them not suppose it makes any difference whether they have arrived in Tralles or in Formiae. If you have an outstandingly faithful slave, employ him in household and private concerns, but don't let him touch any that have to do with the duties of your office or with state business in any shape or form. For much that can safely be entrusted to faithful slaves ought not to be entrusted to them even so, in order to avoid talk and criticism.

Somehow or other as I write I have slipped into the role of mentor, which was not my original intention. Why should I give advice to someone whom I recognize as not inferior to myself in worldly wisdom, especially in this area, and my superior in experience? And yet I had the feeling that you yourself would find more pleasure in doing what you did if it were done on my authority. Well then, here are the foundations of your prestige: first, your own integrity and self-restraint, next a sense of propriety in all your companions, a very cautious and careful selectivity as regards close friendships with Roman residents and with Greeks, and the maintenance of strict household discipline. Such conduct would be creditable enough in our private, everyday lives, but with so wide an authority, amid such a falling-off in moral standards and in a province so rich in temptations, it must surely appear superhuman.

With these principles and this discipline you can safely practise in your decisions and judgements the severity which you have shown in certain matters, by which we have made ourselves some enemies – and very glad I am of it. For you are not to suppose that I pay attention to the grumblings of a fellow called Paconius (not a Greek even, but a Mysian, or rather Phrygian) or the talk of a crazy money-grubber like Tuscenius, whose unsavoury plums you most justly plucked from his disgusting jaws. These and other markedly strict decisions in your province could not easily be sustained against criticism without the highest integrity. So let your judicial rulings be of the strictest, provided that strictness be consistently maintained and never modified by partiality. And yet it is of no great importance that you yourself dispense justice consistently and conscientiously if those to whom you grant some share in this function do not do the like. As it seems to me, the administration of Asia presents no great variety of business; it all depends in the main on the dispensation of justice. The actual knowledge involved, especially in a province, is no problem, but there is need of consistency and firmness to resist even the suspicion of partiality.

Other requisites are readiness to listen, mildness of manner in delivering judgement, conscientiousness in arguing with suitors and answering their complaints. C. Octavius recently gained much public regard by these means.[6] The lictor in his court had nothing to do, the orderly held his tongue, every man spoke as often as he pleased and as long. Perhaps he might have seemed too indulgent, were it not that his indulgence supported his rigour. Sulla's men were obliged to restore what they had stolen by violence and terror. Magistrates who had given wrongful rulings were obliged as private persons to yield obedience conformably to the rules they had made themselves. His rigour

6. As Praetor in 61.

would have seemed harsh, had it not been qualified by a generous seasoning of kindliness.

If such mildness is appreciated in Rome, where people have so much arrogance, such unlimited freedom, such unbridled licence, where moreover there are so many magistrates, so many courts of appeal, where the plebs has so much power and the Senate so much authority, how popular cannot a governor's courtesy be in Asia, with all that multitude of Roman citizens, all those cities and communes, watching the nod of one man – no appeal, no protest, no popular assembly? Only a really great man, gentle by nature and cultivated by instruction and devotion to the highest pursuits, can so behave himself in a position of such power that those under his rule desire no other power than his. Such a one[7] was Cyrus as described by Xenophon,[8] not according to historical truth but as the pattern of a just ruler; in him the philosopher created a matchless blend of firmness and courtesy. With good reason our Roman Africanus[9] used to keep that book always in his hands. It overlooks no aspect of a conscientious and gentle ruler's duty. And if a monarch, who would never be in a private station, so practised these principles, how sedulously ought they to be observed by those to whom official power is granted only for a period, and granted by the laws to which they must eventually return!

I conceive that those who rule over others are bound to take the happiness of their subjects as their universal standard. That this *is* your leading consideration, and has been from the first moment you set foot in Asia, is notorious from consistent report and the talk of all and sundry. Attentiveness to the welfare and needs of those under him is the duty of any ruler, not only over provincials and Roman citizens but even over slaves and dumb animals. I find a universal consensus that you take

7. Supply *ut est* before *Cyrus* in the text.
8. In his *Education of Cyrus*.
9. The younger Scipio Africanus.

all possible pains in that regard. The communes, we are told, are contracting no new debts, and many have been relieved by you of a massive load of old obligations; you have restored a number of ruined and almost deserted cities, including Samos and Halicarnassus, one the most famous city of Ionia, the other of Caria; the towns are free of rioting and faction; you take good care that the government of the communes is in the hands of their leading citizens. Brigandage has been abolished in Mysia, homicides reduced in many areas, peace established throughout the province, banditry quelled not only on the highways and in the countryside but in greater quantity and on a larger scale in the towns and temples; calumny, that cruellest instrument of governors' greed, has been banished, no longer to threaten the reputations, property, and tranquillity of the rich; communal expenses and taxes are equitably borne by all who live within the communal boundaries. You yourself are very easy of access, ready to lend an ear to every grievance, and no man is so poor and forlorn but he is admitted to your house and bedchamber, to say nothing of the tribunal where you receive the public; your entire conduct as governor is free of all trace of harshness and cruelty, entirely pervaded by mercy, gentleness, and humanity.

And then what a boon you conferred on Asia in relieving her from the iniquitous, oppressive Aediles' Tax, thereby making us some powerful enemies. One noble personage is openly complaining that your edict forbidding the voting of public money for shows has picked his pocket of HS200,000. That gives an idea of the sum that would be involved if money were paid out for the benefit of everybody who gave shows in Rome, as had become the practice. However, I found a means of stifling our fellow-countrymen's grumblings on this point – I don't know about Asia, but in Rome my action has been greeted with no little surprise and commendation. I have de-clined money voted by the communes for a temple and memorial to myself. They had voted it enthusiastically in recognition of their great indebtedness to me and the signal benefits of your government; and the taking of money for a temple and memorial is specifically permitted by law. Moreover, the sum contributed would not have vanished into thin air, but would have remained in the form of temple ornaments, presented, as might well be thought, to the Roman People and the Immortal Gods quite as much as to me. This gift – honourable to myself, legally sanctioned, and made with the good-will of the givers – I thought proper to decline, in order, among other reasons, to mitigate the annoyance of those who had lost what nobody owed them and what they had no right to take.

Accordingly, let me urge you to put your whole mind and heart into continuing upon the lines you have followed hitherto; love those whom the Senate and People of Rome have committed to your charge and authority, protect them in every way, desire their fullest happiness. If the luck of the draw had sent you to govern savage, barbarous tribes in Africa or Spain or Gaul, you would still as a civilized man be bound to think of their interests and devote yourself to their needs and welfare. But we are governing a civilized race, in fact the race from which civilization is believed to have passed to others, and assuredly we ought to give its benefits above all to those from whom we have received it. Yes, I say it without shame, especially as my life and record leaves no opening for any suspicion of indolence or frivolity: everything that I have attained I owe to those pursuits and disciplines which have been handed down to us in the literature and teachings of Greece. Therefore, we may well be thought to owe a special duty to this people, over and above our common obligation to mankind; schooled by their precepts, we must wish to exhibit what we have learned before the eyes of our instructors.

The great Plato, a prince among thinkers and scholars, believed that polities would only be happy either when wise and learned men came to rule them or when rulers devoted all their energies to acquiring virtue and wisdom.[10] That is to say, he laid down that this combination of wisdom and power can bring welfare to communities. Perhaps there was a point in time when our state as a whole had such good fortune;[11] at any rate your province surely has it today, with supreme power vested in one who from boyhood has given the greater part of his time and energy to the acquisition of virtue and culture. So see that this year added to your toil may appear in the light of an extension granted for the salvation of Asia. She has been more fortunate in keeping you than we in bringing you home; then make the happiness of the province console our heartache. Nobody could have taken greater pains to deserve the distinctions which have been conferred upon you[12] in perhaps unprecedented measure, and you should take far greater pains to live up to them. I have already written to you what I feel about honours of this kind. I have always considered them worthless if showered indiscriminately, and trivial if conferred from interested motives. But if they were offered as a tribute to your deserts, as is indeed the case, I thought you should make a point of acting up to them. Since you are living with supreme authority and power in cities where you see your virtues consecrated and deified, you will remember in your every decision, ruling, and act what you owe to such honourable tokens of popular sentiment and esteem. That means you will take thought for all, find remedies for men's misfortunes, make provision for their welfare, aiming to be spoken of and thought of as the father of Asia.

Now there is one great obstacle to this your will and endeavour: the tax-farmers. If we oppose them, we shall alienate from ourselves and from the state a class to which we owe a great deal and which we have brought into alliance with the

10. This famous thought comes from Plato's *Republic* (345 D).
11. When Cicero was Consul!
12. By the provincials.

public interest. On the other hand, if we defer to them all along the line, we shall have to close our eyes to the utter undoing of the people for whose interests, as well as survival, it is our duty to care. If we look facts in the face, this is your only really difficult administrative problem. To have clean hands, to restrain all appetites, to keep your subordinates in order, to maintain an even dispensation of justice, to be willing to look into people's problems and listen to them and see them – all that is admirable rather than difficult. It is not a matter of work but of a certain disposition of mind and purpose. How much bitterness the tax-farmer question creates in the provinces has been illustrated for us by the attitude of some of our countrymen over the abolition of Italian customs. It was not the duty they complained of so much as certain maltreatments at the hands of customs officers. Having heard the complaints of Roman citizens in Italy I do not need to be told what happens to provincials at the ends of the earth. So to manage that you satisfy the tax-farmers, especially when they have made a poor bargain with the Treasury,[13] without letting the provincials go to ruin seems to call for judgement more than human – which is to say, it calls for yours.

Now to begin with, the most painful point to the Greeks is that they have to pay taxes at all. And yet they ought not to feel it so very painfully, since without any Roman Empire they were in just the same case under their own institutions, making their own arrangements. They ought not to turn away in disgust at the word 'tax-farmer', seeing that they proved unable to pay their taxes, as fairly allocated by Sulla, on their own without the tax-farmer's intervention. That Greeks in this capacity make no more easy-going collectors than Romans is well seen from the recent appeal to the Senate by the Caunians and all the islands assigned to Rhodes by Sulla, that they should in future pay their taxes to Rome instead of to Rhodes. And so I say that people who have always had to pay taxes ought not

13. As had actually happened; cf. *Letters to Atticus* 17 (1.17).5.

to shudder at the word 'tax-farmer', that such disgust comes ill from people who were unable to pay their tax by themselves, and that those who have what they asked for should not raise objections. Asia must also remember that if she were not in our empire she would have suffered every calamity that foreign war and strife at home can inflict. Since the empire cannot possibly be maintained without taxation, let her not grudge a part of her revenues in exchange for permanent peace and quiet. Now if they will only tolerate the actual existence and name of the tax-farmer with some degree of equanimity, your policy and wisdom will make all else seem easier to bear. In making their compacts they need not worry about the censorial contract, but rather look to the convenience of settling the business and freeing themselves of its annoyance. You yourself can help, as you have admirably done and are doing, by dwelling on the high status of the tax-farmers as a class and how much we[14] owe them, using your influence and moral authority to bring the two sides together without any show of magisterial power and constraint. You may ask it as a favour from people for whom you have done so much and who ought to refuse you nothing, that they be willing to stretch a point or two in order to let us preserve our friendly relations with the tax-farmers unimpaired.

No doubt these exhortations are superfluous. You can do all this yourself without advice from anybody, in fact to a great extent you have done it already. The most important and respectable companies are constantly expressing their gratitude to me, which I find the more agreeable because the Greeks do the same. It is no easy matter to create harmony where there is an opposition of interest and almost of nature.[15] However, I have not written the foregoing to instruct you (you know the world too well to require anyone's advice), but the writing gave me pleasure, the pleasure of dwelling upon your fine

14. Cicero and his brother.
15. I leave out the word *commodis*.

qualities. Though I must admit that this letter has turned out more lengthy than I expected or should have wished.

There is one point on which I shall continue to offer you advice. I shall never, so far as in me lies, let you be praised with a qualification. All who come from out there are loud in praise of your ability, integrity, and courtesy, but they make one reservation – your tendency to lose your temper. In everyday private life this is regarded as the fault of a weak, unstable mind; but nothing looks so ill as the combination of natural acerbity and supreme power. I won't take it upon myself here to expound to you what philosophers are apt to say on the subject of irascibility, for I don't want to take too long, and you can easily find it in many books. It is the proper function of a letter to inform one's correspondent of what he does not know, and that I think I ought not to leave undone.

Pretty well everyone tells us the same tale. They say that no man could be more agreeable than you when you are not out of temper, but that once irritated by some piece of rascality or perverseness you become so worked up that everybody wonders what has become of your gentlemanly self. Not so much by any appetite for glory as by accident of circumstance we have been led into a way of life which will make us a theme of talk for all time to come. So let us take care that, if we can possibly help it, they don't say 'He had one glaring fault.' I am not urging you to change your disposition and eradicate at one pull a deep-rooted habit. That is perhaps difficult to achieve in every nature and particularly at our time of life. I would only suggest, if you cannot avoid the failing altogether because anger seizes your mind before reason can look ahead to prevent it, that you prepare yourself in advance and make a daily resolve not to lose your temper and in moments of extreme exasperation to be particularly careful to restrain your tongue. To do this, I sometimes think, is as great a moral accomplishment as not to be angry at all. The latter is not exclusively a product of moral strength, it sometimes comes of a phlegmatic humour;

whereas to govern one's spirit and speech in anger, or even to hold one's tongue and keep the spiritual disturbance and passion under one's own control, though not the part of the perfect sage, does imply a mind beyond the ordinary.

However, reports are that you have become much milder and more amenable in this respect. We hear of no violent excitement on your part, no abuse or insults – behaviour far removed from literary culture and civilized manners and no less at odds with official authority and dignity. For implacable anger is the extreme of harshness, while appeasable anger is the extreme of levity; which, however, given the choice of evils, is to be preferred to harshness. Well, your first year produced a great deal of criticism in this regard, I imagine because you had not expected to meet with so much injustice, greed, and insolence and found it more than you could tolerate. The second year was a great improvement; habit, reason, and (as I suppose) my letters having made you more patient and gentle. The third year ought to be so impeccable that nobody will be able to find fault with the smallest detail.

And now I no longer exhort and advise, I beg you as a brother to set your whole mind, your entire thought and concern, on gathering universal praise from every quarter. If the talk and public blazoning of our achievements had not been exceptional, nothing extraordinary, nothing beyond the practice of other governors, would be demanded of you. As it is, the lustre and magnitude of the affairs which have engaged us are such that unless we gain the highest credit from your administration it looks as though we shall hardly be able to avoid bitter censure. Consider our situation: all the honest men wish us well, but also demand and expect of us the utmost in conscientiousness and ability; all the rascals, since we have declared unending war on them, will evidently want only the slightest excuse to censure us. Therefore, since so great a theatre has been given for your virtues to display themselves, the whole of Asia[16] no less, a theatre so crowded, so vast, so expertly critical, and with acoustic properties so powerful that cries and demonstrations echo as far as Rome, pray strive with all your might not only that you may appear worthy of what was achieved here[17] but that men may rate your performance above anything that has been seen out there. As chance has decreed, my public work in office has been done in Rome, yours in a province. If my part stands second to none, make yours surpass the rest. Also reflect that we are no longer working for glory hoped for in the future but fighting for what we have gained, and we are more bound to maintain this than we were to seek it.

If I had anything apart from you, I should want no more than this standing which I have already won. But the case is such that, unless all your acts and words out there match my record, I shall feel I have achieved nothing by those toils and hazards of mine, in all of which you took your part. More than any other you have helped me to gain so great a name; assuredly you will work harder than any other to let me keep it. You should not think only of the esteem and judgement of contemporaries but of posterity too; its judgement, to be sure, will be fairer, freed of detraction and malice. Finally, you ought to reflect that you are not seeking glory only for yourself, though even if you were you would not think lightly of it, especially as you have desired to immortalize your name by your splendid works.[18] But you must share that glory with me and hand it on to our children. If you make too light of it, you will run the risk of seeming to begrudge it to your family as well as of caring too little for yourself.

Now I do not wish it to appear as though my words were meant to wake a sleeper; rather, to spur a runner. As in the past,

16. Of course this refers, as elsewhere, to the Roman province so called.
17. By Cicero as Consul.
18. A compliment to Quintus' literary productions.

so to the end you will make all men praise your justice, temperance, strictness, and integrity. But my deep affection inspires me with an almost infinite appetite for your glory. However, after all, you should now know Asia as well as a man knows his own house; you now have a mass of experience to back your excellent judgement. I suppose then that there is nothing tending to credit which you do not best perceive and which does not enter your mind every day without anybody's prompting. But when I read your letters I seem to hear you talk, and when I write to you it is as though I were talking to you. That is why the longer your letters the better I like them, and why I myself often write rather lengthily.

This lastly I beg and urge of you: like good playwrights and hard-working actors, take your greatest pains in the final phase, the rounding off, of your appointed task. Let this third year of your term as governor be like the third act of a play – the most highly finished, best fitted-out of the three. This you will most easily accomplish if you imagine that I, whose single approval has always meant more to you than that of mankind at large, am ever with you, at your side in anything you say or do.

It only remains for me to beg you to pay particular attention to your health, if you value mine and that of all your folk.

2 (I. 2)

CICERO TO HIS BROTHER

Rome, between 25 October and 10 December 59

From Marcus to his brother Quintus greetings.

Statius arrived at my house on 25 October. I was sorry to see him come because you wrote that you would be plucked to pieces by your entourage while he was gone. On the other hand, I felt it just as well to have avoided the curiosity and crowding around there would have been if he came back with you without having made a previous appearance. The talk has exhausted itself. 'Methought to see a mighty man'[19] – such things have now been said a good many times. And I am glad to have got all that over in your absence.

It was not in the least necessary, however, for you to send him to clear himself to me. To begin with, I never suspected him. What I wrote to you about him did not represent my own opinion. But the success and security of all of us in public life rests not only on the truth but on common report, and that is why I have all along kept you informed of what others were saying, not what I myself was thinking. How much talk there was, and how strongly critical, Statius himself found out on his arrival here. He came along just when certain parties were complaining about him to me, and could see how unfriendly talk made his name its principal target.

What used to disturb me most when I heard that he had more to say with you than befitted the weight of your age, official authority, and worldly wisdom – how many people, do you suppose, have asked me to recommend them to Statius? How often do you suppose he himself in talking to me has innocently used phrases like 'I didn't approve of that,' 'I suggested . . . ,' 'I advised . . . ,' 'I warned . . .'? Even if his loyalty in these matters is implicit (which of course I believe, since you are persuaded it is so), the look of the thing, a freedman or slave with so much influence, could not but be highly undignified. I should be wrong if I spoke without good grounds, and wrong if I kept diplomatically silent: please realize that all the grist to the mills of your would-be detractors has been furnished by Statius. Previously I only understood that some people might have been annoyed by your strictness, but after his manumission I saw that those who were had got something to talk about.

19. *Odyssey*, IX.513.

Let me now reply to the letters delivered to me by L. Caesius (I shall do all I can for him since I understand that you so wish). One of them concerns Zeuxis of Blaundus. You say that I have warmly recommended to you an individual who beyond a shadow of doubt murdered his mother. As to that, and to the whole topic, let me tell you one or two things, in case you are surprised that I have become so anxious to curry favour with Greeks. I found that the complaints of these people carried more weight than I liked because of their natural talent for deception; and so I tried in whatever way I could to appease whichever of them I heard complaining about you. First I smoothed down the group from Dionysopolis, who were extremely hostile, and made a friend of their leader, Hermippus, by talking to him and even associating with him on familiar terms. I have showered courtesies on Hephaestius of Apamea, on that little rogue Megaristus of Antandros, on Nicias of Smyrna, on the most arrant good-for-nothings, including Nympho of Colophon. All this I did not do because I have any taste for these specimens or for their whole tribe. On the contrary I am sick and tired of their fribbling, fawning ways and their minds always fixed on present advantage, never on the right thing to do.

But to return to Zeuxis: He was talking about his conversation with M. Cascellius, just the same points as in your letter. So I set myself to stop his gossip and took him into my familiar circle. I don't quite understand this ambition of yours – you write that having sewn up two Mysians in a sack[20] at Smyrna you wanted to show a similar example of your severity in the interior of the province, and for that reason to entice Zeuxis by any means available. Once brought to trial it would not perhaps have been right to let him go, but it was hardly necessary to have him searched for and wheedled into court with soft words, as you put it; particularly as his fellow-Blaundians and

20. The traditional punishment of parricides and matricides.

others give me to understand more and more every day that he is almost more distinguished than his town![21]

It is not as though I am nice only to Greeks. Didn't I try all I knew to propitiate L. Caecilius? What a fellow he is! What fire and fury! Is there anyone except Tuscenius, a hopeless case, whom I haven't mollified? And now down comes Catienus, a mercenary rogue to be sure, but with a Knight's qualification. He too shall be appeased. You bore pretty hard on his father, which I do not criticize – I am sure you had your reasons. But where was the need to write a letter such as you sent Catienus himself: 'that he was building his own gallows, from which you had once before taken him down; you would see to it that he is burned alive to the applause of the whole province'? Why did you have to write to C. Fabius, whoever he may be (that's another letter which T. Catienus is toting around), that 'it was reported to you that taxes were being collected by yon kidnapping villain Licinius and his young sparrowhawk of a son'? You proceed to ask Fabius to burn both father and son alive if he can; if not, he is to send them to you so that they can be burnt up in court. You sent the letter to Fabius as a joke (if you really wrote it), but when folk read it the ferocity of the wording raises a prejudice against you.

If you will recall the advice I have given you in all my letters, you will see that my only criticism has been on the score of harsh language, irritability, and perhaps now and then a lack of care in your official letters. If my counsel had counted more with you in these respects than – shall we say your somewhat hasty temper, or a certain pleasure you take in letting fly, or your gift for pungent and witty expression, we should really have had nothing to regret. You must appreciate the pain I feel when I am told how highly people think of Vergilius and of your neighbour C. Octavius[22] (as for your neighbours on the

21. I understand this to mean that Zeuxis was too insignificant to be worth so much trouble.
22. Governors of Sicily and Macedonia respectively.

other side in Cilicia and Syria,[23] you are not claiming much if you compare yourself favourably with them!). And the distressing thing is that your hands are just as clean as theirs. They put you into the shade by their technique of gaining good-will. And yet they know nothing of Xenophon's Cyrus nor yet his Agesilaus. Nobody ever heard a harsh word from either monarch, autocrats though they were.

Well, I have been telling you all this from the beginning and I am well aware how much good it has done. All the same, in quitting the province, as I understand you are now in process of doing, do leave behind you as pleasant a memory as possible. Your successor[24] is a man of very agreeable manners. Other qualities which you possess will be very much to seek when he arrives. In sending out official letters (I have often written to you about this) you have been too ready to accommodate. Destroy, if you can, any that are inequitable or contrary to usage or contradictory. Statius has told me that they used to be brought to you already drafted, and that he would read them and inform you if they were inequitable, but that before he joined you letters were dispatched indiscriminately. And so, he said, there are collections of selected letters and these are adversely criticized. I am not going to warn you about this now. It is too late for that, and you are in a position to know how many warnings I have given on various occasions and with no lack of particularity. But as I asked Theopompus to tell you at his own suggestion, do see to it through friendly agents (it is easy enough) that the following categories are destroyed: first, inequitable letters; second, contradictory letters; third, letters drafted inappropriately or contrary to accepted usage; and finally, letters insulting to any person. I don't believe all I am told; and if there has been some negligence due to pressure of business, look into it now and set it right. I have read an im-

23. The governor of Syria was Cn. Cornelius Lentulus Marcellinus, Consul in 56. The governor of Cilicia is unknown.
24. T. Ampius Balbus.

proper letter which your nomenclator Sulla is said to have written himself and I have read some angry ones.

The subject of letters is à propos. As I was on this page, Praetor-Elect L. Flavius, a close friend of mine, came to see me. He told me that you had written a letter to his agents which appeared to me quite inequitable, directing them not to touch the estate of L. Octavius Naso, who left Flavius as his heir, until they had paid a sum of money to C. Fundanius; also that you had written directions to the town of Apollonis not to allow Octavius' estate to be touched until Fundanius' debt was paid. This all sounds improbable to me; it is so completely foreign to your usual good judgement. Must the heir not touch the estate? Suppose he denies the debt? Suppose there *is* no debt? Is it usual for a governor to rule that a debt exists? And am *I* not Fundanius' friend and well-wisher, am I not sorry for him? Nobody more. But in some matters the path of justice is not wide enough for favour. Flavius further told me that the letter which he alleged came from you contained a promise 'either to thank them as friends or to make things uncomfortable for them as enemies'. In short, he was much put out and expostulated with me strongly, asking me to write to you most particularly. That I am doing, and I ask you again most earnestly to countermand your order to Flavius' agents about touching the estate, and not to give any further directions to Apollonis against Flavius' interests. I am sure you will do all you can both for Flavius' sake and, no doubt, for Pompey's. Upon my word, I don't wish to appear as obliging Flavius in consequence of your unfairness. On the contrary, I beg you yourself to leave behind you an official declaration in writing in the form of a ruling or a letter which will help Flavius' interests and case. Being most attentive to me and careful of his own rights and dignity, he is greatly put out to find that neither friendship nor justice have counted with you in his favour. I believe that both Pompey and Caesar at some time or other recommended Flavius' interests to you; Flavius himself had written to you, and certainly I did so. So if there is anything you would think proper to do at my request, let this be it. If you love me, spare no pains to ensure that Flavius thanks both you and me as heartily as may be. I could not ask anything of you more urgently.

What you write about Hermia has really vexed me a lot. I had written you a not very brotherly letter – I was annoyed by what Lucullus' freedman Diodotus said, and wrote in some irritation immediately after hearing about the agreement.[25] I wanted to recall it. This unbrotherly letter you must like a good brother forgive.

As for Censorinus, Antonius, the Cassii, and Scaevola, I am very pleased to hear that they are so friendly to you.[26] The remainder of your letter took a graver tone than I could have wished: 'I'll go down with my flag flying',[27] and 'better die once'![28] That is surely overdoing it. My scoldings were full of affection. There *are* some things that I complained of,[29] but of no vast consequence, quite small in fact. Behaving as uprightly as you do, I should never have thought you deserving of the slightest criticism if we did not have many enemies. What I wrote to you in a somewhat warning or reproving strain was written out of the care I take to be always on guard. That I maintain and shall, and I shall continue to ask you to do the same.

Attalus of Hypaepa has been talking to me. He wants you not to stand in the way of his arranging payment of the money decreed for a statue of Q. Publicius. I request accordingly, and

25. The circumstances are unknown.

26. How these young noblemen had shown their friendly feelings is uncertain.

27. Partial quotation of a Greek proverb which means literally: 'Know ye, Poseidon, that the ship when I sink her shall be on an even keel.'

28. From Aeschylus, *Prometheus Bound* (750): 'Better die once for all than be miserable all one's days.'

29. Reading *erant* for *erunt* and *quae* ⟨*questus sum*⟩ *sunt nonnulla*.

would advise you not to wish to be responsible for whittling down or obstructing an honour to so worthy a man and so good a friend of ours. Furthermore, a slave called Licinus (you know him) belonging to our friend Aesopus has run away. He was in Athens with Patro the Epicurean posing as a free man, and passed from there to Asia. Later, one Plato of Sardis, an Epicurean, who is a good deal in Athens and was there when Licinus arrived, having later learned that he is a runaway, arrested him and gave him into custody in Ephesus; but from his letter we are not sure whether the fellow was put into gaol or into the mill. However that may be, he is in Ephesus, so will you please search for him and take good care either to send him to Rome or to bring him with you? Don't consider what he's worth – such a good-for-nothing can't be worth much. But Aesopus is so distressed by the slave's criminal audacity that you can do him no greater favour than by getting him back his property.

Now let me tell you what you are most eager to know. Our free constitution is a total loss, so much so that C. Cato, a young harum-scarum but a Roman citizen and a Cato, had a narrow escape with his life when he addressed a public meeting and called Pompey 'our unofficial Dictator' – he wanted to charge Gabinius with bribery and for several days the Praetors would not let themselves be approached or give him a hearing. It was really touch and go with him. You can see from this what the state of the whole commonwealth is like.

As for my own prospects, however, I do not think I shall lack general support. It is amazing how people are coming forward with declarations and offers and promises. For my own part, I am in good hope and even better courage – hope, because I am confident I shall win; courage, because in the present state of the commonwealth I am not afraid of anything, even an accident. Anyway, this is how things stand: If Clodius takes me to court, all Italy will rally and I shall come out of it with much additional *kudos*; if he tries force, I trust to oppose him with force, supported not only by my friends but by outsiders as well. Everyone is pledging himself and his friends, dependants, freedmen, slaves, even money. My old band of honest men is passionately enthusiastic and loyal. Those who were formerly not so well disposed or not so energetic are now joining the honest men out of disgust with our present tyrants. Pompey is lavish with promises, and so is Caesar. If I take their word, I do not on that account relax my preparations in the slightest. The Tribunes-Elect are my good friends. The Consuls[30] show every sign of good-will. Among the Praetors I can count on Domitius, Nigidius, Memmius, and Lentulus[31] as warm friends and vigorous patriots – others too are well enough, but these are outstanding. Courage then and good cheer! On particulars, I shall send you frequent news of what goes on from day to day.

3 (I. 3)

CICERO TO HIS BROTHER

Thessalonica, 13 June 58

From Marcus to his brother Quintus greetings.

My brother, my brother, my brother! Were you really afraid that I was angry with you for some reason and on that account sent boys to you without a letter, or even did not want to see you?[32] *I* angry with *you*? How *could* I be? As though it was *you* who struck me down, *your* enemies, *your* unpopularity, and not *I* who have lamentably caused *your* downfall! That much-lauded Consulship of mine has robbed me of you, and my children, and my country, and my possessions; I only hope it has robbed you of nothing but myself. Sure it is that you have

30. i.e. Consuls-Elect, L. Calpurnius Piso and A. Gabinius.
31. L. Cornelius Lentulus Crus. Praetors=Praetors-Elect.
32. Cf. *Letters to Atticus* 54 (III.9).1.

never given me cause for anything but pride and pleasure, whereas I have brought you sorrow for my calamity, fear of your own, loss, grief, loneliness. *I* not want to see *you*? No, it was rather that I did not want to be seen by you! You would not have seen your brother, the man you left in Rome, the man you knew, the man who saw you off and said goodbye with mutual tears – you would not have seen any trace or shadow of *him*; only a likeness of a breathing corpse.

Would that you had seen me or heard of me dead before this happened! Would that I had left you as the survivor not of my life only but of my standing! But I call all the Gods to witness that one saying called me back from death – everyone told me that some part of your life was bound up in mine. I was wrong, criminally wrong. If I had died, the fact itself would stand as ample proof of my brotherly love for you. Instead, through my fault you have to do without me and stand in need of others while I am alive, and my voice, which has often defended strangers, is silent when my own flesh and blood is in danger.[33]

As for the fact that my boys came to you without a letter, since you see that anger was not the reason, the reason was surely inertia and an endless stream of tears and grieving. You can imagine how I weep as I write these lines, as I am sure you do as you read them. Can I help thinking of you sometimes, or ever think of you without tears? When I miss you, I do not miss you as a brother only, but as a delightful brother almost of my own age,[34] a son in obedience, a father in wisdom. What pleasure did I ever take apart from you or you apart from me? And then at the same time I miss my daughter, the most loving, modest, and clever daughter a man ever had, the image of my face and speech and mind. Likewise my charming, darling little boy, whom I, cruel brute that I am, put away from my arms. Too wise for his years, the poor child already understood what was going on.

33. Quintus had reason to fear that a charge might be brought against him in connection with his record as governor of Asia.
34. Text doubtful.

Likewise your son, my[35] image, whom my boy loved like a brother and had begun to respect like an elder brother. As for my loyalest of wives, poor, unhappy soul, I did not let her come with me so that there should be someone to protect the remnants of our common disaster, our children.

However, I did write to you as best I could and gave the letter to your freedman Philogonus. I expect it was delivered to you later. In it I urge and ask of you, as in the verbal message brought you by my boys, to go straight on to Rome and make haste. To begin with, I wanted you to stand guard in case there may be enemies whose cruelty is not yet satisfied by our downfall. Secondly, I was afraid of the outburst of grief which our meeting would have brought on. As for parting, I could not have borne it, and I feared the very thing you say in your letter, that you might not endure to be separated from me. For these reasons the heavy affliction of not seeing you, which seems the bitterest, saddest thing that could happen to brothers so affectionate and close as we are, was less bitter and sad than our meeting would have been, and still more our parting.

Now if you can do what I, whom you always thought a strong man, am unable to do, then stand up and brace yourself for the struggle you may have to sustain. I should hope (if any hope of mine counts for anything) that your integrity, the affection in which you are held in the community, and in some degree also the pity felt for myself will bring you protection. If, however, it turns out that your hands are free of that danger, you will doubtless do what you think can be done, if anything, about me. I get many letters from many people on the subject and they make themselves out to be hopeful. But for my own part I can't see any grounds for hope, when my enemies are in power and my friends have either deserted or actually betrayed me. Perhaps the idea of my coming home frightens them as involving blame for their own villainy. But please see how things

35. So the manuscripts. *tuam* ('your') is sometimes read for *meam* ('my').

stand in Rome and make them clear to me. In spite of all, I shall go on living as long as you need me, if you have to go through an ordeal. Live any longer in this kind of life I cannot. No worldly wisdom or philosophic instruction is strong enough to endure such anguish. I know I had the opportunity to die a more honourable and useful death, but that is only one of many chances I let slip. If I were to bewail past mistakes, I should only be adding to your sorrow and exposing my own folly. One thing I ought not and cannot do, and that is to linger on in so miserable and dishonourable an existence any longer than your predicament or a well-grounded hope shall demand. Once I was happy indeed, in my brother, children, wife, means, even in the very nature of my wealth,[36] the equal of any man that ever lived in prestige, moral standing, reputation, influence. Now in my abject ruin I cannot bear to mourn myself and mine much longer.

Why then did you write to me about a bill of exchange?[37] As though your resources were not supporting me at present. Ah, how well I see and feel what a wicked thing I did! You are about to pay your creditors with your heart's blood and your son's, while I squandered to no purpose the money which I received from the Treasury on your behalf.[38] However, both M. Antonius and Caepio[39] were paid the sums you had mentioned. As for me, what I have is enough for my present purposes. Whether I am restored or given up for lost, no more is needed.

If you have any trouble, I advise you to go to Crassus and Calidius. How much faith you should put in Hortensius I don't know. He behaved to *me* most villainously and treacherously, while pretending the warmest affection and sedulously keeping

36. Apart from his inherited fortune this was mainly derived from legacies left by grateful clients.

37. Quintus will have offered to negotiate a bill in Rome, the money to be paid to his brother in Thessalonica.

38. Cf. *Letters to Atticus* 26 (11.6).2.

39. Better known as M. Brutus.

up our daily intercourse. Q. Arrius joined him in this. Through their policies and promises and advice I was left in the lurch and fell into my present plight. But you will keep all this under cover, lest it tell against you. Be careful of one thing (and for that reason I think you should conciliate Hortensius himself through Pomponius): that epigram about the lex Aurelia which was attributed to you when you were standing for the Aedileship,[40] mind it doesn't get established by false evidence.[41] My principal fear is that when people realize how much pity your entreaties and your escape from a prosecution is going to arouse for us, they will attack you the more vigorously. I think Messalla[42] is on your side. Pompey, I think, is still pretending. If only you don't have to put all this to the test! I should pray to the Gods for that if they had not given up listening to my prayers. None the less, I do pray that they may be content with these boundless afflictions of ours, which, however, are free from any stigma of wrong-doing. The whole tragedy is that fine actions have been cruelly penalized.

My brother, I need not commend my daughter (and yours) and our Marcus to your care. On the contrary, I grieve to think that their orphaned state will bring you no less sorrow than me. But while you are safe, they will not be orphans. I swear that tears forbid me to write of other things – so may I be granted some salvation and the power to die in my country! Please look after Terentia too, and write back to me on all matters. Be as brave as the nature of the case permits.

Ides of June, Thessalonica.

40. In 66.

41. It can be supposed that the epigram was offensive to Pompey and Crassus, since the lex Aurelia of 70, revising the Roman jury system, was passed in their Consulship with their support. Cicero seems to have feared that Hortensius might confirm its attribution to Quintus out of spite. As an opponent of the law he would be a credible witness.

42. The Consul of 61, as generally supposed. Perhaps more probably Hortensius' nephew Messalla Rufus, Consul in 53.

CICERO'S LETTERS TO HIS BROTHER QUINTUS

4 (I. 4)

CICERO TO HIS BROTHER

Thessalonica, c. 5 August 58

From Marcus to his brother Quintus greetings.

Dear brother, if a single act of mine has brought you and all my family low, I beg you not to attribute this to wickedness and evil-doing on my part but rather to imprudence and ill-fortune. My only fault lay in trusting men in whom I thought it would be an abomination to deceive me or even imagined that it was not in their interest to do so. My closest, most intimate, most familiar friends were either afraid for themselves or jealous of me. So I lacked nothing, unfortunate that I was, except good faith on my friends' part and good judgement on my own.

If your own innocence and public compassion prove sufficient to protect you from annoyance at this time, you doubtless perceive whether any hope of deliverance is left for me. Pomponius, Sestius, and our Piso have kept me in Thessalonica so far, telling me not to move further away on account of certain developments. But it is because of their letters rather than from any definite hope that I am waiting for the outcome. What am I to hope for, with my enemy[43] wielding great power, my detractors ruling the state, my friends unfaithful, so many jealous of me? As for the new Tribunes, certainly Sestius is most anxious to help me and so, I hope, are Curtius, Milo, Fadius, and Atilius.[44] But Clodius is in strong opposition, and even after he goes out of office he will be able to stir up public meet-

43. Clodius.
44. i.e. Sex. Atilius Serranus Gavianus, originally friendly to Cicero, though in office he joined Clodius. I read *Atilius* for *Gratidius* (there was no Tribune of that name in 57). Editors read *Fabricius*.

ings with the same gang. And someone will be found to cast a veto.

That is not the prospect that was painted to me when I left Rome. I was often told that I could expect a glorious return within three days. You will ask what I thought myself. Well, a combination of factors upset the balance of my mind: Pompey's sudden desertion, the unfriendly attitude of the Consuls, and even the Praetors, the timidity of the tax-farmers, the sight of weapons. The tears of my family and friends forbade me to go to my death, which would certainly have been the most honourable course and the best way of escaping intolerable distresses. But I wrote to you on the subject in the letter I gave to Phaetho.

As matters stand, if public compassion can alleviate[45] our common plight, yours will doubtless be an incredible achievement, thrust down as you are into an abyss of mourning and trouble the like of which no man has ever known. But if we are really lost, oh, the misery of it! I shall have been the ruin of all my family, to whom in time gone by I was no discredit.

But, as I wrote to you earlier, view the situation thoroughly, take your soundings, and write me the truth; that is what our situation, though not your affection, requires. I shall hold on to life as long as I think that it is in your interest for me to do so or that it should be preserved in hope[46] of better things. You will find Sestius very friendly to us. I think Lentulus, who will be Consul, wishes you well. But actions are not so easy as words. You will see what is needed and how things are.

If nobody scorns your loneliness and our common calamity, something will be achievable through you or not at all. But if our enemies start persecuting you too, don't take it lying down. In your case the weapons will be lawsuits, not swords. But I hope there will be none of that. I beg you to write back to me

45. Perhaps read *potes* for *potest*: 'if through public compassion you can alleviate . . .'

46. I retain the manuscript reading *ad spem*.

on all matters and to believe that, however much I may have lost in spirit, or rather in judgement, my affection and family feeling remain the same.

5 (II. 1)

CICERO TO HIS BROTHER

Rome, shortly before 15 December 57

From Marcus to his brother Quintus greetings.

I dispatched a letter this morning which you will have already read. But Licinius was kind enough to call on me this evening after the Senate had risen to give me the opportunity of writing to you an account of the day's proceedings.

The House met in larger numbers than I thought possible in December just before the holiday. Of the Consulars, there were, besides myself and the two Consuls-Elect, P. Servilius, M. Lucullus, Lepidus, Vulcatius, Glabrio. The ex-Praetors were in good force. In all we were about 200. Lupus'[47] speech was awaited with interest. He dealt with the Campanian Land very fully, to an extremely attentive House. You know the material. He covered all my own contributions. There were some barbs to Caesar's address, some insults to Gellius', some complaints to Pompey's – who was not present. It was getting late when he wound up, and he said he would not ask for a debate since he did not wish to put any pressure on members to make themselves enemies. The high words of days gone by and the present silence told him the feeling of the House. He began to dismiss the meeting. Marcellinus observed: 'I must ask you, sir, not to draw any conclusions as to what we now approve or disapprove of from

47. Lupus, who had just come into office as Tribune, later figures as an adherent of Pompey. Hence probably the interest in his speech.

the fact that we have nothing to say. So far as I myself am concerned, and I imagine the same applies to the rest of the House, I am holding my peace because I do not think the question of the Campanian Land can properly be handled in Pompey's absence.' Lupus then said that he would not detain the House.

Racilius then rose and laid the question of the trials before the House, calling on Marcellinus to open the debate. After a powerful indictment of Clodius' arsons, killings, and stonings he proposed that the City Praetor should personally appoint a jury by lot, and that when this process was complete elections should be held; any person obstructing the trials to be regarded as acting contrary to public order. This proposal was warmly approved. C. Cato spoke against it, as did Cassius,[48] amid loud cries of protest when they put the elections before the trials. Philippus concurred with Lentulus. Then Racilius called upon me first of the private members. I spoke at length on the whole issue of P. Clodius' sedition and banditry, arraigning him like a man in the dock with frequent murmurs of approval from the whole House. Antistius Vetus[49] praised my speech at some length – his was not at all a bad performance. He also took up the question of the trials and said that he would regard it as of primary importance. A vote to that effect was about to take place, when Clodius was called and proceeded to talk out the motion. Racilius' insulting and witty attack had infuriated him. Then his roughs suddenly set up quite a formidable shouting from Ambassadors' Lodge[50] and the steps. I believe they had been stirred up against Q. Sextilius and Milo's friends. On that alarm we broke up in haste, amid loud and general protest.

There you have one day's proceedings. The sequel, I suppose,

48. Unknown. Possibly read *Caninius*.

49. Another Tribune, L. Antistius Vetus, to be distinguished from C. Antistius Vetus of *Letters to Atticus* 363 (XIV.9).3 (this has now been established by E. Badian).

50. 'Graecostasis', a platform from which envoys listened to senatorial debates.

will be deferred till January. Racilius is much the best of the Tribunes, but I think Antistius too will be friendly to us. Plancius, of course, is completely devoted.

If you love me, be sure to be cautious and careful about putting to sea in December.[51]

6 (II. 2)

CICERO TO HIS BROTHER

Rome, 17 January 56

From Marcus to his brother Quintus greetings.

Contrary to my habit when writing to you I am dictating this letter instead of writing it myself, not because of pressure of business (though busy I certainly am) but because I have a touch of ophthalmia.

And first I want to excuse myself and accuse you on one and the same count. Nobody has so far asked me whether I have a message for Sardinia, while I think you often have people who ask you whether you have a message for Rome.

As regards what you write to me on behalf of Lentulus[52] and Sestius, I have talked with Cincius. As the matter stands, it's not any too easy. There must be something about Sardinia which arouses dormant memories. Just as Gracchus the Augur[53] after arriving in that province remembered what had happened to him when he held the consular elections in the Campus Martius contrary to the auspices, so you in your Sardinian leisure seem

51. Quintus was going to Sardinia as Legate to Pompey, now in supreme charge of grain supplies.
52. Which Lentulus is uncertain, and we have no further information about the matter under reference.
53. Father of the Gracchi; Cicero tells the story in his treatise *On the Nature of the Gods* (II.10 f.).

to have brought Numisius'[54] ground-plan and the transactions with Pomponius back to your recollection. But so far I have bought nothing. Culleo's auction has taken place, and the property at Tusculum[55] did not find a buyer. If I can get really good terms, perhaps I shall not let it slip. I keep on urging Cyrus about your building[56] and hope he will do a good job. But everything goes slowly because of the prospect of a madman[57] as Aedile. For it looks as though elections will be held without delay – they have been announced for 20 January. However, I don't want you to be anxious. I shall take all manner of precautions.

As for his Alexandrian majesty, the Senate has passed a decree pronouncing it dangerous for him to be restored 'with a host'.[58] For the rest, there has been a tussle in the Senate as to whether Lentulus or Pompey should restore him, and Lentulus looked like winning his point. In that affair I performed my duty to Lentulus to a marvel, at the same time meeting Pompey's wishes in fine style, but the matter was dragged out by the manoeuvring of Lentulus' ill-wishers. Then followed the comitial days during which the House could not meet. What will come of the Tribunes' freebooting I can't prophesy, but I suspect that Caninius will carry his bill by violence. I can't fathom Pompey's wishes in the matter; but everyone sees what his friends want, and the king's creditors are openly putting up money against Lentulus. He certainly seems to have lost the assignment, which I am very sorry for, though he has given me many good reasons to feel annoyed with him[59] if that were not against my conscience.

54. Presumably an architect.
55. Culleo's, not Cicero's.
56. Cf. Letter 8 (II.4).
57. Clodius.
58. Cf. *Letters to his Friends* 12 (I.1).2.
59. Cicero was dissatisfied with Lentulus Spinther's attitude in respect of his indemnities; cf. *Letters to Atticus* 74 (IV.2).4.

If you have sorted matters out over there, I hope you will board ship at the first spell of fair, settled weather and join me. There are numberless things in which I miss you, every day and in every way. Your folk and mine are well.

17 January.

7 (II. 3)

CICERO TO HIS BROTHER

Rome, 12–15 February 56

From Marcus to his brother Quintus greetings.

I gave you the earlier news in my last. Now for the sequel: On the Kalends of February there was a move to postpone the embassies to the Ides. No conclusion reached that day. On 2 February Milo appeared to stand trial with Pompey as supporting counsellor. M. Marcellus spoke (I had asked him) and we came off creditably. Case adjourned to 7 February. Meanwhile the embassies were postponed to the Ides and the House was asked to consider the Quaestors' provinces and the Praetors' establishments. But business was interrupted by numerous complaints about the state of the commonwealth and nothing done. C. Cato gave notice of a bill to relieve Lentulus of his command, and his son put on mourning.

Milo appeared on 7 February. Pompey spoke – or rather tried to speak, for no sooner was he on his feet than Clodius' gang raised a clamour, and all through the speech he was interrupted not merely by shouting but by insults and abuse. When he wound up (and I will say he showed courage; he was not put off, delivered all he had to say, sometimes even managing to get silence by his personal authority) – well, when he wound up, Clodius rose. Wishing to repay the compliment, our side gave him such an uproarious reception that he lost command of thoughts, tongue, and countenance. That lasted till half past one, Pompey having finished just after midday – all manner of insults, ending up with some highly scabrous verse to the address of Clodius and Clodia. Pale with fury, he started a game of question and answer in the middle of the shouting: 'Who's starving the people to death?' 'Pompey,' answered the gang. 'Who wants to go to Alexandria?' Answer: 'Pompey.' 'Whom do you want to go?' Answer: 'Crassus' (who was present as a supporter of Milo, wishing him no good). About 2.15 the Clodians started spitting at us, as though on a signal. Sharp rise in temperature! They made a push to dislodge us, our side counter-charged. Flight of gang. Clodius was hurled from the rostra, at which point I too made off for fear of what might happen in the free-for-all. The Senate was convened in its House, and Pompey went home. I did not attend, however, not wishing to keep mum about so remarkable an incident nor yet to offend the honest men by standing up for Pompey, who was under fire from Bibulus, Curio, Favonius, and Servilius junior. The debate was adjourned to the following day. Clodius had the trial postponed to Quirinus' Day.

On 8 February the Senate met in the temple of Apollo[60] in order that Pompey could be present. Pompey spoke strongly – nothing concluded that day. 9 February, Senate in temple of Apollo. A decree was passed pronouncing the doings of 7 February contrary to public interest. That day C. Cato delivered a broadside against Pompey – a set speech like a prosecuting counsel's with Pompey in the dock. He said many highly laudatory things about me, which I could have done without, denouncing Pompey's treachery towards me. The ill-wishers listened in rapt silence. Pompey replied warmly, making oblique allusion to Crassus and saying plainly that he intended to

60. Outside the ancient city boundary. As holding *imperium* Pompey could come inside only by special dispensation.

take better care of his life than Africanus had done, whom C. Carbo murdered.[61]

So I think big things are on the way. Pompey has information (and talks about it to me) that a plot against his life is on foot, that Crassus is backing C. Cato and supplying Clodius with funds, and that both are getting support both from Crassus and from Curio, Bibulus, and his other enemies. He says he must take very good care not to be caught napping, with the meeting-going public pretty well alienated, the nobility hostile, the Senate ill-disposed, and the younger generation ill-conditioned. So he is getting ready and bringing up men from the country. Clodius on his side is reinforcing his gang in readiness for Quirinus' Day. With the same date in view we have much the advantage even with Milo's own forces, but a large contingent is expected from Picenum and Gaul, which should further enable us to make a stand against Cato's bills concerning Milo and Lentulus.

On 10 February Sestius was charged with bribery by an informer, Cn. Nerius of the tribe Pupinia, and on the same day with breach of the peace by a certain M. Tullius. He was unwell, so, as was only proper, I called on him immediately and promised him my services without reservation. And I have acted accordingly, contrary to what people were expecting in the belief that I was justifiably annoyed with him.[62] So I figure in his eyes and everyone else's as an eminently forgiving and grateful character. And I shall so continue. The same informer Nerius has produced as deputies Cn. Lentulus Vatia and C. Cornelius of the tribe Stellatina. The same day the Senate passed a decree to the effect that the political clubs and caucuses should be dissolved and a bill put through providing that persons not complying with this ordinance be liable to the same penalty as those guilty of breach of peace.

61. In 129. But murder was never proved.
62. The reason is unknown; cf. the first paragraph of the next letter.

On 11 February I defended Bestia on a bribery charge before Praetor Cn. Domitius in mid Forum. There was a large crowd in court. In the course of my speech I came to the occasion on which Bestia saved Sestius' life when he was lying covered with wounds in the temple of Castor. I took the favourable opportunity to lay down a foundation for my defence of Sestius against the charges which are being got up against him and pronounced a well-deserved eulogy, which was received with great approval by all. Sestius was highly pleased. I tell you all this because you have often referred in your letters to the desirability of preserving good relations with him.

I am writing this before dawn on 12 February. This evening I shall be dining with Pomponius at his wedding.[63]

In the rest of my affairs it is as you foretold when I was far from hopeful – my prestige and influence flourishes. This restitution, in which we both share, is due, my dear brother, to your patience, courage, devotion, and, let me add, your personal charm.

Piso's house (the Liciniana) near the wood[64] has been rented for you, but I hope you will be moving into your own in a few months' time, after the Kalends of July. The Lamiae have taken your house in Carinae – nice, clean tenants. Since your letter from Olbia I have heard nothing from you. I am anxious to know how you are and how you amuse yourself, and above all to see you as soon as possible.

Take care of your health, my dear brother, and don't forget that it's Sardinia where you are, winter time though it be.[65]

15 February

63. To Pilia.
64. Reading uncertain.
65. The climate of Sardinia was notoriously unhealthy, more so, naturally, in summer than in winter.

8 (II. 4)

CICERO TO HIS BROTHER

Rome, mid March 56

From Marcus to his brother Quintus greetings.

Our friend Sestius was acquitted on 14 March, and by a unanimous vote, which was politically of great importance as showing that no difference of opinion exists in a case like this. I have often noticed your anxiety lest I gave a handle to a hostile critic who might accuse me of ingratitude if I did not put up with his unreasonableness in certain respects with the best of grace. Well, you may rest assured that my conduct in that trial has made me pass for a model of gratitude. By my defence I have more than discharged what was due to this peevish personage, and I cut up his overt adversary Vatinius just as I pleased to the applause of Gods and men,[66] which was what he wanted more than anything. What is more, our friend Paulus, who appeared as a witness against Sestius, undertook to prosecute Vatinius if Licinius Macer[67] did not get on with the job; on which Macer rose from Sestius' benches and promised not to fail him. In short, that bullying ruffian left the court much disconcerted and unnerved.

Your son Quintus, who is a fine boy, is getting on famously with his lessons. I notice this more now because Tyrannio is teaching at my house. Building of both our houses goes briskly forward. I have paid your contractor half his money. I hope we shall be under the same roof before winter. I hope we have settled matters with Crassipes about our Tullia, who loves you very much indeed. But it is the two days after the Latin Festival (now ended), which are holy days, and he is just leaving town.

66. In the speech *In Vatinium*.
67. i.e. the poet and orator C. Licinius Macer Calvus.

9 (II. 5)

CICERO TO HIS BROTHER

Rome, March 56

★★★ As for the *abondance* you often talk about, I want it
moderately; that is to say, if the animal comes my way I shall be
glad to snap it up, but if it stays in hiding I don't intend to flush
it out. I am building in three places and refurbishing the rest. I
live on a rather more handsome scale nowadays than I used – it
was called for. If I had you with me, you[68] would take second
place to the builders for a spell! But all this too I hope we shall
soon be talking over between us.

The situation in Rome is as follows: Lentulus makes an
excellent Consul, and his colleague does not stand in his way –
yes, really good, I have never seen a better. He has blocked all
the comitial days – even the Latin Festival is being repeated, and
no lack of Supplications either. So pernicious bills are blocked,
especially Cato's.[69] Our friend Milo has played that patron of
gladiators and beast-fighters a fine trick. Cato had bought some
beast-fighters from Cosconius and Pomponius and never
appeared in public without their armed escort. He could not
feed them and was having difficulty in keeping them. Milo got
to know, and employed an agent to buy the troupe from Cato,
a man who was not a crony of his own and so could do it without arousing suspicion. No sooner had they been led off than
Racilius (the only Tribune worth the name at present) gave the
show away, announcing by prearrangement with Milo that
these men had been bought for himself and putting out an
advertisement that he was going to sell 'Cato's troupe' by
auction. There was great amusement over that advertisement.

68. I read *dares* for *darem*.
69. Cf. *Letters to his Friends* 15 (1.5a). The references are throughout to
the Tribune, C. Cato.

Well, Lentulus has kept this fellow Cato away from legislation, as also some others who have given notice of bills about Caesar – monstrous things, and nobody to veto them. As for Caninius' campaign regarding Pompey, it has fallen quite flat. The proposal finds little favour in itself, Pompey is criticized because of his friendship with P. Lentulus,[70] and frankly his position is not what it was. He has incurred some unpopularity with the vicious elements, the dregs of the mob, because of Milo, while the honest men find him lacking in many respects and blameworthy in many others. The only fault *I* have to find with Marcellinus is his excessive asperity towards Pompey. But the Senate does not disapprove, which makes me all the more glad to withdraw from the Senate-House and public affairs altogether.

In the courts I stand where I stood. My house is as full of callers as in my heyday. One unfortunate incident happened through Milo's imprudence, about Sex. Cloelius[71] – I was against a prosecution at the present time and with weak prosecutors. It only needed three more votes in a deplorable jury. The people are demanding another trial and he will have to be brought back – they won't tolerate it, and look upon him as already convicted since he was almost found guilty by a jury of his own men. In this affair too Pompey's unpopularity stood in our way. The Senators acquitted him by a large margin, the Knights were tied, the Paymaster Tribunes voted guilty. But to make up for this misadventure, my enemies are being convicted every day. Sevius ran on the rocks to my great satisfaction, and the rest are being broken up.[72] C. Cato has told

70. i.e. for acting disloyally by intriguing to get the Egyptian assignment transferred to himself.

71. Read *Cloelio* for *Caelio* etc. in the manuscripts (*Clodio* edd.).

72. The distinction is not wholly clear, but it may be that Sevius (an unknown; most editors read *Servius*, mistakenly identifying with Servius Pola) had been condemned for some non-political offence. His fate, then, was a kind of accident, whereas the other Clodians had been prosecuted by their political enemies on public grounds.

a public meeting that he won't allow elections to be held if his days for moving legislation in the Assembly are blocked. Appius has not yet got back from Caesar.

I am waiting for a letter from you with the greatest impatience. I know that the sea has been closed to shipping up till now, but they say that certain persons arrived in Ostia bringing glowing accounts of you and your great reputation in the province. They also say you are giving out that you will cross at the first sailing. I hope so, and although naturally it is yourself I most want, I am none the less expecting a letter in advance.

Goodbye, dear brother.

10 (II. 6)

CICERO TO HIS BROTHER

En route *to Anagnia*, *9 April 56*

From Marcus to his brother Quintus greetings.

I sent you a letter[73] the other day telling you that our Tullia was betrothed to Crassipes on 4 April, along with the rest of the news, public and private. Subsequent items are as follows: On the Nones of April the Senate decreed HS40,000,000 to Pompey as Grain Commissioner. The same day there was a warm debate on the Campanian Land – the shouting in the House was like at a public meeting. The shortage of funds and the high price of grain made the question more acute. I must not fail to mention that M. Furius Flaccus, a Roman Knight and a scoundrel, was expelled from the Capitoline College and the Guild of Mercury,[74] he being present and throwing himself at the feet of every member in turn.

73. Not extant.
74. The *Capitolini* were in charge of the Capitoline Games held every Ides of October. The *Mercuriales* were a corporation of merchants.

On 6 April I gave a dinner for Crassipes to celebrate the engagement. Your and my boy Quintus (a very good boy) could not come because of a very slight indisposition. On the 8th I went to see him and found him quite recovered. He talked to me at length and in the nicest way about the disagreements between our ladies. It was really most entertaining. Pomponia has been grumbling about you too, but we will talk of this when we meet.

On leaving the boy I went over to your site. Work was going ahead with a crowd of builders. I said a few animating words to Longilius the contractor, and he convinced me that he wants to give us satisfaction. Your house will be splendid. One can see more now than we could judge from the plan. Mine too will be built rapidly.

I dined that evening at Crassipes' and after dinner had myself carried to Pompey's, not having been able to meet him during the day because he had been away – I wanted to see him because I was leaving Rome next day and he had a trip to Sardinia in view. So I met him and asked him to send you back to us as soon as possible. 'Straight away,' said he. He would be leaving, he said, on 11 April and taking ship from Labro[75] or Pisae. Now as soon as he arrives, my dear fellow, be sure to take the next boat, provided the weather is suitable.

On 9 April I dictated this letter before daylight and am writing the rest on the road, expecting to stay the night with T. Titius near Anagnia. Tomorrow I intend to stay at Laterium, and then, after five days in the Arpinum area, go on to Pompeii. I shall have a look at my Cumae place on the way back, and so to Rome (since Milo's trial has been scheduled for the Nones of May) on the 6th, then, as I hope, to see you, my dearest and sweetest of brothers. I thought it best to hold up the building at Arcanum pending your arrival.

Be sure to keep well, my dear fellow, and come as soon as you can.

75. No place of this name is otherwise recorded.

11 (11. 7)

CICERO TO HIS BROTHER

Rome, shortly after 15 May 56

From Marcus to his brother Quintus greetings.

At last, your delightful letter! I have been waiting for it so impatiently, and of late apprehensively too. I must tell you that this is the only letter I have had from you since the one dispatched from Olbia which your sailor brought.

Let all else be kept for talk in person, as you say, but one thing I cannot let wait: on the Ides of May the Senate refused Gabinius a Supplication – a magnificent performance! Procilius takes his oath that this has never happened to anyone before.[76] Outside the House it is heartily applauded. To me it is agreeable in itself, and the more so because it was done in my absence – an unbiased judgement, without any aggressive action or influence on my part. I did not attend because it had been reported that the Campanian Land would be debated on the Ides and the day following, as indeed it was. On this question I am muzzled.[77] But I am writing more than I intended – we shall talk.

Goodbye, my best and most longed-for of brothers, and hurry you home. Our boys make the same plea of you. Oh, and of course you will come to dinner when you arrive.

76. In fact there seems to have been only one precedent, that of T. Albucius, Governor of Sardinia *c.* 104.
77. Cf. *Letters to friends* 20 (1.9)5 ff.

12 (II. 8)

CICERO TO HIS BROTHER

Rome, shortly after 11 February 55

From Marcus to his brother Quintus greetings.

I thought you would like Canto II,[78] but I'm very glad you liked it so very much as you say in your letter. You remind me of Indifference[79] and advise me to remember Jupiter's speech at the end of the Canto.[80] Yes, I remember. I wrote it all for myself more than for the rest of the world.

However, the day after you left I paid Pompey a late-night visit in company with Vibullius and spoke to him about those buildings and inscriptions.[81] He answered very kindly and held out great hopes, saying that he would like to discuss it with Crassus and advising me to do the same. I accompanied Consul Crassus from the Senate to his house. He undertook to do his best and said there was something Clodius wanted to get just now through Pompey and himself; if I did not put a spoke in his wheel, he thought I could gain my point without a fight. I put the whole business in his hands and said I would do just as he thought fit. Young P. Crassus, who is devoted to me as you know, was present during our talk. As for what Clodius wants, it's a Free Commissionership (if not through the Senate, then through the Assembly) either to Byzantium or to Brogitarus or

78. Of the poem *On my Vicissitudes*. Cf. *Letters to his Friends* Vol. I, p. 68.

79. I translate a Greek word taken from Stoic terminology and conjectured here by W. Sternkopf in place of *non curantia* in the manuscripts, which seems to be an attempt to render it in Latin. Cicero also uses the word in *Letters to Atticus* 37 (II.17) and in his *Academica* (II.130).

80. Jupiter will have advised the poet to leave politics and devote himself to letters; see end of next paragraph.

81. The reference is obscure, but cf. n. 141.

both.[82] There's plenty of money in it, but that doesn't trouble me too much – even if I don't get what I'm after. However, Pompey has talked to Crassus, and they seem to have taken the thing on. If they do it, fine! If not, let us return to our Jupiter.

On 11 February the Senate passed a decree about bribery on Afranius' motion, which was the one I proposed myself when you were here. But to the loudly voiced disappointment of the House the Consuls did not pursue the proposal of certain members who, after concurring with Afranius, added that the Praetors should remain private citizens for two months after election. There was a flat repudiation of Cato.[83] The fact is, they are all-powerful and want everybody to know it.

13 (II. 9)

CICERO TO HIS BROTHER

Cumae(?), 55(?)

From Marcus to his brother Quintus greetings.

What, *you* afraid of interrupting me? To start with, even if I were occupied in the way you think, you know what 'interrupting an idler' is![84] But upon my word it looks as though you

82. As Tribune Clodius had brought about the recall of some Byzantine exiles and had got Brogitarus appointed High Priest of Cybele at Pessinus. He now proposed to go and 'collect'. Though his business was private, the 'Free Commissionership' would give him official status.

83. Since the Praetors for 55 had not been elected in the previous year they would, failing special provision, take office immediately after election and so become immune from prosecution for electoral malpractice. M. Cato was a candidate, in opposition to the Consuls, Pompey and Crassus, who secured his defeat. He was, however, later elected for the following year.

84. I translate my conjecture *tu scis quid sit interpellare otiantem*, by which Cicero may be supposed to allude to a saying that to interrupt an

are giving me a lesson in this kind of thoughtfulness, for which I have no use when it comes from you. No, no, I hope you will interpose and interrupt and talk me down and talk me out! Nothing would please me better. No moonstruck poet is so willing to recite his latest effusions as I to listen to you talking on any topic, public or private, country or town. It was my stupid diffidence that stopped me from taking you along when I left Rome. You put up an unanswerable excuse the first time, the ill health of our little boy; so I held my tongue. Then again it was the boys, and I said nothing. And now your most agreeable letter bothers me a little, because it looks as though you were afraid, and still are, of being a bother! I should quarrel with you if brotherly love permitted. But mark my words; if ever I suspect anything of the kind again – well, I'll say only this: I shall be afraid when we are together of bothering *you*. That touches you on the raw, doesn't it? Well, that's the way it goes: 'whoso evil speaketh . . .'[85] (I'll never say 'evil doth').

As for our friend Marius, I assure you I should have thrown him into the litter – not the one Asicius[86] had from King Ptolemy (I remember that occasion when I was transporting him from Naples to Baiae in Asicius' eight-bearer palanquin with a hundred swordsmen following; Marius knew nothing about this escort and I laughed till I cried when he suddenly opened the curtains and we both almost collapsed – he with fright and I with laughter). Well, as I say, I should certainly have taken him along to sample the subtlety of his old-time wit and civilized conversation, but I did not like to invite an invalid

---

idle man was to do him a service. Private study or literary work came under the heading of *otium* ('leisure, idleness').

85. The Greek verse part of which Cicero quotes is from a lost work of Sophocles: 'If what you did was terrible, so must what you suffer be terrible also.'

86. Charged with the murder of the chief of a delegation from Ptolemy the Piper's revolted subjects, he was successfully defended by Cicero.

to a draughty house, still not even roughly finished. It would be a special treat for me to enjoy his company here too – I can tell you that Marius as my neighbour is the pride and glory of my property at Pompeii. I shall take care that Anicius' place is ready for him. As for me, bookworm though I be, I can live with the carpenters, a philosophy which I get, not from Mt Hymettus, but from our native Peak.[87] Marius is not so tough, either in health or nature. As for interruptions, I shall borrow from you people just so much time for writing as you allow, and I hope you don't allow any; that way, if I do nothing, you will be to blame instead of my own laziness.

I am sorry you take the political situation overmuch to heart and that you are a better citizen than Philoctetes, who being wronged wanted to see such sights as are evidently painful to you.[88] Be a good fellow, and hurry over. I shall comfort you and wipe away all sorrows. And bring Marius, if you love me. But make haste, both of you.

The kitchen garden is in good shape.[89]

14 (II. 10)

CICERO TO HIS BROTHER

Rome, early February 54

From Marcus to his brother Quintus greetings.

Your tablets[90] clamorously demanded this letter. Otherwise,

87. Literally 'from our Arx', reading *arce nostra* (written *arcenra*) for the meaningless *araxira* in the manuscripts. There was a place called Arx ('citadel') in the neighbourhood of Arpinum. Cicero means that he did not need Greek philosophy to teach him to put up with inconvenience; early training in his native hill country had done that.

88. Evidently an allusion to a lost play. Sophocles' *Philoctetes* contains nothing relevant.

89. The meaning of the Latin (*hortus domi est*) is uncertain.

90. See Glossary of Terms.

in actual material the day of your departure offers virtually no subject for my pen. But when we are together we are seldom at a loss for talk, and in the same way our letters must sometimes just ramble on.

Well then, the liberties of the good folk of Tenedos have been chopped by their own axe;[91] nobody came to their defence except myself, Bibulus, Calidius, and Favonius. You got an honourable mention from the men of Magnesia by Mt Sipylus; they said you were the only one to stand up to L. Sestius Pansa's demand.[92] If there is anything you ought to know on the remaining days, or for that matter if there is nothing, I shall still write you a daily line. On the 12th I shall not fail you, nor Pomponius either.

Lucretius' poetry is as you say – sparkling with natural genius, but plenty of technical skill.[93] If you read Sallust's *From Empedocles*,[94] I'll rate you both more and less than ordinary humanity.[95]

91. The people of Tenedos seem to have petitioned the Senate for the status of a 'free' community, and to have been summarily refused. The exact origin of the proverbial expression 'axe of Tenedos' is variously explained, but has to do with the eponymous hero of the island, Tenes, who was supposed to have introduced a peculiarly drastic legal code.

92. Nothing is known of Pansa or his demand. He may have been a tax-farmer.

93. According to St Jerome Cicero edited Lucretius' poem *On the Nature of the Universe* after the poet's death.

94. Presumably a Latin translation of the fifth-century philosopher-poet Empedocles. The identity of the translator is unknown.

95. Literally: 'I shall think you a *man* (*virum*), but not a human being.'

15 (II. 11)

CICERO TO HIS BROTHER

Rome, c. 13 February 54

From Marcus to his brother Quintus greetings.

I am glad my letters give you pleasure, though just now I should not have had any subject to write about if I had not had a letter from you.

Appius called a thinly attended meeting of the Senate on the 12th, but it was so chilly that the outcry forced him to dismiss us. As for His Majesty of Commagene,[96] I quite settled his hash and so Appius is paying me extravagant court both in person and through Pomponius. He sees that if I take the same tone in other matters he will have a lean February.[97] I poked fun at the king comically enough, not merely twisting that little town on the Bridge of Euphrates out of his grip but raising a storm of laughter by my jibes at the purple-bordered gown he got during Caesar's Consulship: 'Now as for his request for the renewal of the honours accorded to him, far be it from me to suggest that this House should gainsay his right to give the purple-bordered gown an annual redyeing. But I appeal to members of the nobility here present: you gentlemen drew the line at Oxnose; are you going to accept Commagene ointment?'[98] You perceive the genre and the theme. I cut so many jokes at this

96. Antiochus. He had received the kingdom, formerly part of Syria, when Pompey set up the Roman province at the end of the war against Mithridates.

97. The Senate dealt with foreign delegations in February. As Consul Ap. Claudius Pulcher was in a position to help them gain their petitions, for which, as Cicero implies, he would expect to be paid.

98. It seems that in 59 the king had been accorded the right to wear the purple-bordered gown (*toga praetexta*) worn by Roman curule

inglorious monarch's expense that he was totally exploded.
Appius, as I say, was alarmed by this procedure and is smother-
ing me in courtesies. It would be the easiest thing in the world to
spoke the other wheels. But no, I shall not offend him,

lest upon Jove he cry,
Guardian of Troth, and all the Greeks convoke[99]

– that is, the intermediaries in our reconciliation.

I shall do my best for Theopompus. As for Caesar, I forgot to
tell you – yes, I understand what kind of a letter you have been
waiting for. But he wrote to Balbus that the parcel containing
Balbus' letter and mine was delivered to him completely water-
logged so that he doesn't even know that a letter from me was
inside. But he had made out a few words in Balbus' letter, to
which he replies as follows: 'I see you have written something
about Cicero which I cannot make out. But so far as I could
follow it by guesswork, it looked like something I should have
wished rather than hoped for.'[100] So I proceeded to send Caesar

magistrates, perhaps on a particular annual occasion; and that the
Senate had been asked to renew or confirm it. The conjecture *qui
Burrhinum* for *quibus r(h)enum* assumes a double pun in Cicero's usual
manner. There was a medicament *commagenum*, made from a herb
commagene; and there was a herb *burrhinon* (*burrhinum*, 'oxnose'; it was
otherwise called *bucranion*, 'oxskull'). The missing link will be a low-
born person named or nicknamed *Burrhinus*, whose election to a
magistracy was resented or ridiculed by the nobility – unless, as suggested by T. P. Wiseman, one Burrienus (or, more likely, Burrenus),
City Praetor in 83, is relevant.

99. A quotation from an unknown Latin play. 'Jove, Guardian of
Troth' (Jupiter Hospitalis) = Zeus Xenios, defender of the laws of
hospitality. The 'Greeks' do not, as commentators naïvely suppose,
represent actual Greeks, but, as Cicero expressly says, the intermediaries
who had recently reconciled him with Appius, principally Pompey; cf.
Letters to Atticus 124 (VII.1)3, where, likewise in quotations, the 'Trojan
men and dames' stand for public opinion and 'Polydamas' for Atticus.

100. This no doubt referred to Q. Cicero's desire for a command in
Caesar's army.

a copy of my letter. And don't be put off by his joke about being hard up. I replied that he had better not spend his last penny depending on *my* strong-box, and some more banter on the same lines – familiar but not undignified. All reports speak of his special regard for me. The letter replying to the point you have in mind should just about coincide with your return to Rome.

I shall write you day-by-day news-letters always provided you supply the couriers. But there's a hard frost ahead. In fact Appius stands in grave danger of seeing his house become a bonfire.[101]

16 (II. 12)

CICERO TO HIS BROTHER

Rome, 14 February 54

From Marcus to his brother Quintus greetings.

Your 'black snow' made me laugh,[102] and I am very glad to find you so cheerful and ready for a joke. I agree with you about Pompey, or rather you agree with me, for, as you know, I have been chanting your Caesar's praises this long while past. Believe me, he is grappled to my heart and *I* have no intention of disengaging.

Well, now for the Ides. It was the tenth day for Caelius.[103]

101. There is an untranslatable joke here, in the word *urerentur*, which can mean 'may be burned' or 'may be frostbitten'. The meaning is, of course, that Appius' unpopularity was such that a mob might set his house on fire.

102. The point of Quintus' joke is uncertain.

103. An interval of at least ten days was required between arraignment and trial. Nothing is known of the trial here in question.

Domitius[104] didn't have a complement of jurors. I'm afraid that horrible savage Servius Pola may join the prosecution, for our friend Caelius is vigorously assailed by the Clodian clan.[105] There's nothing for certain so far, but we are apprehensive.

That same day a well-attended Senate gave audience to the delegation from Tyre. Numerous Syrian tax-farmers appeared in opposition. Gabinius was hauled over the coals in lively style, but the tax-farmers were harried by Domitius for having escorted him on horseback.[106] Our friend Lamia went a little far. When Domitius said: 'All this is the fault of you Roman Knights. You give lax verdicts,' Lamia retorted: 'We give verdicts, and you give testimonials!'[107] Nothing was concluded that day before nightfall ended the session.

According to Appius' interpretation, he is not debarred by the lex Pupia from holding meetings of the Senate on the comitial days following the Feast of Quirinus, and is actually obliged, as laid down in the lex Gabinia, to hold a meeting every day from the Kalends of February to the Kalends of March for the hearing of embassies.[108] So it's thought that the elections[109] are pushed away into March. All the same, the Tribunes say they intend to bring Gabinius' action before the Assembly on these coming comitial days.

I rake together all I can find to put some news in my letter, but, as you see, I am simply out of matter. So I come back to Callisthenes and Philistus – I can see you have been wallowing

104. A Praetor; or possibly the Consul, L. Domitius Ahenobarbus, mentioned below.

105. Already in 56 Caelius Rufus had been defended by Cicero on a charge instigated by his former mistress Clodia, sister to P. Clodius.

106. Ptolemy the Piper had finally been restored to his throne by Gabinius, now governor of Syria.

107. Cf. *Letters to his Friends*, Vol. I, p. 65.

108. Cf. n. 97.

109. Of magistrates for the current year, whether Praetors or Aediles is uncertain.

in them. Callisthenes is a vulgarian, a 'bastard'[110] author, as certain of his fellow-countrymen have put it. But the Sicilian is capital – full of matter, penetrating, concise, almost a miniature Thucydides. But which of his books you have had (there are two works), or whether you have had them both, I don't know. I prefer his *Dionysius*. Dionysius is a grand old fox and on very familiar terms with Philistus. You add a question – shall you embark on history? You have my full encouragement. And since you are furnishing couriers, you shall have today's chronicle on the Lupercalia.

Have a perfectly delightful time with our young man.

17 (II. 13)

CICERO TO HIS BROTHER

Cumae or Pompeii, May 54

From Marcus to his brother Quintus greetings.

Up to date I have received two letters from you, one dispatched just as we said goodbye,[111] the other from Ariminum; the further letters which you say you sent I have not received.

Except that I lack your company I am in other respects having quite a pleasant time at Cumae and Pompeii and shall be staying in those places till the Kalends of June. I am writing the political book[112] I mentioned earlier, and a pretty sticky, laborious job it is. However, if it turns out satisfactory, the time will have been well spent. If not, I'll toss it into the sea, which is before my eyes as I write, and attack something else, since I can't do nothing.

110. Reading *nothum* for *notum* ('familiar'). In his treatise *On the Orator* (II.58) Cicero says that Callisthenes wrote history 'almost in the fashion of a rhetorician'.
111. Quintus had left to join Caesar for service in Gaul.
112. *On the Republic.*

I shall carefully attend to your charges, both in conciliating people and in not estranging certain persons. But my greatest concern will be to see your boy (*our* boy) every day, which goes without saying, and to look into what he is learning as often as possible. If he is willing to accept it, I shall even offer my services as his teacher, having gained some practice in this employment in bringing our younger boy[113] forward during this holiday season.

On your side, as you say in your letter (though even if you did not say so I know you are doing it most conscientiously), you will of course take care to sort out my commissions and follow them up and do them. When I get back to Rome I shall not let a single courier of Caesar's leave without a letter for you. At present (you will forgive me) there was nobody to take a letter until this M. Orfius, a Roman Knight who is connected with me both on personal grounds and because he comes from the town of Atella, which you know to be under my patronage. So I recommend him to you warmly. He is a man of distinction in his own community and of influence even outside it. Be sure to treat him handsomely and so attach him to yourself. He is a Military Tribune in your army. You will find him grateful and attentive.

Let me earnestly beg you to be very kind to Trebatius.

18 (II. 14)

CICERO TO HIS BROTHER

Rome, beginning of June 54

From Marcus to his brother Quintus greetings.

On 2 June, the day I got back to Rome, I received your letter dispatched from Placentia, and then another dispatched the

113. Young Marcus.

following day from ⋆,[114] together with a letter of Caesar's full of all manner of friendly attention, thoughtfulness, and charm. The things you speak of are indeed important, or rather *most* important, tending powerfully, as they do, to great *kudos* and the highest prestige. But take the word of one you know: what I value most in these matters I already have, and that is, first, yourself so dedicated to the support of our common standing, and second, such affection for me on Caesar's part. That means more to me than all the distinctions he wants me to expect at his hands. The letter he sent along with yours pleased me beyond words. He begins by saying how delighted he was at your arrival and the memory of old affection, then goes on to promise that, knowing how sorely I shall miss you, he will make me glad that in your absence from me you are with him rather than anywhere else.

It is good brotherly advice you give me to make Caesar the one man I exert myself to please, but *now* upon my word the horse is willing. Yes, that I shall do enthusiastically. It often happens to travellers in a hurry that after getting up rather later than they intended they put on speed and thus arrive at their destinations faster even than if they had been astir in the middle of the night. So perhaps with me. In cultivating this man's friendship I have been asleep a long while, though I must admit that you often tried to wake me up. Now I shall compensate my slowness by putting my horse to a gallop – and not just my horse but my poetic chariot, since you say my poem[115] meets with his approval. All you have to do is to give me Britain to paint. I'll use your colours with my brush. And yet . . . Where can I spy the spare time, especially if I stay in Rome, as he asks me to do? Well, I'll see. Perhaps love alone will conquer all obstacles. It often does.

114. 'Blanden(n)o' in the manuscripts; but no place of that name is known.

115. An epic poem addressed to Caesar which Cicero had begun, and eventually finished; cf. Letter 27 (III.7)6.

He actually thanks me for sending him Trebatius, very wittily and kindly, saying that in all his multitudinous entourage there wasn't a man who could draw up a bail-bond. I asked him for a Tribunate for M. Curtius – if I had asked Domitius he would have thought I was making game of him, it's his daily grumble that he can't even appoint a Military Tribune; he even made a joke in the Senate to the effect that his colleague Appius had gone to Caesar for the gift of a Tribune's commission – but for next year. That is how Curtius himself wanted it.[116]

Rest assured that in public life and in my personal feuds I am and shall be just what you recommend, softer than the lobe of your ear. Public affairs stand as follows: there is some hope of elections, but doubtful; some suspicion of a Dictatorship, but that too not definite; peace reigns in the Forum, but it's the peace of a senile community rather than a contented one. In the Senate my speeches are of a nature to win agreement from others rather than from myself.

> Such are the sorry works of woeful war.[117]

19 (II. 15)

CICERO TO HIS BROTHER

Rome, end of July 54

From Marcus to his brother Quintus greetings.

This time it will be best-quality pen and ink and ivory-finished paper, since you say you could hardly read my last letter. No, my dear fellow, it was for none of the reasons you

116. Cf. p. 317 and *Letters to his Friends* 26 (VII.5)2.
117. From Euripides' *Suppliant Women* (119).

suppose. I was neither busy nor upset nor annoyed with anybody. It's just that I always take the first pen that comes to hand as though it was a good one.

But now, my best and sweetest of brothers, pay careful attention while I answer that very down-to-earth passage in this same short letter. You ask me to reply in brotherly candour, without concealment or dissimulation or attempt to spare your feelings, to tell you, that is, whether you should hurry back as we had agreed or stay on (given sufficient reason) with a view to disembarrassing yourself. My dear Quintus, if you were enquiring about my wishes on some small matter, I should leave it to you to do as you chose, but at the same time make my own wishes clear. In this matter, however, I take it that you are really asking how I expect next year to turn out: well, definitely a peaceful year for me, or at any rate a very well-protected one. My house, the Forum, the demonstrations in the theatre declare as much every day. And I am not making the mistake I made once before in my consciousness of the forces behind me.[118] What gives me confidence is that I am in Pompey's and Caesar's good graces. But if the madman[119] breaks out in some wild attempt, everything is ready to crush him.

This is my true feeling and judgement, written after a careful survey. You must have no misgivings; I forbid it as a brother, not because that is what you want to be told. To enjoy the pleasure we take in each other's society I should wish you to come home at the time you stated originally, but above that I put what you think to be in your own interest. I also attach great importance to your *abondance* and the liquidation of your debts. Be sure of one thing: once free of embarrassments, we shall be the most fortunate folk in the world, given health. Our habits being what they are, the gaps are small, and if health holds, to fill them is no problem.

118. Reading *nec labor, ut quondam, conscientia* (or *confidentia?*) *copiarum nostrarum*.

119. Clodius.

Bribery is rampant again, dreadful, worse than ever before. On the Ides the rate of interest rose from 4 to 8%[120] because of a coalition between Memmius and the Consuls with Domitius.[121] Scaurus on his own can hardly defeat this. Messalla is a tired horse. I do not speak in hyperbole: they are settling to distribute ten million sesterces among the first Century. It is a flaming scandal. The candidates for the Tribunate have agreed among themselves to deposit HS500,000 each with M. Cato and make him referee of the elections, anyone contravening his rulings to be condemned by him. If these elections go through without corruption, Cato will have achieved more on his own than all the laws and all the juries.

20 (II. 16)

CICERO TO HIS BROTHER

Rome, late August 54

From Marcus to his brother Quintus greetings.

When you get a letter from me in the hand of one of my secretaries you are to infer that I did not have a minute to spare; when in my own, that I had – a minute! For let me tell you that I have never in my life been more inundated with briefs and trials, and in a heat-wave at that, in the most oppressive time of the year. But I must put up with it, since you so advise. I shall not let it appear that *I* have disappointed your[122] joint hopes and plans; and if that prove difficult, at any rate I shall reap a

120. Literally 'from 1/3 to 2/3%' (monthly).
121. There were four candidates for the Consulship of 53: M. Aemilius Scaurus, Cn. Domitius Calvinus, C. Memmius, and M. Valerius Messalla Rufus. On the coalition cf. *Letters to Atticus* 91 (IV.17)2.
122. Quintus' and Caesar's.

rich harvest of influence and prestige from my labour. So I follow your wishes. I take care to offend nobody, to be highly regarded even by those who deplore our having become so closely involved with Caesar, and an object of much attention and friendly feeling from non-partisans or from those whose sympathies actually lie this way. There has been a debate in the Senate lasting a number of days on the bribery question. The most drastic action was called for, the candidates for the Consulship having gone to intolerable lengths. I did not attend. I have decided not to come forward to cure the ills of the body politic without powerful backing.

The day I write this letter Drusus has been acquitted of collusive prosecution by the Paymaster-Tribunes. The overall majority was four, the Senators and Knights having found him guilty. This afternoon I shall be defending Vatinius – an easy matter. The elections have been put off to September. Scaurus' trial[123] will proceed straight away, and I shall not let him down.

I don't at all approve of Sophocles' *Banqueters*,[124] though you evidently gave an entertaining performance.

Now I come to what ought perhaps to have been put first. How pleased I was to get your letter from Britain! I dreaded the Ocean and the island coast. Not that I make light of what is to come, but there is more to hope than to fear, and my suspense is more a matter of anticipation than of anxiety. You evidently have some splendid literary material – the places, the natural phenomena and scenes, the customs, the peoples you fight, and, last but not least, the Commander-in-Chief! I shall be glad to help you, as you ask, in any way you wish, and I shall send you the verses you ask for (an owl to Athens!).[125]

But see here, you seem to be keeping me in the dark. Tell me,

123. For extortion in Sardinia; cf. *Letters to Atticus* 89 (IV.16)6, 90 (IV.15)9, 91 (IV.17)3.

124. Sophocles wrote a satyric play so entitled, but Cicero's meaning is obscure.

125. Cf. *Letters to his Friends*, n. 515.

my dear fellow, how does Caesar react to my verses?[126] He wrote to me that he read the first Canto and has never read anything better than the earlier part, even in Greek, but finds the rest, down to a certain point a trifle 'languid'. The truth, please! Is it the material or the style he doesn't like? No need for you to be nervous – my self-esteem won't drop a hair's-breadth. Just write to me *en ami de la vérité* and in your usual fraternal way.

21 (III. 1)

CICERO TO HIS BROTHER

Arpinum and Rome, September 54

From Marcus to his brother Quintus greetings.

Escaped from the great heat-wave (I don't remember a greater), I have refreshed myself on the banks of our delightful river at Arpinum during the Games period, after putting our fellow-tribesmen in the hands of Philotimus.

I was at Arcanum on 10 September. There I saw Mescidius and Philoxenus and the stream which they are bringing over not far from the house. It was flowing merrily enough, particularly in view of the severe drought, and they said they would be collecting a considerably larger volume of water. All was well at Herus'.[127]

On the Manilius property[128] I found Diphilus, slower than – Diphilus. However, he had nothing left to do except for the baths, promenade, and aviary. I was very pleased with the house, because the paved colonnade is a most imposing feature;

126. The poem *On my Vicissitudes*.
127. 'Herus' was probably the bailiff (therefore a slave). But the name is unexampled. Perhaps it should be 'Herius'.
128. Seemingly near Arcanum and recently acquired by Quintus.

it struck me only this visit, now that its whole range is open to view and the columns have been cleared. All depends on the elegance of the stucco, and that I shall attend to. The paving seemed to be going nicely. I did not care for some of the ceilings and gave orders to alter them.

They say you have written instructions for a small court in a certain area of the colonnade. I like that area better as it is. I don't think there is enough space for a small court, and it is not very usual to have one except in buildings which contain a larger court. Nor could it have adjoining bedrooms and suchlike appurtenances. As it is, it will make a handsome vault or a very good summer-room. But if you feel otherwise, please write back as soon as possible.

In the baths I moved the sweat-bath into the other corner of the dressing-room because in the original position its steam-pipe lay immediately underneath the bedrooms. I was very pleased with a largish bedroom and another bedroom for winter; they are a good size and well situated on the side of the promenade next the baths. The columns placed by Diphilus are neither straight nor properly aligned. He will pull them down, of course. One day he may learn how to use a rule and plumb-line. To be sure, I hope Diphilus' job will be finished in a few months. Caesius, who was with me at the time, is keeping a very watchful eye on it.

From there I set off straight down Steer Street to the Fufidius farm which I bought for you from Fufidius in Arpinum last market day for HS101,000. I never saw a shadier place in summer. There is running water all over and plenty of it. In fact Caesius thinks you will irrigate thirty-five acres of meadow with ease. For my part I'll promise what I better understand, that you will have an exceptionally charming country house when certain extras have been put in – a fish-pond, fountains, a palaestra, a ★ wood. I hear you want to keep this Bobilius[129] place. You

129. Another property, called after its previous owner. But the name may be corrupt – perhaps 'Babullius'.

will decide for yourself what you think best about that. ★[130] says that with the water taken off, and the right to the water legally certified, and a servitude placed on the property, we can still keep our price if we wanted to sell. I had Mescidius with me. He says he agreed with you on three sesterces per foot,[131] and that he has measured the distance by walking as 3,000 paces. It looked more to me, but I will guarantee that the money could not be better invested. I had sent for Cillo from Venafrum, but that very day at Venafrum a tunnel had fallen in, crushing four of his fellow-slaves and pupils.

On the Ides of September I was at Laterium. I examined the road, which I thought good enough to be a public highway, except for 150 paces (I measured it myself) from the little bridge at Furina's[132] temple leading to Satricum. In that stretch powdered earth has been used instead of gravel (that will be altered) and that part of the road has a steep uphill gradient. But I saw that no other direction was possible, especially as you did not want to take it through either Locusta's land or Varro's. Varro had made the road in front of his property in good style, whereas Locusta has not touched his section. I shall tackle him in Rome and think I shall get him moving. At the same time I shall ask M. Taurus, who is now in Rome, about taking a conduit through his farm – I hear he has made you a promise.

Your bailiff Nicephorus impressed me very favourably. I asked him whether you had given him any instructions about that little bit of building at Laterium of which you had spoken to me. He answered that he had contracted to do the job himself for HS10,000, but that you had later made considerable additions to the work and none to the price, so he had done nothing about it. For my part, I am really strongly in favour of making the additions you proposed. True, the house at present

130. The name in the manuscripts appears as 'Calibus'. Purser's correction *Camillus* is the most plausible.

131. For the construction of an aqueduct.

132. Or Furrina, an ancient Roman goddess of whom little is known.

has an air of high thinking which rebukes the wild extravagance of other country houses; but still that addition will be pleasant. I commended the gardener. He has covered everything with ivy, the foundation-wall of the house and the intervals between the columns in the promenade, so that the Greek statues look as though they were doing ornamental gardening and advertising their ivy. Then there is the little dining-room which is cool and mossy to a degree.

That's about all from the country. Philotimus and Cincius are pushing on with the finishing touches to your house, but I often put in an appearance myself, which is easy to do. So please set your mind at rest on that score.

I pardon your continual enquiries about young Quintus, but I hope you on your side will pardon me if I refuse to admit that you love him any more than I do myself. I only wish he could have been with me these days at Arpinum, which he wanted and I no less. So I'd like you to write to Pomponia, if you see fit, and ask her to come with me when I make an excursion and bring the boy. I shall do wonders if I have him by me on vacation – in Rome there isn't a moment to breathe. You know I gave you my word earlier gratis, so you can imagine what will happen now that you have offered me such a splendid fee.

I come now to the letter which I received at Arpinum in several instalments – three letters were delivered to me in one day, apparently dispatched by you simultaneously. One, which was rather long, began by noting that my letter to you bore an earlier date than the one to Caesar. It sometimes happens unavoidably that when Oppius has arranged to send couriers and been given a letter from me, he is held up by something unexpected and dispatches it unavoidably later than he had arranged; and once the letters are handed in, I don't trouble about getting the date changed.

You write about Caesar's warm affection for us. You will cherish that, and I shall do everything in my power to increase it. As regards Pompey, I am and shall be careful to do what you advise. You say you are grateful for my licence to stay on; I miss you very sorely indeed, but still I am partially glad of it. I don't understand your purpose in sending for Hippodamus and certain others. Every one of these gentry expects a present from you to the value of a property in the suburbs. But you don't have to mix up Trebatius in that category. *I* sent him to Caesar, who has already done all I expected of him. If he has not done all that Trebatius expected, I am not obliged to answer for anything and I likewise absolve and acquit you of all responsibility for him. I am tremendously pleased that you say you are rising in Caesar's good graces every day. Balbus, who you say is your helper in this, is the apple of my eye. I am glad that you and my friend Trebonius are such good friends.

As for what you write about the Tribunate, I did request one for Curtius[133] and Caesar wrote to me personally in so many words that one was waiting for Curtius, mentioning his name; and he took me to task for my backwardness in making such requests. If I make one for anybody else (and I have told Oppius to write to Caesar accordingly), I shall not mind a refusal, seeing that the people who pester me *do* mind *my* refusing them. I have a regard for Curtius, as I told himself, not only because you ask me but because of your testimonial, for your letter made it clear to me how zealous he was for my restoration.

As to British matters, I see from your letter that we have no cause for alarm nor for rejoicing either. On public affairs, which you want Tiro to write up for you, I have hitherto written rather perfunctorily because I know that everything, from greatest to least, is reported to Caesar.

I have answered the big letter, now for the little one: First you tell me about Clodius' letter to Caesar. I think Caesar was right to say no to the request you so affectionately made of him and not to write a single word to that embodiment of mis-

133. Cf. Letter 18 (II.14)3.

chief.[134] Next, as to Calventius Marius' speech,[135] I am surprised that you think I should write a rejoinder to that, especially as nobody will read it if I don't reply, whereas all the school-children learn mine against him by heart as though it was part of their lessons. I have begun the work which you are waiting for,[136] but I can't finish it this trip. I have completed the speeches for Scaurus and for Plancius[137] according to demand. I have broken off the poem addressed to Caesar which I had begun, but for you I shall write what you ask[138] (since the very springs are now athirst),[139] if I get any time.

Now I come to the third letter. You say that Balbus will be coming to Rome in good time with a goodly company and that he will be with me constantly until the Ides of May; much obliged, and much pleased to hear it. And then on the same letter, as often in the past, you urge me to go on winning friends and working. I shall. But when are we going to start living?

A fourth letter was delivered to me on the Ides of September, which you dispatched from Britain on 10 August. There was really nothing new in it except about *Erigona*[140] (and when I get her from Oppius I shall send you my opinion, though I don't doubt I shall like her) and (this I almost forgot) about the person who you say wrote to Caesar about the applause for Milo.

134. Quintus in brotherly solicitude had urged Caesar to rebuke or restrain Clodius; but Caesar had thought it best not to reply at all, a decision which M. Cicero approves.

135. L. Calpurnius Piso, Consul in 57, whose maternal grandmother was an Insubrian Gaul named Calventius. Cicero's speech against him, delivered in 55, compares him (naturally to his disadvantage) with Marius, who was responsible for Metellus Numidicus' exile in 100; cf. *in Pisonem*, 20. Piso had evidently published a speech in reply to Cicero's.

136. The treatise *On the Republic*.

137. Part of the former and the whole of the latter are extant.

138. Cf. Letter 24 (III.4)3.

139. Cicero affects to consider Quintus a better poet than himself; cf. ibid.

140. A tragedy composed by Quintus.

Well, I am quite happy that Caesar should think the applause was tremendous. In point of fact, it was; though applause for him seems in a way like applause for me.

Also, a very old letter was delivered to me, a late arrival, in which you remind me about the temple of Tellus and Catulus' portico.[141] Work is going diligently forward on both. I have even put up your statue in the former. You also remind me about a place in the suburbs, but I was never very eager for one and my house now affords me that amenity.

When I returned to Rome on 18 September I found the roof on your house finished. You had not wished it to have any gables above the living-rooms. It now slopes handsomely down to the roof of the lower portico.

Our boy has not been idle with his tutor in rhetoric during my absence. You need have no anxiety about his progress, for you know his abilities and I see his keenness. All else that concerns him I take upon myself and regard as my responsibility.

So far there are three groups out to prosecute Gabinius: L. Lentulus, the Flamen's son, who has already brought a charge of lèse-majesté; Ti. Nero, with some good assistant-prosecutors; and Tribune C. Memmius,[142] with L. Capito. Gabinius arrived in the neighbourhood of Rome on 19 September. It was an ignominious homecoming with hardly a soul to welcome him. But the courts being what they are nowadays I dare not feel confident about anything. He has not yet been charged with extortion because Cato is ill. Pompey is putting a lot of pressure on me for a reconciliation, but so far he has got nowhere, nor ever will if I keep a scrap of personal independence. I am waiting impatiently for a letter from you. It is untrue that I had anything to do with the coalition between the

141. The latter, adjoining Cicero's house on the Palatine, had been destroyed by Clodius. Cicero seems to have been in charge of restoring both.
142. To be distinguished from his relative and namesake, the consular candidate.

consular candidates, as you say you have heard. In view of the nature of the bargains struck in that coalition, which were subsequently made public by Memmius, no honest man could decently have had a hand in it. Besides, it would not have been right for me to take part in coalitions from which Messalla was excluded. He is very pleased with the support I am giving him in all ways. I think Memmius is pleased too. Even Domitius has had many favours from me, things he wanted or asked of me. Scaurus is under a great obligation to me for defending him. So far both the date of the elections and the result are highly uncertain.

Just as I was folding up this letter, couriers arrived from you – on the 20th, twenty-seven days' journey. How anxious I was! And how distressed to read Caesar's charming letter – the more charming the letter, the more distress I feel at the blow which has befallen him. But to come to your letter: First, once again I approve of your staying on, especially as you have discussed it, as you say, with Caesar. I am surprised that Oppius has had any dealings with Publius[143] – I did not want it. Further on in your letter you say that I am to be appointed Pompey's Legate on the Ides of September.[144] That is news to me. I have written to Caesar to say that neither Vibullius nor Oppius has brought any message from Caesar to Pompey about my staying in Rome. What was the reason? Well, it's true that I held Oppius back, because the leading role belonged to Vibullius; Caesar had talked to him in person on the subject, only written to Oppius. No, I cannot have any second thoughts where Caesar is concerned. He comes next with me after you and our children, and only just after. I think I am wise in this (after all, it is time for some wisdom), but my affection is truly kindled.

After I had written these last lines which are in my own hand, your son came over to us for dinner, as Pomponia was dining out. He gave me your letter to read, which he had received

143. Clodius.
144. Cf. *Letters to his Friends*, n. 142.

shortly before – a charming, serious letter upon my word, in the manner of Aristophanes.[145] I was quite delighted with it. He also gave me the other letter, in which you tell him to stick close to me and regard me as his teacher. How pleased they made him these letters, and me likewise! He is the most charming boy, and no one could be fonder of me. I dictated the above to Tiro at dinner, in case the different handwriting may surprise you.

Annalis was very grateful for your letter, grateful to you for taking trouble on his behalf and at the same time for honestly advising him for his own good. P. Servilius senior, speaking of a letter which he says he has had from Caesar, intimates that he is very much obliged to you for having spoken so kindly and with such particularity about his friendly feelings towards Caesar.

When I got back to Rome from Arpinum I was told that Hippodamus had set out to join you. I cannot say that I was surprised by his lack of consideration in leaving to join you without a letter from me. I say only that it vexed me. You see, it had been in my mind for a long time, from what you had written to me, that if there was anything which I wanted conveyed to you with extra care I should give it to him; for in those letters which I send you in the ordinary way the fact is that I write practically nothing which would be awkward if it fell into the wrong hands. Now[146] I am reserving myself for Minucius and Salvius and Labeo. Labeo will either leave late or stay here. Hippodamus did not even bid me goodbye.

T. Pinarius sends me an amiable letter about you, saying that he takes great pleasure in your letters, your conversation, and, not least, your dinners. I always liked him, and his brother is much in my company. So go on being nice to the young man.

I have had this letter in my hands for many days past, and so collected many items at different times. For instance: T. Anicius

145. Probably the comic poet rather than the grammarian.
146. *nunc* seems to have fallen out of the text before *Minucio*.

has often told me that he would not hesitate to buy a suburban property for you if he found one. This talk of his surprises me in two ways. I think it strange that you should write to him about buying a suburban property, whereas not only do you not write about it to *me* but you write in a different sense. I also think it odd that when you write to him you don't remember anything about those letters of his which you showed me at Tusculum or the precept of Epicharmus ('Find how he behaves to others'), that in fact you have as it were obliterated (?), so I suppose, his whole face and talk and mind. But it's your affair. As to suburban property, make sure that I know your wishes, and mind he doesn't do something idiotic.

What else? Oh yes, Gabinius entered Rome after dark on 27 September and today at two o'clock, when he had to appear to answer a charge of lèse-majesté on C. Alfius' order, he was almost crushed by a huge, hostile assembly of the whole people. He cuts the sorriest of figures, but Piso runs him close. I am thinking of putting a marvellous episode into Canto II of my 'Vicissitudes' – Apollo in the assembly of the Gods foretelling the return of the two generals, one of them after losing his army, the other after selling it.

Caesar dispatched a letter to me from Britain on the Kalends of September which I received on 27 September, giving a good enough account of the British campaign. He says that, in case I might wonder why I got no letter from you, you were not with him when he got to the coast. I have not replied, not even to congratulate him, because of his bereavement.[147]

Once again, my dear fellow, I beg you take care of your health.

147. Caesar's daughter and Pompey's wife Julia had recently died.

22 (III. 2)

CICERO TO HIS BROTHER

Rome, 11 October 54

From Marcus to his brother Quintus greetings.

On the evening of 10 October Salvius left for Ostia by boat with the articles you wanted sent to you from Rome. That same day Memmius[148] gave Gabinius a rare pasting at a public meeting; Calidius was not allowed to say a word in his defence. The day following the day that is about to break as I write Memmius, Ti. Nero, and the Antonius brothers (Gaius and Lucius, sons of Marcus) will plead before Cato for the right to prosecute Gabinius. We think it will go to Memmius, though Nero is remarkably keen. In a word, he is properly under pressure – unless our friend Pompey spoils the sport to the disgust of God and man.

Now let me tell you about the fellow's insolence – something to give you a little pleasure in this twilight of the commonwealth. After giving out wherever he went that he was claiming a Triumph and then (good general that he is) suddenly bursting into the enemy capital[149] at night, he didn't trust himself inside the Senate. Not until[150] the statutory tenth day, on which he was required to report the number of sacrificial victims and soldiers, did he creep into a very thin House.[151] As he was about

148. The Tribune.

149. Literally 'into a city' (or 'into Rome'; *in urbem* can mean either) 'full of enemies'.

150. *interim* ('meanwhile') in the manuscripts seems to be wrong. I have conjectured *inde primo*.

151. By entering Rome Gabinius had forfeited his claim to a Triumph, which, in any case, could hardly be taken seriously after the Senate's refusal of his Supplication. Cicero's remarks are therefore ironical. It

to leave he was detained by the Consuls and the tax-farmers brought in. Attacked from all sides as he was, I hit him hardest. Unable to stand it, he called out 'exile' in a quavering voice. Thereupon (Gods above, it was the most flattering thing that ever happened to me) the Senate rose like one man, shouting and physically bearing down on him. The tax-farmers shouted as loud and moved as smartly. To put it in a nutshell, every man of them behaved as though he was you. Outside the House nothing has ever been more talked of. However, I refrain from prosecuting him myself – with difficulty I can assure you, but I refrain. I don't want a fight with Pompey (what's coming over Milo is enough) and there are no juries any more. I'm afraid of a fiasco. And then people are so malicious – I'm nervous that he might gain some advantage with myself as prosecutor. And I don't despair of seeing the thing go through without me, and in some degree with my assistance.

All the candidates for the Consulship have been charged with bribery: Domitius by Memmius,[152] Memmius by Q. Acutius (a good, well-instructed young man), Messalla by Q. Pompeius, Scaurus by Triarius. Something big is on the way, for it looks like the end of either the men or the laws. Efforts are being made to prevent the trials, and there's the prospect of an Interregnum. The Consuls are eager to hold elections, but the defendants don't want them, especially Memmius, because he hopes that when Caesar arrives he will be elected. But he is in remarkably low water. It seems a certainty for Domitius and Messalla. Scaurus has gone flat. Appius says definitely that he will take over from our friend Lentulus[153] without a *lex*

would seem that a general claiming a Triumph was required to give notice within ten days of arrival in the area of Rome how many sacrificial victims he proposed to immolate and how many soldiers would be taking part. The reading *hostium* ('enemies') in Watt's text, instead of *hostiarum* ('victims'), has practically no manuscript authority and is otherwise unsatisfactory.

152. Probably the candidate rather than the Tribune.

153. As governor of Cilicia.

curiata. I almost forgot to say that he was magnificent that day against Gabinius – charged him with lèse-majesté. Members volunteered (?),[154] while Gabinius never said a word.

So much for public affairs. At home all is well. As to the home itself, the contractors are making reasonably good progress.

23 (III. 3)

CICERO TO HIS BROTHER

Rome, 21 October 54

From Marcus to his brother Quintus greetings.

You may take my secretary's handwriting as a sign of how busy I am. I tell you, there is not a day on which I don't make a speech for the defence. So practically everything I do or think about I put into my walking-time.

Our affairs stand as follows: Domestically they are as we wish them. The boys are well, keen at their lessons and conscientiously taught. They love us and each other. The finishing touches to both our houses are in train, but your country residences at Arcanum and Laterium are already all but complete. Furthermore, I wrote to you in full detail about the water and the road in one of my letters,[155] omitting nothing. But I am very anxious and worried by the fact that for more than seven weeks now I have heard nothing either from you or from Caesar. Not a letter, not even a rumour has trickled in from that part of the world. Sea and land out there both make me anxious now, and, as usual when people one is fond of are concerned, I am continually imagining the worst. I won't ask you

154. Literally 'names were given'; but the meaning is uncertain.
155. Letter 21 (III.1).

to write to me about yourself and about what is going on, for you never lose an opportunity; but I do want you to know that I have never been so impatient for anything in my life as I am for a letter from you as I write these lines.

Now let me tell you about politics. Day by day election-days are cancelled by declarations of contrary omens, to the great satisfaction of all honest men. That is because the Consuls are in very bad odour owing to the suspicion that they have sold themselves to the candidates. All four consular candidates have been charged. The cases are difficult to defend, but I am working hard to save Messalla, and that involves the survival of the others. P. Sulla has charged Gabinius with bribery, with his stepson Memmius, his brother Caecilius,[156] and his son Sulla as assistant-prosecutors. L. Torquatus put in a rival claim to prosecute and everyone was glad it failed. You will want to know what is happening about Gabinius. We shall know about the lèse-majesté in three days' time. In that trial he is weighed down by his unpopularity with all classes, and the witnesses are most damaging; the prosecutors are extremely ineffective, the jury is a mixed bag, the President, Alfius, is responsible and firm, Pompey is urgently trying to influence the jurors. I don't know what will happen, but I don't see any place for him in the community. I take a moderate attitude as to his ruin, and a very easy one as to the outcome of events.

That is about all my news. I will add one thing: your (our) boy Quintus is greatly devoted to his tutor in rhetoric, Paeonius, a very good experienced man, I think; but, as you are aware, my method of instruction is a little more scholarly and abstract. Accordingly, I don't want Quintus' progress and the teaching he is getting held up; and the boy himself seems to find the declamatory mode more attractive and agreeable. We have been through it ourselves, so let us allow him to follow in our footsteps. I am confident he will reach the same goal. All the same, when I take him away with me somewhere in the

156. L. Caecilius Rufus, Praetor in 57.

country, I shall introduce him to my method and practice. You have offered me a big fee, and it won't be my fault if I don't earn it.

Do write to me in full detail where you will be spending the winter and with what prospects.

24 (III. 4)

CICERO TO HIS BROTHER

Rome, 24 October 54

From Marcus to his brother Quintus greetings.

Gabinius has been acquitted. To be sure, the prosecutor Lentulus and his assistants were stutterers and the jury was a disgrace. None the less, but for Pompey's incredible lobbying and importunity, also the formidable rumour of a Dictatorship, he would not have answered, not even to Lentulus. Even with such a prosecutor and such a jury he was found guilty by 32 votes out of 70 cast. To be sure, this trial has caused so much scandal that he looks likely to go under in the forthcoming trials, especially for extortion. But you see that we have neither commonwealth nor Senate nor courts of justice, and that none of us has any standing. Further as to the jury, two ex-Praetors sat on it, Domitius Calvinus (who openly voted for acquittal for all to see) and ★[157] (when the votes had been counted he slipped off and was the first to bring the good news to Pompey).

Some, like Sallustius, say I ought to have prosecuted. Was I to trust myself with such a jury as this? How should I have looked if he had got away with me conducting the business? But I had

157. The manuscripts have 'Cato'; but M. Cato, who was Praetor in 54, is impossible, C. Cato, Tribune in 56, equally so. Gutta, who appears to have been a candidate for the Consulship of 52 favoured by Pompey (cf. p. 336), is a possibility.

other reasons. Pompey would have felt that it was a fight between him and me, and that the stake was, not Gabinius' survival, but his own prestige. He would have entered Rome, it would have come to a feud. I should have looked like Pacideianus matched against Aeserninus the Samnite.[158] He might have bitten off my ear, and he would certainly have made it up with Clodius. No, I strongly approve of my decision, especially if you don't disapprove of it. Think of what Pompey did. I had shown extraordinary zeal for his advancement, I was under no obligation to him, whereas his to me were unlimited; and yet he couldn't tolerate (I will use no harsher phrase) my political disagreement with himself, and though less powerful then than now he showed what he could do to me at the height of my career. *Now*, when I don't even trouble about having power and the state certainly has none and Pompey alone is all-powerful, was I to lock horns with Pompey himself? For that is what I should have had to do. I don't believe you would have had me take that upon myself. 'One thing or the other,' says that same Sallustius. 'You ought to have defended him and yielded to Pompey's insistence' (he certainly begged me earnestly to do that). What a charming friend Sallustius is! He thinks I ought to have chosen between a dangerous feud and eternal disgrace. For my part, I like this middle way. And I am glad to remember that after I had given my evidence very gravely in accordance with my honour and conscience the defendant said that if he was allowed to remain in the community he would make me amends. Nor did he ask me a single question.

As for the verses you want me to write for you, I lack the leisure, but I also lack divine *afflatus*, which[159] calls not only for time but for a mind free of all anxiety. For I am not altogether

158. Two gladiators in the time of Lucilius. Pacideianus was the more skilful, Aeserninus the more powerful.

159. I translate a reading proposed in *Proceedings of the Cambridge Philological Society*, 7 (1961), p. 4.

without anxiety about next year, though I have no fear. And furthermore, truly without false modesty, I recognize you as my superior in that line of authorship.

As regards filling the gaps in your Greek library and exchanging books and acquiring Latin ones, I should very much like all this done, especially as I too stand to benefit. But I have nobody I can employ on such business, not even for myself. Books, at least such as one would like to have, are not on the market and they can't be obtained except through an expert who is willing to take trouble. However, I'll give an order to Chrysippus and talk to Tyrannio. I shall enquire what Scipio has done about the Treasury,[160] and shall pay what appears proper. As to Ascanio, you will do what you wish – I don't interfere. You are wise to be in no hurry about a suburban property, though I do encourage you to get one.

I am writing this on 24 October, the opening day of the Games, as I leave for Tusculum. I am taking my son with me, to work, not to play. The reason I go no further away, as[161] I should have liked to do, is that I want to put in an appearance for Pomptinus, whose Triumph is on 2 November. And there will be some little trouble, for Praetors Cato and Servilius are threatening to forbid it. I don't know what they can do (he will have Consul Appius with him and most of the Praetors and Tribunes), but threaten they do, especially Q. Scaevola, 'breathing war'.[162]

Take care of your health, my sweetest and dearest of brothers.

160. Nothing is known about this business, but cf. p. 332.
161. Read *quod vellem* for *quam vellem*.
162. Greek. (The Latin equivalent is in *Letters to Atticus* 389 (xv.11).1); cf. Aeschylus, *Agamemnon*, 375, Quintus of Smyrna, 1. 343.

25 (III. 5)

CICERO TO HIS BROTHER

Tusculum, end of October or beginning of November 54

From Marcus to his brother Quintus greetings.

You ask what has become of the work[163] which I started to write when I was at Cumae. Well, I have not been and am not idle, but several times already I have changed the whole plan and framework. I had two Books in which I presented a conversation held during the nine-day holiday in the Consulship of Tuditanus and Aquilius,[164] the speakers being Africanus (shortly before his death), Laelius, Philus, Manilius, P. Rutilius, Q. Tubero, and Laelius' sons-in-law, Fannius and Scaevola. The conversation, distributed over nine days and nine Books, concerned the ideal constitution and the ideal citizen. The composition of the work was going forward very nicely and the high rank of the participants lent weight to their words. But when these two Books were read to me at Tusculum in Sallustius' hearing, he pointed out that these matters could be treated with much more authority if I spoke of the state in my own person. After all, he said, I was no Heraclides of Pontus but a Consular, one who had been involved in most important state affairs. Speeches attributed to persons so remote in time would appear fictitious. In my earlier work on the theory of oratory, he said, I had tactfully separated the conversation of the orators from myself, but I had put it into the mouths of men whom I had personally seen. Finally, Aristotle's writings on the state and the pre-eminent individual are in his own person.

This shook me, all the more so as I was debarred from touching upon the greatest upheavals in our community because they

163. On the Republic.
164. 129 B.C.

took place after the lifetimes of the interlocutors. In point of fact that was my object at the time, to avoid giving offence in any quarter if I came into contact with our own period. Now, while avoiding this, I shall speak myself in conversation with you; none the less I shall send you what I had begun when I return to Rome. I think you will appreciate that it cost me some heartburning to give up those two Books.

Caesar's affection as expressed in his letter pleases me beyond anything, but I set no great store by the promises he holds out. I am not thirsty for honours nor do I hanker after glory. I look forward to his lasting good-will more than to the outcome of his promises. And yet I live constantly toiling to win friends as though I *were* looking forward to what I do not ask.

As for your request about writing verses, my dear fellow, you cannot believe how short I am of time; and frankly I am not sufficiently stimulated by the theme on which you want me to poetize. Do you ask me for tides[165] and things which I myself cannot even imagine – you, who have excelled everyone in this kind of descriptive eloquence? Even so I should do it as best I could, but, as you are very well aware, poetry calls for a certain *élan* of which the times we live in quite deprive me. To be sure, I am withdrawing from all political concerns and giving myself up to literary work; all the same, I will tell you something which I assure you I used to want to hide from you of all people. My sweetest brother, it wrings my heart to think that we have no commonwealth, no courts of justice, and that these years of my life which ought to be passing in the plenitude of senatorial dignity are spent in the hurly-burly of forensic practice or rendered tolerable by my studies at home. As for my childhood dream, 'Far to excel, out-topping all the rest,'[166] it has perished

165. Reading *ampoteis* (Greek) *et ea quae*. Quintus had invited Cicero to describe British natural phenomena in verse (cf. p. 312), including the ocean tides.

166. Cf. *Letters to his Friends*, n. 809. *pollon* ('far') is here substituted for *aien* ('always').

utterly. Some of my enemies I have refrained from attacking, others I have actually defended. My mind, even my animosities, are in chains. And in all the world Caesar is the only man who cares for me as much as I could wish, or (as others would have it) who wants *me* to care for *him*.[167] And yet nothing of all this is so painful but that I find many consolations to make life easier day by day. But the greatest consolation will be for us to be together. As it is, I have to bear the heavy burden of your absence on top of the rest.

If I had defended Gabinius, as Pansa thought I ought to have done, it would have been my undoing. Those who hate him (and this includes all categories of society) would have begun to hate me – the very person on whose account they hate *him*.[168] I held my horses to admiration, I think, doing just so much as everyone saw I had to do. And in the final sum I am resolutely facing in the direction of tranquillity and peace, as you advise.

As for the books, Tyrannio is a dawdler. I shall speak to Chrysippus. But it is a laborious business and needs somebody who will take a lot of trouble. I know that from my own experience of trying very hard and making no headway. As for the Latin ones, I don't know where to turn, the copies are made and sold so full of errors. None the less, I shall not neglect to do what can be done.

*,[169] as I wrote to you earlier, is in Rome and reports himself as infinitely obliged to you, which is very gratifying.[170] I think our business has been settled by the Treasury during my absence.

You write that you have finished off four tragedies in sixteen days; and are *you* trying to borrow anything from someone else? And are you asking for *Sailors* when you have written an

167. Reading *qui a me amari vellet*.

168. As largely to blame for Cicero's exile.

169. 'Crebrius', according to the manuscripts, which are probably corrupt.

170. Reading *et, quod valde iuvat, omnia debere tibi renuntiat*.

Electra and a ★?[171] Don't be so lazy. And don't suppose that the old maxim 'know thyself' was made only to reduce conceit; it also tells us to know our strong points. But please send me these new ones and *Erigona*. There are your two last letters answered.

In Rome and especially on the Appian Way near the temple of Mars we are having extraordinarily heavy floods. Crassipes' promenade has been swept away along with a great number of residences and shops. The vast expanse of water stretches as far as the public fish-pond. Homer's lines are much quoted:

> An autumn day, when Zeus most mightily
> Doth rain, in ire against unrighteous men,

pat as they are to Gabinius' acquittal:

> Who, rendering crooked judgements openly,
> Drive justice out nor reck of wrath divine.[172]

But I am resolved not to trouble myself about such matters. When I get back to Rome I shall write to you what I observe, especially about the Dictatorship, and shall send letters to Labienus and Ligurius.

I am writing this before dawn by the light of a little lamp with a wooden stand, which delights me because they say you had it made when you were in Samos.

Goodbye, my sweetest and best of brothers.

171. On this passage see *Proceedings of the Cambridge Philological Society*, 7 (1961), p. 5.
172. *Iliad*, XVI.385-8.

26 (III. 6)

CICERO TO HIS BROTHER

Rome, end of November 54

From Marcus to his brother Quintus greetings.

I have no answer to make to your earlier letter, which is full of spleen and grumblings (you say you gave another in similar vein to Labienus the previous day, but that has not yet arrived); for the letter which followed it obliterated all my vexation. I only warn and beg you amid these annoyances and labours and privations to be mindful of our purpose when you went to Gaul. They were no trifling or ordinary advantages that we had in view. What would have seemed worth the price of our separation? Our object was to gain reliable, comprehensive support for our public position and status from the good-will of a very fine and very powerful person. Our capital is invested in hope rather than in money; if that hope were to be abandoned,[173] all else would be saved only to be lost later on. Accordingly, if you will frequently carry your mind back to our old reasoned purpose and hope, you will find it easier to put up with your military labours and the other irritants – which, however, you will lay aside when you so desire; but the time is not yet ripe for that, though it is already drawing near.

I would also advise you not to trust anything to a letter which might embarrass us if it became public property. There are many things of which I had sooner be ignorant than informed, if the information carries risk. I shall write to you at greater length when, as I hope, my boy is himself again and my mind is easy. On your part please see to it that I know to whom I ought

173. Reading *qua relicta reliqua*.

to give the letter which I shall then be sending – should it be Caesar's couriers, so that he forwards it to you straight away, or Labienus'? For where those Nervii of yours live and how far they are away from us I don't know.

It gave me much pleasure to learn from your letter of the courage and dignity of Caesar's bearing in his great sorrow.[174] As for your command that I finish that poem addressed to him which I had begun, my time is much distracted and my mind far more so, but since Caesar knows from my letter to you that I have started on something, I shall go back to what I began and finish it during these leisure days of Supplications. I am very glad that thanks to them our friend Messalla and the others have been relieved of annoyance, and when you folk reckon him as certain of election along with Domitius you don't at all run counter to our opinion. I make myself responsible to Caesar for Messalla's behaviour. But Memmius pins hopes on Caesar's return to Italy, wherein I fancy he is making a mistake. Here at any rate he is in the cold. Scaurus was thrown over by Pompey some time ago.

Business has been adjourned and the elections brought to an Interregnum. There is talk of a Dictator, disagreeable to the honest men; what they are saying is to me still less agreeable. But the whole idea is viewed with alarm, and at the same time it's falling flat. Pompey categorically denies any desire for it. Talking to me himself earlier on he did not use to deny it. It looks as though Hirrus will make the proposal (Gods, what an ass he is! How he loves himself – in which regard he has no competitor!). He got me to frighten off Crassus Junianus,[175] who is at my service. Does he want it or doesn't he? Hard to tell, but if Hirrus is the mover, he will never persuade the world that

---

174. Julia's death.

175. A Tribune in 53. His full name seems to have been P. Licinius Crassus Junianus (Brutus) Damasippus.

he doesn't. At present they are talking of nothing else in the way of politics; certainly nothing is a'doing.

The funeral of Serranus, Domitius' son,[176] took place on 23 November, a very sad occasion. His father spoke a eulogy of my composition.

Now about Milo: Pompey does nothing to help him and everything to help Gutta.[177] He says that he will see to it that Caesar throws his weight that way. This appalls Milo, as well it may, and he is almost in despair should Pompey become Dictator. If he assists anyone vetoing the Dictatorship with his organized band he fears Pompey's hostility, whereas if he doesn't give such assistance he's afraid it will be carried through by force. He is preparing some most magnificent Games, in fact they will cost as much as any that ever were – which is double and triple folly, for (a) nobody asked him, (b) he had previously given a splendid show, (c) he can't afford it; or rather more than triple because (d) he could have seen himself as an executor, not an Aedile.[178]

That's about all. Take care of your health, my dearest brother.

27 (III. 7)

CICERO TO HIS BROTHER

Rome, December 54

From Marcus to his brother Quintus greetings.

It would not have been right for me to take any of the courses

176. Reading with Münzer *Domiti* for *domestici*. The deceased will have been a son of L. Domitius Ahenobarbus adopted by an Atilius Serranus.

177. Otherwise unknown, unless he is the ex-Praetor mentioned in Letter 24; see n. 157. Milo was standing for the Consulship of 52.

178. Reading *vel quia non postulatos* and *vel magis quam ter, quia potuerat*. But the meaning of *magistrum*, translated 'executor', is uncertain.

with regard to Gabinius which you, in the warmth of your affection, have been considering. 'Then let the earth yawn wide for me.'[179] What I did I did, as everybody feels, with the utmost responsibility and moderation. I have neither borne hard on him nor lent a helping hand. I spoke forcibly on the witness-stand but otherwise held my peace. As for the outcome of the trial, shocking and detrimental as it was, I took it with complete composure. Now at long last I have gained this much: the evils in our public life and the licence of bold, bad men, which used to make me boil with rage, now leave me quite unmoved. For the men and the times could not be worse than they are; so, since public affairs can no longer yield any pleasure, I don't know why I should get my temper up. I have sources of joy in my writings and studies, the leisure of my country houses, and above all else in our children. Milo is my only worry, but I hope his Consulship will put an end to that. I shall make as big an effort in that as I made for my own, and you will help from over there, as you are doing. In this matter, unless sheer violence breaks loose, everything is in good shape with one exception – his pocket. That alarms me. 'Mad he is, past all bearing'[180] – planning a show to cost HS ★. His unwisdom in this one particular I shall restrain as best I can, and your force of character[181] should enable you to do the like with effect.

As for the changes in the coming year, I did not mean you to understand anything in the nature of private alarm, I was referring to the general state of the commonwealth. Even though I have no responsibility, I cannot be indifferent. How cautious I want you to be in what you write you may infer from the fact

179. *Iliad*, IV.182=VIII.150.

180. *Iliad*, VIII.355.

181. The conjecture *Nerviorum*, adopted in Watt's text for *nervorum*, would mean that Quintus, whose winter headquarters were among the Nervii, could get rich at their expense and so come to Milo's assistance. *sustinebo*, translated 'I shall restrain', will then have to mean 'I shall support'.

that in writing to you I don't mention even overt political disorders, for fear of the letters getting intercepted and giving offence in any quarter. So I want you to ease your mind of private concern. I know how anxious you are apt to be about public affairs.

I expect to see our friend Messalla made Consul; if by an Interrex he will not be on trial, if by a Dictator he will still be in no danger.[182] Nobody hates him, Hortensius' ardour[183] will have a powerful effect, and Gabinius' acquittal is regarded as a statute of impunity. *En passant*, nothing has so far been done about a Dictator after all. Pompey is away, Appius is stirring the pot, Hirrus making ready, many vetoes are being counted, the public is indifferent, the leaders are opposed, I lie low.

Thank you very much for your promise of slaves.[184] As you say, I am indeed short-handed, both in Rome and on my estates. But, my dear fellow, please don't consider anything to do with my convenience unless it is absolutely convenient and easy for *you*.

I was amused to hear about Vatinius' letter,[185] but I may tell you that he is so attentive to me that I not only swallow those insolences of his but digest them too.

The epic to Caesar which you urge me to finish, finished it I have, a delectable piece, so it seems to *me*. But I am looking for a trustworthy courier for fear it share the fate of your *Erigona*, the only traveller from Gaul under Caesar's government who found the road unsafe. And she at least had an excellent dog to protect her![186]

182. If the elections were held by an Interrex in 53 (as ultimately happened) Messalla would take office immediately the result was declared and would be immune from prosecution at least until the end of his term. But even if they were held before the end of the year Messalla was not likely to be convicted.

183. Hortensius was Messalla's uncle.

184. From Gaul or Britain.

185. Probably a letter to Caesar which had been shown to Quintus.

186. Reading *quid si canem tam bonum non haberet?*, literally 'What

What, demolish the building?[187] I like it better every day. The lower portico and its rooms are coming on particularly well. As for Arcanum, we need Caesar's good taste, or even better taste than his upon my word! Those busts of yours, the palaestra, the fishpool, the canal, call for a multitude of Philotimi – not Diphili![188] However, I shall visit them myself, and send people over, and give instructions.

You would be more indignant about Felix's will than you are if you knew. The document which he thought he signed, in which you were firmly down for a twelfth share, he did not in fact sign, being misled by an error of his own and of his slave Sicura's;[189] the one he signed was contrary to his wishes. But to the devil with him! So long as we stay healthy!

I love your son as you ask and as he deserves and as I ought, but I am letting him go because I don't want to take him away from his teachers and because his mother ★ is leaving. Without her I am terrified of the young fellow's appetite! But we are a great deal together all the same.

I have answered all your points. My best and most delectable of brothers, goodbye.

---

would have happened to her if she didn't have such a good dog?' The messenger who brought Quintus' tragedy *Erigona* to Italy seems to have been attacked on the road. Erigone's dog Maera was proverbially faithful, an Athenian Gelert.

187. Apparently on the Manilius property; see p. 313.

188. Cicero had a poor opinion of Diphilus' competence as an architect; cf. p. 314. Philotimus was concerned in work on Quintus' house in Rome (p. 316).

189. The name seems impossible; perhaps 'Scurra', epigraphically attested as a slave-name (='buffoon', 'wag').

INTRODUCTION TO CICERO'S LETTERS
TO MARCUS BRUTUS

BORN in 85, M. Junius Brutus was adopted in early life by a maternal uncle, so that his name became for official purposes Quintus (Servilius) Caepio Brutus. But the original style remained in general use among his contemporaries and posterity. His natural father was a nobleman supposedly descended from Rome's first Consul, who held office under the Marians and was killed by Pompey in 78 for his part in an insurrection against the post-Sullan regime. His mother, Servilia, not only belonged to a patrician family with wide aristocratic connections but was half-sister to Marcus Cato and, according to general report, Julius Caesar's mistress. A second marriage and the marriages of three resulting daughters linked her and her son to yet other leading families and individuals. Brutus himself married a daughter of Appius Claudius Pulcher, whose other daughter was the wife of Pompey's elder son (Brutus later divorced her to marry Cato's daughter, the 'Portia' of Shakespeare's *Julius Caesar*). The great account in which he was held by his contemporaries is partly attributable to the extent and brilliance of these family connections.

But Brutus' personal qualities and attainments were far out of the ordinary. An austere intellectual with a deep interest in Greek philosophy, he became as a young man one of the foremost public speakers of the day in the so-called 'Atticist' manner, which aimed at simple elegance in opposition to Ciceronian orotundity. Moreover, he did nothing by halves. 'When he wants something,' said Julius Caesar of Brutus, 'he wants it badly.'

In 58 he accompanied his uncle Cato on a special mission to supervise the annexation of Cyprus to the Roman Empire. In 53 he served as Quaestor under his father-in-law, Appius

Claudius, the governor of Cilicia, and in 49 as Legate to Cicero's successor in the same province, Publius Sestius. The Civil War had now broken out and Brutus passed from Cilicia to Pompey's camp in Greece, where Cicero wrote of him to Atticus as 'zealous in the cause'. But after Pharsalia he was not only pardoned by Caesar but taken into favour, being made governor of Cisalpine Gaul in 46 and City Praetor in 44. Early that year a plot was hatched to assassinate the Dictator, which took effect on 15 March. Brutus was its leader, along with his brother-in-law, C. Cassius Longinus, and a distant kinsman, Decimus Brutus.

The conspirators seem to have planned no further than the act. Mark Antony, the surviving Consul, soon showed a disposition to step into Caesar's shoes. His ascendancy was challenged by Caesar's heir, the eighteen-year-old Octavian, while Brutus and Cassius, the 'Liberators' as they were called, remained helpless spectators until the autumn, when they left for the East. There it was a very different story. The Caesarian commanders in Syria and Egypt, whether from republican sympathies or lack of personal ambition, handed over to Cassius, while Brutus took possession of Greece, defeating and capturing Antony's brother Gaius. By the spring of 43 the 'Liberators' were in control from the Euphrates to the Adriatic. Despite all appeals, they made no effort to come to the rescue of the republican cause in Italy, preferring to wait to be attacked by the new coalition of Antony and Octavian. The end came at Philippi in October 42. Brutus and Cassius perished and the Roman Republic perished with them.

Atticus, who was on friendly terms with Cato and his circle, found himself much drawn to Cato's gifted nephew, and through Atticus an intimacy arose between Brutus and Cicero. It may have ripened when they were together in Pompey's army, and after Cicero's return to Rome in the autumn of 47 we find it fully established. It was publicly signalized *inter alia* by Cicero's dialogue on the history of Roman oratory, to which he gave Brutus' name, and by the dedication of the *Orator*, a work of which he was particularly proud.

Apart from four (or, as I believe, five) letters of recommendation in the collection *ad Familiares* the extant correspondence between Cicero and Marcus Brutus consists of one 'Book' and a portion of another, twenty-six letters in all. They date from March or April to July 43. The first five (= 'Book' II) are known only from an edition printed in 1528, the manuscript which contained them being no longer extant.

The genuineness of the whole collection was impugned in the eighteenth century and long remained in doubt. It is now generally recognized, with the possible exception of Letters 24 (I.16) and 25 (I.16). For Brutus' sake one would be glad to assign to a later forger these repetitious and unjust diatribes, made purportedly from the security of Macedonia against the man who was upholding the Republic in Italy by the only means open to him at the ultimate cost of his life. But proof is lacking.

Watt's Oxford Text of 1958 is again the basis of my translation.

CICERO'S LETTERS TO
MARCUS BRUTUS

LETTERS TO M. BRUTUS

I (I or II. I)

CICERO TO M. BRUTUS

Rome, c. 1 April 43

From Cicero to Brutus greetings.

As I write, the ultimate crisis is thought to be upon us. Gloomy letters and messengers are coming in about our friend Decimus Brutus. They do not disturb *me* overmuch, for I cannot possibly lack confidence in our armies and generals, nor do I subscribe to the majority opinion – I do not judge unfavourably of the loyalty of the Consuls, which is under strong suspicion; though in certain respects I could have wished for more wisdom and promptitude. Had that been forthcoming, we should have had public order restored a while ago. You are well aware of the importance of the right moment in political affairs, and what a vast difference it makes whether the same decree or enterprise or course of action be adopted before or after. If only all the strong measures decreed during this turmoil had been carried through the day I proposed them, and not put off from one day to the next or dragged out and procrastinated *after* action upon them had been taken in hand, we should now have no war.

My dear Brutus, I have done for our country all that lies with one who stands where I, by judgement of Senate and People, stand today. I have not only given all that can fairly be demanded of a man – good faith, vigilance, patriotism; for these are what it is everybody's duty to render. But I conceive that something more is required of one whose voice is heard among leading statesmen, namely wisdom. And having presumed to take the helm of state, I should hold myself no less to blame if any counsel I gave the Senate were inexpedient than I should if it were dishonest.

I know you receive full and accurate reports of events both past and current. As coming from myself, I should like you to be well aware that *my* mind is in the fighting line – I am not looking over my shoulder, unless it so happen that the interests of the community make me turn my head; but the minds of the majority are looking back, to you and Cassius. So, Brutus, I would have you adjust yourself to the realization that it will be your duty either to improve our body politic, should the present conflict go well, or to restore it, should we meet with a reverse.

2 (III or II. 3)

M. BRUTUS TO CICERO

Dyrrachium, 1 April 43

From Brutus to Cicero greetings.

I am eagerly waiting for a letter from you written after the news of my doings and of Trebonius' death, not doubting that you will set out your views for me. By a dastardly crime we have lost a fine Roman and have been ousted from a province, which is neither easy to regain nor will the thing be the less shameful and outrageous if it *can* be regained.[1]

Antonius[2] is still with me, but upon my word I am moved by

1. Reading *quam neque reciperari facile est neque . . . erit si potest reciperari.*
2. Mark Antony's brother Gaius. Appointed governor of Macedonia, he had been defeated and taken prisoner by Brutus.

CICERO'S LETTERS TO MARCUS BRUTUS

his pleas and I am afraid that the fanaticism of certain people may pick him off. I am really troubled. If I knew what course you favoured I should not be worried, for I should be satisfied that it was best. So please let me know your opinion as soon as possible.

Our friend Cassius holds Syria and the Syrian legions. He was called in by Murcus and Marcius and the army itself. I have written to my sister Tertia[3] and my mother to tell them not to make this splendid success of Cassius' public before consulting with you and before you think proper.

I have read your two speeches,[4] the one on the Kalends of January and the one you delivered against Calenus. You won't be waiting for me to praise them.[5] I don't know whether these pieces say more for your spirit or for your genius. I am now willing to let them be called by the proud name of 'Philippics',[6] as you jestingly suggested in one of your letters.

My dear Cicero, I have now two needs: money and reinforcements. The latter you can provide by arranging for a contingent of troops to be sent to me from Italy either by way of a secret understanding with Pansa or through action in the Senate. The former is a necessity, as much for the other armies as for mine, which makes me all the sorrier that we have lost Asia. I hear that Dolabella's oppression of the province makes Trebonius' murder no longer appear the worst of his savageries. However, Antistius Vetus[7] has given me financial help.

Your son Cicero earns my approval by his energy, endur-

3. Wife of Cassius.

4. The Fifth and Seventh Philippics.

5. Reading *non* for *nunc*, which would mean 'Now, no doubt, you expect me to praise them'. Despite *Letters to Atticus* 115 (VI.1).7, Brutus is not likely to have written anything so churlish.

6. After Demosthenes' speeches against Philip of Macedon.

7. C. Antistius Vetus had been in charge of Syria until succeeded by Staius Murcus. Probably late in 44 he (if it is the same man) entered into Brutus' service, handing over the tribute money which he was bringing back to Rome. Cf. Letter 16 (XIX or I.11).

ance, hard work, and unselfish spirit, in fact by every kind of service. Indeed he seems never to forget whose son he is. I cannot make you think more of one whom you so deeply love than you already do, but trust my judgement in assuring yourself that he will have no need to exploit your renown in order to attain his father's honours.

Kalends of April, Dyrrachium.

3 (II or II. 2)

CICERO TO M. BRUTUS

Rome, 11 April 43

From Cicero to Brutus greetings.

From Plancus' letter,[8] of which I think you have been sent a copy, you will have been able to perceive his fine spirit of patriotism as well as the legions, auxiliaries, and resources at his disposal. On the other hand I suppose that letters from your own circle will already have made evident to you the irresponsibility, fickleness, and consistently unpatriotic attitude of your connection Lepidus, who hates his relatives by marriage only one degree less than his brother.[9]

We are anxiously waiting for news from Mutina, where the whole situation is at ultimate crisis-point. All hope lies in relieving Brutus. We are in grave fear for him.

Here I have trouble enough on my hands with that madman Servilius. I put up with him longer than suited my dignity, but I did that for the public sake, not wishing to give traitors a rallying-point – a semi-lunatic, to be sure, but a nobleman; though rally to him they do none the less. Still I thought he had

8. *Letters to his Friends* 371 (x.8).
9. L. Aemilius Paulus, Consul in 50.

better not be estranged from the national cause. Well, my patience with him is at an end. His insolence reached the point that he treated everybody else like slaves. He flared up in an incredible passion over Plancus' matter and battled with me for two days. I quashed him so effectively that I hope he will mend his manners once and for all. Just when this combat was at its height on 9 April a letter was delivered to me in the Senate from our friend Lentulus[10] about Cassius and the legions and Syria. I read it out at once and Servilius, along with several more (there are a number of prominent persons who are thoroughly disloyal), collapsed. But Servilius bitterly resented my gaining my point about Plancus. He is a political monstrosity, but will not last long, take my word.

4 (IV or II. 4)

CICERO TO M. BRUTUS

Rome, 12 April 43

From Cicero to Brutus greetings.

After giving a letter to Scaptius on the morning of 11 April I received that same evening yours dispatched from Dyrrachium on the Kalends of April. So on the morning of the 12th, having been informed by Scaptius that the persons to whom I gave my letter yesterday have not yet left but are leaving directly, I am scribbling these few words in the hubbub of my morning levée.

I am happy about Cassius and congratulate the commonwealth, and myself too in that against Pansa's angry opposition I proposed that Cassius should take military action against Dolabella. Indeed I ventured to maintain that he was already engaged in such action without any decree of ours. I also said

10. The younger Lentulus Spinther. The letter is not extant.

what I thought proper about yourself. The speech[11] will be sent to you, since I see you enjoy my Philippics.

With regard to your question about Antonius, I think he should be held in custody until we know what happens to Brutus. From the letter you have sent me it seems that Dolabella is oppressing Asia and behaving there abominably. Now you have written to several people that Dolabella was refused admission by the Rhodians. If he has approached Rhodes, then I suppose he has left Asia. If that is so, I would advise you to remain where you are, but if he has got possession of Asia I would advise you to pursue him there.[12] I do not think you can do better at this time.

You say you are in want of two necessities, reinforcements and money. It is hard to make any suggestion. No financial resources occur to me as available for your use other than those which the Senate has decreed, namely that you should borrow sums from civic bodies. So far from Pansa assigning you anything from his own army or levies he is not happy that so many volunteers are joining you, because, as I for my part suppose, he thinks that no forces are too large for the issues which are being determined in Italy – but as many suspect, because he does not want even you to be too strong. *I* have no such suspicion.

You say you wrote to your sister Tertia and your mother telling them not to make Cassius' successes public before I thought proper. Evidently you were afraid, and with good reason, that Caesar's party, as it is still called, would be much upset by the news. But the matter was common knowledge before we got your letter. Even your own couriers had brought letters to many of your friends. Accordingly, it was not advisable to suppress it, particularly as that was impossible; and even had it been possible, I should have been in favour of publication rather than concealment.

If my son Marcus has all the qualities with which you credit

11. The Eleventh Phillippic.
12. Reading *a te* for *at*.

him, I am naturally no less glad than I ought to be. And if your affection for him makes you exaggerate, the very fact of your caring for him makes me exceedingly happy.

5 (V or II. 5)

CICERO TO M. BRUTUS

Rome, 19 (?) April 43

From Cicero to Brutus greetings.

I expect you have heard from your own people about your letter which was read out in the Senate on the Ides of April and Antonius'[13] letter which was read at the same time. None of them thinks more of you than I do, but there was no need for everyone to tell you the same tale. There *is* need for me to tell you my views about the nature of this war, how I judge and what I advise.

My general political aims have always been identical with yours, my dear Brutus; my policy in certain matters (not in all) has perhaps been a little more forceful. You know I have always held that the commonwealth should be freed from monarchy, not merely from a monarch. You took a milder view, no doubt to your own eternal credit. But we have realized to our bitter distress, and are realizing to our grave peril, what the better course would have been.[14] In the period we have lately been through your supreme object was peace – which could not be accomplished with words; mine was freedom, for without freedom peace is meaningless. I thought that peace itself could be achieved by war and weapons. Men with the zeal to demand them were not lacking, but we checked their enthusiasm and

13. C. Antonius (see below).
14. i.e. Mark Antony should have been killed along with Caesar.

damped down their ardour. And so matters reached the point that, if some higher power had not inspired Caesar Octavian, we should have lain at the mercy of an abandoned villain, Mark Antony. How desperate a struggle with him is going on at this moment you see. Obviously there would have been none, if Antony's life had not then been spared.

But I leave all this aside. That memorable, almost god-like deed of yours is proof against all criticisms; indeed it can never be adequately praised. Latterly you have appeared in a new and sterner guise. In a short time and by your own efforts you have got an army – forces, legions in sufficient strength. Ah, that was news, that was a letter! The Senate was in transports, the whole community afire. I have never seen anything so universally applauded. News was still awaited about Antonius' remnants – you had despoiled him of the greater part of his horse and foot. That too came out according to our prayers. Your dispatch, read out in the Senate, declares the valour of the soldiers and their commander, and the zealous efforts of your friends, including my son. If your people here had thought fit that a motion be made on the dispatch, and if it had not arrived at a moment of great confusion after Consul Pansa's departure, a thank-offering to the Gods, just and due, would have been decreed.

And then! On the morning of the Ides of April along runs Pilius Celer. What a personage, in heaven's name! So responsible, so consistent, such a fine political record! Two letters he brings, one in your name, the other from Antonius, and delivers them to Tribune Servilius, who hands them to Cornutus. They are read out to the Senate. 'Antonius, Proconsul'! That produced a sensation, as though it had been 'Dolabella, Imperator' – and couriers *had* arrived from Dolabella, but nobody like Pilius with the courage to produce the letter or deliver it to the magistrates. Your letter was read, brief but distinctly mild in tone as regards Antonius. The House was greatly surprised. As for myself, it was not clear to me what I ought to do. If I called this letter a forgery, it might turn out that you had approved it; whereas to acknowledge it as genuine would be bad for your prestige. So that day passed in silence. On the following, after talk had become rife and the sight of Pilius had given strong and general offence, I must admit that I opened the game, with a good deal to say about 'Antonius, Proconsul'. Sestius followed me and supported the cause, pointing out what a dangerous position his son and mine would be in if they had taken up arms against a Proconsul. You know Sestius. He supported the cause. Others spoke as well. Our friend Labeo remarked that your seal was not on the letter, that it was not dated, and that you had not written to your own people as you usually do. He drew the conclusion that the letter was forged, and, if you wish to know, the House agreed with him.

Now, Brutus, it is for you to judge of the whole character of the war. Clearly lenience is to your liking and you think it is the most rewarding policy. Admirable! But the place for clemency is usually found, and ought to be found, in other matters and circumstances. In the present situation what is to be done, my friend? The hopes of needy desperados hang over the temples of the Immortal Gods. What is at issue in this war is our existence; no more, no less. Whom are we sparing? What are we about? Are we concerned for men who, if they win the day, will wipe us out without a trace? For what difference is there between Dolabella and any one of the three Antonii? If we spare any of them, we have been too hard on Dolabella.[15] That this is the sentiment of the Senate and People of Rome comes from the logic of the situation, but also in large measure from my advice and influence. If you do not approve of this attitude, I shall defend your view, but I shall not relinquish my own. Men expect from you neither laxity nor cruelty. It is easy to strike a balance; you need only be strong with the leaders and generous to the rank and file.

I hope you will keep my son at your side as much as possible,

15. Who had been declared a public enemy.

my dear Brutus. He will find no better training in manly excellence than by watching and imitating you.

19 (?) April.

6 (VIII or I. 2a)

CICERO TO M. BRUTUS

Rome, 20 (?) April 43

★ ★ ★ I am delighted that you find the army and the cavalry so loyally disposed towards you. If you get any news of Dolabella, you will inform me, as you say. I am glad that I had the forethought to leave you free to decide about making war on him. That was important for the state, as I recognized at the time, and I now consider that it was important for your prestige.

You say that I ★ ★ ★ [16] to attack the Antonii and commend the same. I don't doubt that you think so. But I am far from approving the distinction you draw when you say that we should be keener to prevent civil wars than to wreak vengeance on the defeated. I strongly disagree with you, Brutus. I consider myself as merciful a man as you, but salutary severity is better than the hollow appearance of mercy. If we want to be merciful, we shall never be without a civil war. However, that is your problem. I can say of myself what Plautus' father says in *Song of Sixpence*

My time is nearly over. You're the party most concerned.[17]

Believe me, Brutus, you and your friends will be overwhelmed if you do not take care. You will not always have a people and a Senate and a leader of the Senate as they are today. You may take this as a Delphic oracle. Nothing can be more true.

20 (?) April.

16. The manuscript reading makes no sense and has not been satisfactorily corrected.

17. *Trinummus*, 319.

7 (IX or I. 3)

CICERO TO M. BRUTUS

Rome, c. 21 April 43

From Cicero to Brutus greetings.

Our affairs are in better shape. I am sure your correspondents
have informed you of what has occurred. The Consuls have
proved such as I have often described them to you. As for the
boy Caesar, his natural worth and manliness is extraordinary.
I only pray that I may succeed in guiding and holding him in
the fulness of honours and favour as easily as I have done
hitherto. That will be more difficult, it is true, but still I do not
despair. The young man is persuaded (chiefly through me)
that our survival is his work; and certain it is that if he had not
turned Antony back from Rome, all would have been lost.

Three or four days before this splendid victory the whole
city fell into a panic, and poured out with wives and children
to join you; but on 20 April they recovered and would now
like you to come over here instead. That day I reaped the
richest of rewards for my many days of labour and nights of
wakefulness – if there is any reward in true, genuine glory. The
whole population of Rome thronged to my house and escorted
me up to the Capitol, then set me on the rostra amid tumultuous
applause. I am not a vain man, I do not need to be; but the
unison of all classes in thanks and congratulations does move
me, for to be popular in serving the people's welfare is a fine
thing. But I would rather you heard all this from others.

Please keep me very particularly informed about your doings
and plans, and take care that your generosity does not look like
laxity. It is the feeling of the Senate and People of Rome that no
public enemies ever deserved the harshest penalties more than
those Romans who have taken up arms against their country in
this war. In all my speeches I punish and harry them with the

approval of all honest men. Your view on the matter is for you to determine. Mine is that the three brothers are in one and the same boat.

8 (X or I. 3a)

CICERO TO M. BRUTUS

Rome, 27 (?) April 43

From Cicero to M. Brutus greetings.

We have lost two good Consuls – but 'good' is as much as one can say. Hirtius fell in the moment of victory after winning a great battle a few days earlier. Pansa had fled after receiving wounds which were too much for him. Brutus and Caesar are in pursuit of the remnant of the enemy. And all those who have followed Mark Antony's lead have been pronounced public enemies. Most people interpret that decree of the Senate as applying to those whom you have captured or whose surrender you have accepted. For my part I used no harsh language in making a proposal about C. Antonius by name, having made up my mind that the Senate should learn of his case from yourself.

27 (?) April.

9 (XIII or I. 5)

CICERO TO M. BRUTUS

Rome, 5 May 43

From Cicero to Brutus greetings.

In a debate of 27 April on military operations against those who have been declared public enemies, Servilius made a speech mostly about Ventidius, but he also moved that Cassius should take action against Dolabella. I concurred, and proposed in addition that you should take military action against Dolabella if you thought it expedient and in the public interest; but that, if you could not do so with benefit to the commonwealth and did not think it in the public interest, you should keep your army where it now is. The Senate could not pay you a greater compliment than to let you decide for yourself what course you judge most advantageous to the state. My personal feeling is that if Dolabella has a following, a camp, anywhere to make a stand, you should move against him as a matter of loyalty and prestige. We know nothing about our friend Cassius' forces. No letters have arrived from him nor have we any report on which we can firmly rely. I am sure you appreciate how important it is that Dolabella should be crushed, so that he pay for his crime and so that the traitor chiefs in flight from Mutina do not have a rallying point. You may remember from my previous letters that I held this view at an earlier stage, although at that time your camp was our harbour of refuge and your army our vital reserve. Now that our dangers are, as I hope, safely over, we ought to be all the more concerned about crushing Dolabella. But you will give careful thought to all this and come to a wise conclusion. If you see fit, please let me know what you have decided and what you are doing.

I should like our Marcus to be co-opted into your College.[18] I think that candidates at elections to priesthoods can be admitted *in absentia*. It has been done before. C. Marius was elected Augur under the lex Domitia when he was in Cappadocia, and no later law has made this any the less permissible in the future. Also the lex Julia, the most recent law on priesthoods, reads as follows: 'Whosoever shall stand or whose candidature shall be admitted.' That clearly implies that the candidature of one not personally standing is admissible. I have written to him on this subject telling him to abide by your

18. That of Pontiffs.

judgement, as in all matters. And you must decide about Domitius and our young friend Cato.[19] However, even though candidature *in absentia* is allowable, everything is easier for those on the spot. But if you decide that you ought to go to Asia, there will be no chance of fetching our young men back for the elections.

To be sure, I thought everything would go more quickly with Pansa alive. He would have had his new colleague elected at once, and then the elections for the priesthoods would have been held before the praetorian elections. Now I expect a long delay because of the auspices, since so long as we have a single patrician magistrate the auspices cannot revert to the patriciate.[20] It is certainly a very confused situation. I hope you will inform me of your views on the whole matter.

5 May.

10 (XI or I. 4)

M. BRUTUS TO CICERO

Dyrrachium, c. 7 May 43

From Brutus to Cicero greetings.

How delighted I am to learn of the successes of our friend Brutus and the Consuls it is easier for you to imagine than for me to write. I applaud and rejoice at all of it, but especially the fact that Brutus' break-out not only brought safety to himself but also made a major contribution to the victory.

You tell me that the three Antonii are in one and the same boat, and that my view is for me to determine. My only con-

19. Sons of L. Domitius Ahenobarbus and M. Porcius Cato, now serving with Brutus.

20. Thus creating an Interregnum and making possible the holding of consular elections.

clusion is that the Senate or the People of Rome must pass judgement on those citizens who have not died fighting. You will say that my calling men hostile to the state 'citizens' is an impropriety in itself. On the contrary, it is quite proper. What the Senate has not yet decreed, nor the People ordered, I do not take it upon myself to prejudge; I do not make myself the arbiter. This much I maintain: in dealing with a person[21] whose life circumstances did not oblige me to take I have neither despoiled him cruelly nor indulged him laxly, and I have kept him in my power for the duration of the war.

In my judgement it is much more honourable and from a public standpoint allowable to refrain from bearing hard on the unfortunate than to make endless concessions to the powerful which may whet their appetite and arrogance. In which regard, my excellent and gallant friend, whom I love so well and so deservedly both on my own account and on that of the commonwealth, you seem to me to be trusting your hopes too fondly. The moment somebody behaves well you seem to set no bounds to your favours and concessions, as though a mind corrupted by largesse could not possibly be swayed to bad courses. Your heart is too good to take offence at a warning, especially where the common welfare is at stake. But you will do as you think best. I too, when you have informed me ★ ★ ★.

II (XII or I. 4a)

M. BRUTUS TO CICERO

Camp, 15 May 43

★ ★ ★ Now, Cicero, now is the time to act so that our joy over Antony's collapse does not turn out an illusion and so that the excision of one evil does not always generate a new and worse one. If anything untoward happens now, to our surprise or

21. C. Antonius.

with our tolerance, we shall all be to blame, but you more than any; for the Senate and People of Rome not only allows but desires you to exercise an authority as great as can belong to any one man in a free community. You should live up to that by thinking wisely as well as loyally. Moreover, the only form of wisdom (of which you have enough and to spare) felt to be lacking is restraint in bestowing honours. All else you have in such ample measure that your qualities can be compared with any of the great men of history. This one thing only, which comes from a grateful and generous heart, people criticize: they would like to see your generosity tempered by caution and moderation. The Senate ought not to grant any man a favour which might serve as a precedent or a support to evil-designing persons. Accordingly, I am alarmed about the Consulship. I fear your young friend Caesar may think he has climbed too high through your decrees to come down again if he is made Consul. Antony made use of the apparatus of monarchy left behind by another to make himself a monarch. What do you suppose will be the mentality of one who thinks himself in a position to covet any office of power with the backing, not of a slaughtered tyrant, but of the Senate itself? So I shall applaud your good fortune and foresight when, and only when, I begin to feel assurance that Caesar is going to be satisfied with the extraordinary honours that have come his way. You may ask whether I am going to make you answerable for somebody else's misdoings. Indeed I am, if they could have been foreseen and prevented. I only wish you could see into my heart, how I fear that young man.

After I wrote the above, we heard that you have been elected Consul. The day I see that, I shall begin to envisage a true commonwealth, relying on its own strength. Your son is well and has been sent to Macedonia in advance with a force of cavalry.

Ides of May, from camp.

12 (XIV or I. 6)

M. BRUTUS TO CICERO

Camp in Lower Candavia, 19 May 43

From Brutus to Cicero greetings.

Don't wait for me to thank you. That has long since become inappropriate in our relationship, which has developed into so close a friendship.

Your son is not with me. We shall meet in Macedonia – he has orders to take a squadron of cavalry from Ambracia through Thessaly. I have written to him to meet me at Heraclea. When I see him, since you leave it in our hands, we shall take counsel together about his returning to stand for election or about recommending him for the office.

I very particularly recommend to you Pansa's doctor, Glyco, who is married to our friend Achilleus' sister. We hear that Torquatus[22] suspects him in connection with Pansa's death and that he is being kept in custody like a parricide. That is quite incredible. Pansa's death hit nobody harder. Besides he is a well-conducted, decent fellow, who would not be likely to be driven to crime even by self-interest. I beg you, and very earnestly (for our friend Achilleus is no less disturbed about it than he should be), to get him out of custody and keep him safe. I regard this as a matter of private obligation for me, of equal importance to any other.

As I was writing you these lines, a letter was delivered to me from C. Trebonius' Legate Satrius giving the news that Dolabella has been cut to pieces and put to flight by Tillius and Deiotarus. I am sending you a letter in Greek from a certain Cicereius, sent to Satrius.

Our friend Flavius has chosen you as arbiter in the dispute he

22. Pansa's Quaestor.

has about an inheritance with the township of Dyrrachium. I beg you, Cicero, and so does Flavius, to settle the matter. There is no question but that the town owed money to the person who made Flavius his heir. The townspeople don't deny it, but say that Caesar made them a present of the debt. Don't let a wrong be done to my friend by your friends.[23]

19 May from camp in lower Candavia.

13 (VI or I. 1)

CICERO TO M. BRUTUS

Rome, May (?) 43

From Cicero to Brutus greetings.

L. Clodius,[24] Tribune-Designate, has a high regard for me, or rather (to put it with more *empressement*) a great affection. Since I am satisfied of that, I don't doubt that you, knowing me as well as you do, conclude that I have an affection for *him*. Nothing to my way of thinking becomes a human being less than not to respond to a challenge of affection. I think Clodius suspects, and is very sorry to suspect, that something has been passed to you by your people, or rather through ill-wishers of *his*, to set your mind against him. As I think you know, my dear Brutus, it is not my habit to make assertions about another person lightly. That is a dangerous thing to do – people's real sentiments are so often concealed and their dispositions so complex. But Clodius' mind is an open book to me, and my opinion is formed. There are many indications, but they need

23. As to Cicero's relations with the town of Dyrrachium cf. *Letters to his Friends* 7 (XIV.2) and 8 (XIV.1).

24. Not necessarily or even probably identical with Ap. Pulcher's Prefect of Engineers in 51.

not be put into writing. After all, I don't want this to seem like a formal deposition rather than a letter.

He was advanced by Antony, in which favour you had a large share. Accordingly, he would have wished him well, compatibly with *my* welfare. But being, as you know, very far from a fool, he realizes that things have come to the point where both cannot survive, and so he prefers me. As for yourself, he speaks and feels about you in the most friendly way. So if anybody has written or talked to you amiss about him, let me beg you again to trust me, who am in a better position to judge than that somebody-or-other, and have a greater regard for you. Believe that Clodius is a very good friend of yours and as good a citizen as a man of thorough sound sense and excellent worldly position ought to be.

14 (VII or I. 2)

CICERO TO M. BRUTUS

Rome, c. 20 June 43

From Cicero to Brutus greetings.

I had already written and sealed a letter to you when one from you was delivered to me full of news, the most surprising item being that Dolabella has sent five cohorts to the Chersonese. Are his forces so ample that after we were told he was in flight from Asia he is trying to lay hands on Europe? And what did he expect to achieve with five cohorts when you have five legions, excellent cavalry, and large auxiliary forces? I hope those cohorts are now yours, since the bandit has been thus crazy.

I strongly commend your prudence in not moving your army from Apollonia and Dyrrachium before you heard of Antony's rout, Brutus' break-out, and the victory of the

Roman People. You say that thereafter you decided to march your army into the Chersonese and not allow the authority of the Roman People to be flouted by a criminal and a public enemy. That is for your own prestige and the national interest. You further write of a mutiny in the Fourteenth Legion and of C. Antonius' treachery. You will take what I say in good part: I approve of the severity of the soldiers more than of your ★ ★ ★

15 (XVI or I. 8)

CICERO TO M. BRUTUS

Rome, May or June (?) 43

From Cicero to Brutus greetings.

I have recommended many persons to you, and needs must. For our best men and citizens are most eager for your good opinion and all gallant spirits want to give you enthusiastic service. Nor is there a man who does not believe that my authority and influence counts for a great deal with you. But I recommend to you nobody more earnestly than C. Nasennius, a townsman of Suessa. He was First Centurion of the eighth cohort in the Cretan War[25] under General Metellus. Thereafter he has been busy with his private affairs, but is now moved by party loyalty and your outstanding prestige to wish to take some position of authority by your appointment. I commend him to you, Brutus, as a brave gentleman, a man of worth and (if that is at all relevant) of wealth too. You will greatly oblige me if you handle him so that he can thank me on account of what you do for his benefit.

25. In 68–67.

16 (XIX or I. 11)

M. BRUTUS TO CICERO

Camp, June 43

From Brutus to Cicero greetings.

Antistius Vetus' patriotic spirit is such that I do not doubt he would have shown himself a most ardent champion of our common liberties both against Caesar and against Antony had he been able to meet the occasion. When he encountered Dolabella, who had soldiers and horse, in Greece, he preferred to face any danger from the plots of a totally unscrupulous bandit rather than let it be thought that he had been forced to give money to such an arrant scoundrel or had given it willingly. To me, on the other hand, he voluntarily promised and gave HS2,000,000 out of his own funds and, what is worth much more, put himself in my way and joined me.

I wished to persuade him to remain in his camp as commander-in-chief and defend the commonwealth. He decided that he could not do that since he had dismissed his army. But he gave an assurance that he would take a commission as Legate and return to us if the Consuls were not going to hold praetorian elections. I strongly urged him, being the loyal citizen that he is, not to put off his candidature to a later date. His conduct should have won the gratitude of all who regard this army as in the service of the commonwealth and of yourself above all, who are defending our freedom with so much spirit and glory and will enjoy so great a prestige if our plans are crowned with the success we hope for.

Also, my dear Cicero, I ask you personally as a friend to be kind to Vetus and to desire his advancement. Although nothing can deter him from his purpose, your praise and indulgence can stimulate him to cling more closely and steadfastly to his intention. You will be obliging me greatly.

17 (XXV or I. 17)

M. BRUTUS TO ATTICUS

Camp, June (?) 43

From Brutus to Atticus greetings.

You tell me that Cicero is surprised that I never comment on his proceedings. Since you press me, I will tell you what I think at your insistence. I know that Cicero has always acted with the best intentions. I am as sure of his patriotism as of anything in the world. But in certain respects he has acted – shall I say 'clumsily', of the most worldly-wise of men? Or shall I say 'with a desire to ingratiate' of one who for his country's sake did not hesitate to incur the enmity of Antony in the fulness of his power? I don't know how to put it to you, except simply to say that the boy's ambition and lawlessness have been stimulated rather than checked by Cicero; and that he goes so far in this indulgence as not to refrain from offensive expressions which recoil upon himself in two ways. For he took more than one life, and he must confess himself an assassin before he says what he says against Casca (in Casca's case imitating Bestia in his own). Because we are not bragging every hour about the Ides of March like Cicero with his everlasting Nones of December,[26] is he in any better position to revile a splendid action than Bestia and Clodius when they used to attack his Consulship?

Our friend Cicero in his gown boasts to me that he has taken the brunt of Antony's war. What good is that to me if the price claimed for crushing Antony is to be succession to Antony's place, and if our champion against that evil has emerged in support of another evil, which is likely to be more firmly based and deeply rooted – if we allow it? His present activities make one begin to wonder whether it is despotism he is afraid of or a particular despot, Antony. For my part I don't feel grateful to

26. The Catilinarian conspirators were executed on 5 December 63.

anybody who does not object to slavery as long as his master is not angry with him. Triumph, pay for his troops, encouragement in every decree not to let modesty deter him from coveting the position of the man whose name he has assumed – is that worthy of a Consular, of Cicero?

Since I have not been permitted to hold my tongue, you will have to read what cannot but be disagreeable to you. I know how much pain it has cost me to write these lines. I am not unaware of your political views and how little hope you have of healing the commonwealth even if its freedom is established. I am not criticizing you, Atticus, upon my word. Your age and habits and children[27] make you loth to move, as I saw from the episode of our friend Flavius[28] among other things.

But to get back to Cicero. What difference is there between him and Salvidienus? What more would Salvidienus propose? You may say that he is afraid even now of the remnants of the civil war. So afraid of a war that is as good as over that he sees no cause for alarm in the power of a leader of a victorious army and the rashness of a boy? Or does he do it just because he thinks that the boy's greatness makes it advisable to lay everything at his feet now without waiting to be asked. What a foolish thing is fear! When precaution consists in summoning and inviting the very thing you are afraid of, when you might have been able to avoid it! We dread death and banishment and poverty too much. For Cicero I think they are the ultimate evils. So long as he has people from whom he can get what he wants and who give him attention and flattery he does not object to servitude if only it be dignified – if there is any dignity in the sorriest depth of humiliation.

27. Atticus' daughter was his only child; cf. *Letters to his Friends*, n. 1001.

28. Cornelius Nepos writes that C. Flavius asked Atticus to take the lead in raising a fund for Caesar's assassins by subscription from the Knights. Atticus refused, though he said that his private fortune was at Brutus' disposal (*Life of Atticus*, 8.3f.).

Octavius may call Cicero his father, ask his opinion on everything, flatter him, thank him, but it will be plain to see that the words contradict the realities. It is an outrage to human feeling to regard as a father one who does not even count as a free man. And yet that is his goal and purpose, that is the result which our excellent friend impatiently pursues – for Octavius to be gracious to him! For myself, I no longer allow any value to those arts in which I know Cicero is so well versed. What do they do for him, all his copious writings in defence of national freedom, on dignity, on death, banishment, and poverty? Philippus seems to be much cleverer on these subjects. He has been less ready to make concessions to his stepson[29] than Cicero who makes them to a stranger. So let him stop his boasting which is an aggravation of our distresses. For what is it to us that Antony has been defeated, if his defeat meant that somebody else stepped into his shoes? – though your letter suggests some uncertainty even now.

By all means let Cicero live, since he can live so, as a helpless petitioner, if his age and honours and past achievements don't put him to shame! No slavery will be so comfortable that *I* shall be turned away from waging war against the thing itself, that is to say against monarchy, and extraordinary commands, and despotism, and power which sets itself above the laws – however good a man, as you say, Antony[30] may be, though I have never thought so. But our forbears were not willing that even a parent should be a master.

If my affection for you were not as great as Cicero believes Octavius' regard for himself I should not have written to you in this strain. I am sorry that you are now vexed, fond as you are of all your friends and especially of Cicero. But you may be sure that there has been no falling off in my personal feelings, though my judgement has changed considerably. After all, we

29. L. Marcius Philippus married Octavian's mother Atia after the death of her first husband.

30. So the manuscripts; but Brutus seems to be referring to Octavian.

cannot be expected not to think of things the way we see them.

I wish you had told me what matches are in view for our dear Attica. I could have put down for you something of my own views. Your concern for my Porcia's health is only what I should have expected. Finally, I shall be glad to do as you ask. My sisters make the same request. I shall get to know the man and find out his intentions.

18 (XVIII or I. 10)

CICERO TO M. BRUTUS

Rome, June 43

From Cicero to Brutus greetings.

We have heard nothing from you as yet, not even a rumour to tell us that you have been apprised of the Senate's resolution and are bringing your army to Italy. The public interest urgently demands that you do this, and quickly. For our internal malady grows worse every day, and the enemies within the gates give us as much trouble as those outside. They existed, it is true, from the beginning of the war, but they used to be more easily put down. The Senate was more resolute, animated by my proposals and exhortations. Pansa was there to take a sufficiently strong and stern line with these gentry, his father-in-law[31] especially. As Consul he did not lack spirit from the outset nor loyalty at the end. In the fighting at Mutina Caesar's conduct gave no room for criticism, Hirtius' gave some.[32]

You might say of the fortune of this war

'Unsettled', when our luck is in;
When out, we call it 'fair'.[33]

31. Q. Fufius Calenus, Antony's leading supporter in the Senate.
32. The nature of the criticism is uncertain.
33. Cf. *Letters to Atticus* 73 (IV.I).8.

The national cause was victorious. Antony's forces were cut to pieces and himself driven out. Then Brutus made so many mistakes that the victory somehow slipped through our fingers. Our generals failed to pursue the demoralized, unarmed, wounded enemy, and Lepidus was given time to let us experience in a graver crisis the irresponsibility he has so often demonstrated. Brutus' and Plancus' armies are good but raw, and they have large, very loyal contingents of Gaulish auxiliaries. But Caesar, who has so far been guided by my counsels and is a fine young man in himself, remarkably steady, has been prodded by certain persons with rascally letters and shifty go-betweens into a very confident expectation of the Consulship. As soon as I had an inkling of that, I wrote him letter after letter of warning and taxed those friends of his who seemed to be backing his ambition to their faces, and I did not scruple to expose the origins of these criminal designs in open Senate. The Senate and magistrates behaved as well as I can remember in any context. In the case of an extraordinary office for a powerful individual – or let us say a *very* powerful individual, since power now resides in armed force – it is unheard of that *nobody*, no Tribune nor other magistrate nor private person, should appear as sponsor. But with all this steadiness and courage, the community is anxious. The fact is, Brutus, we are made a mockery by the caprices of the soldiers and the insolence of generals. Everybody demands as much political power as he has force behind him. Reason, moderation, law, tradition, duty count for nothing – likewise the judgement and views of the citizen body and respect for the opinion of those who come after us.

Foreseeing this long beforehand I was making my escape from Italy when the report of your manifestos recalled me. But it was you, Brutus, at Velia, who urged me forward. Grieved though I was to be returning to the city from which you, her liberator, were taking flight – something which had happened to me too in the days gone by in circumstances of similar peril and sadder fortune – I proceeded none the less and returned to

Rome. There, quite unsupported, I shook Antony's position and strengthened the defence against his nefarious arms which Caesar's judgement and prestige had put in our way. If he remains loyal and obeys me, I think we shall have means enough to defend ourselves. But if the advice of miscreants carries more weight with him than mine, or if the frailty of his years proves unequal to the heavy burden of affairs, all hope lies in you.

Therefore, I beg you, hurry here and free with your army the commonwealth of which you are the liberator in virtue of your courage and self-devotion rather than in the actual event. Everyone will rally like one man to your side. Write to Cassius and urge him to do the same. Hope of liberty lies nowhere but in your and his headquarters. To be sure, we have strong armies and generals in the west. For my part, I still think that we can rely on this young man, but so many folk are pushing him the wrong way that I am sometimes afraid of his changing his position.

I have given you a complete picture of the state of the commonwealth, such as it is at the time of dispatching this letter. I hope for better things in the future. If it turns out otherwise (which Heaven forfend!), I shall grieve for the commonwealth, which ought to be everlasting. For myself, how little time remains!

19 (XVII or I. 9)

CICERO TO M. BRUTUS

Rome, June 43

From Cicero to Brutus greetings.

I should do you the same office as you did for me in my

bereavement and write you a letter of consolation if I did not know that you have no need in your grief of the remedies with which you alleviated mine.[34] And I hope you find healing in your own case easier than you found it in mine. It is not like so great a man as you to be unable to do the very thing he recommended to another. The arguments which you assembled and my respect for yourself held me back from undue sorrowing. For when you thought I was taking the blow less bravely than a man should, especially one who was in the habit of consoling others, you wrote and taxed me in terms more severe than you are accustomed to use. And so, esteeming your judgement highly and fearing you were right, I pulled myself together and felt that all I had learned and read and been taught gained added weight from your authority.

At that time I owed nothing except to duty and nature; but now *you* have your obligations to the public and the limelight, as they say. Not only your army but all Romans, one might almost say all nations, have their eyes upon you. It would not be seemly if the man who makes us all braver were himself seen to be broken in spirit. You have indeed suffered a blow (the like of what you have lost was nowhere on earth) and you must grieve in so heavy a calamity. To lack all sense of grief might be more pitiable than grief itself. But moderation in grief, which is expedient for other men, is for you a necessity.

I should write more but that as written to *you* this is already too much. We are waiting for you and your army. Without that it looks as though we shall hardly be sufficiently free, even though everything else goes as we wish. I shall be writing more on the situation in the letter which I intend to give to our friend Vetus and shall then perhaps have more solid news.

34. Brutus' wife Porcia had died.

20 (XV or I. 7)

M. BRUTUS TO CICERO

Camp, May or June 43

From Brutus to Cicero greetings.

How dear L. Bibulus should be to me nobody can judge better than you, who have been through so much struggle and care for our country's sake. His own qualities and our connection ought to make you his friend. So I do not think I need write at length. My good-will ought to weigh with you, provided it be legitimate and in pursuance of a necessary obligation. He has decided to stand for Pansa's vacancy.[35] You cannot do a favour to anyone closer to you than I am, nor can you nominate a worthier candidate than Bibulus.

As for Domitius and Apuleius, it is superfluous for me to write when they are so strongly commended to you by their own persons. But you do have a duty to put your prestige behind Apuleius. However, he shall have a letter to himself to sing his praises. As for Bibulus, don't let him out of your care. He is already a fine fellow and, believe me, he can develop into one on whom the praises of the select few like yourself will be fitly bestowed.

21 (XXI or I. 13)

M. BRUTUS TO CICERO

Camp, 1 July 43

From Brutus to Cicero greetings.

The fears of the rest of the world make me apprehensive

35. In the College of Pontiffs.

about M. Lepidus. If he tears himself away from us (I hope the general suspicion that he will is hasty and unjust), I beg and implore you, Cicero, in the name of our friendship and your good-will towards me, to forget that my sister's children are Lepidus' sons and to regard me as having replaced him as their father. If you grant so much, I am sure there is nothing you will hesitate to do on their behalf. Others may stand on different terms with their kith and kin, but nothing I can do for my sister's children can satisfy my desire or my duty. And what mark of favour can honest men confer upon me (that is, if I am worthy of any such), how am I going to help my mother and my sister and these children, if you and the rest of the Senate will not let their uncle Brutus count against their father Lepidus?

Anxiety and vexation make it impossible for me to write to you at length, nor do I have to. After all, if I need words to rouse and strengthen you in a matter so important and close to my heart, there is no hope of your doing what I ask and what is right. So don't expect a lengthy appeal. Just look at *me*. You ought to grant me this both as a private individual, my very close friend Cicero, and as the great Consular you are, private connections apart. Please write back as soon as you can and let me know your intention.

Kalends of July, from camp.

22 (XX or I. 12)

CICERO TO M. BRUTUS

Rome, July 43

From Cicero to Brutus greetings.

Although I shall be giving a letter to Messalla Corvinus presently, I did not want our friend Vetus to join you without a letter from me.

CICERO'S LETTERS TO MARCUS BRUTUS

The commonwealth is in the gravest peril, Brutus, and after our victory we are forced to join battle once more. That has happened because of the criminal folly of M. Lepidus. Many things distress me at this time by reason of the care for the commonwealth which I have taken upon myself, but nothing has distressed me more than my inability to comply with your mother's and your sister's entreaties. As for yourself (which is what matters to me most), I believe I shall have no difficulty in justifying my conduct.

Lepidus' case can in no way be distinguished from Antony's, and is universally judged to be even less defensible than his, in that after the Senate had honoured him with the highest distinctions and only a few days after sending a splendid letter to that body, Lepidus suddenly let in the remnants of the enemy and, not content with that, is waging war energetically by land and sea. What will be its outcome who can say? So when we are asked to extend compassion to his children, not a word is said to suggest that *we* shall not be punished to extremity if the children's father is victorious, which Jupiter forfend!

Not that I do not recognize the harshness of visiting the sins of the fathers upon the children. But the laws have very wisely ordained this in order that parental affection may better dispose the fathers to the commonwealth. Therefore it is Lepidus who is cruel to his children, not those who declare Lepidus a public enemy. If he laid down his arms and was found guilty on charges of breaking the peace, against which he would certainly have no defence, his children would suffer the same penalty – his property being forfeit. Not but what Lepidus, Antony, and the other public enemies are threatening all of us with this very reprisal against which your mother and sister are pleading on behalf of the children, and with many others more cruel.

Accordingly, we pin our best hope at this time on you and your army. It is of great moment to the national cause and to your own glory and prestige that, as I have written before, you return to Italy as soon as possible. The commonwealth sorely needs your strength and your counsel.

Following your letter I have gladly made a friend of Vetus in view of his good-will and outstanding services to you; and I have found him most zealous and loyal to you and to the commonwealth. I hope to see my son Marcus shortly, since I trust that you will quickly come to Italy and he will be with you.

23 (XXII or I. 14)

CICERO TO M. BRUTUS

Rome, 14 July 43

From Cicero to Brutus greetings.

Your short letter – I say 'short', but it was not really a letter at all. Does Brutus write me only three lines in times like these? Better nothing at all. And you think *I* should have written more. Which of your friends ever joined you without a letter from me? And which of my letters lacked weight? If they have not been delivered to you, I think your letters from home have not been reaching you either. You say you will give Marcus a longer letter. Right, but this one too should have been fuller. Now when you wrote to me about Marcus' leaving you I immediately pushed out couriers and a letter to Marcus telling him to rejoin you even if he had already returned to Italy. No other course is more agreeable to me or more honourable to him. To be sure, I had written to him more than once that by dint of a great effort on my part, the elections to priesthoods were put off till next year. I exerted myself to bring that about both for Marcus' sake and for that of Domitius, Cato, Lentulus, Bibulus, and others. I wrote the same to you, but apparently you had not yet heard of it when you dispatched that tiny letter to me.

So I ask you with all urgency, my dear Brutus, not to send my son Marcus away but to bring him back with you. And this latter you should do any day now if you have any thought for the commonwealth which you were bred to serve. For the war is reborn through Lepidus' criminal behaviour, and no small war either. Caesar's army, which used to be excellent, is not only no help but forces us to ask urgently for *your* army. Once the latter touches Italian soil, every Roman who can legitimately be so called will betake himself to your camp. True, we have Brutus in fine combination with Plancus. But you well know how uncertain are the minds of men, tainted with party spirit, and the results of battles. Even if we win, as I hope we shall, the guidance of your counsel and prestige will be greatly needed. So come to our assistance, in God's name, and do so as soon as you can. Be sure that you did your country no greater service on the Ides of March, when you lifted the yoke of servitude from the backs of your fellow-countrymen, than you will do her if you come quickly.

14 July.

24 (XXIII or I. 15)

CICERO TO M. BRUTUS

Rome, July 43

From Cicero to Brutus greetings.

Messalla is with you. However carefully I write, I cannot hope to explain the current proceedings and situation more precisely in a letter than he will expound them with his excellent and comprehensive knowledge, and his ability to present you with all the facts in lucid and well-chosen terms. For I do assure you, Brutus (not that there is any need for me to tell you what you already know, but I cannot pass over such all-round excellence in silence) – I assure you that in uprightness, resolution, concern, and patriotic zeal the like of Messalla does not exist. In him the gift of eloquence, which he possesses in a quite astonishing degree, hardly seems worth commending. And yet his good sense is specially conspicuous in that very sphere, for he has trained himself in the strictest school of oratory with serious judgement and a great deal of technical skill. He is so industrious and indefatigably studious that his pre-eminent natural ability seems a secondary qualification.

But my affection carries me too far. It is not my purpose in this letter to praise Messalla, especially to you, my friend, who know his worth as well as I and who know those very pursuits which I am eulogizing better than I do. My one consolation in the distress I feel at parting with him is that he is going to join you, my *alter ego*, is doing his duty, and seeking no mean laurels. But enough of this.

Now I come rather belatedly to a letter of yours in which, while paying me a number of compliments, you find one fault, namely that I am excessive and, so to speak, prodigal in voting honours. This you criticize; someone else perhaps might tax me with undue harshness in the infliction of punishments – or perhaps you would charge me with both. If so, I am anxious that you should be thoroughly acquainted with my judgement on either point. I will not just quote the saying of Solon, one of the Seven Wise Men and the only one to write a code of law. He said that a state depends on two things, reward and punishment. There is, of course, a due limit in both, as in all other things, a sort of balance in each of the two categories. But it is not my purpose to discuss so wide a theme here. I do, however, think it appropriate to reveal the principle which I have followed in the proposals I have made to the Senate during this war.

You will not have forgotten, Brutus, that after Caesar's death and your memorable Ides of March I said that you and your associates had left one thing undone and that a mighty storm was brewing over the commonwealth. You had driven away a great plague, wiped a great blot from the honour of the Roman people, and won immortal glory for yourselves; but the apparatus of monarchy descended to Lepidus and Antony, one more of a weathercock, the other more of a blackguard, both afraid of peace and hostile to domestic tranquillity. We had no force to pit against their passionate desire for a political upheaval. The community had risen unanimously in defence of freedom, but we appeared too bold, and you and your friends may perhaps have shown greater wisdom in leaving the city you had liberated and in asking nothing of Italy when she proffered you her enthusiastic support. And so, seeing that Rome was in the hands of traitors, that neither you nor Cassius could live there in safety, and that the city was crushed by Antony's armed force, I thought that I too had better go elsewhere. A community crushed by ruffians, with all hope of rendering help cut off, is a hideous spectacle. But my spirit, anchored as ever upon the love of country, could not endure separation from her perils. Halfway to Greece, when the Etesians should have been blowing, the South Wind carried me back to Italy, as though dissuading me from my plan. I saw you at Velia, and was deeply distressed. For you were retiring, Brutus – retiring, since our friends the Stoics say that the Wise Man never flees. On returning to Rome I immediately set myself in opposition to Antony's wickedness and folly. Having stirred him up against me, I embarked upon a policy to free the commonwealth – a truly Brutine policy, since such aspirations run in your family.

The sequel is long and not to be recounted here, since it is about myself. All I will say is that this young man Caesar, thanks to whom (if we choose to admit the truth) we are still alive, drew his inspiration from my counsels. I have given him no honours, Brutus, but what were due and necessary. When we first began to call freedom back, before even D. Brutus' superlative valour had visibly come into action, our only protection was this lad, who had thrust Antony away from our necks. What honour ought we *not* to have voted him? However I at that time paid him a verbal tribute, and that in moderation, and voted him military authority. That no doubt seemed an honour at his age, but it was necessary since he had an army; for what is an army without military authority? Philippus voted him a statue, Servius the right to stand for office in advance of the legal age, a privilege which was later extended by Servilius. Nothing seemed too much at the time.

But for some reason it is easier to find good-will in the hour of danger than gratitude in victory. There came that most joyful day of D. Brutus' liberation, which happened also to be Brutus' birthday. I proposed that Brutus' birthday should be entered in the Calendar beside that day, following the precedent of our ancestors who paid that compliment to a woman, Larentia,[36] at whose altar in Velabrum you Pontiffs offer sacrifice. In trying to confer that on Brutus I wished the Calendar to contain a permanent record of a most welcome victory. That day I realized that gratitude has considerably fewer votes in the Senate than spite. During these same days I showered honours (if you like to put it that way) on the dead, Hirtius and Pansa, even Aquila. Who shall blame me, unless he forgets the bygone danger once the fear is laid aside? Besides the grateful memory of benefit I had another reason, one of advantage to posterity: I wanted memorials of the public hatred for those bloodthirsty rebels to stand for all time. I suspect that another proposal of mine is less to your liking – your friends, excellent persons but lacking political experience, did not like it either – namely that Caesar be granted leave to enter Rome in ovation. For my part (but perhaps I am mistaken, though it is not my way to be particularly pleased with my own performances), I do not think I have made a better proposal in the course of this war. Why that is so I had better not

36. Acca Larentia, a figure of early Roman legend. Various stories are told about her.

reveal, or I might seem more far-sighted than grateful. I have said too much as it is; so let us pass on.

I voted honours to D. Brutus and to L. Plancus. It is a noble mind that is attracted by glory; but the Senate too has shown good sense in using every means, provided it be honourable, to draw this man and that to the aid of the state. But there is Lepidus. Oh yes, we are blamed there – we set up a statue for him in the rostra and then pulled it down. We tried to bring him back from treason by honouring him, but our wisdom was defeated by the folly of a thoroughly irresponsible individual. Not but what the setting up of Lepidus' statue did less harm than the pulling down did good.

That's enough about honours. Let me now say a little about punishment. Your letters have often let me understand that you would like to earn praise by your clemency towards those you have defeated in war. For my part, I look upon anything that comes from you as wise. But to waive the punishment of crime (for that is what is called 'pardoning'), even if it is tolerable in other contexts, I consider to be fatal in this war. Of all the civil wars in our commonwealth that I remember there has not been one in which the prospect of some form of constitution did not exist whichever side won. In this war I should not like to be positive about what constitution we shall have if we win, but there will certainly be none ever again if we lose. Accordingly I proposed stern measures against Antony and against Lepidus too, not so much for vengeance's sake as to deter the criminals among us by terror from attacking our country in the present and to leave an object-lesson for the future, so that none shall be minded to imitate such madness. To be sure this proposal was no more mine than everybody's. One feature seems cruel, the extension of the penalty to innocent children. But that is an ancient rule, found in all communities. Even Themistocles' children lived in poverty. If the same penalty applies to citizens judicially condemned, how could we take a more lenient line with public enemies? And what complaint can anyone have of me who must needs admit that he would have treated me more harshly had he won?

There you have the rationale of my proposals so far as this category of honours and punishments is concerned. Of my speeches and votes on other matters I think you have heard.

But all this is not particularly crucial; what *is* extremely crucial, Brutus, is that you come back to Italy with your army as soon as possible. You are most eagerly awaited. As soon as you touch Italian soil there will be a universal rally to your side. If we win the day, as won it we had most gloriously if Lepidus had not had a craving to destroy everything, including himself and his family, we need your prestige to establish some sort of civic settlement. Whereas if a contest is still to come, our best hope lies in your prestige and the strength of your army. But for heaven's sake hurry! You know how much depends on timing and on speed.

I expect you will hear from your mother and sister about the pains I am taking on behalf of your sister's children. In this I am taking more account of your wishes, which mean a great deal to me, than of my own consistency, as some people see it. But I want to be and seem consistent in my affection for you more than in anything else.

25 (XXIV or I. 16)

M. BRUTUS TO CICERO

July (?) 43

From Brutus to Cicero greetings.

I have read a small part of your letter to Octavius, sent to me by Atticus. Your devoted concern for my welfare gave me no novel pleasure, accustomed as I am (indeed it happens every day) to hear of some loyal and complimentary action or words of yours in support of our public standing. But that same extract from your letter to Octavius in which you write about us gave me all the distress of which my mind is capable. You thank him on public grounds in such a fashion, so imploringly and humbly – I hardly know what to write; I am ashamed of the situation, of what fortune has done to us, but write I must. You commend our welfare to him. Better any death than such welfare! It is a downright declaration that there has been no abolition of despotism, only a change of despot. Read over your words again and then dare to deny that these are the pleadings of a subject to his king. You say that the one thing asked and expected of him is his good wishes for the welfare of those citizens of whom the honest men and the Roman People think well. What if he should refuse? Shall we cease to exist? And indeed it would be better not to exist than to exist on his sufferance. I really do not believe that the Gods have so turned their faces away from the welfare of the Roman People that Octavius has to be begged on behalf of the welfare of any citizen, let alone on behalf of the liberators of the world – it pleases me to be grandiloquent, nor is that out of place in addressing people who do not know in each particular case what fears it is right to entertain and what favours it is right to ask.

Do you admit, Cicero, that Octavius has such power and are you his friend? If you care for me, do you want me to be seen in Rome when in order to make that possible I have to be recommended to the good graces of this boy? Why do you thank him if you think you have to ask him to wish or to suffer us to survive? Are we to consider him as having done us a kindness in preferring that he himself rather than Antony should be the person to whom such requests must be addressed? Is he our champion against the despotism of another or that other's substitute? If the former, does anybody petition him to let the benefactors of our country survive? It is this weakness and despair, for which the blame rests no more with you than with everybody else, that brought Caesar to dream of monarchy, that persuaded Antony after Caesar's death to try to step into the shoes of the man we killed, and that now has raised this boy so high that *you* think the survival of men like ourselves has to be gained by pleading and that we shall be safe through the compassion of an individual (and he scarcely yet a grown man) or not at all. If we remembered that we are Romans, miscreants would not be bolder to become our masters than we to stop them, and Antony would not have been incited by Caesar's monarchy rather than deterred by his death.

As a Consular, one who has put down such atrocious crimes (though I fear that in suppressing them you have only delayed the disaster for a short time), how can you look back on what you have achieved and at the same time give your approval to *this*, or if not approval, a tolerance so submissive and ready as to present the appearance of approval? What private quarrel did you have with Antony? It was surely because he demanded that men's safety should be begged from himself, that we to whom he owed his own liberties should hold civic status by his grace and favour, that he should dispose of the commonwealth as he chose – that was why you thought we should look for weapons with which to prevent his despotism, only, as it seems, in order that after stopping him we should ask someone else to let himself be put in Antony's place. Or was it that rights of ownership over the commonwealth should belong to the commonwealth itself? Perhaps, though, it was not servitude but a particular servile situation that we rejected. And yet we could have had a good master in Antony under whom to put up with our condition. Not only that, we could have enjoyed all the favours and honours we wanted as his partners. What would he have refused to men in whose tolerance he would have seen the best guarantee of his régime? But nothing was worth the surrender of our loyalties and liberties.

This very boy, who is apparently incited by Caesar's name against Caesar's killers – what would he not give, if there were room for bargaining, in return for our support for the power which I suppose will indeed be his, since we want to keep our lives and our money and be called Consulars? Caesar will have perished for nothing (why did we rejoice at his death if we were going to be slaves just the same after he was dead and gone?), if no care is taken. But may the Gods and Goddesses take away everything I have sooner than my determination that nobody shall have more power than the Senate and the laws with my consent. That I did not tolerate in the case of the man I killed, I shall not concede it to his heir, I should not concede it to my own father if he came back to life. Do you believe that a personage without whose permission we can have no place in your community is going to leave the rest their liberties? And how is it possible for your petition to be granted? You ask his good wishes for our welfare. Do you think we are getting welfare if we get our lives? How can we get welfare if we let status and liberty go? Or do you think that to live in Rome is to be a citizen? That is a matter of condition, not of place. I had no citizenship in Caesar's lifetime until after I resolved upon his assassination, nor can I be in exile anywhere so long as I hate to be a slave and suffer indignities more than all other evils. In Greece when tyrants are suppressed their children suffer the same penalty. Here is one who has taken the tyrant's name, and he is being asked to agree to the survival of the avengers and suppressors of despotism. Is not that a relapse into the same old darkness? Should I wish to see a community, or think it worthy of the name, that cannot take freedom when handed on a platter and rammed down its throat, and has more fear of the name of a liquidated monarch borne by a boy than confidence in itself, though it has seen the possessor of unlimited power liquidated by the courage of a few individuals?

No, do not in future commend me to your Caesar, nor yourself either, if you will listen to me. You must set great store by the years that can remain to a man of your age if you are going to humble yourself before that boy on their account.

Have a care, furthermore, lest the admirable line you have taken and are taking against Antony, in which your courage is so highly praised, come to look like fear. For if you see in Octavius one whom you can suitably petition for our welfare, you will appear to have acted not in avoidance of a master but in search of a more friendly one. I fully approve of your praise of his conduct so far. It *is* praiseworthy, provided he entered on it in opposition to someone else's irregular power and not in furtherance of his own. But when you judge that he has the right to be begged not to refuse his good wishes for our welfare, and even yourself accord it to him, you are setting too high a price on his services. You are making him a present of what (thanks to him, as it seems) belongs to the state. Nor has it occurred to you that if Octavius merits any honours because he is making war on Antony, those who have cut out the evil growth of which you are now left with the remnants can never be recompensed by the Roman people as richly as they deserve, even if every imaginable reward be heaped upon them at once.

How much more attention people pay to their fears than to their memories! Antony is alive and fighting, whereas what could and had to be done about Caesar is finished and no one can put back the pieces. And so it is Octavius whose decision about ourselves is awaited by the Roman People, and it is we whose welfare must apparently be asked of a single individual.

For my part, to return to the point I have already made, I am not one to make petitions. I would rather trim to size those who claim the right to receive them. Or else I shall stay far away from a society of serfs, and wherever I can live as a free man there for me shall be Rome. And I shall pity all of you for whom life has a sweetness from which neither years nor honours nor the courage of other men can take away. I shall think myself so happy, if only I always cling steadfastly to this intention, that I shall regard my patriotism as well rewarded. For what is better than to be indifferent to the vicissitudes of life, content with freedom and the memory of deeds well done? But assuredly I shall not submit to the submissive or be defeated by defeatists. I shall try every expedient and never abandon my efforts to draw our society away from thraldom. If deserved good fortune follow the enterprise, we shall all be glad. If not, *I* shall still be glad. My life cannot be better spent than in such actions and thoughts as conduce to the liberation of my fellow-countrymen.

As for yourself, Cicero, I ask and urge you not to grow weary or discouraged, and in forestalling present evils always to be alert for those which, unless measures are taken beforehand, may insinuate themselves into the future. Do not imagine that the free and gallant spirit with which you have championed the state both as Consul and Consular has any value without steadiness and consistency. I must acknowledge that proven merit makes harder demands than merit still unrecognized. Previous good performances are required as due, and if it turns out otherwise we become indignant critics, as though those performances had deceived us. That Cicero should resist Antony is most creditable; but because the Consul that was is felt to guarantee the Consular that is, no one is surprised. But if the same Cicero changes in relation to others the policy he has applied so firmly and nobly in expelling Antony, he will not only rob himself of future laurels but will make his past lose its lustre. No act is great in itself, unless inspired by reasoned judgement. On nobody does the role of patriot and defender of freedom sit more fittingly in virtue of your spirit, your record, and the eager demand of all.

Therefore Octavius is not to be asked to wish us well. Instead, rouse yourself! Believe that the community in which you achieved so much will be free and respected if only the people have leaders to resist the designs of wicked men.

26 (XXVI. or I. 18)

CICERO TO M. BRUTUS

Rome, 27 July 43

From Cicero to Brutus greetings.

I have often urged you by letter to come to the aid of the commonwealth and bring your army over to Italy as soon as possible, and I was under the impression that those close to you were in no doubt on this point. On 25 July that very wise and watchful lady your mother, whose every care begins and ends with you, requested me to visit her. Naturally I did so without delay. On my arrival I found Casca, Labeo, and Scaptius already there. Your mother put the question: What did I think? Should we send for you and did we consider this to be in your best interests, or was it better that you should take your time and hold back? I said in answer what I thought, that it was in the highest degree advantageous to your prestige and reputation that you should lend support to our tottering and almost collapsing commonwealth at the earliest possible moment.

Every imaginable evil chance has dogged us in this war. Victorious armies have refused to pursue a fleeing enemy. An army commander in good standing, eminent in public distinction and private fortune, with a wife and children, related by marriage to you and your brother-in-law, has declared war on the commonwealth. I might add 'in the face of a unanimous Senate and People', were it not that the mischief within the gates remains so strong. As I write I am in great distress because it hardly looks as though I can make good my promises in respect of the young man, boy almost, for whom I went bail to the commonwealth. Responsibility for someone else's mind and sentiment, especially in matters of great importance, is more burdensome and difficult than the pecuniary kind. That can be discharged and the loss of money can be borne. But how is one to discharge a pledge to the state if the person for whom one has made it is quite happy to leave his backer to pay? However, I hope I shall still hold him, though many people are pulling the other way. The natural quality seems to be there, but it is an impressionable age and there are plenty of would-be agents of corruption. They are confident of dazzling his good disposition by dangling in front of him the glitter of a false distinction. So this care is added to my load. I must move every engine at my disposal to hold the young man, or else be judged guilty of indiscretion. And yet, where is the indiscretion? I bound the one on whose behalf I gave the pledge rather than myself. The state has no reason to find fault with that pledge. Its subject proved the steadier in his public actions both from natural disposition and because of my promise.

However, unless I am perhaps mistaken, our knottiest political problem is shortage of money. The honest men become more obdurate every day at the mention of a special levy. The proceeds of the 1%,[37] thanks to the scandalously low returns put in by the wealthy folk, are entirely absorbed in the bounties of the two legions. Yet limitless expenses hang over us both for the armies which are now defending us and for yours. It looks as though our friend Cassius will be able to arrive tolerably well furnished. But these and many other matters I want to discuss with you in person, and that soon.

About your sister's children, my friend, I did not wait for you to write. To be sure the progress of time is leaving the case uncompromised for you to handle, for the war will be protracted. But from the outset, when I could not prophesy the length of the war, I pleaded the children's cause in the Senate, as I think you will have been able to learn from your mother's letters.

37. Income tax, imposed by the Senate.

There shall never be any matter on which I shall not speak and act in accordance with what I take to be your wish and concern, even at the hazard of my life.

27 July.

APPENDIX I

(i) Roman Dates

UNTIL Julius Caesar reformed the calendar the Roman year consisted of 355 days divided into twelve months, all of which bore the Latin forms of their present names except Quintilis (= July) and Sextilis (= August). Each month had 29 days, except February with 28 and March, May, July, and October with 31. The first, fifth and thirteenth days of each month were called the Kalends (*Kalendae*), Nones (*Nonae*), and Ides (*Idus*) respectively, except that in March, May, July, and October the Nones fell on the seventh and the Ides on the fifteenth. I have kept these names in translation.

The calendar was adjusted by means of 'intercalation'. At the discretion of the College of Pontiffs, usually every other year, an 'intercalary' month of 23 or 22 days was inserted after 24 or 23 February. But in the years immediately before the Civil War the College neglected this procedure, so that by 46 the calendar was well over two months in advance of the sun. Julius Caesar rectified the situation by inserting two 'intercalary' months totalling 67 days between November and December of that year in addition to the traditional one in February. He also gave the months their present numbers of days, thus almost obviating the need for future intercalations, though in 1582 a further discrepancy had to be met by the institution of a Leap-Year.

(ii) Roman Money

The normal unit of reckoning was the sesterce (HS), though the denarius, equal to 4 sesterces, was the silver coin most generally in use. Differences of price structure make any transposition into modern currency misleading, but very roughly HS25 may be taken as equivalent to the debased pound sterling of 1974. Sometimes sums are expressed in Athenian currency. The drachma was about equal to the denarius, the mina (100 drachmae) to HS400, and the talent

(60 minae) to HS2,400. The Asiatic cistophorus was worth about 4 drachmae.

(iii) Roman Names

A Roman bore the name of his clan (*gens*), the *nomen* or *nomen gentilicium*, usually ending in *-ius*, preceded by a personal name (*praenomen*) and often followed by a *cognomen*, which might distinguish different families in the same *gens*: e.g., Marcus Tullius Cicero. The *nomen* was always, and the *cognomen* usually, hereditary. Sometimes, as when a family split into branches, an additional *cognomen* was taken: e.g., Publius Licinius Crassus Dives. Other additional *cognomina* were honorific, sometimes taken from a conquered country as Africanus or Numidicus, or adoptive (see below). Women generally had only the one clan-name (e.g., Tullia), which they retained after marriage.

Only a few personal names were in use and they are generally abbreviated as follows: A. = Aulus; Ap(p). = Appius; C. = Gaius; Cn. = Gnaeus; D. = Decimus; L. = Lucius; M. = Marcus; M'. = Manius; N. = Numerius; P. = Publius; Q. = Quintus; Ser. = Servius; Sex. = Sextus; Sp. = Spurius; T. = Titus; Ti. = Tiberius (I omit one or two which do not occur in our text). The use of a *praenomen* by itself in address or reference is generally a sign of close intimacy, whether real or affected, but in the case of a rare or distinctive praenomen, as Appius and Servius, this is not so.

The practice of adoption, of males at any rate, was very common in Rome. According to traditional practice the adopted son took his new father's full name and added his old *nomen gentilicium* with the adjectival termination *-ianus* instead of *-ius*: e.g., C. Octavius, adopted by C. Julius Caesar, became C. Julius Caesar Octavianus. But in Cicero's time the practice had become variable. Sometimes the original name remained in use.

A slave had only one name, and since many slaves came from the East, this was often Greek. If freed, he took his master's *praenomen* and *nomen*, adding his slave-name as a *cognomen*: e.g., Tiro, when freed by M. Tullius Cicero, became M. Tullius Tiro. Occasionally the *praenomen* might be somebody else's. Atticus' slave Dionysius became M. Pomponius Dionysius in compliment to Cicero (instead of Titus).

Much the same applied to Greek or other provincials on gaining Roman citizenship. Such a man retained his former name as a *cognomen* and acquired the *praenomen* and *nomen* of the person to whom he owed the grant: e.g., the philosopher Cratippus became M. Tullius Cratippus after Cicero had got Caesar to give him the citizenship.

APPENDIX II

Consuls, 68–43 B.C.

68 L. Caecilius Metellus
    Q. Marcius Rex

67 C. Calpurnius Piso
    M'. Acilius Glabrio

66 M'. Aemilius Lepidus
    L. Vulcatius Tullus

65 L. Aurelius Cotta
    L. Manlius Torquatus

64 L. Julius Caesar
    C. Marcius Figulus

63 M. Tullius Cicero
    C. Antonius

62 D. Junius Silanus
    L. Licinius Murena

61 M. Pupius Piso Frugi
    M. Valerius Messalla Niger

60 Q. Caecilius Metellus Celer
    L. Afranius

59 C. Julius Caesar
    M. Calpurnius Bibulus

58 L. Calpurnius Piso Caesoninus
    A. Gabinius

57 P. Cornelius Lentulus Spinther
    Q. Caecilius Metellus Nepos

56 Cn. Cornelius Lentulus
        Marcellinus
    L. Marcius Philippus

55 Cn. Pompeius Magnus
    M. Licinius Crassus

54 L. Domitius Ahenobarbus
    Ap. Claudius Pulcher

53 Cn. Domitius Calvinus
    M. Valerius Messalla

52 Cn. Pompeius Magnus
        (Sole Consul)
    . . . .
    Q. Caecilius Metellus Pius
        Scipio

51 Ser. Sulpicius Rufus
    M. Claudius Marcellus

50 L. Aemilius Paulus
    C. Claudius Marcellus

49 C. Claudius Marcellus
    L. Cornelius Lentulus Crus

48 C. Julius Caesar
    P. Servilius Isauricus

47 Q. Fufius Calenus
    P. Vatinius

46 C. Julius Caesar
    M. Aemilius Lepidus

45 C. Julius Caesar (Sole Consul)
    . . . .
    Q. Fabius Maximus (suffect)
    C. Trebonius (suffect)
    C. Caninius Rebilus (suffect)

44 C. Julius Caesar
    M. Antonius
    . . . .
    P. Cornelius Dolabella (suffect)

43 C. Vibius Pansa Caetronianus
    A. Hirtius

GLOSSARY OF PERSONS

The glossaries cover the whole correspondence, but references are to the *Letters to his Friends*, unless otherwise stated. A number of unimportant names are omitted. 'Nobles' are marked with an asterisk.

ACASTUS: Slave of Cicero's.

ACCIUS: Late second-century writer of Latin tragedies.

ACIDINUS: See MANLIUS.

ACILIUS (M. Acilius Caninus?): Caesarian officer, Proconsul in Sicily 46–45.

M'. ACILIUS Glabrio: Consul in 67.

ADIATORIX: Son of a Galatian Tetrarch under Deiotarus' suzerainty.

AEGYPTA: Freedman, apparently of Cicero's.

L. AELIUS Lamia: Hereditary friend of Cicero's. As a prominent Knight, was banished from Rome by Gabinius in 58 for championing Cicero's cause. Later entered the Senate, becoming Aedile in 45 and probably Praetor in 43.

*L. AELIUS Tubero: Friend and marriage connection of Cicero's and one of Q. Cicero's Legates in Asia. His son prosecuted Q. Ligarius in 45, Cicero defending.

M. AEMILIUS Avianianus: Friend of Cicero's known only from letters of recommendation.

*M'. AEMILIUS Lepidus: Consul in 66. Seems to have died in Italy during the Civil War.

*M. AEMILIUS Lepidus: Consul in 46 and one of Caesar's leading followers. After Caesar's death succeeded him as Chief Pontiff and became governor of Narbonese Gaul and Hither Spain in 44–43. Joined Antony and became Triumvir, Consul again in 42, and governor of Africa in 40–36. Forced by Octavian to retire from public life.

*L. AEMILIUS Paulus: Elder brother of the above and Consul in 50. Allegedly bought by Caesar. Probably neutral in the Civil War, he was proscribed by the Triumvirs but escaped to end his days in Miletus.

*M. AEMILIUS Scaurus: (1) Consul in 115 and Leader of the Senate.

*(2) His son, Praetor in 56. As candidate for the Consulship in 54 was successfully defended by Cicero on a charge of extortion in his province (Sardinia), but found guilty in a second trial for bribery (Cicero still defending) and disappeared into exile.

AESOPUS: See CLODIUS.

L. AFRANIUS (nicknamed 'Aulus' son'): Lieutenant of Pompey, who 'bought' him the Consulship of 60. Later governed Further Spain as Pompey's Legate and fought on his side in the Civil War. Perished in Africa after Caesar's victory in 46.

AFRICANUS: See CORNELIUS Scipio.

AGESILAUS: King of Sparta c. 401–360.

AHALA: See SERVILIUS.

C. ALBANIUS: Father-in-law of P. Sestius (manuscripts sometimes, and editors usually, call him Albinius).

ALEDIUS: Friend of Cicero's brother(?)-in-law Publilius in 46–45 and a strong Caesarian.

ALEXANDER: Of Ephesus, called Lychnus ('The Lamp'), perhaps contemporary with Cicero. Among other activities wrote poems on astronomy and geography, the latter named after the three continents.

ALEXIO: (1) Atticus' bailiff (?) in Epirus. (2) Cicero's doctor, who died in 45.

ALEXIS: Favourite slave or freedman of Atticus.

C. ALFIUS Flavus: Praetor (?) in 54.

A. ALLIENUS: Friend of the Ciceros. Praetor in 49 and a supporter of Caesar.

C. AMAFINIUS: Probably the first writer on Epicureanism in Latin, usually thought to have 'flourished' early in the first century.

AMMONIUS (Hammonius): Minister of Ptolemy the Piper and later (if the two are one) of Cleopatra.

T. AMPIUS Balbus: Praetor in 59 and governor of Asia the following year, then transferred to Cilicia. Henchman of Pompey and friend of Cicero, who probably obtained permission for him to return to Italy in 46.

C. ANICIUS: Senator and friend of Cicero.

T. ANICIUS: Agent of Q. Cicero.

M. ANNEIUS: Legate of Cicero in Cilicia.

T. ANNIUS Milo: As Tribune in 57 stoutly championed Cicero's recall and raised armed bands against Clodius. Candidate for the Consulship in 53, was condemned after Clodius' murder in January 52 and retired to Massilia. In 48 returned to Italy to take part in Caelius Rufus' rising and was killed.

ANTEROS: Name of one or more slaves in the Cicero family.

ANTIOCHUS: (1) Of Ascalon, contemporary Greek philosopher. Succeeded Philo as head of the Academy. (2) Literary clerk of Atticus. (3) King of Commagene.

ANTISTHENES: Disciple of Socrates and founder of the Cynic school.

Pacuvius 'ANTISTIUS' Labeo: One of Caesar's assassins, later Legate of M. Brutus, he ordered his slave to kill him after Philippi. His name was probably Pacuvius Labeo (praenomen unknown).

C. ANTISTIUS Reginus: Legate of Caesar in Gaul, apparently in charge of the western coast of Italy in 49 along with the younger Hortensius.

C. ANTISTIUS Vetus: Caesarian officer, in charge of Syria in 44. In 43 an Antistius Vetus figures as a friend of Brutus with republican sympathies. A C. Antistius Vetus was Consul-Suffect in 30 and became owner of Cicero's villa at Puteoli. Whether these are two or one is doubtful.

*C. ANTONIUS: (1) Caesar's colleague in the Consulship of 63, having previously been expelled from the Senate for rapacity and insolvency. Governor of Macedonia in 62–60. Condemned after his return to Rome, went into exile but lived to become Censor (!) in 42. Mark Antony was his nephew. *(2) Brother of Mark Antony. A Caesarian officer in the Civil War, became Praetor in 44. Captured in 42 by Brutus in Greece and later executed.

*L. ANTONIUS: Youngest brother of Mark Antony. Quaestor in 50 to Q. Minucius Thermus in Asia, Tribune in 44, and Consul in 41, when he and Antony's wife Fulvia started an unsuccessful war against Octavian in Italy. His life was spared but probably ended soon afterwards.

M. ANTONIUS: (1) Grandfather of Mark Antony, Consul in 99, and a celebrated orator. *(2) Mark Antony. Caesar's Quaestor in 52 and one of his principal lieutenants in the Civil War. Tribune in 49. Consul with Caesar in 44 and would-be successor to his power, he eventually formed the Triumvirate of 43 along with Octavian and Lepidus. Later quarrelled with Octavian and committed suicide after defeat at Actium (31).

APELLA: Freedman of M. Fabius Gallus (several other persons of this name crop up).

APELLES: The most famous painter of antiquity (late fourth-century).

APOLLODORUS: Of Athens. Second-century writer of a historical chronicle in verse.

APPIUS: See CLAUDIUS.

M. APULEIUS: One of Gabinius' would-be prosecutors in 54, Augur and Quaestor in 45, Consul in 20.

AQUILA: See PONTIUS.

C. AQUILIUS Gallus: Praetor in 66 and an eminent jurist.

ARCHIAS: See LICINIUS.

ARCHILOCHUS: Seventh-century poet, famous for the virulence of his lampoons.

ARCHIMEDES: Third-century mathematician.

ARIARATHES: Brother of the following, whom in 42 he succeeded as Ariarathes X. Later deposed and probably killed by Antony.

ARIOBARZANES III: Succeeded his murdered father as King of Cappadocia in 52. Killed by Cassius' orders in 42.

ARISTARCHUS: Homeric critic and keeper of the Alexandrian library in the earlier second century.

ARISTIPPUS: Of Cyrene. Pupil of Socrates and author of a hedonistic system of philosophy.

ARISTOPHANES: (1) Fifth-fourth-century Athenian comic dramatist. (2) Grammarian, Aristarchus' predecessor as head of the Alexandrian library.

ARISTOTLE: The great fourth-century philosopher and polymath.

ARISTOXENUS: Pupil of Aristotle, especially noted for his works on music.

ARISTUS: Brother of Antiochus of Ascalon, whom he succeeded as head of the Academy.

C. ARRIUS: Cicero's neighbour at Formiae.

Q. ARRIUS: Henchman of M. Crassus. He seems to have been exiled in 52 and dead by 46.

ARTAVASDES: King of Armenia. Dethroned by Antony in 34 and subsequently executed.

ARTAXERXES I: King of Persia with whom Themistocles took refuge.

ASCLAPO: Doctor who treated Tiro at Patrae in 50–49.

C. ASINIUS Pollio: Born about 76, Praetor in 45, Consul in 40. Soldier, orator, tragic dramatist, and historian. Governor of Further Spain at the time of Caesar's death, he joined Antony in 43 and remained his supporter, but lived on under Augustus until A.D. 5.

C. ATEIUS Capito: As Tribune in 55 an ally of Cato, but after expulsion from the Senate in 50 supported Caesar. A close friend of Cicero.

L. ATEIUS Capito: Senator in 51.

ATHENODORUS: (1) The Bald. Stoic philosopher of Tarsus, brought to Rome by Cato. (2) Son of Sandon. Also a Stoic philosopher, tutor to the future Emperor Augustus.

ATILIUS: Early writer of Latin comedy.

C. ATIUS Paelignus: Pompeian officer.

ATTICA: See CAECILIA.

ATTIUS Dionysius: Friend of Cicero and Cornificius.

P. ATTIUS Varus: Pompeian officer. In 49 irregularly took over the province of Africa, which he had previously governed. Defeated and killed Curio. Probably fell at Munda.

Aulus' son: See AFRANIUS.

*AURELIA Orestilla: Wife of Catiline, 'in whom no respectable person ever found anything to praise except her good looks' (Sallust).

AURELIUS: Apparently acting as agent for M. Tullius Montanus in 44. Perhaps one of the brothers for whom Cicero wrote a recommendatory letter (Letter 59 (XIII. 40)).

*L. AURELIUS Cotta: Consul in 65. A relative of Caesar's mother, he took no part in the Civil War and later seems to have been at Caesar's disposition. After Caesar's murder retired from public life.

*M. AURELIUS Cotta: Governor of Sardinia in 49.

P. AUTRONIUS Paetus: Elected Consul in 66 but deprived of office by a conviction for bribery. Condemned in 62 for complicity with Catiline, he went into exile in Greece.

C. AVIANIUS Evander: Freedman of Aemilius Avianianus and distinguished sculptor.

C. Avianius Flaccus: Corn-merchant of Puteoli, well known to Cicero.

Q. Axius: Wealthy Senator. A collection of Cicero's letters to him was extant in antiquity.

Balbus: See Cornelius.

Basilus: See Minucius.

Bassus: See Caecilius.

Bibulus: See Calpurnius.

Brogitarus: Galatian, son-in-law of Deiotarus. In return for a bribe Clodius as Tribune had him made Priest of the Great Mother at Pessinus with the title of king.

Brutus: See Junius.

Bursa: See Munatius.

Caecilia Attica: Atticus' daughter, born probably in 51.

*Caecilia Metella: Wife of the younger P. Lentulus Spinther and perhaps daughter of Clodia ('Ox-Eyes').

Q. Caecilius: Atticus' maternal uncle, a Roman Knight. Died in 58 leaving Atticus his heir.

Statius Caecilius: Early writer of Latin comedy.

Q. Caecilius Bassus: Former Pompeian who raised a mutiny in 46 against Caesar's governor of Syria and took command of his troops.

C. Caecilius Cornutus: (1) Tribune in 61 and Praetor in 57, when he supported Cicero's recall. (2) Perhaps son of the foregoing, City Praetor in 43. Committed suicide when Octavian seized Rome.

*L. Caecilius Metellus: Tribune in 49.

*Q. Caecilius Metellus Celer: As Praetor in 63 cooperated with Cicero against Catiline. Governor of Cisalpine Gaul in 62, Consul in 60. Died in 59. His wife was the notorious Clodia ('Ox-Eyes').

*Q. Caecilius Metellus Creticus: Consul in 69. Gained his honorific cognomen by conquering and annexing Crete (68–65).

*Q. Caecilius Metellus Nepos: Younger brother of Celer. Served with Pompey in the East. As Tribune in 62 agitated against Cicero and was suspended from office. Consul in 57 and then governor of Hither Spain. Celer and Nepos were P. Clodius' half-brothers.

*Q. CAECILIUS Metellus Numidicus: Consul in 109. In 100 he went into voluntary exile rather than swear an oath to uphold legislation by the demagogue Saturninus, and was brought back the following year.

*Q. CAECILIUS Metellus Pius Scipio: A Scipio Nasica adopted by a Metellus (Numidicus' son), 'vaunting an unmatched pedigree, yet ignorant as well as unworthy of his ancestors, corrupt and debauched in the way of his life' (R. Syme). Became Pompey's father-in-law and colleague in the Consulship of 52. After Pompey's death led the Republican forces in Africa and committed suicide after Thapsus.

A. CAECINA: Friend of Cicero, of noble Etruscan family; noted orator and author among other things of a treatise on divination by lightning.

CAELIUS: A debtor of Faberius.

M. CAELIUS Rufus: Born c. 88. Placed by his father under Cicero's patronage and successfully defended by him on a criminal charge in 56. Tribune in 52, Curule Aedile in 50. One of the leading speakers of his time. Previously an opponent of Caesar, he changed sides just before the outbreak of the Civil War and was made Praetor in 48. As such started an agitation in favour of debtors ending in an attempted rising against Caesar in which he and his partner Milo lost their lives.

CAEPIO: See M. JUNIUS Brutus.

CAERELLIA: A friend of Cicero's later years, considerably his senior, with philosophical interests. His letters to her, allegedly of a risqué character, were extant in antiquity.

CAESAR: See JULIUS.

L. CAESIUS: Member of Q. Cicero's entourage in Asia, later employed on his building operations near Arpinum.

M. CAESIUS: Aedile of Arpinum in 46.

CALDUS: See COELIUS.

CALENUS: See FUFIUS.

M. CALIDIUS: Distinguished orator. As Praetor in 57 supported Cicero's recall. A Caesarian in the Civil War, he died as governor of Cisalpine Gaul in 47.

CALLISTHENES: Latter-fourth-century historian.

*L. CALPURNIUS Bestia: (1) Tribune in 62 and enemy of Cicero.
*(2) Friend of Cicero, defended by him in 56. Some identify
the two.

*L. CALPURNIUS Bibulus: Son of the following. Joined his step-
father Brutus in 43 but after Philippi served Antony, dying as
governor of Syria in 32.

*M. CALPURNIUS Bibulus: As Consul in 59 opposed Caesar's legis-
lation, shutting himself in his house and 'watching the skies'.
Governor of Syria in 51–50. Died of overstrain while com-
manding Pompey's fleet in 48. Married Cato's daughter
Porcia, later wife of Brutus.

*C. CALPURNIUS Piso: Consul in 67, then governor of Transalpine
and Cisalpine Gaul. Defended by Cicero on a charge brought
in this connection in 63.

*L. CALPURNIUS Piso Caesoninus: Consul in 58, when he took a
line unfriendly to Cicero. Hence a bitter attack (extant) in 55.
As Censor in 50 tried to moderate his colleague Appius
Pulcher's harsh measures. Neutral in the Civil War (Caesar
was his son-in-law), he opposed Antony in 44 but in 43 tried
to promote an understanding.

*C. CALPURNIUS Piso Frugi: Tullia's first husband. Quaestor in 58,
he died before Cicero's return from exile.

CALVINUS: See DOMITIUS.

CALVUS: See LICINIUS Macer.

C. CAMILLUS: An expert on business law, friend of Atticus and
Cicero.

P. CANIDIUS Crassus: Consul-Suffect in 40. Commanded Antony's
land forces at Actium and was executed by Octavian.

L. CANINIUS Gallus: Friend of Cicero, who defended him in 55.
As Tribune in 56 he worked for Pompey's appointment to
replace Ptolemy the Piper on his throne. Died in 44.

C. CANINIUS Rebilus: Caesarian officer and one-day Consul in 45.

Ti. CANNUTIUS: As Tribune in 43 bitterly hostile to Antony.
Escaped proscription, but was later executed by Octavian.

CANUS: See GELLIUS.

CARBO: See PAPIRIUS.

D. CARFULENUS: Able Caesarian officer who, after Caesar's death, opposed Antony as Tribune in 44. Commanded Martian Legion at the battle of Forum Gallorum, in which he was reported killed.

CARNEADES: Second-century philosopher and head of the 'New' Academy.

T. CARRINAS: Caesarian acquaintance of Cicero's in 45. Perhaps the praenomen should be Gaius (C.) to identify him with a Consul-Suffect of 43 who played a considerable role in the Triumviral period.

CASSIUS Barba: Caesarian officer, later supporter of Antony.

*C. CASSIUS Longinus: As Quaestor took charge of Syria after Crassus' death at Carrhae in 53. Gained a success against invading Parthians in 51. As Tribune in 49 joined Pompey. Pardoned and favoured by Caesar, he became Praetor in 44 and one of the leading conspirators against Caesar's life. Subsequently organized forces against the Triumvirs in the East and perished with Brutus at Philippi in 42. Married to Brutus' half-sister, Junia Tertulla.

*L. CASSIUS Longinus: Brother of the above but a Caesarian, Tribune in 44.

*Q. CASSIUS Longinus: Cousin of the foregoing. Formerly a favourite with Pompey, as Tribune in 49 he supported Caesar. His misgovernment of Hither Spain (49–47) provoked mutiny and his attempted assassination. Recalled by Caesar, he died at sea.

C. CASSIUS Parmensis: Quaestor in 43. According to the historian Velleius (who may, however, have confused him with someone else) he was one of Caesar's assassins and the last of them to die (killed at Athens after Actium). Probably the author of elegies mentioned by Horace (*Epistles*, 1. 4.3).

M. CASSIUS Scaeva: As a Centurion in 48 his epic courage is recorded by Caesar. It seems to have been matched by his rapacity.

CASTRICIUS: A person with whom Q. Cicero had financial dealings.

CATILINE: See SERGIUS.

CATIUS: Native of Cisalpine Gaul and author of a treatise or treatises on Epicureanism.

CATO: See PORCIUS.

CATULUS: See LUTATIUS.

CELER: See CAECILIUS Metellus and PILIUS.

CENSORINUS: See MARCIUS.

CEPHALIO: Letter-carrier in 49–47.

CHAERIPPUS: Friend, or perhaps freedman or client, of Q. Cicero, probably to be distinguished from a friend of Cornificius mentioned in letters addressed to the latter.

CHRYSIPPUS: (1) Third-century Stoic philosopher. (2) Freedman in charge of Cicero's library. (3) See VETTIUS.

CICERO: See TULLIUS.

L. CINCIUS: Man of business and confidential agent of Atticus.

CINEAS: Minister of King Pyrrhus and author (or rather epitomizer) of a work on strategy.

CINNA: See CORNELIUS.

L. (?) CISPIUS Laevus: Officer (not necessarily Legate) of Plancus in 43.

Ser. CLAUDIUS: Roman knight and scholar, half-brother or cousin to Papirius Paetus. Drew up a list of Plautus' authentic plays.

*C. CLAUDIUS Marcellus: (1) Praetor in 80. *(2) Son of the foregoing. As Consul in 50 in opposition to Caesar, but neutral in the Civil War. Married Caesar's great-niece Octavia. *(3) Cousin of the foregoing and Consul in 49. A naval commander under Pompey in 48, he seems to have died before Pharsalia.

*M. CLAUDIUS Marcellus: Brother of Gaius (no. 3), Consul in 51. A steady though not fanatical opponent of Caesar, he joined Pompey in the war but retired to Mytilene after Pharsalia. Publicly pardoned by Caesar in 46 (hence Cicero's extant speech of gratitude), he was murdered by a friend on his way home.

*Ti. CLAUDIUS Nero: One of Tullia's suitors in 50, he served and held office under Caesar. Praetor in 42, died after various vicissitudes about 35. His wife Livia married Octavian; his son became Octavian's (Augustus') successor, the Emperor Tiberius.

*Ap. CLAUDIUS Pulcher: As Praetor in 57 at enmity with Cicero but later reconciled. Consul in 54, he became Cicero's predecessor as governor of Cilicia. Censor in 50. Supported Pompey in the Civil War, but died before Pharsalia. One of his daughters married Pompey's elder son, another M. Brutus.

*Ap. CLAUDIUS Pulcher (maior): Son of Gaius. Probably served under Caesar in Gaul. After Caesar's death joined Antony, but temporarily regretted it. Later a Triumviral partisan and Consul in 38.

*Ap. CLAUDIUS Pulcher (minor): Younger brother of the above, adopted by his uncle Appius. In 51 figured in the proceedings following C. Pulcher's conviction (this distribution of the two young Appii, due to Mommsen, is generally accepted but not certain).

*C. CLAUDIUS (CLODIUS) Pulcher: Brother of Appius. Legate of Caesar in Gaul, Praetor in 56, then governor of Asia. Condemned for extortion after his return, he may have remained in exile until 43.

CLITARCHUS: Third-century author of a history of Alexander the Great.

*CLODIA (CLAUDIA, 'Ox-Eyes'): Sister to C. Claudius Pulcher (Clodius; above) and wife of Metellus Celer; probably the 'Lesbia' to whom Catullus wrote his love-poems. Perhaps owner of a suburban property which Cicero wanted to buy in 45. The Clodia mentioned in Letters to Atticus, 172 (IX.6)3 may have been her sister.

L. CLODIUS: 'Prefect of Engineers' to Ap. Pulcher in 51.

CLODIUS Aesopus: Great tragic actor, well known to Cicero personally. His son (mentioned also by Horace) was a notorious reprobate.

*P. CLODIUS Pulcher: Younger brother of Appius and Gaius. As Tribune in 58 drove Cicero into exile and remained his archenemy. From then until his death in an affray with Milo in 52 he was a power in politics through his popularity with the Roman mob and organized street-rowdyism. Often called Publius or Pulchellus ('Little Beauty', 'Pretty-boy') in Cicero's letters.

Sex. CLOELIUS: P. Clodius' chief lieutenant and gang-organizer. Traditionally known as Sex. Clodius after an error in some inferior manuscripts.

CLUATIUS: An architect.

M. CLUVIUS: Wealthy banker of Puteoli from whom Cicero inherited an estate there.

COCCEIUS: Perhaps an agent or surety of Dolabella's, possibly one of the brothers L. and M. Cocceius Nerva, prominent in the Triumviral period (see NERVA).

*C. COELIUS Caldus: Quaestor to Cicero in 50 and left by him in charge of Cilicia.

Q. CONSIDIUS: Wealthy old Senator in 59. Q. Considius Gallus of Letter 431 (XII. 26) may have been a relative, as also the following.

M. CONSIDIUS Nonianus: Praetor perhaps in 52; named by the Senate in 49 as Caesar's successor in Cisalpine Gaul.

C. COPONIUS: Praetor in 49 and Pompeian naval commander in 48.

Q. CORNELIUS: Jurist, teacher of Trebatius Testa.

L. CORNELIUS Balbus: (1) Native of Gades (Cadiz), received Roman citizenship in 72 through L. Cornelius Lentulus Crus. Attached himself to Caesar, becoming his confidential agent and financial adviser, and later to Octavian. Appointed Consul-Suffect in 40, not having held (at least until Caesar's death) any previous magistracy. Present at Atticus' death-bed in 32. (2) Nephew of the foregoing. In Caesar's entourage during the Civil War, he became Quaestor in 44, serving under Pollio in Spain. Rose to Consular rank under Augustus and triumphed in 19.

*L. CORNELIUS Cinna: Consul in 87. Expelled from Rome he reestablished himself by military force and after Marius' death remained at the head of affairs until his own death in 84.

*P. CORNELIUS Dolabella (after adoption Cn. Cornelius Lentulus Dolabella?): Defended by Cicero on two capital charges, he married Tullia in 50, but was divorced in 46. A favoured follower of Caesar (despite demagogic activities as Tribune in 47), whom he succeeded as Consul in 44. After some wavering joined Antony and left for his province of Syria late in the year. On the way killed C. Trebonius, governor of Asia and one of Caesar's assassins. Soon afterwards committed suicide to avoid capture by Cassius.

C. CORNELIUS Gallus: Distinguished poet, friend of Pollio and Virgil. After high promotion from Augustus his career ended in disgrace and suicide.

*CORNELIUS Lentulus: Son of Dolabella and Tullia, born in January 45; lived only a few months.

*L. CORNELIUS Lentulus: Son of the Flamen, L. Lentulus Niger. Unsuccessfully prosecuted Gabinius in 54.

*L. CORNELIUS Lentulus Crus: Praetor in 58 (friendly to Cicero), Consul in 49. After Pharsalia fled to Egypt, where he was murdered in prison.

*Cn. CORNELIUS Lentulus Marcellinus: Consul in 56. Not heard of thereafter.

*L. CORNELIUS Lentulus Niger: Flamen of Mars. Died in 55.

*P. CORNELIUS Lentulus Spinther: (1) As Consul in 57 took a leading part in Cicero's restoration. Governor of Cilicia 56–54. Supported Pompey in the Civil War. Taken prisoner by Caesar at Corfinium and released, he joined Pompey in Greece. Put to death in Africa in 46, perhaps by Caesar's orders. The name Spinther, derived from an actor who resembled him, is used by Cicero only for his son. *(2) Son of the foregoing. Falsely claimed to have taken part in Caesar's murder. Went to Asia in 43 as Trebonius' Quaestor, after whose death he was active in support of Brutus and Cassius. Probably put to death after Philippi.

CORNELIUS Nepos: Friend of Atticus and Cicero. Author of a short biography of the former in his book *On Famous Men*.

*P. CORNELIUS Scipio Aemilianus Africanus: Destroyer of Carthage in 146 and leading Roman statesman, idealized by Cicero, who gave him the chief role in his dialogue *On the Republic*.

*Faustus CORNELIUS Sulla: Son of the Dictator. Served with distinction in the East under Pompey, whose daughter he married. Active Republican in the Civil War, killed in Africa.

*P. CORNELIUS Sulla: (1) Nephew of the Dictator. Elected to the Consulship in 66 along with P. Autronius and deprived of office for the same reason, he retired to Naples. Defended in 62 by Cicero in an extant speech on a charge of complicity in Catiline's plot. Prominent after Caesar's victory, he enriched himself by buying confiscated property. Died in 46. *(2) Son of the foregoing. It was probably he rather than his father who held military commands in the Civil War, including that of Caesar's right at Pharsalia.

*L. Cornelius Sulla Felix: The Dictator. Held supreme power in Rome from 82 till his abdication in 79. Died in 78.

Q. Cornificius: (1) Praetor in 67 or 66 and a fellow-candidate with Cicero for the Consulship of 63. (2) Son of the above. Quaestor in 48, he served Caesar in and after the Civil War. Governor of Africa 44–42, until defeated and killed by the neighbouring governor, T. Sextius. A notable orator and poet, friend and correspondent of Cicero.

Cornutus: See Caecilus.

L. Cossinius: Like his friend Atticus a Roman Knight and landed proprietor in Epirus, with a role in Varro's dialogue *On Agriculture*.

Cotta: See Aurelius.

Crassipes: See Furius.

Crassus: See Licinius.

Craterus: Attica's doctor, a celebrated physician mentioned by Horace and Galen.

Cratippus: Eminent philosopher of the Peripatetic (Aristotelian) school, mentor of young M. Cicero at Athens, Cicero obtained him Roman citizenship from Caesar.

Crispus: See Marcius.

Culleo: See Terentius.

Curio: See Scribonius.

M'. Curius: Roman businessman resident at Patrae, a close friend of Atticus and later of Cicero.

M. Curtius: Recommended by Cicero to Caesar for a military Tribunate in 54.

Curtius Nicias: A noted scholar. In 45–44 closely attached to Dolabella, who perhaps introduced him to Cicero. Sometimes identified with a despot of Cos, his native island, during Antony's régime.

C. Curtius Postumus: A vigorous Caesarian, almost certainly the C. Rabirius Postumus whom Cicero defended in an extant speech in 56.

Cyrus: (1) Founder of the Persian empire. Xenophon's *Education of Cyrus* is a highly idealized account of him. (2) See Vettius.

Cytheris: See Volumnia.

DAMASIPPUS: Well-known art expert who, as we learn from Horace, went bankrupt and turned Stoic philosopher.

DECIMUS: See JUNIUS.

DEIOTARUS: Tetrarch of part of Galatia, made king by Pompey, whom he supported in the Civil War. Caesar let him keep his throne and acquitted him on a charge of attempted assassination (Cicero's defence is extant). Died about 40 in extreme old age. His son and namesake, also given the royal title by the Senate, probably predeceased him.

DEMETRIUS: (1) A freedman of Pompey (*Letters to Atticus* 86 (IV.11) I). (2) A freedman, probably of Atticus (*Letters to Atticus* 371 (XIV.17)1). (3) Of Magnesia, a contemporary littérateur, author of a book *On Concord*. (4) A tiresome personage, perhaps identical with No. 1, perhaps an influential freedman of Caesar's (Letters 184–6 (XVI.19, 22, 17)). (5) Caesarian officer in 49 (Letter 149 (VIII.15)). (6) Megas, a Sicilian recommended by Cicero in 46. (7) Of Phalerum, late-fourth-century Athenian orator and statesman.

DEMOCRITUS: Fifth-century philosopher, developed the atomic theory of the universe.

DEMOSTHENES: Great fourth-century Athenian orator and patriot.

DICAEARCHUS: Pupil of Aristotle and like him a polymath, author of works on philosophy, history, literature, etc.

DIODOTUS: (1) Stoic philosopher and Cicero's teacher. Lived in Cicero's house for many years and died leaving him his money. (2) Freedman of Lucullus.

DIOGENES: Greek friend or agent of Caelius Rufus, sent out to Cilicia in 51.

DIONYSIUS: (1) Fourth-century despot of Syracuse. (2) His son and successor. (3) Freedman and librarian of Cicero, pilfered his books and ran away. (4) See ATTIUS, POMPONIUS.

DIPHILUS: (1) An actor. (2) An architect.

DOLABELLA: See CORNELIUS.

*Cn. DOMITIUS Ahenobarbus: Son of the following. Returned to Italy after Pharsalia. Later a partisan of Antony (Shakespeare's Enobarbus), whom he finally deserted. Consul in 32.

*L. DOMITIUS Ahenobarbus: Cato's brother-in-law and bitter opponent of Caesar. Captured at Corfinium in 49 and released, he stood siege in Massilia but fled before the town fell to Caesar's forces. Commanded Pompey's left at Pharsalia and was killed in flight.

*Cn. DOMITIUS Calvinus: Consul in 53. Probably condemned for bribery and restored from exile by Caesar. Held high commands in the war, and a second Consulship and Triumph after Caesar's death.

DRUSUS: See LIVIUS.

DURIS: Historian, 'flourished' c. 300.

L. EGNATIUS Rufus: Roman Knight with whom Cicero and his brother had financial dealings.

Q. ENNIUS: Third-second-century Latin poet.

EPAMINONDAS: Theban soldier and statesman, killed in the battle of Mantinea (362).

EPHORUS: Fourth-century historian.

EPICHARMUS: Sixth-century Sicilian writer of comedy.

EPICURUS: Fourth-century philosopher.

ERATOSTHENES: Third-century savant, head of the Alexandrian library and founder of scientific geography.

EROS: Slave (perhaps of Philotimus) or freedman who looked after Cicero's finances in 45-44.

EUPOLIS: Athenian writer of comedy, contemporary with Aristophanes.

EURIPIDES: Athenian writer of tragedy.

EUTRAPELUS: See VOLUMNIUS.

Q. FABERIUS: Caesar's Secretary, served Antony after Caesar's death.

FABIUS: A lover of Clodia's, perhaps identical with Q. Fabius Maximus.

C. FABIUS: Legate of Caesar and friend of Atticus. Seems to have died in 49.

M. FABIUS Gallus: Usually but wrongly called Fadius. Friend of Cicero, author, Epicurean, connoisseur of art.

*Q. FABIUS Maximus: Supporter of Caesar and Consul-Suffect in 45. Died in office.

Q. FABIUS Vergilianus: Legate to Ap. Pulcher in Cilicia. Perhaps the Q. Fabius who brought Pompey a message in 49 (*Letters to Atticus* 161A (VIII.11A)).

L. FADIUS: Aedile of Arpinum in 44.

T. FADIUS: Cicero's Quaestor in 63, Tribune in 57 (supported Cicero's recall), probably Praetor in a later year. Condemned for bribery in 52.

*C. FANNIUS: Anti-triumviral Tribune in 59, probably Praetor later, governor of Asia in 49. Proscribed in 43, he fled to Sex. Pompeius and later to Antony.

*FAUSTA: Sulla's daughter and wife of C. Memmius, later of Milo.

FAUSTUS: See CORNELIUS Sulla.

M. FAVONIUS: Follower of Cato. Fled from Pharsalia with Pompey. Later pardoned by Caesar, but proscribed in 43 and put to death at Philippi.

FIGULUS: See MARCIUS.

FLACCUS: See VALERIUS.

FLAMINIUS Flamma: Debtor mentioned in 45.

C. FLAVIUS: Friend and 'Prefect of Engineers' to M. Brutus. Fell at Philippi.

L. FLAVIUS: As Tribune in 60 acted in Pompey's interest. Praetor in 58. The Caesarian officer of *Letters to Atticus* 190 (x.1).2 may or may not be the same.

FUFIDIUS: The Fufidii were a prominent family in Arpinum.

Q. FUFIUS Calenus: Tribune in 61, Praetor in 59. Served under Caesar in Gaul and the Civil War. Governor of Greece in 48, Consul in 47. After Caesar's death supported Antony in Rome. Disliked by Cicero, who had known and respected his father.

*FULVIA: Wife of P. Crassus, Curio, and Antony.

C. FUNDANIUS: Friend and apparently ex-client of Cicero.

FUNISULANUS: Twice mentioned as carrying a letter from Atticus to Cicero.

T. FURFANUS Postumus: Friend of Cicero and governor of Sicily in 46–45.

*FURIUS Crassipes: Married Tullia about 55, soon afterwards divorced. Quaestor in Bithynia, perhaps in 54.

C. FURNIUS: Friend of Cicero, Tribune in 50. A Caesarian, he served as Munatius Plancus' Legate in 43 and later supported Mark Antony and his brother Lucius. Pardoned and dignified by Octavian, he lived to see his son Consul in 17.

A. Gabinius: Military lieutenant and political supporter of Pompey. As Consul in 58 backed Clodius against Cicero. As governor of Syria restored Ptolemy the Piper to his throne in 55. Went into exile in 54 after conviction on charges of extortion. Reappears as Caesar's Legate in 48. Died in 47.

Galba: See Sulpicius.

M. Gallius: Along with his brother prosecuted Calidius in 51. Identifiable with an ex-Praetor and partisan of Antony in 43.

Q. Gallius: Brother of the foregoing, both being sons of a former client of Cicero's, Q. Gallius. Probably Praetor in 43, deposed from office by Octavian.

Gallus: See Fabius.

L. Gavius: Agent of Brutus in Cappadocia 50–49.

Gellius Poplicola: Brother of L. Gellius Poplicola, Consul in 72, and a follower of Clodius. F. Münzer wished to identify him with Q. Gellius Canus (or Kanus), a close friend of Atticus, saved by him from proscription in 43. The L. Gellius of Letter 398 (x.17)3 may be his nephew, Consul in 36.

Glabrio: See Acilius.

Gnaeus: See Pompeius.

Graeceius: Friend of Cassius and D. Brutus.

Hammonius: See Ammonius.

Hegesias: Third-century rhetorician, regarded as the creator of the 'Asiatic' style of oratory, one feature of which was a fondness for short, staccato sentences.

Heraclides: Of Pontus. Pupil of Plato, author of works on a variety of subjects, mostly in dialogue form.

Hermia(s): Apparently a slave of Cicero's or of his brother's.

Herodes: An Athenian, probably of high rank, acquainted with Atticus and Cicero.

Herodotus: Fifth-century historian.

Hesiod: Early Greek poet.

Hilarus: Four freedmen of this name occur in the Letters.

Hipparchus: Second-century astronomer and geographer.

Hirrus: See Lucilius.

A. Hirtius: Caesarian officer, Praetor in 46 and Consul in 43 until his death at Mutina. Man of letters and gourmet. Nine or more books of his correspondence with Cicero were extant in antiquity.

T. HORDEONIUS: Member of a Campanian merchant family and co-heir to the estate of M. Cluvius.

*Q. HORTENSIUS Hortalus: (1) Consul in 69 and before Cicero Rome's leading forensic orator. A devoted friend of Atticus, his relations with Cicero varied. Died in 50. *(2) Son of the foregoing and on bad terms with him. Joined Caesar in the Civil War, who made him Praetor and governor of Macedonia. Joined Brutus in 43. Put to death after Philippi by Antony in reprisal for the execution of his brother Gaius.

HOSTILIUS Saserna: Three brothers of this name, Gaius, Lucius, and Publius, served in Caesar's armies. One of them was with Antony at Mutina.

HYPSAEUS: See PLAUTIUS.

ISOCRATES: Fourth-century Athenian rhetorician.

JUBA: King of Numidia, allied with the Pompeians in the Civil War.

*C. JULIUS Caesar: The Dictator.

*L. JULIUS Caesar: (1) Distant relative of the above. Consul in 64 and Legate in Gaul, he stood neutral in the Civil War. Proscribed in 43, he was saved by his sister, Antony's mother Julia. *(2) Son of the above. After acting as messenger in abortive peace negotiations early in the Civil War he joined Pompey. Killed after Thapsus, perhaps at Caesar's orders.

*C. JULIUS Caesar Octavianus: Caesar's great-nephew and adopted son. Later Triumvir and Emperor Augustus.

*JUNIA: Half-sister of Brutus and wife of Lepidus.

*JUNIA Tertia (or Tertulla): Sister of the above and wife of C. Cassius. Her funeral in A.D.22 is described by Tacitus.

L. JUNIUS Brutus: Rome's first Consul, who drove out the last king, Tarquin the Proud.

*M. JUNIUS Brutus: Sometimes called (Q. Servilius) Caepio (Brutus) after adoption by his uncle Q. Servilius Caepio. On his career see the introductory note on pp. 341 f.

*D. JUNIUS Brutus Albinus: Not closely related to the above. Served under Caesar in Gaul and the Civil War, governor of Transalpine Gaul in 48–46. Regarded by Caesar with special favour and named as Consul for 42 along with L. Plancus, he became a leading conspirator against his life. Later besieged by Antony at Mutina in his province of Cisalpine Gaul, after Antony's defeat and escape he too crossed the Alps to join Plancus. When the latter went over to Antony he fled, but was killed by a Celtic chieftain on Antony's orders.

*D. JUNIUS Silanus: Consul in 62. Married Brutus' mother Servilia by whom he had three daughters (see JUNIA).

*M. JUNIUS Silanus: Officer of Lepidus in 43, who (probably) sent him to Antony at Mutina but later disavowed him. Consul in 25.

*M. JUVENTIUS Laterensis: Praetor in 51. As Lepidus' Legate killed himself when his chief joined Antony.

*JUVENTIUS Talna: Friend of Cicero's, whose son came into consideration as a future husband for Attica. The rascally juryman at Clodius' trial mentioned in *Letters to Atticus* 16 (1.16)6 is no doubt another man.

KANUS: See GELLIUS.

LABEO: See 'ANTISTIUS'.

D. LABERIUS: Roman Knight, author of mimes.

T. LABIENUS: Tribune in 63. Caesar's principal lieutenant in Gaul, but deserted him at the outbreak of the Civil War and fought against him to the end. Killed at Munda.

D. LAELIUS: Family friend and supporter of Pompey. Allowed to return to Italy after Pharsalia.

*C. LAELIUS Sapiens: Consul in 140 and life-long friend of the younger Scipio Africanus.

*LAENAS: Perhaps Popilius Laenas, Senator and friend of Caesar.

LAÏS: Famous Corinthian courtesan.

LAMIA: See AELIUS.

LATERENSIS: See JUVENTIUS.

LENTULUS: See CORNELIUS.

LEONIDES: Athenian, apparently of high position, who kept an eye on M. Cicero junior in 45–44.

LEPIDUS: See AEMILIUS.

GLOSSARY OF PERSONS

LEPTA: See PACONIUS.

LIBO: See SCRIBONIUS.

A. LICINIUS Archias: Poet, author of some surviving epigrams. Cicero successfully defended his title to Roman citizenship in an extant speech (62).

*L. LICINIUS Crassus: Consul in 95 and one of the greatest Roman orators.

*M. LICINIUS Crassus: (1) Consul in 70 and 55. Joined Pompey and Caesar in 60 to form the so-called First Triumvirate. Left for Syria late in 55. Defeated and killed at Carrhae in 53 leading an invasion of Parthia. *(2) Son (probably younger) of the above.

*P. LICINIUS Crassus: Son (probably elder) of the 'Triumvir'. Much attached to Cicero in his early days, he served brilliantly under Caesar in Gaul. Went out to Syria with his father and was killed at Carrhae. In the *Brutus* Cicero seems to blame him for the disaster.

*P. LICINIUS Crassus Dives: See *Cicero's Letters to Atticus*, p. 98, n. 147. He was Praetor in 57.

*L. LICINIUS Lucullus Ponticus: Lieutenant of Sulla and Consul in 74. In 73–66 waged a brilliant series of campaigns against King Mithridates of Pontus, ending ingloriously through disaffection in his army. After supersession by Pompey returned to Rome to live in ease and luxury until his death in 56.

*M. LICINIUS Lucullus: (1) See TERENTIUS. *(2) Son of Ponticus. Died at Philippi, or soon afterwards.

C. LICINIUS Macer Calvus: Son of C. Licinius Macer (see *Cicero's Letters to Atticus*, p. 39, n.15); a distinguished orator and poet.

Q. LIGARIUS: Pompeian, defended in 45 by Cicero before Caesar in an extant speech. Allowed to return to Rome he joined the conspiracy against Caesar.

T. LIGARIUS: Brother of the above. He and another brother perished in the proscriptions of 43.

A. LIGURIUS: Caesarian officer and friend of Cicero's.

L. LIVINEIUS Regulus: Friend of Cicero, at some time Praetor; later exiled.

L. LIVINEIUS Trypho: Freedman of the above.

*M. Livius Drusus Claudianus: Father of Augustus' wife Livia, originally a Claudius Pulcher. Successfully defended by Cicero in 54. Praetor or President of Court in 50. Owner of suburban estate coveted by Cicero in 45. Killed himself in his tent at Philippi.

M. Lollius Palicanus: Tribune in 71. Mob orator and agitator against the post-Sullan régime.

Cn. Lucceius: Member of a locally aristocratic family of Cumae, friend of Cicero and Brutus.

L. Lucceius (son of Quintus): Praetor in 67 and unsuccessful candidate for the Consulship in 60. On amicable terms with Cicero, he remained one of Pompey's most intimate friends until Pharsalia. Pardoned by Caesar, he may have died in the proscriptions of 43. Cicero admired his historical work, which was perhaps never published.

P. Luccius: Friend of Cornificius (wrongly called Lucceius).

C. Lucilius: Roman satirist late in the second century.

C. Lucilius Hirrus: Great-nephew (probably) of the above and cousin to Pompey. Tribune in 53, he annoyed Cicero by standing against him for the Augurate. Defeated in 51 in his candidature for the Aedileship. Followed Pompey in the Civil War but survived to lend Caesar 6,000 fish for his triumphal banquet in 45 and flee proscription in 43–42. A great landowner and in Cicero's opinion an egregious ass.

Lucius: See Saufeius.

Q. Lucretius: Whether certain Lucretii mentioned in the Letters are identical and whether they are to be identified with Q. Lucretius Vespillo, who commanded a Pompeian squadron in the Adriatic and lived to become Consul in 19, is doubtful.

T. Lucretius Carus: One of Rome's greatest poets. His work *On the Nature of Things* is an exposition of Epicurus' physical philosophy.

Lucullus: See Licinius.

Lupus: (1) Friend of D. Brutus. (2) See Rutilius.

*Q. Lutatius Catulus: (1) Colleague of Marius as Consul in 102, killed by his orders in 87. *(2) Son of the foregoing. Consul in 78 and leading conservative figure until his death in 61 or 60.

Lysippus: Fourth-century sculptor.

LYSO: Friend and host of Cicero at Patrae.

P. MAGIUS Cilo: Friend and murderer of M. Marcellus.

MAMURRA: 'Prefect of Engineers' to Caesar and a *nouveau riche*. Savagely lampooned by Catullus.

M'. MANILIUS: (1) Consul in 149, one of Rome's great jurists. ★(2) Friend of Trebatius Testa, also a jurist and probably descended from the foregoing.

★MANLIUS Acidinus: Student at Athens in 45, perhaps identical with Horace's friend Torquatus.

★A. MANLIUS Torquatus: Praetor perhaps in 70 and friend of Cicero, who tried through Dolabella to get Caesar's permission for him, as an ex-Pompeian living in Athens, to return to Italy. After Caesar's death an active republican, he was befriended by his old friend Atticus after Philippi.

★L. MANLIUS Torquatus: Of a different branch of the family, Praetor in or before 49. Also friend of Cicero, who made him the Epicurean spokesman in his *De Finibus*, and of Atticus. Perished in Africa in 46. A writer of erotic verse, he is almost certainly the bridegroom in Catullus' Wedding Ode.

★T. (?) MANLIUS Torquatus: Apparently son of Aulus, mentioned in letters to Atticus of 45–44. Probably to be distinguished from Pansa's Quaestor in 43.

MARCELLINUS: See CORNELIUS Lentulus.

MARCELLUS: See CLAUDIUS.

MARCIANUS: See TULLIUS.

★L. MARCIUS Censorinus: Partisan of Caesar, then of Antony. Got possession of Cicero's house on the Palatine after its owner's murder.

C. MARCIUS Crispus: Caesarian officer. Proconsul in Bithynia in 45–44. Brought three legions to help Staius Murcus in Syria against Caecilius Bassus.

★L. MARCIUS (?) Figulus: Commanded Dolabella's fleet in 43.

★L. MARCIUS Philippus: (1) Consul in 91. Censor under Cinna's régime, but joined Sulla when he returned to Italy. ★(2) Son of the foregoing. Consul in 56. Husband of Caesar's niece and Cato's father-in-law, he took no part in the Civil War. Counselled caution to his stepson Octavian in 44. A moderating influence in the struggle between the Senate and Antony.

C. MARIUS: Of Arpinum. Great general, seven times Consul, destroyer of invading northern tribes. Driven into exile by Sulla in 88, returned to Rome by force in 87 and killed off numbers of opponents before his own death early the following year.

'C. MARIUS': An impostor, who in 45 claimed to be grandson of the above. Executed by Antony in 44.

M. MARIUS: Friend, correspondent, and perhaps relative of Cicero, resident near Pompeii.

P. MATINIUS: Agent of Brutus in Cilicia in 51–50.

C. MATIUS: Old friend of Cicero's, closely attached to Caesar, whom he accompanied in Gaul without official rank. Cicero calls him by nicknames referring to his baldness.

MAXIMUS: See FABIUS.

MEGABOCCHUS: Friend and contemporary of P. Crassus, he committed suicide at Carrhae.

MEMMIUS: Stepson of P. Sulla, associated with him in a proposed prosecution of Gabinius in 54. Perhaps identical with the following.

C. MEMMIUS (son of Gaius): Tribune in 54.

C. MEMMIUS (son of Lucius): First husband of Sulla's daughter Fausta, who was a ward of L. Lucullus, hence perhaps an enemy of the two Luculli. An erratic political career ended in exile after conviction for bribery in 52. Noted orator and poet, generally supposed to be the friend to whom Lucretius dedicated his poem *On the Nature of Things*.

L. MESCINIUS Rufus: Cicero's Quaestor in Cilicia. Seems to have joined Pompey in the Civil War but was allowed to return to Italy in 46.

MESSALLA: See VALERIUS.

C. MESSIUS: Pro-Ciceronian Tribune in 57 and adherent of Pompey; but in 46 Legate to Caesar in Africa.

METELLUS: See CAECILIUS.

METRODORUS: A doctor, probably a freedman of Cicero's.

MILO: See ANNIUS.

M. MINDIUS: Brother (?) of L. Mescinius Rufus.

L. MINUCIUS Basilus: Legate of Caesar in Gaul and the Civil War and Praetor in 45, joined the conspiracy in 44. Murdered by his slaves the following year. A friend of Cicero, he may or may not be identical with a person or persons here and there referred to as 'Minucius'.

*Q. MINUCIUS Thermus: Governor of Asia in 51–50. A Pompeian in the Civil War and proscribed in 43, he escaped to join Sex. Pompeius and then Antony.

*MUCIA: Pompey's third wife and half-sister to the Metelli, Celer and Nepos.

*Q. MUCIUS Scaevola: (1) The Augur. Consul in 117, died in 87. Cicero knew him well. *(2) Pontifex Maximus. Consul in 95. A great jurist and a model governor of Asia, also well known to Cicero until his murder by the Marians in 82. *(3) Perhaps grandson of the Augur. After Tribunate in 54 served on Ap. Pulcher's staff in Cilicia, but a Caesarian in the Civil War. Author of erotic verse.

L. MUMMIUS Achaicus: Consul in 146 and destroyer of Corinth.

C. MUNATIUS Plancus: See PLOTIUS.

L. MUNATIUS Plancus: Family friend of Cicero. Served under Caesar in Gaul and the Civil War. City Prefect during Caesar's absence in 46–45. As governor of Transalpine Gaul (except the Narbonensis), he finally joined Antony in 43. Consul in 42. Changed sides again before Actium and became Censor in 22.

T. MUNATIUS Plancus Bursa: Brother of the above. Tribune in 52 and follower of Clodius, he was successfully prosecuted by Cicero as a ringleader in the riots following Clodius' death. In exile joined Caesar, who brought him back in 49. Later an active supporter of Antony.

MURCUS: See STAIUS.

MURENA: See TERENTIUS.

Cn. NAEVIUS: Early Roman epic and dramatic poet.

NASICA: See CAECILIUS Metellus Pius Scipio.

L. NASIDIUS: Republican naval commander in 47.

NATTA: See PINARIUS.

NEPOS: See CAECILIUS Metellus and CORNELIUS.

NERO: See CLAUDIUS.

NERVA: Officer under Lepidus, perhaps one of the brothers C. and

M. Cocceius Nerva prominent in the Triumviral period (see also COCCEIUS).

NICIAS: See CURTIUS.

P. NIGIDIUS Figulus: As a Senator assisted Cicero in 63. Praetor in 58. Joined Pompey in the Civil War and died in exile in 45. A prolific writer on various branches of learning, he was chiefly remembered as an astrologer and magician.

L. NINNIUS Quadratus: Member of a distinguished Campanian family. Opposed Clodius as Tribune in 58.

M. NONIUS (Struma?): Probably governor of Macedonia in 50.

M. NONIUS Sufenas: Tribune in 56. Sometimes identified with the above.

OCELLA (L. Livius Ocella?): Friend of Cicero and Atticus, sometime Praetor.

Servius OCELLA: Subject of a Roman scandal in 50.

OCTAVIANUS or OCTAVIUS: See JULIUS.

C. OCTAVIUS: Father of Augustus. Praetor in 61, succeeded C. Antonius as governor of Macedonia. Died in 58.

*M. OCTAVIUS: Caelius Rufus' colleague as Curule Aedile in 50. Active as a Pompeian admiral in the Civil War he probably perished in Africa.

A. OFFILIUS: Jurist, pupil of Ser. Sulpicius. Probably one of Cluvius of Puteoli's heirs in 45.

OPPII: Probably bankers, from Velia in southern Italy.

C. OPPIUS: Roman Knight, friend and agent of Caesar, usually mentioned in conjunction with Cornelius Balbus and like him a friend of Atticus and Cicero.

L. OPPIUS: Subject of several letters of recommendation in 47–46. Was in business at Philomelium and agent of Egnatius Rufus.

ORESTILLA: See AURELIA.

ORODES: King of Parthia 57–37.

OTHO: (1) L. Roscius Otho, Tribune in 67. (2) Co-heir to the estate of one Scapula which included a suburban property coveted by Cicero in 45.

OVIA: In some sort of financial relationship with Cicero in 45 and later co-heir to Cluvius of Puteoli's estate.

PACIAECUS: See VIBIUS.

Q. PACONIUS(?) Lepta: Cicero's 'Prefect of Engineers' in Cilicia.

PACORUS: Son of and eventually co-ruler with Orodes, King of Parthia. Killed in battle in 38.

PAETUS: See PAPIRIUS.

PALICANUS: See LOLLIUS.

PANAETIUS: Eminent second-century Stoic philosopher, friend of the younger Scipio Africanus.

PANSA: See VIBIUS.

*Cn. PAPIRIUS Carbo: Leading Marian, killed by Pompey after surrender in 82.

L. PAPIRIUS Paetus: Wealthy resident of Naples and an old friend of Cicero.

Q. (?) PATISCUS: Apparently a Roman businessman in Asia, then a Caesarian officer, in 43 a Republican Proquaestor taking part in naval operations in the East (if these are identical).

PATRO: Successor of Phaedrus as head of the Epicurean school at Athens, old friend and protégé of Atticus and Cicero.

PAULUS: See AEMILIUS.

Q. PEDIUS: Caesar's nephew or great-nephew. Died in office as Octavian's colleague in the Consulship of 43.

Sex. PEDUCAEUS: (1) Praetor in 77, then governor of Sicily. Cicero served under him as Quaestor. (2) Son of the foregoing and intimate friend of Atticus. References in the Letters, except when explicitly to the father, are probably to the son, whom Cicero sometimes calls simply 'Sextus'.

M. PETREIUS: Sometime Praetor, Legate of C. Antonius in 62, when he commanded the government forces in the final battle against Catiline. Legate to Pompey in Spain 55–49. After the collapse of the Pompeian armies there continued to fight against Caesar and committed suicide in Africa.

PHAEDRUS: Patro's predecessor as head of the Epicurean school. Cicero as a boy heard him lecture in Rome.

PHALARIS: Sixth-century tyrant of Agrigentum in Sicily, notorious for his cruelty.

PHAMEA: Uncle or grandfather of Tigellius. Nothing proves that he was a freedman, as often supposed.

PHANIA(s): Freedman of Ap. Pulcher.

PHARNACES: (1) Son of Mithridates the Great of Pontus and King of Bosporus. Recovered his father's kingdom in 48 and defeated Caesar's lieutenant, Domitius Calvinus. Caesar 'came, saw, and conquered' him the following year. (2) Clerk of Atticus.

PHILIPPUS: See MARCIUS.

PHILISTUS: Fourth-century historian of Sicily.

PHILO: (1) Of Larissa. Antiochus' predecessor as head of the Academic school of philosophy. (2) Freedman of Caelius Rufus, sent out to Cilicia in 51.

PHILOGENES: Freedman of Atticus, employed in financial transactions with Cicero.

PHILOTIMUS: (1) Freedman of Terentia, up till 50 much employed by Cicero in financial business. (2) Clerk of Cicero (it is not always possible to be sure which of the two is meant).

PHILOXENUS: Slave or freedman of Q. Cicero.

PHOCYLIDES: Sixth-century author of versified maxims, which he prefaced: 'This also says Phocylides.'

PILIA: Atticus' wife, married in 56. May have died in 44.

Q. PILIUS Celer: Relative, probably brother, of the above. Supported Caesar in the Civil War and brought letters from M. Brutus and C. Antonius to the Senate in 43. Cicero thought well of him as a speaker.

*L. PINARIUS Natta: Brother-in-law of Clodius, to whom as Pontifex in 58 he gave his services in connection with Cicero's house. The family was immemorially old. Several other Pinarii, probably not of aristocratic origin, crop up in the Letters, not safely to be sorted out.

PINDARUS: Possibly the freedman by whose hand Cassius died after Philippi at his own orders.

PISISTRATUS: Sixth-century 'tyrant' of Athens, type of a 'benevolent despot'.

PISO: See CALPURNIUS and PUPIUS.

PLAETORIUS: The identity of persons of this name occurring in the Letters is doubtful.

Cn. PLANCIUS: Befriended Cicero when Quaestor in Macedonia in 58. Curule Aedile in 54, defended by Cicero on a bribery charge in an extant speech. Last heard of in 45 as a Pompeian awaiting pardon in Corcyra.

PLATO: Fourth-century Athenian philosopher, founder of the Academy.

A. PLAUTIUS: See PLOTIUS.

*P. PLAUTIUS Hypsaeus: Leading adherent and at one time Quaestor of Pompey. Candidate for the Consulship in 53. Pompey let him be condemned on a bribery charge in 52.

PLAUTUS (T. Maccius Plautus): Early writer of Latin comedy.

A. PLOTIUS (or Plautius): City Praetor in 51. Identifiable with a Legate of Pompey in 67, who became Tribune, Curule Aedile, and probably governor of Bithynia in 49–48.

POLA: See SERVIUS Pola.

POLLA: See VALERIA.

POLLEX: Slave of Cicero.

POLLIO: See ASINIUS.

POLYBIUS: Second-century historian.

POLYCLES: Three sculptors of that name are recorded, one in the fourth-century, the other two in the second.

POLYDAMAS: Senior Trojan in the *Iliad*.

A. POMPEIUS Bithynicus: Friend of Cicero, Propraetor in Sicily in 44–42. Accepted Sex. Pompeius as co-governor, who later had him executed.

*Cn. POMPEIUS Magnus: (1) Pompey the Great. *(2) Elder son of the foregoing, killed in Spain after the battle of Munda.

*Sex. POMPEIUS Magnus: Younger son of Pompey the Great. After Caesar's death revived the war in Spain, then came to terms with Lepidus. Eventually gained control of Sicily and was a thorn in Octavian's flesh until defeated in 36. Fled to the East and after further adventures was captured and executed by an officer of Antony's.

*Q. POMPEIUS Rufus: Sulla's grandson, but an associate of P. Clodius, condemned for his part as Tribune in 52 in the riots following Clodius' murder. His prosecutor was Caelius Rufus, who later befriended him when he was living in poverty in Bauli.

Cn. POMPEIUS Theophanes: Of Mytilene, a protégé of Pompey, with whom he had much influence, and author of a history of Pompey's campaigns.

POMPONIA: Sister of Atticus, married to Q. Cicero from about 70 until their divorce in 45 or 44.

T. POMPONIUS Atticus (Q. Caecilius Pomponianus Atticus): Cicero's friend and correspondent.

M. POMPONIUS Dionysius: Learned freedman of Atticus and tutor to the young Ciceros.

C. POMPTINUS: Praetor in 63, then governor of Narbonese Gaul, where he crushed a tribal revolt. Finally granted a Triumph in 54. Legate to Cicero in Cilicia.

PONTIUS: Several persons of this name occur. The following can be distinguished:

L. PONTIUS: Owner of a villa in the Trebula district, where Cicero stayed when travelling between Rome and Brundisium.

PONTIUS Aquila: Tribune in 45 and assassin of Caesar. Legate to D. Brutus in 43. Killed at Mutina.

PONTIUS Titinianus: Son by birth of the Senator Q. Titinius. Joined Caesar at Brundisium in 49.

*PORCIA: (1) Cato's sister, wife of L. Domitius Ahenobarbus. Died in 45. (2) Cato's daughter, married first to M. Bibulus, then to M. Brutus. Died, allegedly by suicide, in 43.

*C. PORCIUS Cato: As Tribune in 56 at first opposed, then supported Pompey (perhaps leagued with Crassus). Tried and acquitted in 54.

*M. PORCIUS Cato: (1) 'Of Utica'. Leader of conservative opposition to the 'First Triumvirate'. Later made common cause with Pompey against Caesar, and after Pompey's death became the life and soul of continuing resistance. Committed suicide at Utica after the republican defeat in 46. Family connections included Servilia (half-sister), her son Brutus, M. Bibulus, L. Domitius, and Hortensius. *(2) Son of the foregoing, who left Cicero and Atticus as his guardians. Killed at Philippi.

POSIDONIUS: Stoic philosopher and polymath, resident in Rhodes.

*POSTUMIA: Wife of Ser. Sulpicius Rufus.

L. (?) POSTUMIUS: Follower of Cato. As his subordinate (Quaestor?) instructed to take over Sicily in 49.

POSTUMUS: See CURTIUS.

PROCILIUS: Perhaps Tribune in 56, under prosecution in 54. May or may not be identical with the author mentioned in Letters to Atticus 22 (II.2)2.

PROTOGENES: Fourth-century painter.

PTOLEMY XII: Called 'The Piper', King of Egypt. Driven out by his subjects in 58, restored by Gabinius in 55, died in 51.

PUBLILIA: Cicero's ward and second wife, married towards the end of 46, divorced a few months later.

PUBLILIUS: Relative, probably brother, of the above.

PUBLILIUS Syrus: Contemporary writer of mimes. A collection of maxims taken from his work survives.

PUBLIUS, PULCHELLUS, PULCHER: See CLODIUS.

*M. PUPIUS Piso Frugi: Friend of Cicero's youth, to whom he gave a role in his De Finibus. After his Consulship in 61 (severely criticized by Cicero) he disappears.

PYRRHUS: King of Epirus. Campaigned against Rome in 281–275. Wrote a treatise on tactics.

T. QUINTIUS Scapula: Leader of a mutiny against Caesar in Spain.

L. RACILIUS: Tribune in 56.

REBILUS: See CANINIUS.

REGINUS: See ANTISTIUS.

REGULUS: See LIVINEIUS.

RHINT(H)ON: Fourth-century writer of mock-tragedies.

L. ROSCIUS Fabatus: Served with Caesar in Gaul. Praetor in 49 and peace intermediary. Reported dead at the battle of Forum Gallorum.

Q. ROSCIUS Gallus: Rome's greatest comic actor, friend and client of Cicero.

T. (?) RUFRENUS: Officer in Lepidus' army in 43. Apparently Tribune the following year.

RUFUS: See CAELIUS, MESCINIUS, SEMPRONIUS.

*P. RUTILIUS Lupus: Tribune and supporter of Pompey in 56. Praetor in 49. Served under Pompey in Greece in 48.

Cn. SALLUSTIUS: Friend of Cicero and Atticus.

P. SALLUSTIUS: Perhaps brother of the above.

Q. SALVIDIENUS Rufus: Partisan of Octavian. After a distinguished career accused of preparing to desert to Antony and committed suicide in 40.

SALVIUS: (1) Literary slave of Atticus'. (2) Influential freedman of Caesar's.

SASERNA: See HOSTILIUS.

L. SAUFEIUS: Friend of Atticus, who saved his property in the Proscriptions. A devoted Epicurean and prolific writer on the subject.

SCAEVA: See CASSIUS.

SCAEVOLA: See MUCIUS.

M. SCAPTIUS: (1) Agent of Brutus in Cilicia 51–50. (2) Presumably relative of the foregoing, looked after Brutus' interests in Cappadocia.

SCAPULA: (1) Deceased owner of an estate which Cicero wished to buy in 45. (2) See QUINTIUS.

SCAURUS: See AEMILIUS.

SCIPIO: See CAECILIUS and CORNELIUS.

C. SCRIBONIUS Curio: (1) Consul in 76, notable general and orator. Died in 53. *(2) His son, Cicero's friend and correspondent. After some variations appeared as Tribune in 50 in the role of a fervent optimate, but suddenly went over to Caesar, allegedly for a vast bribe. Led expedition to Africa in 49, where he was defeated and killed.

SCROFA: See TREMELLIUS.

M. SEIUS: Roman Knight and man of business, supporter of Caesar. Mentioned by Varro and Pliny the Elder as a noted producer of poultry, etc.

Q. SELICIUS: Friend of Lentulus Spinther, perhaps identical with a wealthy money-lender mentioned in letters to Atticus.

C. SEMPRONIUS Rufus: Acquaintance of Cicero, apparently exiled in 50 and restored by Antony after Caesar's death. Mentioned by Horace as an ex-Praetor and gourmet.

*C. SEMPRONIUS Tuditanus: The father and son (Consul in 129) of that name are the subject of one of Cicero's historical queries.

C. SEPTIMIUS: (1) Secretary to M. Bibulus in 59. (2) Praetor in 57.

SERAPIO: (1) Author of a work on mathematical geography, after Eratosthenes and perhaps before Hipparchus. (2) Owner (?) of a ship in 49.

*L. SERGIUS Catilina: Cicero's rival for the Consulship in 64. Plotted a *coup d'état* in 63, killed in battle the following year.

*Servilia: Mother of M. Brutus, half-sister of Cato, allegedly mistress of Caesar, and close friend of Atticus.

*M. Servilius: Tried in connection with C. Claudius Pulcher's conviction in 50. The republican Tribune of 43 who later served as Legate under Cassius and Brutus may be the same.

Q. Servilius: Friend of Ap. Pulcher.

*C. Servilius Ahala: Ancestor of M. Brutus (through his mother and adoptive father), who as Master of the Horse in 439 killed one Sp. Maelius, suspected of plotting to become despot in Rome.

*P. Servilius Isauricus: Earlier an associate of Cato and married to his niece, he joined Caesar in the Civil War and became Consul in 48. Governor of Asia 46–44. Moderate opponent of Antony after Caesar's death, but later reconciled. Consul again in 41.

*P. Servilius Vatia Isauricus: Father of the above. Consul in 79 and Proconsul in Cilicia in 78–74, he gained his triumphal cognomen by operations against the Isaurian mountaineers. Died in extreme old age in 44.

Servius: See Sulpicius.

Servius Pola: Professional prosecutor.

L. Sestius: Probably Quaestor in 44 and later a faithful follower of M. Brutus. None the less became Consul in 23 and recipient of a Horatian Ode.

P. Sestius: Father of the above. Quaestor in Macedonia in 62. As Tribune in 57 took a leading part in promoting Cicero's recall. Defended on charges in this connection by Cicero in 56 (speech extant). Later Praetor and Cicero's successor as governor of Cilicia in 49. Went over to Caesar after Pharsalia. Supported Cicero in 43, but kept his life and status in the thirties. A notoriously wearisome speaker.

Sextilius: Four persons of this name may be distinguished in the Letters, identification of any one of them with any other being doubtful. But C. Sextilius Rufus, Quaestor (?) in Cyprus in 49, may be the Sextilius Rufus who commanded Cassius' fleet in 43; and Q. Sextilius, Milo's friend in 57, could be the Pompeian over whose expropriation Cicero waxed indignant in 44.

SEXTUS: See PEDUCAEUS and POMPEIUS.

SICCA: Friend of Cicero's, often mentioned in letters to Atticus and Terentia, perhaps a fellow-Arpinate and Cicero's 'Prefect of Engineers' in 63.

SILANUS: See JUNIUS.

P. SILIUS: Governor of Bithynia in 51–50 and owner of a property which Cicero wished to buy in 45.

SIRO: Epicurean philosopher who lived in Naples and became Virgil's teacher.

P. SITTIUS: Roman Knight, who left Italy for Further Spain and then Mauretania in 64, where, according to our sources, he became a military adventurer. In 57 condemned in absence on an unknown charge. Brought a force to join Caesar in 46 and received a principality in reward. Murdered in 44.

SOCRATES: Plato's teacher and principal speaker in his dialogues.

SOLON: Sixth-century Athenian statesman and law-giver.

SOPHOCLES: Fifth-century Athenian tragic dramatist.

C. SOSIUS: Praetor in 49.

SPARTACUS: Leader of a slave rebellion in 73–71.

SPINTHER: See CORNELIUS Lentulus.

SPURINNA: Haruspex (diviner from entrails). Warned Caesar that his life was in danger before his assassination.

L. STAIUS Murcus: Legate of Caesar's. Proconsul in Syria in 44. Active at sea on behalf of the republicans. After Philippi joined Sex. Pompeius, who eventually put him to death.

STATIUS: Slave, then freedman, of Q. Cicero.

SUFENAS: See NONIUS.

SULLA: See CORNELIUS.

*Ser. SULPICIUS Galba: Legate to C. Pomptinus, then to Caesar in Gaul. Praetor in 54. Supported Caesar in the Civil War and joined the conspiracy in 44. Fought under Pansa at the battle of Forum Gallorum. Probably killed in 43.

*Ser. SULPICIUS Rufus: (1) Friend and contemporary of Cicero's and one of the most famous of Roman jurists. Consul in 51, he worked to avoid the coming clash with Caesar, but in 49 after initial wavering joined Pompey (the common view that he remained neutral is mistaken). After Pharsalia he retired to Samos, but was appointed governor of Achaia by Caesar in

46. Died in 43 on a mission to Antony. ★(2) His son. Joined Caesar's army at Brundisium in March 49, but further part in the war is unknown. After Caesar's death a republican and probably a victim of the Proscriptions.

TALNA: See JUVENTIUS.

TARCONDIMOTUS: Ruler (later king) in the Amanus mountains. Died at Actium fighting for Antony.

TERENCE (P. Terentius Afer): Second-century writer of Latin comedy.

TERENTIA: Cicero's wife from about 80 to 46.

TERENTIUS: Several persons with this name cannot be traced outside the passages where they occur.

Q. TERENTIUS Culleo: Tribune in 58 and friend of Pompey. Lepidus' officer Culleo in 43 may have been his son or a younger relative.

P. TERENTIUS Hispo: Friend of Cicero, worked for a tax-farming company (or companies) in Asia and Bithynia.

M. TERENTIUS Varro: Of Reate, the most learned and prolific author of his time. Born in 116. After a distinguished military and political career under Pompey's aegis, he gave up the republican cause after Pharsalia and became head of Caesar's new library. Narrowly escaping proscription in 43 he lived till 27 in tireless literary activity. Of his vast and varied output only a small part, and perhaps the least interesting, survives apart from fragments.

M. TERENTIUS Varro Gibba: See the recommendatory letter, 277 (XIII.10). He was Tribune in 43 and executed at Philippi.

★M. TERENTIUS Varro Lucullus: Brother by birth of L. Lucullus and an almost equally distinguished soldier. Consul in 73, triumphed for victories in the Balkans. Died not long after Lucius.

★A. TERENTIUS Varro Murena: Friend of Cicero and Ap. Pulcher.

TERTIA, TERTULLA: See JUNIA.

TESTA: See TREBATIUS.

THEMISTOCLES: Athenian leader in the Persian War of 481–479. Later exiled and took refuge with the King of Persia.

THEOPHANES: See POMPEIUS.

THEOPHRASTUS: Pupil of Aristotle and prolific writer on philosophy, politics, and natural science.

THEOPOMPUS: (1) Of Chios. Fourth-century historian noted for censoriousness. (2) Of Cnidus. Writer on mythology and friend of Caesar.

THERMUS: See MINUCIUS.

THRASYBULUS: Athenian statesman, who overthrew the oligarchy in 403.

THUCYDIDES: Fifth-century historian of the Peloponnesian War.

THYILLUS: Poet, three of whose epigrams survive in the Greek Anthology.

TIGELLIUS: A Sardinian, favourite of Caesar and later of Octavian.

TIGRANES: King of Armenia 95–c. 55.

C. TILLIUS Cimber: One of Caesar's assassins. Later as governor of Bithynia supported Brutus and Cassius. Probably died at Philippi.

TIMAEUS: Fourth-third-century historian.

TIMOLEON: Democratic leader in Sicily in the fourth century.

TIRO: See TULLIUS.

Q. TITINIUS: A wealthy Senator.

P. TITIUS: Tribune in 43 and proposer of the law establishing the Triumvirate. Died in office (other Titii crop up sporadically).

TORQUATUS: See MANLIUS.

TRABEA: Writer of Latin comedy.

TRATORIUS: Friend of Cornificius in 43.

C. TREBATIUS Testa: Of Velia. Friend and correspondent of Cicero, about twenty years his junior, recommended by him to Caesar in 54. Supported Caesar in the Civil War and lived to a ripe old age. Cicero's *Topica* is dedicated to him. Eminent jurist.

L. TREBELLIUS: As Tribune in 47 resisted Dolabella's radical economic programme, thus acquiring the cognomen 'Fides' ('Good Faith', 'Credit'). Officer under Antony in 43.

C. TREBONIUS: Tribune in 55, put through a law extending Caesar's term of command. Legate to Caesar in Gallic and Civil Wars and Praetor in 48. Governor of Further Spain 47–46. Consul-Suffect 45. Joined the conspiracy in 44. Brutally murdered by Dolabella shortly after his arrival in Asia as governor. Friend and correspondent of Cicero.

Cn. TREMELLIUS Scrofa: Praetor in the sixties and governor of Crete in 51–50. A leading character in Varro's dialogue *On Agriculture*.

TRIARIUS: See VALERIUS.

TRYPHO: See LIVINEIUS.

TUBERO: See AELIUS.

TUDITANUS: See SEMPRONIUS.

*TULLIA: Cicero's daughter. Died February 45.

L. TULLIUS: Legate to Cicero in Cilicia.

M. TULLIUS: Cicero's Secretary in Cilicia.

M. TULLIUS Cicero: (1) The orator. *(2) His son.

Q. TULLIUS Cicero: (1) Brother of the orator. (2) His son, Cicero's and Atticus' nephew.

TULLIUS Marcianus: He and the following accompanied young M. Cicero to Athens in 45. They were probably connections or dependants of the family.

L. TULLIUS Montanus: See the foregoing.

M. TULLIUS Tiro: Slave of Cicero, manumitted in 53, a confidential secretary and literary assistant. After Cicero's death devoted himself to propagating his work and memory.

TULLUS: See VULCATIUS.

D. TURULLIUS: Assassin of Caesar, probably Proquaestor to Tillius Cimber in 43. Later joined Antony and was executed by Octavian.

TUTIA: Considered as a possible match for the younger Quintus.

TYRANNIO: Of Amisus, originally called Theophrastus. Settled in Rome about 68 and became rich and well known as a scholar and teacher. Wrote on grammatical and literary subjects. The geographer Strabo was his pupil.

Paula (Polla) VALERIA: Of the Triarius family. Married D. Brutus in 50.

VALERIUS: (1) Called the interpreter. Probably to be distinguished from (2) A friend of Cicero and Trebatius, writer of mimes, possibly identical with the following.

L. VALERIUS: Lawyer friend of Cicero.

P. VALERIUS: (1) Businessman or tax-farmer in Cilicia in 50. (2) Friend at whose villa near Rhegium Cicero stayed in 44.

*C. VALERIUS Flaccus: Son of the following. On staff of Ap. Pulcher in 51. Killed fighting in Pompey's army at Dyrrachium in 48.

*L. VALERIUS Flaccus: Praetor in 63 and governor of Asia. Defended by Cicero in 59 in an extant speech.

*M. VALERIUS Messalla Corvinus: Son of the following. At Athens with young M. Cicero in 45. Distinguished orator and one of the great figures of the Augustan period.

*M. VALERIUS Messalla Niger: As Consul in 61 took an optimate line, but later a supporter of Pompey. Censor in 55–54, apparently died shortly before the Civil War.

*M. VALERIUS Messalla Rufus: Brother-in-law to Sulla and Hortensius' nephew, friend of Atticus and Cicero. Consul in 53, later condemned for electoral malpractice and rehabilitated by Caesar. After Caesar's death lived in scholarly retirement to an advanced age. Wrote on augury.

C. VALERIUS Triarius: Apparently fell on the Pompeian side at Pharsalia. Cicero gave him a role in the *De Finibus*.

P. VALERIUS Triarius: Brother of the above.

VARRO: See TERENTIUS.

P. VATINIUS: Tribune in 59, carried through legislation on Caesar's behalf. Praetor in 55, Consul in 47, governor of Illyricum, triumphed in 42. Cicero attacked him in an extant speech, but in 54 became reconciled under pressure and defended him in court. From then on they remained on good terms.

P. VENTIDIUS Bassus: From humble beginnings rose to a Consulship (Suffect in 43) and Triumph (33). Antony's lieutenant in 43, fought for L. Antonius against Octavian in 40, as Proconsul won important successes against the Parthians.

C. VERGILIUS: Friend of Cicero, but as governor of Sicily refused him admittance in 58. Identifiable with a republican officer in Africa whose life was spared after surrender to Caesar and with a co-heir to the Scapula estate.

C. VESTORIUS: Businessman of Puteoli, friendly with Atticus and Cicero (who was apt to make fun of his lack of culture).

VETTIENUS: Businessman with whom Cicero had transactions in 49–44.

L. VETTIUS: Roman Knight from Picenum, who turned informer

against his Catilinarian associates in 63–62 and was prosecuted and imprisoned for making false charges against Caesar. Revealed or fabricated a plot against Pompey's life in 59. Died mysteriously in prison.

VETTIUS Chrysippus: an architect, freedman of the following.

VETTIUS Cyrus: a well-known architect.

VETUS: See ANTISTIUS.

L. VIBIUS Paciaecus: He and his father were prominent men in Further Spain. Served under Caesar in his final Spanish campaign.

C. VIBIUS Pansa Caetronianus: Son of one of Sulla's victims, served under Caesar in Gaul. Tribune in 51. Governed Bithynia and Cisalpine Gaul under Caesar. Consul in 43, died of wounds received in the battle of Forum Gallorum.

L. VIBULLIUS Rufus: Henchman of Pompey and his 'Prefect of Engineers' in 49.

C. VISELLIUS Varro: Cicero's cousin, son of a notable jurist and himself versed in law.

VOLUMNIA Cytheris: Freedwoman of the following and a well-known actress. Mistress of Mark Antony and allegedly the Lycoris to whom Virgil's friend Cornelius Gallus wrote love poems.

VOLUMNIUS: A Senator, perhaps identical with L. Volumnius Flaccus, bearer of a message from D. Brutus to the Senate in 43.

P. VOLUMNIUS Eutrapelus: Roman Knight and celebrated wit. After Caesar's death an adherent of Antony, probably his 'Prefect of Engineers' in 43–42.

Q. VOLUSIUS: On Cicero's staff in Cilicia.

L. VULCATIUS (or VOLCACIUS) Tullus: (1) Consul in 66. In and after the Civil War his political moderation seems to have turned into subservience to Caesar.*(2) His son, Praetor in 46 and governor of Cilicia (?) in 44. Consul with Octavian in 33.

XENO: (1) Friend and agent of Atticus in Athens. (2) Of Apollonia, commended by Atticus to Cicero in 51.

XENOCRATES: Pupil of Plato and third head of the Academy.

XENOPHON: Fifth–fourth-century Athenian historian.

ZENO: Founder of Stoicism.

GLOSSARY OF PLACES

Some names are omitted as generally familiar or explained in the notes. Italics are used for modern equivalents.

ACHAIA: Southern Greece.

ACTIUM: Promontory on the mainland south of Corfù.

AECULANUM: Town on the Appian Way, east of Beneventum.

AEGINA: Island on the Saronic Gulf, south-west of Athens.

AEMILIAN WAY: Roman road running north-west from Ariminum through Mutina.

AENARIA (*Ischia*): Island off Naples.

AESERNIA: Town in central Italy, about 30 miles east of Arpinum.

AETOLIA: District of Greece, north-west of the Gulf of Corinth.

AFRICA: (1) The continent. (2) The Roman province, part of modern Tunisia.

ALABANDA: Town in Caria.

ALBA: (1) Alba Longa north-east of Rome (Mt Albanus = *Monte Cavi*). (2) Alba Fucens in central Italy near Lake Fucino.

ALLOBROGES: Chief tribe of Narbonese Gaul.

ALSIUM (*Palo*): Town on the coast of Etruria.

ALYZIA: Greek town south of Actium.

AMANUS: Mountain range separating Cilicia from Syria.

AMBRACIA: Town in southern Epirus.

ANAGNIA (*Anagni*): Town about 25 miles west of Arpinum.

ANTANDRUS: Town in Mysia.

ANTILIBANUS: Range of mountains in Syria.

ANTIOCH: Capital of Syria, about 40 miles west of modern Aleppo.

ANTIUM (*Anzio*): Coast town south of Rome, where Cicero owned a house.

APAMEA: Town in Phrygia.

APOLLONIA: Town on the western coast of the province of Macedonia.

APOLLONIS: Town in Asia Minor, north-east of Smyrna.

APPIA: Town in Phrygia.

APPIAN WAY: The great road linking Rome with Brundisium.

APPII FORUM: Town on the Appian Way about 40 miles from Rome.

APULIA: District in south-eastern Italy.

AQUINUM (*Aquino*): Town just south of Arpinum.

ARABIA FELIX: The Arabian peninsula.

ARADUS: Island town off the coast of Syria.

ARCADIA: Central district of the Peloponnese.

ARCANUM: Village between Aquinum and Arpinum.

ARGENTEUS (= 'Silver', *Argens*): River in Narbonese Gaul.

ARGENTEUS, PONS (= 'Silverbridge'): Bridge over the above.

ARRETIUM: *Arezzo* in Etruria.

ASIA: (1) The continent. (2) The Roman province, comprising the western part of Asia Minor.

ASTURA: Small island (joined to the mainland) off the coast south of Antium, where Cicero had a villa.

ATELLA: Town in Campania.

ATTICA: Territory of Athens.

AVENTINE: One of the Seven Hills of Rome, south of the Palatine.

BAIAE: Famous resort on the Bay of Naples, near Cumae.

BAREA: Town on the Spanish coast south of New Carthage (*Cartagena*).

BAULI: Seaside resort near Baiae.

BELLOVACI: Gallic tribe.

BENEVENTUM (*Benevento*): Important town on the Appian Way about 30 miles east of Capua.

BITHYNIA: Region in north-western Asia Minor; as a Roman province (Bithynia and Pontus) stretching much further east.

BLAUNDUS: Town in western Asia Minor about 120 miles east of Smyrna.

BOEOTIA: Greek territory north of Attica.

BONONIA: *Bologna*.

BOVILLAE: Ancient Latin town on the Appian Way about 11 miles from Rome.

BRUNDISIUM (*Brindisi*): Adriatic port in the heel of Italy.

BUTHROTUM: Town on the coast of Epirus opposite Corfù. Atticus had an estate near by.

BYLLIS: Town in Illyricum.

CAIETA (*Gaeta*): Port of Formiae.

CALACTE: Town on the northern coast of Sicily.

CALATIA: Campanian town between Capua and Beneventum.

CALES (*Calvi*): Town in northern Campania.

CALPE: Modern Cape of Gibraltar.

CAMERIUM (*Camerino*): Town in the Umbrian Apennines.

CAMPANIA: District south of Latium.

CANDAVIA: District in Illyricum (modern Albania) to the east of
      Dyrrachium.

CANUSIUM: Apulian town between Arpi and Brundisium.

CAPENA, PORTA: Entrance to Rome from the Appian Way.

CAPENA: Town in Etruria north-east of Veii.

CAPITOL: Highest of the Roman Hills, overlooking the Forum.

CAPPADOCIA: Kingdom in east-central Asia Minor.

CAPUA: Chief town of Campania.

CARIA: Region in south-western Asia Minor.

CARINAE: District of Rome north of the Colosseum.

CARTEIA: Spanish coast town near modern Gibraltar.

CASILINUM: Modern Capua, about three miles west of ancient
      Capua.

CASSIOPE: Town in the north-east of Corfù.

CASTRUM TRUENTINUM: Coast town about 60 miles south of
      Ancona.

CASTULO, Pass of: Pass in the Sierra Morena.

CATINA (*Catania*): Town on the eastern coast of Sicily.

CAUNUS: Town in Caria.

CEOS: Aegean island, one of the Cyclades.

CERAMICUS: District of Athens.

CERMALUS: A depression in the Palatine Hill, towards the Tiber.

CHAONIA: District of Epirus.

CHERSONESE: The Gallipoli peninsula.

CHIOS: Large island in the Aegean, not far from Smyrna.

CIBYRA: Town in south-western Asia Minor.

CILICIA: (1) Coastal strip in south-eastern Asia Minor. (2) Roman
      province comprising the whole southern coast, much of the
      interior, and the island of Cyprus.

CINGULUM (*Cingoli*): Inland town in Picenum.

CIRCEII: Town on the promontory west of Tarracina.

CISALPINE GAUL: 'Gaul this side of the Alps', i.e., northern Italy between the Alps and the Apennines.

CLATERNA (*Quaderna*): Town in Cisalpine Gaul, on the Aemilian Way between Bononia and Forum Cornelii.

CLITERNUM: Town in central Italy.

COLCHIS: Region bordering the south-eastern coast of the Black Sea.

COLOPHON: Town on the coast of Asia Minor near Ephesus.

COMMAGENE: Kingdom situated west of the Euphrates between Syria and Cappadocia.

COMUM (*Como*): Town on the southern shore of Lake Como, re-founded by Julius Caesar (Novum Comum).

CORCYRA (*Corfù*): Island off the coast of Epirus.

CORDUBA: *Cordova*, in southern Spain.

CORFINIUM: Chief town of the Paeligni, east of Lake Fucino.

CORYCUS: Town on the coast of Cilicia.

COSA (*Ansedonia*): Town on the coast of Etruria.

CROMMYACRIS ('Onion Cape'): Headland on the north coast of Cyprus.

CROTON: Town on the east coast of modern Calabria.

CULARO: *Grenoble*.

CUMAE (*Cuma*): Coastal town a few miles west of Naples. Cicero had a villa in its territory.

CYBISTRA: Town in the south-eastern corner of Cappadocia.

CYRRHESTICA: District of Syria, north-east of Antioch.

CYZICUS: Town on the Asiatic coast of the Propontis (*Sea of Marmora*).

DELOS: Aegean island, in the Cyclades.

DERBE: Town in Isauria.

DERTONA (*Tortona*): Town in Liguria.

DIONYSOPOLIS: Town in Phrygia.

DYRRACHIUM (*Durazzo*): Town on the western coast of the Roman province of Macedonia.

ELEUSIS: Town in Attica where the Mysteries were celebrated.

ELIS: Town in the west of the Peloponnese.

EPHESUS: On the western coast of Asia Minor, chief town of the province of Asia.

EPIDAURUS: Town on the eastern coast of the Peloponnese opposite Piraeus.

EPIPHANEA: Town in Cilicia.

EPIRUS: District of north-western Greece opposite Corfù.

EPOREDIA (*Ivrea*): Town in the foot-hills of the Pennine Alps.

EQUUS TUTICUS: Town in central Italy about 20 miles north of Beneventum (also called Equum (or Aequum) Tuticum).

ETRURIA: *Tuscany*.

FABRATERIA (VETUS and NOVA): Towns in Latium.

FALERNUM: District in northern Campania.

FICULEA: Town 5 miles north-east of Rome. Atticus had a villa between there and Nomentum (*La Mentana*).

FIRMUM (*Fermo*): Town near the Adriatic coast between Ancona and Castrum Truentinum.

FORMIAE (*Formia*): Town on the coast of Latium close to the Campanian border. Cicero had a villa near by.

FORUM CORNELIUM (or CORNELII): Town about 20 miles down the Aemilian Way east from Bononia.

FORUM GALLORUM: Village between Mutina and Bononia.

FORUM JULII (*Fréjus*): Town on the coast of Narbonese Gaul.

FORUM VOCONIUM (or VOCONII): Town in Narbonese Gaul between Pons Argenteus and Forum Julii.

FREGELLAE: Latian town destroyed in 125 and replaced by Fabrateria Nova.

FRUSINO (*Frosinone*): Latian town a few miles north-west of Fabrateria Nova.

FUNDI (*Fondi*): Latian town on the Appian Way between Tarracina and Formiae.

GADES: *Cadiz*.

GALATIA: District or kingdom in the east of Asia Minor, north of Cappadocia. The inhabitants were descended from Gaulish invaders.

GETAE: Tribe inhabiting modern Rumania.

HAEDUI: Gallic tribe.

HALAESA: Town in northern Sicily.

HALES (*Alento*): River in south-west Italy on which the town of Velia was situated.

HALICARNASSUS: Town in Caria.

HELLESPONT: The modern Dardanelles.

HERACLEA: (1) Town in Caria. (2) Town on the north coast of the Propontis (*Sea of Marmora*).

HERCULANEUM: Town near Pompeii.

HISPALIS: *Seville.*

HYDRUS (*Otranto*): Port in the heel of Italy south of Brundisium.

HYMETTUS: Mountain near Athens.

HYPAEPA: Town in Asia Minor, north-east of Smyrna.

ICONIUM (*Konya*): Town in Lycaonia.

IGUVIUM (*Gubbio*): Umbrian town on the western slope of the Apennines.

ILIUM: = Troy, near the southern entrance of the Hellespont.

ILLYRICUM: Region bordering the Adriatic from Epirus to the Gulf of Trieste.

INALPINI: Inhabitants of the Alps.

INSUBRES: Tribe of Cisalpine Gaul.

INTERAMNA (*Terni*): Town on the river Nar in Central Italy.

INTIMILII: Tribe of Liguria.

IONIA: Area on the western coast of Asia Minor settled by Ionian Greeks.

ISARA (*Isère*): River, tributary of the Rhône.

ISAURIA: Region south of Lycaonia in southern Asia Minor.

ISSUS: Cilician town on gulf of the same name in the south-eastern corner of the province.

LACEDAEMON: Another name for Sparta.

LANUVIUM: Latian town just off the Appian Way about 20 miles from Rome.

LAODICEA: (1) Town in the south-west of Phrygia. (2) Town in Syria on the coast south of Antioch.

LARINUM (*Larino*): Town in northern Apulia.

LATERIUM: Village between Arpinum and Anagnia where Q. Cicero had a property.

LATIUM: Territory to the south and east of Rome.

LAVERNIUM: Place in the neighbourhood of Formiae.

LESBOS: Large island in the northern Aegean.

LEUCAS: Town on the island of the same name between Actium and Alyzia.

LEUCATA (*Cape Ducato*): South-western extremity of the island of Leucas, south of Actium.

LILYBAEUM (*Marsala*): Town at the western end of Sicily.

LITERNUM (*Tor di Patria*): Coast town just north of Cumae.

LOCRI: Town in the toe of Italy.

LUCA (*Lucca*): Town in north-western Etruria.

LUCERIA (*Lucera*): Apulian town to the west of Arpi.

LUCRINE LAKE (*Lago Lucrino*): Lagoon adjoining the Gulf of Baiae.

LUSITANIA: Region of south-western Spain.

LYCAONIA: Region in central Asia Minor between Phrygia and Cappadocia.

LYCIA: Region on the southern coast of Asia Minor between Caria and Pamphylia.

MAGNESIA BY MT SIPYLUS: Town north-east of Smyrna.

MALEA (*Malia*): Headland at the south-eastern end of the Peloponnese.

MANTINEA: Town in Arcadia, scene of famous battle between Spartans and Thebans.

MARSI: People living near Lake Fucino in central Italy.

MASSILIA: Greek city, now Marseilles.

MEGARA: Town on the Isthmus of Corinth.

MIDAÏUM: Town in Phrygia.

MILETUS: Town on the west coast of Asia Minor, south of Ephesus.

MINTURNAE: Town a few miles south-east of Formiae.

MISENUM: Headland bounding the Bay of Naples to the north.

MOPSUHESTIA (= 'Hearth of Mopsus'): Town in the extreme east of Cilicia.

MULVIAN BRIDGE (*Ponte Molle*): Bridge across the Tiber above Rome.

MYLASA: Chief town of Caria.

MYRINA: Town on the coast north of Smyrna.

MYSIA: Region of north-western Asia Minor.

MYTILENE: Principal town of Lesbos.

NAR (*Nera*): River of central Italy.

NARBO (*Narbonne*): Roman colony in the west of Narbonese Gaul.

NARBONESE GAUL: Old Roman province in southern France.

NARES LUCANAE: Mountain pass in south-west Italy, five miles south-east of modern Acerno.

NARONA: Roman colony in Dalmatia.

NERVII: Tribe of north-eastern Gaul (Belgium).

NESIS (*Nisida*): Island off the coast between Puteoli and Naples.

NICAEA: Town in Bithynia.

NOLA (*Nola*): Inland town of Campania about 20 miles north-east of Capua.

NYSA: Town in Caria.

OLBIA (*Terranova*): Town in Sardinia.

OPUS: Town in Greece.

OSTIA (*Ostia*): Port of Rome.

PAESTUM (*Pesto*): Town on the western coast of Italy, south of Salerno.

PALATINE: Large hill south of the Forum, where according to tradition Rome began. A number of prominent people had houses on it, including Cicero.

PALTOS: Town on the coast of Syria, south of Laodicea.

PAMPHYLIA: Region on the south coast of Asia Minor between Lycia and Cilicia.

PANHORMUS: *Palermo*.

PAPHOS: Town in Cyprus.

PARIUM: Town on the Asiatic side of the Hellespont.

PARMA (*Parma*): Town in northern Italy.

PATRAE (*Patras*): Town on the northern coast of the Peloponnese.

PELLA: Town in Macedonia.

PELLENE: Greek town west of Sicyon.

PERGE or PERGA: Town on the coast of Pamphylia west of Side.

PESSINUS: Town in the west of Galatia.

PETRINUS: Mountain and district near Sinuessa.

PHILOMELIUM: Town in south-east Phrygia.

PHLIUS: Town in the Peloponnese.

PHRYGIA: Region in the middle of western Asia Minor.

PICENUM: Territory bordering the Adriatic south of Ancona.

PINDENISSUM: Town of the 'Free Cilicians' in the Amanus mountains.

PIRAEUS: Port of Athens.

PISAE: *Pisa*.

PISAURUM (*Pesaro*): Town on the coast of the Adriatic south of Ariminum.

PISIDIA: Region in south-west Asia Minor north of Pamphylia.

PLACENTIA (*Piacenza*): Town on the Po in northern Italy.

POLLENTIA (*Polenza*): Inland town in Liguria.

POMPEII: Town on the Bay of Naples where Cicero had a villa.

POMPTINE MARSHES: District adjoining the coast south of Rome.

PONS ARGENTEUS: See ARGENTEUS.

PONTUS: Region in north-eastern Asia Minor.

PORTA CAPENA: See CAPENA.

PRAENESTE (*Palestrina*): Latian town about 20 miles east of Rome.

PUTEOLI (*Pozzuoli*): Town east of Naples on the Bay. Cicero inherited an estate there in 45.

PYRAMUS: River in eastern Cilicia.

QUIRINAL: One of the Seven Hills of Rome.

REATE (*Rieti*): Sabine town south of Interamma.

REGIUM (*Reggio*): Town at the toe of Italy.

REGIUM (LEPIDI, *Reggio Emilia*): Town on the Aemilian Way west of Mutina.

SABINI: People of central Italy, with a reputation for old-fashioned frugality and virtue.

SACRA VIA: Street adjoining the north side of the Forum.

SALAMIS: Town in Cyprus.

SAMAROBRIVA: *Amiens*.

SAMNIUM: Region of central Italy.

SAMOS: Aegean island close to Ephesus.

SATRICUM: Place (village?) near Laterium.

SEGOVIA: Besides modern Segovia in Spain several other towns were so called.

SELEUCIA: City close to the right bank of the Tigris, near the site of ancient Babylon.

SELEUCIA PIERIA: Syrian coastal town west of Antioch.

SICYON: Greek town west of Corinth.

SIDE or SIDA: Harbour town in Pamphylia.

SIDON: Coastal town in Phoenicia (Lebanon).

SIGEUM: Town at the entrance of the Hellespont near ancient Troy.

SINUESSA (*Mondragone*): Town on the coast south of Formiae.

SIPONTUM: Coastal town in Apulia near modern Manfredonia.

SOLONIUM: Area south of the Ostian Way about 12 miles from Rome.

STABIAE: Town on the Bay of Cumae a few miles south of Pompeii.

STATIELLENSES: A Ligurian tribe on the northern slopes of the Apennines. Their chief town, Aquae Statiellae (*Acqui*), lay between Dertona and Pollentia.

SUESSA (*Sessa*): Latian town between Minturnae and Sinuessa.

SUNIUM: Promontory (and 'deme') south of Athens.

SYBOTA: Town on the coast of Epirus opposite a little archipelago of the same name between Corfù and the mainland.

SYNNADA: Town in Phrygia.

TARENTUM (*Taranto*): Town on the south coast of Italy.

TARICHEAE: Town in lower Galilee.

TARRACINA (*Terracina*): Town on the coast of Latium at the southern end of the Pontine Marshes.

TARSUS: Chief town of Cilicia proper.

TAUROMENIUM (*Taormina*): Town on the east coast of Sicily.

TAURUS: Mountain range in south-eastern Asia Minor.

TEANUM (APULUM): Town in the north of Apulia.

TEANUM (SIDICINUM, *Teano*): Inland town in Campania, a few miles south-west of Cales.

TENEDOS: Island south of the Hellespont.

THESPIAE: Town in Boeotia.

THESPROTIA: District in Epirus in which Atticus' estate was situated.

THESSALONICA: *Salonika*.

THESSALY: Region in Greece, south of Macedonia and east of Epirus.

THURII: Town near the Tarentine Gulf at the north-eastern end of the toe of Italy.

THYAMIS: River of Epirus bordering (or flowing through) Atticus' estate.

THYRREUM: Inland town east of Leucas.

TIBUR (*Tivoli*): Town in Latium 18 miles east of Rome.

TRALLES: Town in Caria.

TREBULA: The district of Trebula, near Calatia, bordered the Appian Way about 25 miles from Pompeii.

TRES TABERNAE (= 'Three Cottages'): Station on the Appian Way between Lanuvium and Forum Appii.

TUSCULUM: Latian town near modern Frascati. Cicero spent much time at his villa near by.

TYBA: Town in Cyrrhestica.

TYNDARIS (*Tindaro*): Town on the north coast of Sicily.

ULUBRAE: Small town bordering the Pontine Marshes.

UMBRIA: Region of central Italy east of Etruria.

UTICA: Chief town of the province of Africa.

VADA (*Vado*): Town on the coast of Liguria about 30 miles west of Genoa.

VARDAEI: Illyrian tribe.

VEII: Tuscan town a few miles north of Rome.

VELABRUM: District of Rome south of the Capitol.

VELIA: Town in south-western Italy south of Paestum. Also an area on the Palatine.

VELINE LAKE: Near Interamna.

VENAFRUM (*Venafro*): Town in northern Campania.

VENUSIA (*Venosa*): Town in western Apulia on the Appian Way.

VERCELLAE (*Vercelli*): Town in Cisalpine Gaul.

VESCINUM: District named from the ancient town of Vescia, on the slopes of Mt Massicus including the town of Sinuessa.

VIBO (*Bivona*): Town on the western coast of modern Calabria.

VICETINI: Inhabitants of Vicetia (*Vicenza*) in Venetia.

VIENNE (Latin VIENNA): Town in Narbonese Gaul on the east bank of the Rhône.

VOCONTII: People of Narbonese Gaul between the Rhône and the Alps.

VOLATERRAE (*Volterra*): Town in Etruria.

VOLSCI: Ancient Latin tribe. Arpinum was in their territory.

ZOSTER: Cape in Attica between Piraeus and Sunium.

GLOSSARY OF TERMS

ACADEMY (*Academia*): A hall (*gymnasium*) and park at Athens sacred to the hero Academus, in which Plato established his philosophical school. Hence Plato's school or system of philosophy, which went through various phases after his time. The terminology became confused, but Cicero recognized the 'Old Academy of Plato and his immediate successors and the 'New' Academy of Arcesilas and Carneades, which maintained the uncertainty of all dogma and to which he himself professed to belong. In his own times this was modified by his teachers Philo of Larissa and Antiochus of Ascalon, the latter of whom claimed to represent the 'Old' Academy with a system akin to Stoicism. Cicero gave the name 'Academy' to a hall which he built on his estate at Tusculum.

AEDILE (*aedilis*): Third in rank of the regular Roman magistracies. Four at this time were elected annually, two Curule and two Plebeian. They were responsible for city administration and the holding of certain public Games. The chief magistrates in some municipalities were also so called.

ASSEMBLY: I sometimes so translate *populus* or *comitia*, as describing the Roman people convened for electoral or legislative purposes. There were several different sorts varying with the convening magistrate and the business to be done.

ATTIC(ISM): One use of the word was in connection with Roman oratory. In Cicero's time a movement principally represented by Calvus and M. Brutus favoured an austere style like that of the Athenian Lysias.

AUGUR: The priestly College of Augurs were official diviners interpreting signs (mostly from the flight and cries of wild birds or the behaviour of the Sacred Chickens) before major acts of public (and sometimes private) business. The College, like that of Pontiffs, was in practice almost a preserve of the nobility, so that for a 'new man' like Cicero membership was a coveted social distinction.

AUSPICES (*auspicia*): Divination from birds or other signs was officially necessary as a preliminary to major acts by magistrates, who were said to 'have auspices', i.e., the power of taking them.

BACCHUS' DAY (*Liberalia*): The festival of Liber Pater, commonly identified with the Greek god Dionysius or Bacchus, and Libera on 17 March. It was the usual day for a coming of age ceremony.

BOARD OF FOUR: Municipalities (not Roman colonies) were commonly governed by four principal magistrates (*quattuorviri*), divided into two pairs (*duoviri*), and a senate of *decuriones*.

BONA DEA: See GOOD GODDESS.

BOY (*puer*): Male slaves of any age were so called, as in later times.

CAMPANIAN LAND (DOMAIN – *ager Campanus*): Fertile land in Campania, originally confiscated by Rome in 211 and leased to small tenants. Caesar as Consul passed a bill (the Campanian Law) to distribute it among Pompey's veterans and the Roman poor.

CAMPUS (MARTIUS): The plain adjoining the Tiber on which assemblies of the Centuries were held, often for elections.

CENSOR: Two magistrates usually elected every five years for a tenure of eighteen months. They revised the roll of citizens, with property assessments, also the rolls of Knights and Senators, removing those deemed guilty of misconduct. They further supervised public contracts, including the lease of revenues to the tax-farmers, and issued decrees as guardians of public morals.

CENTURIES, ASSEMBLY OF (*comitia centuriata*): Form of assembly in which voting took place by 'Centuries', i.e., groups unequally composed so as to give preponderance to birth and wealth. It elected Consuls and Praetors, and voted on legislation proposed by them. The first Century to vote (*centuria praerogativa*) traditionally had a determining effect on the rest.

CENTURION: See LEGION.

COHORT: See LEGION.

COMITIAL DAYS: Days in the Roman calendar on which the popular assemblies (*comitia*) could legally be held. The Senate was normally not allowed to meet on these days.

GLOSSARY OF TERMS

COMITIUM: An area north of the Forum where assemblies were held.

COMMISSION, FREE or VOTIVE: See LEGATE.

COMPITALIA: See CROSSWAYS' DAY.

CONSUL: Highest of the annual Roman magistrates. Two were elected, usually in July, to take office on the following 1 January.

CONSULAR: An ex-Consul. The Consulars made up a corps of elder statesmen to whom the Senate would normally look for leadership.

CROSSWAYS' DAY (*Compitalia*): Festival in honour of the Lares Compitales (gods of the crossroads) held annually soon after the Saturnalia on a day appointed by the Praetor.

CURIATE LAW (*lex curiata*): A law passed by the Curies (*curiae*), the oldest form of Roman assembly. In Cicero's time it survived only in form, each of the thirty Curies being represented by a lictor, but still had certain legislative functions, notably the passage of laws to confirm the executive authority (*imperium*) of individual magistrates; but the precise nature of these laws is much in doubt.

CURULE CHAIR (*sella curulis*): Ivory chair, or rather stool, of state used by regular 'curule' magistrates, i.e., Consuls, Praetors, and Curule Aediles, and certain others.

DICTATOR: A supreme magistrate with quasi-regal powers appointed to deal with emergencies under the early Republic; his second-in-command, the Master of the Horse, was appointed by himself. The office was revived to legitimize the autocratic régimes of Sulla and of Julius Caesar.

EDICT: A public announcement or manifesto issued by a magistrate. The name applied to the codes issued by City Praetors and provincial governors at the beginning of their terms setting out the legal rules which they intended to follow.

EPICUREANISM: A materialistic school of philosophy named after its founder Epicurus, much in vogue among the Roman intelligentsia in Cicero's time.

EQUESTRIAN ORDER: See KNIGHTS.

ETESIAN WINDS (*etesiae*): Northerly winds which blew every year during the Dog-days.

FASCES: Bundles of rods carried by lictors in front of magistrates as a symbol of authority. Those of victorious generals were wreathed in laurel.

FLAMEN: Priest in charge of the cult of a particular deity. There were fifteen, three (those of Jupiter, Mars, and Quirinus) being superior to the rest.

FORUM: The chief square of Rome, centre of civic life.

FREEDMAN (*libertus*): A 'manumitted' slave.

GAMES (*ludi*): Gladiatorial and other shows, some recurring annually and supervised by magistrates, others put on for an occasion by private individuals. Of the former the Roman Games (*ludi Romani*) were held from 5 to 19 September, the Games of Apollo (*ludi Apollinares*) from 5 to 13 July. 'Greek Games' seem to have consisted of performances of Greek plays in the original language.

GOOD GODDESS (*Bona Dea*): A goddess whose worship was confined to women. Her yearly festival was held in the house of a Consul or Praetor and supervised by his wife.

GOWN (*toga*): Formal civilian dress of a Roman citizen. The gown of boys and curule magistrates (*toga praetexta*) had a purple hem. At sixteen or seventeen on coming of age a boy was given his White (or 'Manly') Gown (*toga pura, toga virilis*).

GREEK GAMES: See GAMES.

GREEKS: In Cicero's time the word was loosely used to include the more or less hellenized inhabitants of Western Asia and Egypt as well as those of Greece proper and the old Greek settlements elsewhere.

HONEST MEN: So I translate Cicero's *boni* ('good men', *les gens de bien*), a semi-political term for people of substance and respectability, supporters of the established order. Their opposites he calls *improbi* ('rascals').

IMPERATOR: Commander of a Roman army. But at this period the title was conferred on Generals by their soldiers after a victory and retained until they relinquished their *imperium*.

IMPERIUM: Literally 'command'; the executive authority appertaining to higher magisterial and promagisterial office.

INTERCALATION: See Appendix I(i).

INTERREGNUM: If through death or otherwise the consular office stood vacant and no patrician magistrates holding *imperium* were in office, an Interrex was appointed from among the patrician members of the Senate to exercise consular functions for five days. He was then replaced by another Interrex, and so on until new Consuls could be elected.

KNIGHTS (*equites*): In effect non-Senators of free birth possessing property over a certain level. They were regarded as forming a class of their own (*ordo equestris*) with special privileges and insignia.

LATIN FESTIVAL (*Feriae Latinae*): Movable annual festival of the Romano-Latin League held on Mt Alba. Its date was determined from year to year by the Consuls.

LECTURE HALL (*gymnasium*): The Greek gymnasium was originally a sports ground containing a *palaestra* (see below). But literature, philosophy, and music were also taught in them.

LEGATE (*legatus*): A provincial governor took several Legates, normally Senators, on his staff as deputies. Caesar in Gaul made them commanders of legions. The duties might, however, be purely nominal. The Senate could also appoint its members to 'free' or 'votive' (i.e., to discharge a vow) *legationes*, thus enabling them to travel abroad with official status. I sometimes translate with 'commission(er)'. The word can also be used for any kind of envoy.

LEGION: Roman army unit with a full complement of 6,000 men divided into ten cohorts. Each legion was officered by six Military Tribunes. Each cohort had six Centurions, the highest in rank being called *primi pili* (Chief Centurion). The ensign of a Legion was an eagle, and each cohort had its standard (*signum*).

LÈSE-MAJESTÉ (*maiestas*): The term *maiestas* covered acts 'in derogation of the majesty of the Roman People', as of magistrates or governors exceeding the bounds of their authority.

LEX CORNELIA (*de provinciis*): Law of Sulla regulating provincial administration.

LEX CURIATA: See above, CURIATE LAW.

LEX GABINIA: A law of 67 or 58 forbidding or restricting loans from Roman citizens to provincials.

LEX JULIA (*de provinciis*): Consular law of Caesar's on provincial administration.

LEX JUNIA-LICINIA: A law of 62 requiring that copies of proposed legislation be deposited in the Treasury.

LEX POMPEIA: Pompey's law against electoral corruption in 52.

LEX ROSCIA: A law of 67 assigning the first fourteen rows in the theatre to the Knights (the Senate sat below in the Orchestra).

LEX SCANTINIA: A law of uncertain date penalizing homosexual acts committed upon persons of free birth.

LIBERALIA: See BACCHUS' DAY.

LICTOR: Official attendant of persons possessing magisterial authority (*imperium*), the number varying with the rank.

LUPERCALIA: Fertility festival on 15 February held in a cave below the Palatine Hill by the Luperci. There were two Colleges of these until 45-44, when Caesar added a third called the *Luperci Iulii*.

MANUMISSION: Process of freeing a slave. This could be done either formally or informally ('between friends'), but in the latter case the master could revoke it at will.

MILE (*mille passus*): The Roman mile was 1,618 yards.

MIME (*mimus*): Type of entertainment with dancing, music, and dialogue which became highly popular in the first century B.C. It was considered more sophisticated and risqué than the Atellan Farce, which it virtually superseded.

MINERVA'S DAY (*Quinquatrus*): Festival of Minerva on 19 March.

NOBILITY: Practically, a noble (*nobilis*) at this period meant a direct descendant of a Consul in the male line. In the early Republic the Roman community was divided into patricians and plebeians, the former holding a virtual monopoly of political power. But after the Consulship was thrown open to plebeians in the fourth century many plebeian families became 'noble', and the remaining patricians were distinguished chiefly by their ineligibility to hold both Consulships in one year and for the plebeian offices of Tribune and Plebeian Aedile.

NOMENCLATOR: A slave whose duty it was to remind his master of the names of clients and acquaintances whom he happened to meet.

OPS: Roman goddess in whose temple on the Capitol Caesar deposited the state treasure.

OPTIMATES: Literally 'those belonging to the best' – the leading conservatives in the Senate and their supporters throughout the community. Sometimes the term is practically equivalent to the 'honest men' (*boni*), though more purely political in its implications.

OVATION: A lesser form of Triumph.

PALAESTRA: A space surrounded by colonnades, found in all *gymnasia*. Literally 'wrestling-school' (Greek).

PATRICIANS: See NOBILITY.

PAYMASTER-TRIBUNES (*tribuni aerarii*): At this time probably a class similar to the Knights but with a lower property qualification. Under the lex Aurelia of 70, juries were composed in equal numbers of Senators, Knights, and Paymaster-Tribunes.

PLEBEIANS: See NOBILITY.

PONTIFF (*pontifex*): These formed a priestly College in general charge of Roman religious institutions (including the Calendar), presided over by the Chief Pontiff (*pontifex maximus*), who was Julius Caesar from 63 until his death.

PRAETOR: Second in rank of the annual magistracies. Eight were elected at this period until Caesar increased the number to twenty. The City Praetor (*praetor urbanus*) was in charge of the administration of justice between Roman citizens, others presided over the standing criminal courts. After his year of office a Praetor normally went to govern a province as Propraetor or Proconsul.

PRAETORIAN COHORT (*cohors praetoria*): A special military unit forming a general's bodyguard.

PREFECT: Officer appointed by a magistrate (usually as provincial governor) for military or civil duties. These might be only nominal, the appointment merely conferring official status and privileges. The 'Prefect of Engineers' (*praefectus fabrum*) acted as adjutant to his chief – no longer any connection with engineers.

PROCONSUL (*pro consule*): 'Acting Consul', one who, not holding the office, exercised consular authority outside Rome by senatorial appointment. Similarly Propraetor (*pro praetore*) and Proquaestor (*pro quaestore*).

PROSCRIPTION (*proscriptio*): A procedure first employed by Sulla, then by the Triumvirs in 43. Lists of names were published, the persons thus 'proscribed' being declared outlaws and their goods confiscated. Their killers were rewarded, their protectors punished.

QUAESTOR: The first stage in the regular 'course of offices', election to which carried life-membership of the Senate. Since Sulla's time twenty were elected annually. The two City Quaestors (*quaestores urbani*) had charge of the Treasury and the Quaestors assigned to provincial governors (usually by lot) were largely concerned with finance.

QUARTAN: A fever recurring every third day; less grave therefore than a tertian, which recurred every other day.

QUIRINUS' DAY (Quirinalia): Festival in honour of Quirinus (the deified Romulus, founder of Rome) on 17 February.

RESOLUTION (*auctoritas*): A decree of the Senate vetoed by a Tribune was sometimes recorded under this name.

ROSTRA: The speakers' platform in the comitium, so called from the beaks (*rostra*) of captured warships which decorated it.

SATURNALIA: Festival of Saturn beginning on 17 December, marked by merrymaking reminiscent of modern Christmas, to which it contributed some elements.

SECRETARY: I so translate (with a capital letter) Latin *scriba*. The 'scribes' were a corporation of civil servants working in the Treasury and otherwise. City magistrates and provincial governors might be assigned official Secretaries for their personal assistance. Private clerks were called *librarii*.

SENATE: Governing body of the Roman Republic, numbering about 600 (increased to 900 by Caesar) and composed of magistrates and ex-magistrates.

SHEPHERDS' DAY (*Parilia*): Festival of the god and goddess Pales, protectors of flocks and herds, on 21 April.

SOOTHSAYING: For *haruspicina*, an Etruscan system of divination from the entrails of sacrificial animals, from portents, and from lightning. Some of its practitioners (*haruspices*) seem to have been organized as a body of sixty and were consulted officially.

SOPHIST: A professional 'wise man', making money as a teacher and lecturer, often itinerant.

STOICISM: Philosophical school, named from the portico (*stoa*) in which its founder, Zeno of Citium (*c.* 300), taught. Cato was its most prominent Roman adherent in Cicero's time.

SUMPTUARY LAW: A series of laws during the Republic attempted to impose restrictions on luxury spending, especially on food. One was enacted by Julius Caesar in 46.

SUPPLICATION (*supplicatio*): A thanksgiving ceremony decreed by the Senate in honour of a military success, the number of days varying according to the importance of the victory. It was generally regarded as a preliminary to a Triumph.

TABLETS (*codicilli*): Wooden tablets coated with wax and fastened together with thread, used for memoranda and short notes.

TAX-FARMERS (*publicani*): Roman taxes, as on grazing-land in the provinces or excise, were largely farmed out by the Censors to private companies who bid for the right of collection. The capitalists in Rome as well as their local agents were called *publicani*. In political terms *publicani* and Knights often amount to the same thing.

TELLUS: Earth-goddess, whose temple was one of the meeting-places of the Senate.

TESTIMONIAL: Renders *laudatio* (= 'eulogy') in one of its senses. It was customary for defendants to ask prominent persons to offer witness to their good character in court either orally or in writing.

TETRARCH: Literally 'ruler over a fourth part'. In Cicero's time many minor eastern princes were called by this title.

TOGA: See GOWN.

TREASURY (*aerarium*): The Roman state treasury was in the temple of Saturn in the Forum, managed by the City Quaestors with the assistance of Secretaries.

TRIBE (*tribus*): A division, mainly by locality, of the Roman citizen body. The number had risen over the centuries from three to thirty-five (four of them 'urban', the rest 'rustic'). Assemblies voting by tribes (*comitia tributa*) elected magistrates below Praetor and could pass legislation proposed by Tribunes.

TRIBUNE: (1) Of the Plebs. A board of ten, originally appointed to protect plebeians from patrician high-handedness. They had wide constitutional powers, the most important being that any one of them could veto any piece of public business, including laws and senatorial decrees. They could also initiate these. They took office on 10 December. (2) Military: See LEGION. (3) See PAYMASTER-TRIBUNES.

TRIUMPH: Victory celebration by a general on his return to Rome. Permission had to be granted by the Senate.

UNIFORM: Magistrates leaving to take command of armies wore the general's red cloak (*paludamentum*) and were said to set out *paludati*.

VALUATION (*aestimatio*): Process by which a debtor's property could be transferred to his creditor in settlement. Caesar made such transfers compulsory on terms favourable to the debtor.

WEAL: The goddess Salus, who had a temple on the Quirinal Hill near Atticus' house.

MAPS

THE ROMAN

BRITAIN

R. Rhine

GALLIA
COMATA

R. Rhone

GALLIA
NARBONENSIS

Massilia

GALLIA
CISALPINA
Verona

ILLYRICU

Rubicon
Ariminum

Numantia

Ilerda

Narbo

R. Iura

Albintimilium

Rome

FURTHER
SPAIN

NEARER
SPAIN

SARDINIA

Tartessus
Gades

Sisapo

Munda

Thurii

SICILY Mylae

Leon

Utica

Syra

Carthage

Agrigentum

NUMIDIA

AFRICA

Thapsus

0   100   200   300   English Miles

EMPIRE 51 B.C.

—— Boundaries of provinces
- - - Boundaries of the empire

SCYTHIANS

Borysthenes

R. Danube

BLACK SEA

ARMENIA MINOR MAJOR

PONTUS

BITHYNIA · Zela

GALATIA

· Pessinus

· Carrhae

ASIA

CILICIA

· Laodicea Tarsus

· Side

R. Euphrates

SYRIA

Pamphylia CYPRUS

· Citium · Apamea

Paphos

CRETE

Cyrene

Alexandria Ascalon

CYRENE

EGYPT R. Nile

GREECE AND THE
BALKANS

Scales

0 20 40 60 80 100 120 140 160
English miles

0 20 40 60 80 100 120 140 160
Roman miles

to Milvian Bridge and the North

VIA FLAMINIA

FIELD OF MARS
(CAMPUS MARTIUS)

QUIRINAL

"Sheepfold"

R. Tiber

Theatre of
Pompey

Capitol

CARINAE

Forum

VIA SACRA

VIA NOVA

VIA AURELIA

PALATINE

JANICULUM

AVENTINE

Porta Capena

to Arpinum and
Campania

VIA LATINA

VIA APPIA (to Campania)

1 Temple of Jupiter
2 Temple of Saturn
3 Temple of Castor
4 Senate House
5 Temple of Concord
6 Regia (official residence of High Priest)

ROME
in the late Republic

ITALY and SICILY

0   50   100   150   200 Miles

CONCORDANCE

This concordance covers all three volumes of this translation of Cicero's correspondence. In the letters to Brutus the numbering in the translation is the same as that of standard modern editions.

Letters to Atticus

Latin	This translation	Latin	This translation
I. 1	10	II. 7	27
I. 2	11	II. 8	28
I. 3	8	II. 9	29
I. 4	9	II. 10	31
I. 5	1	II. 11	32
I. 6	2	II. 12	30
I. 7	3	II. 13	33
I. 8	4	II. 14	34
I. 9	5	II. 15	35
I. 10	6	II. 16	36
I. 11	7	II. 17	37
I. 12	12	II. 18	38
I. 13	13	II. 19	39
I. 14	14	II. 20	40
I. 15	15	II. 21	41
I. 16	16	II. 22	42
I. 17	17	II. 23	43
I. 18	18	II. 24	44
I. 19	19	II. 25	45
I. 20	20	III. 1	46
II. 1	21	III. 2	48
II. 2	22	III. 3	47
II. 3	23	III. 4	49
II. 4	24	III. 5	50
II. 5	25	III. 6	51
II. 6	26	III. 7	52

CONCORDANCE

Latin	This translation	Latin	This translation
III. 8	53	IV. 15	90
III. 9	54	IV. 16	89
III. 10	55	IV. 17	91
III. 11	56	IV. 18	92
III. 12	57	IV. 19	93
III. 13	59	V. 1	94
III. 14	58	V. 2	95
III. 15	60	V. 3	96
III. 16	61	V. 4	97
III. 17	62	V. 5	98
III. 18	63	V. 6	99
III. 19	64	V. 7	100
III. 20	65	V. 8	101
III. 21	66	V. 9	102
III. 22	67	V. 10	103
III. 23	68	V. 11	104
III. 24	69	V. 12	105
III. 25	70	V. 13	106
III. 26	71	V. 14	107
III. 27	72	V. 15	108
IV. 1	73	V. 16	109
IV. 2	74	V. 17	110
IV. 3	75	V. 18	111
IV. 4	76	V. 19	112
IV. 4a	78	V. 20	113
IV. 5	80	V. 21	114
IV. 6	83	VI. 1	115
IV. 7	77	VI. 2	116
IV. 8	79	VI. 3	117
IV. 8a	82	VI. 4	118
IV. 9	85	VI. 5	119
IV. 10	84	VI. 6	121
IV. 11	86	VI. 7	120
IV. 12	81	VI. 8	122
IV. 13	87	VI. 9	123
IV. 14	88	VII. 1	124

Latin	This translation	Latin	This translation
XII. 10	247	XII. 43	284
XII. 11	249	XII. 44	285
XII. 12	259	XII. 45	290
XII. 13	250	XII. 46	287
XII. 14	251	XII. 47	288
XII. 15	252	XII. 48	289
XII. 16	253	XII. 49	292
XII. 17	255	XII. 50	291
XII. 18	254	XII. 51	293
XII. 18a	256	XII. 52	294
XII. 19	257	XII. 53	295
XII. 20	258	XIII. 1	296
XII. 21	260	XIII. 2	297
XII. 22	261	XIII. 2a	301
XII. 23	262	XIII. 2b	304
XII. 24	263	XIII. 3	308
XII. 25	264	XIII. 4	311
XII. 26	265	XIII. 5	312
XII. 27	266	XIII. 6	310
XII. 28	267	XIII. 6a	310
XII. 29	268	XIII. 7	314
XII. 30	270	XIII. 7a	315
XII. 31	272	XIII. 8	313
XII. 32	271	XIII. 9	317
XII. 33	269	XIII. 10	318
XII. 34	273	XIII. 11	319
XII. 35	274	XIII. 12	320
XII. 36	275	XIII. 13–14	321
XII. 37	276	XIII. 14–15	322
XII. 37a	277	XIII. 16	323
XII. 38	278	⎰ XIII. 17	324
XII. 38a	279	⎱ XIII. 18	325
XII. 39	280	XIII. 19	326
XII. 40	281	XIII. 20	328
XII. 41	283	XIII. 21	351
XII. 42	282	XIII. 21a	327

Latin	This translation	Latin	This translation
XIII. 22	329	XIV. 5	359
XIII. 23	331	XIV. 6	360
XIII. 24	332	XIV. 7	361
XIII. 25	333	XIV. 8	362
XIII. 26	286	XIV. 9	363
XIII. 27	298	XIV. 10	364
XIII. 28	299	XIV. 11	365
XIII. 29	300	XIV. 12	366
XIII. 30	303	XIV. 13	367
XIII. 31	302	XIV. 13A	367A
XIII. 32	305	XIV. 13B	367B
XIII. 33	309	XIV. 14	368
XIII. 33a	330	XIV. 15	369
XIII. 34	350	XIV. 16	370
XIII. 35–6	334	XIV. 17	371
XIII. 37	346, 340	XIV. 17A	371A
XIII. 38	341	XIV. 18	373
XIII. 39	342	XIV. 19	372
XIII. 40	343	XIV. 20	374
XIII. 41	344	XIV. 21	375
XIII. 42	354	XIV. 22	376
XIII. 43	335	XV. 1	377
XIII. 44	336	XV. 1a	378
XIII. 45	337	XV. 2	379
XIII. 46	338	XV. 3	380
XIII. 47	339	XV. 4	381
XIII. 47a	352	XV. 4a	382
XIII. 48	345	XV. 5	383
XIII. 49	347	XV. 6	386
XIII. 50	348	XV. 7	374
XIII. 51	349	XV. 8	385
XIII. 52	353	XV. 9	387
XIV. 1	355	XV. 10	388
XIV. 2	356	XV. 11	389
XIV. 3	357	XV. 12	390
XIV. 4	358	XV. 13	416

CONCORDANCE

CONCORDANCE

Letters to Friends

Latin	*This translation*	Latin	*This translation*
V. 10*a*.3	256	VII. 1	24
V. 10*b*	258	VII. 2	52
V. 11	257	VII. 3	183
V. 12	22	VII. 4	199
V. 13	201	VII. 5	26
V. 14	251	VII. 6	27
V. 15	252	VII. 7	28
V. 16	187	VII. 8	29
V. 17	23	VII. 9	30
V. 18	51	VII. 10	33
V. 19	152	VII. 11	34
V. 20	128	VII. 12	35
V. 21	182	VII. 13	36
VI. 1	242	VII. 14	38
VI. 2	245	VII. 15	39
VI. 3	243	VII. 16	32
VI. 4	244	VII. 17	31
VI. 5	239	VII. 18	37
VI. 6	234	VII. 19	334
VI. 7	237	VII. 20	333
VI. 8	235	VII. 21	332
VI. 9	236	VII. 22	331
VI. 10.1–3	223	VII. 23	209
VI. 10.4–6	222	VII. 24	260
VI. 11	224	VII. 25	261
VI. 12	226	VII. 26	210
VI. 13	227	VII. 27	148
VI. 14	228	VII. 28	200
VI. 15	322	VII. 29	264
VI. 16	323	VII. 30	265
VI. 17	324	VII. 31	267
VI. 18	218	VII. 32	113
VI. 19	262	VII. 33	192
VI. 20	247	VIII. 1	77
VI. 21	246	VIII. 2	78
VI. 22	221	VIII. 3	79

Latin	*This translation*	Latin	*This translation*
VIII. 4	81	IX. 23	198
VIII. 5	83	IX. 24	362
VIII. 6	88	IX. 25	114
VIII. 7	92	IX. 26	197
VIII. 8	84	X. 1	340
VIII. 9	82	X. 2	341
VIII. 10	87	X. 3	355
VIII. 11	91	X. 4	358
VIII. 12	98	X. 5	359
VIII. 13	94	X. 6	370
VIII. 14	97	X. 7	372
VIII. 15	149	X. 8	371
VIII. 16	153	X. 9	379
VIII. 17	156	X. 10	375
IX. 1	175	X. 11	382
IX. 2	177	X. 12	377
IX. 3	176	X. 13	389
IX. 4	180	X. 14	384
IX. 5	179	X. 15	390
IX. 6	181	X. 16	404
IX. 7	178	X. 17	398
IX. 8	254	X. 18	395
IX. 9	157	X. 19	393
IX. 10	217	X. 20	407
IX. 11	250	X. 21	391
IX. 12	263	X. 21a	392
IX. 13	311	X. 22	423
IX. 14	326	X. 23	414
IX. 15	196	X. 24	428
IX. 16	190	X. 25	403
IX. 17	195	X. 26	424
IX. 18	191	X. 27	369
IX. 19	194	X. 28	364
IX. 20	193	X. 29	426
IX. 21	188	X. 30	378
IX. 22	189	X. 31	368

Latin	This translation	Latin	This translation
X. 32	415	XI. 29	335
X. 33	409	XII. 1	327
X. 34	396	XII. 2	344
X. 34a	400	XII. 3	345
X. 35	408	XII. 4	363
XI. 1	325	XII. 5	365
XI. 2	329	XII. 6	376
XI. 3	336	XII. 7	367
XI. 4	342	XII. 8	416
XI. 5	353	XII. 9	421
XI. 6	343	XII. 10	425
XI. 6a	356	XII. 11	366
XI. 7	354	XII. 12	387
XI. 8	360	XII. 13	419
XI. 9	380	XII. 14	405
XI. 10	385	XII. 15	406
XI. 11	386	XII. 16	328
XI. 12	394	XII. 17	204
XI. 13	388	XII. 18	205
XI. 13a	418	XII. 19	206
XI. 13b	381	XII. 20	339
XI. 14	413	XII. 21	429
XI. 15	422	XII. 22	346
XI. 16	434	XII. 22a	357
XI. 17	435	XII. 23	347
XI. 18	397	XII. 24	361
XI. 19	399	XII. 24.3	430
XI. 20	401	XII. 25	373
XI. 21	411	XII. 25a	383
XI. 22	427	XII. 26	431
XI. 23	402	XII. 27	432
XI. 24	412	XII. 28	374
XI. 25	420	XII. 29	433
XI. 26	410	XII. 30	417
XI. 27	348	XIII. 1	63
XI. 28	349	XIII. 2	314

Latin	This translation	Latin	This translation
XIII. 73	273	XV. 6	112
XIII. 74	269	XV. 7	99
XIII. 75	60	XV. 8	100
XIII. 76	62	XV. 9	101
XIII. 77	212	XV. 10	108
XIII. 78	275	XV. 11	118
XIII. 79	276	XV. 12	102
XIV. 1	8	XV. 13	109
XIV. 2	7	XV. 14	106
XIV. 3	9	XV. 15	174
XIV. 4	6	XV. 16	215
XIV. 5	119	XV. 17	214
XIV. 6	158	XV. 18	213
XIV. 7	155	XV. 19	216
XIV. 8	164	XV. 20	208
XIV. 9	161	XV. 21	207
XIV. 10	168	XVI. 1	120
XIV. 11	166	XVI. 2	121
XIV. 12	159	XVI. 3	122
XIV. 13	169	XVI. 4	123
XIV. 14	145	XVI. 5	124
XIV. 15	167	XVI. 6	125
XIV. 16	163	XVI. 7	126
XIV. 17	162	XVI. 8	147
XIV. 18	144	XVI. 9	127
XIV. 19	160	XVI. 10	43
XIV. 20	173	XVI. 11	143
XIV. 21	165	XVI. 12	146
XIV. 22	172	XVI. 13	40
XIV. 23	171	XVI. 14	41
XIV. 24	170	XVI. 15	42
XV. 1	104	XVI. 16	44
XV. 2	105	XVI. 17	186
XV. 3	103	XVI. 18	219
XV. 4	110	XVI. 19	184
XV. 5	111	XVI. 20	220

CONCORDANCE

CONCORDANCE

Letters to Quintus

Latin	This translation	Latin	This translation
I. 1	1	II. 11 (10)	15
I. 2	2	II. 12 (11)	16
I. 3	3	II. 13 (12)	17
I. 4	4	II. 14 (13)	18
II. 1	5	II. 15 (14)	19
II. 2	6	II. 16 (15)	20
II. 3	7	III. 1	21
II. 4 (4.1–2)	8	III. 2	22
II. 5 (4.3–7)	9	III. 3	23
II. 6 (5)	10	III. 4	24
II. 7 (6)	11	III. 5 (5–7)	25
II. 8 (7)	12	III. 6 (8)	26
II. 9 (8)	13	III. 7 (9)	27
II. 10 (9)	14		

MORE ABOUT PENGUINS
AND PELICANS

Penguinews, which appears every month, contains details of all the new books issued by Penguins as they are published. It is supplemented by our stocklist which includes around 5,000 titles.

A specimen copy of *Penguinews* will be sent to you free on request. Please write to Dept EP, Penguin Books Ltd, Harmondsworth, Middlesex, for your copy.

In the U.S.A.: For a complete list of books available from Penguins in the United States write to Dept CS, Penguin Books, 625 Madison Avenue, New York, New York 10022.

In Canada: For a complete list of books available from Penguins in Canada write to Penguin Books Canada Ltd, 2801 John Street, Markham, Ontario L3R 1B4.